The Fourth Morningside Papers

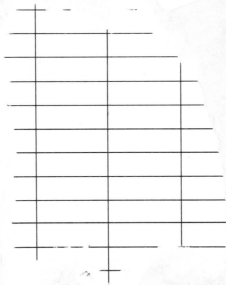

THE FOURTH MORNINGSIDE PAPERS

PETER GZOWSKI

M&S

Canadian Cataloguing in Publication Data

Gzowski, Peter
  The fourth Morningside papers

Includes index.
ISBN 0-7710-3731-7

1. Morningside (Radio program). I. Title.
II. Title: Morningside (Radio program).

PN1991.3.C3G95 1991   791.44'72   C91-095146-2

McClelland & Stewart Inc.
The Canadian Publishers
481 University Avenue
Toronto, Ontario
M5G 2E9

Printed and bound in Canada

CONTENTS

A Tip of Both My Hats

As I hope regular listeners (and readers) will know by now, both *Morningside*, CBC Radio's daily three hours, and the books that arise from it are works of collegiality, and the fact that I have survived nine years as the host of the program and had my picture on the cover of (now) four volumes of *Papers* is more a tribute to the people who surround me than it is a reflection of my own talents. The producers – there has never been a better collection than that which put together the two seasons represented here – make the radio; the editors make the books. If there were justice, in fact, Laurie McGaw's cover painting, especially this time, would have Edna Barker in the foreground and not me. Edna has worked on all the *Papers*; her role grows stronger, her judgement surer, her touch defter, each time out. Close behind her, as she is close behind me in everything I do, would be Shelley Ambrose. Shelley was a working journalist before she signed on as my assistant, and I am as pleased as she must be that the *Papers* allow her to keep her editing skills at play. In this collection, the three chapters of letters from abroad – a department of *Morningside* she also produces on the air – are particularly hers. Shelagh Rogers, whose editorial eye is as astute as her voice is melodious, would be in the picture, too, as would Lynn Reilly, who deciphered all the handwriting (none more difficult than mine) and key-boarded all the poetry and prose; Wendy Thomas, our dauntless copy editor; Meg Taylor, who read the proofs; and Larry St. Aubin, a young film maker who occasionally mans the *Morningside* reception desk and somehow also finds time to be a kind of Shelley's Shelley. Gill Howard, with whom I live, works in the daytime and may well know *Morningside* and its audience as well through the letters I have asked her to read as she does from replays and holiday mornings. My thanks, as always, to all of them, and of course, to everyone at M&S.

The Usual Note About My Fellow Authors

Once again, we've made every effort to obtain the permission of all the people whose letters, essays, poems and insights make up the chapters of this collection. Once again, there remain a few we haven't been able to reach. And some of them – we *still* can't find Heather Allen, who appears not yet to have emerged from the steaming jungle of Zaire – are either a step behind or a step ahead of their mail. People do move – even those whose addresses we can read. I beg their understanding. It still seems better to risk their annoyance this way than their disappointment at being left out.

Words & Music of "Out Past the Timberline," page 35 – Murray McLauchlan ©1983 Gullwing Music Limited/Sold For A Song/MCA Music Canada, a division of MCA Canada Ltd. (CAPAC). Rights Administered by MCA Music Canada, a division of MCA Canada Ltd. (CAPAC). Used By Permission. All Rights Reserved.

And a Grateful Dedication

To Patsy Pehleman, whose name scarcely appears in these pages, but without whom . . . etc. In nine seasons at *Morningside*, I've been extraordinarily lucky in the executive producers I've worked with. But never more so than in the two seasons represented here – Patsy's.

Whistling Down the Northern Lights

I never have gone to the James Bay; I never go to it; I never shall. But somehow I'd feel lonely without it.

– Stephen Leacock, "I'll Stay In Canada," 1936

IN THE SPRING of 1991, just as the two seasons of radio reflected in this book were drawing to a close, I slipped away from the *Morningside* studio for a game of golf.

The round I was headed for was not an ordinary one. It was in the land that Stephen Leacock never saw – well beyond "the James Bay." To get to it, I took, first, a limousine to Pearson airport in Toronto, where I was joined by three of the people I was going to play with, the television actors Cynthia Dale and Pat Mastroianni and the country singer Colleen Peterson. From Pearson, we flew to Ottawa, where we rendezvoused with some more prospective golfers who had flown in from various corners of the country. From Ottawa, our party – nearly a dozen of us now, including two people from *Morningside* and my own incomparable assistant Shelley Ambrose – boarded a First Air jet for a three-hour ride north to Baffin Island. We stopped briefly in Iqaluit, picking up still more players (northerners, this time) and dropping in on the Elders' Centre, where, over tea, those of us who had come from the south were presented with honorary "Q-numbers," the Inuit's ironic twist on the old dog-tags issued by the government to make up for their traditional lack of sur-names. (Q stands for *Qallunaaq*, the Inuktitut word for white person.) From Iqaluit, we flew still farther north, over the dra-matic rocks and fjords of the Baffin, to Pond Inlet, some four hundred miles inside the Arctic Circle. By the time we were in the air towards Pond, our party had grown to perhaps twenty golfers (we were still not sure how many intended to play and how many would just tag along) who ranged in background from Colin James, the young blues star from Vancouver, still wearing his black jeans and cowboy boots ("Can someone lend me a black leather parka?" he had asked Shelley), to Steven Kakfwi, the minister of education of the Northwest Territories, and in golfing skills from Randy Gregg, the doctor and former Edmonton Oiler, who, like many hockey players, hits the ball a mile, to Sheree Fitch, the children's poet from New Brunswick, who, to my knowledge, had not so much as picked up a putter before her trip to the Baffin.

At Pond, we had a couple of days of acclimatization. In the unrelenting, twenty-four-hour sunlight, our energy levels seemed to rise. We rode snowmobiles across the endless, shining land-scape, our hearts pounding as fiercely as our kidneys, and returned at midnight to join the villagers in a dance. We scaled a glimmering blue iceberg, the size of a triplex, trapped in Eclipse Sound. We listened to the elders' tales of the old whaling days, before the *Qallunaaq* came. We met a man who had guided the first Mounties across the barrens, rubbing their feet for warmth and, when they had all returned to the comfort of the settlement, found himself once again treated as an inferior. We joined the people of the hamlet – Pond Inlet has a population of nine hundred and fifty, ninety-five per cent of whom are Inuit – in a feast of raw and frozen char, raw and frozen caribou and freshly slaughtered seal, the meat as red as rubies, the organs a purply brown, and, one afternoon, tried our hands at throwing harpoons at targets in the snow, and cracking the long whips used to steer dog teams. Squatting on caribou skins in Takijualik School, we swapped stories with the children, Sheree Fitch offering up one of her tongue-twisting poems ("Mabel Murple's house is purple, so are Mabel's ears") and, in turn, stumbling over the Inuktitut word for parka, *qulittaujaq*, until the child whose story had included it told her to make a sound like a raven. Our cultures often tumbled together – as when Colin James's rendition of Bob Dylan's "When I Paint My Masterpiece," which he sang after our feast of raw protein, was followed by (and drew the same applause as) two Inuit throat-singers, or when we found graffiti at the top of the iceberg, or tried to write our names in syllabics on a Macintosh computer. The Inuit kids – fifty per cent of the population of Pond is under sixteen – engaged Randy in what seemed to be one continuous game of road hockey, forming such a solid swarm around his towering, six-foot-four frame that Shelley took to calling him "the man with no legs." Cynthia – "Olivia," to everyone in Pond, after her character on *Street Legal* and Pat – "Joey" of *Degrassi High* – appeared to sign every piece of paper in town, and when the paper was full, many of the shirts, hats, plaster casts and, on at least one occasion, bare knees. Colin, who had had to borrow a guitar from a local teenager to sing at the feast, repaid the debt by giving the guitar's owner a long, personalized seminar on blues licks and was so enchanted by his pupil's enthusiasm that he immediately began making arrangements to send one of his own amplifiers to Pond. But more often we, the southerners, just wondered in the ways of the north, revelling in its heart-aching beauty and the shy warmth of its people, and feeling, curiously, at home.

On golf day, we took dog sleds on the last lap of the journey that had begun by limo, sweeping out across the ice of Eclipse Sound, past the trapped iceberg – the people had asked that the ice not be scraped too close to shore, so that their traditional route home from their hunting camps wouldn't melt too early – towards our course. Twenty miles across the sound, the mountains of Bylot Island glistened in the Arctic sun, the site, we were told, of the world's most northerly dinosaur bones. The yelping of the dogs mixed with our cries of delight as we clambered off our *qamutiks* and saw the ice sculptures – a whale appeared to be diving into the sound, with only its graceful tail sticking up in the air – with which the carvers of Pond had adorned the first tee. Golf clubs, borrowed from Yellowknife, awaited us in a snow house – an *igluvigaq*. The man who had built the course, with its snow-lined fairways and scraped "greens" (whites, really, with brightly coloured flags planted in the holes), read us the rules. "Balls landing in an *aglu* (a seal breathing hole) are lost. . . . Balls taken by ravens or polar bears may be replaced without penalty." We split into foursomes as varied as our backgrounds. Ann Mee-kitjuk Hanson, the deputy commissioner of the Northwest Territories, who had been Annie E7-121 in her nomadic childhood on the land (the "E" stood for Eastern; the 7 denoted the Lake Harbour region of Baffin Island), played with Dr. Gregg, who wore his own Q-number now (Q-1021), along with the gigantic ring that marked five Stanley Cup victories; Pat Mastroianni was in the same foursome as Joanna Awa, *Morningside*'s Iqaluit correspondent, and herself a star in Pond, where she had grown up (earlier in her visit, Joanna had talked movingly of her experiences sniffing glue under the school steps, before she had discovered her considerable skills as a broadcaster); Susan Nattrass, the Olympic trap-shooter who lives in Halifax now (and heads the athletic department at Saint Mary's University), played with Jacob Anaviapik, the hamlet manager, in whose life as a hunter guns played an equally significant, if somewhat different, role.

After an appropriate prayer, we walked to our various tees and waited for the signal to start. In just a couple of hours – though there was no hurry, since dark wouldn't come until August – we played our nine holes and gathered at the *igluvigaq* for bannock, tea and a celebratory poem by Sheree. I shot a forty-three, better than I usually do on grass, but well back of the thirty-nine recorded by Randy Gregg. Randy's score, I presume, will stand forever, since by June the course at Pond Inlet, with its *igluvigaq* pro shop and its first-tee sculptures, would melt, never to be played again.

Two days later, back in Toronto, I wrapped up my ninth season as host of *Morningside*. On the final program, I talked, as usual, politics and current affairs, read some letters with Shelagh Rogers, said summer farewells to our regular columnists and my producers, and listened to the music of the Barenaked Ladies, a gang of young Ontario musicians who are neither–bare naked, that is, nor ladies. But the sounds and sights of Pond Inlet lingered in my mind. They stayed there in the days and weeks that followed. On Canada Day, I returned to *Morningside* to help present a three-hour special that the producer Terry MacLeod had put together about our northern journey. But even that could not empty my mind of the images – the *experience* – of the Baffin. My trip to Pond Inlet, though not my first to the Canadian north, had begun to crystal-lize some thoughts I had been having about the country. After the *Morningside* season ended, I made some more forays into the landscape: west to Winnipeg and east to the Maritimes, among other places. These trips, too, were ostensibly about golf–or golf and literacy, which are combined in the series of events I was attending. But the thoughts that had begun to build in Pond Inlet were echoed and strengthened wherever I went. And, weeks after I had returned from the north, as I pondered the contents of this anthology and the seasons of broadcasting it represents, they would not go away.

THIS IS, as its title makes clear, the fourth collection of letters to and moments from CBC Radio's national morning program (after *The Morningside Papers, The New Morningside Papers* and *The Latest Morningside Papers*, I stopped being cute and turned to the numbering system I should have used in the first place). In many respects, it is simply a continuation of what all the *Papers* have been, the ruminations of what I am convinced is the smartest and most literate audience in the world over a couple of years of radio, in this case the seasons that stretched from the autumn of 1989 to the spring of 1991. Like their predecessors, the *Fourth Papers* are a mixture of private and public affairs. Many of the letters are personal insights, stories, really, that people wanted to share (*Morningside* continued to be, as I once described it, a kind of village bulletin-board to the nation) or, as with Lavinia Glass's jolly treatise on the Shirleys of Bellefield, Manitoba, fabrications that pleased their authors to pass along. Others are responses to subjects that arose on the program: the pleasures of Gravenstein apples, the intelligence of ravens, the existence of snow fleas. Still others, once again, reflect events that made news in the seasons in which they were written: the mind-numbing slaughter of female engineering students in Montreal in December of 1989, the slumping economy, the environment, the fierce onslaught and fiercer resolution of the Gulf War.

For all those reasons, the *Fourth Papers* are probably no less (if no more) as fair a measure of much of what was on Canadians' minds for a couple of years than any of the editions that preceded them. But the radio seasons of 1989-90 and 1990-91 also encompassed an extraordinary time in Canadian history – a time when the country itself threatened to come apart at the seams. Those politics coloured much of what was on the *Morningside* air, as they did much of what was in the newspapers, in the magazines and on television. In time, in the office we began to refer to Canada's political crisis simply as "The Subject," and sometimes we would work as hard to avoid inundating our listeners with still more constitutional developments – "We need a *hootenanny*," I remember someone saying in the story meeting that led to one of our most successful programs – as we did to try to explain what was happening.

The anger and the tension people were feeling also showed up in our mail, which was crankier than I could ever remember it. People poured out their frustrations with politics and politicians. They were grouchy with the media, too. They chastised us – and me – for being both too sympathetic to Quebec and too blind to its aims. They accused us and our panelists of being too right wing, too left wing, too wimpish, too strident. These were still not the majority of letters to *Morningside* – far from it, in fairness – but there were enough of them in almost every morning's pile of mail that, even without all the other evidence that was around us, we could feel the country in trouble. When, on my travels, people would pay me the highest compliment that *Morningside* receives – which, thank heavens, they still did from time to time – which is that the program (together with the network that carries it) is "one of the few things holding the country together," I could only reply wistfully that we weren't doing a very good job, were we?

THE GREATEST STRESS, of course, was around the borders of Quebec. Whether or not the rest of the country had intended it as such – and I for one was and remain convinced that the signal sent was not the signal received – Quebeckers saw the rejection of the Meech Lake accord, in the summer of 1990, as a rejection of them. The tide of Quebec nationalism, which had first been evident in the late fifties and early sixties, which had crested and appeared to break with the referendum of 1980, and which had appeared to recede as Quebeckers turned their energies towards the economy (I remember hearing in the mid-eighties that the daughter of a leading separatist was studying business at L'Ecole des Hautes Etudes at the University of Montreal and thinking that there, at last, it was all over) now rushed back with unprecedented force. Suddenly, a *majority* of Québécois wanted out. On a plane trip from Vancouver to Toronto, I sat with a very senior civil servant, a Quebecker, whom I had come to know through the literacy movement but who had been seconded, along with many of his colleagues, into the federal government's constitutional scramble, and heard him lament how his own mother had felt hurt by Meech Lake and was now, he said forlornly, an eighty-year-old *indépendantiste*. On St. Jean Baptiste Day, the Monday after the collapse of Meech, a hundred thousand Québécois, many waving pale blue fleurs-de-lis, gathered at Ile Ste-Hélène in Montreal, to sing their own songs into the summer air. Watching them on television, listening to scores of thousands of voices joining in the chorus of Michel Rivard's "*Je voudrais voir la mer*," it was difficult not to think that they were on their way to nationhood – if in fact they were not already there. It was hard not to be envious. It was impossible not to be sad.

Just as dramatically, a significant proportion of the rest of the population – the polls varied, but the feelings were consistently strong – seemed prepared to let them go. In the west (or at first in the west, for it was later to make huge inroads into Ontario as well), Preston Manning's Reform Party rose on a wave of resentment, much of which – whatever the protestations of its unruffable and personable leader – was resentment of Quebec. The two founding nations had not been as rancorous with one another since the conscription crises of the two world wars – and those crises, for all the anger they had unleashed, had never really threatened, as the post-Meech Lake bitterness did, the very fibre of the alliance.

"Alliance"? Between "the founding nations"? In the early nineties that understanding of Canada, if it had ever been valid, was increasingly difficult to regard as definitive. French Canada remained French, all right; more than five million Quebeckers out of a total population of just over six million told 1986 census takers they were of French origin. But the non-Quebec parts of Canada, for which, significantly, on *Morningside* as elsewhere, people struggled to find a sobriquet (TROC, for The Rest Of Canada? COQ, for Canada Outside Quebec?), could no longer be looked on as "English." English-*speaking*, perhaps (and certainly as opposed to French-speaking). But not English. The patterns of immigration since World War Two had altered forever the idea of a nation of displaced British and Scots, eating their fish and chips and longing for home. The 1986 census reported 3.5 million Canadians with mother tongues other than English or French, and 2.3 million as still speaking those languages at home. Majority cultures? Only in the Maritimes (still British) and in the *pur laine* of Quebec was there any majority at all. The rest was a quilt of minorities. Whatever we thought of the government's *policy* of multi-culturalism – and it was a subject that rankled many of the people who were to shout out their anger to Keith Spicer and his colleagues in 1991 – we had become a multi-cultural society.

As well, in the vast mosaic that stretched (in particular) west from the Quebec-Ontario border, it was harder and harder to make the case for French as a *second* language. There were more Italians than French Canadians in Toronto, more Ukrainians in Edmonton, more Asians in British Columbia. In the city where I grew up, to take a more specific example, Galt, Ontario, as it was then – it is Cambridge now – there were, in 1990, six times as many people who listed Portuguese as their mother language as listed French. Or, to take another, I remember going to visit the then-premier of British Columbia, Bill Vander Zalm, in his riding office in suburban Richmond. The office was in a shopping plaza, and as we chatted in its second-floor boardroom, I looked out the window at the signs for Chinese doctors, Vietnamese restaurants and Italian groceterias, with nary a syllable of French among them, wondering not that the premier had not fought harder for the Quebec case at Meech Lake but that he had been sympathetic to it at all.

All this, of course, underlay the stresses Meech Lake had sought to assuage. If the premier of Quebec considered himself as the spokesman for one "founding nation" in negotiation with another, the other premiers saw things differently; to them (and they were right), English-speaking Canada was not a single polit-ical body – certainly it had no single spokesperson – it was a con-glomerate of nine individual constituencies. The creaking old metaphor of the marriage ("Can this marriage be saved?" my favourite fencing partner Lise Payette and I discussed yet again at the Canadian Association of Journalists' meeting in Montreal) was, in a changed and changing Canada, useful only from the Quebec view. In TROC, Canada wasn't an agreement between two entities, it was an arrangement among ten.

What *did* Quebec want? Even this hoariest of Canadian political questions seemed – to some of us at least – to require a new answer. It was as if many of the changes the country had made since the days of the Quiet Revolution had been based on a false premise. What Quebec had wanted, we had understood – for the Laurendeau-Dunton commission told us so in the sixties, and it had been the policy of every prime minister and every government that had held power since – was to play its own role in a "bilingual" nation. Not bilingual in the sense that every citizen had command of two languages; no one, contrary to the extremists of reaction, ever believed that, just as no one had ever wanted to shove French – or English – down anyone else's throat. But *reasonably* bilingual, a country where, within the bounds of common sense, every citizen could live, be educated and be accommodated by the government in whichever of the two official languages he or she chose. Gradually over the years that followed Laurendeau-Dunton, we had moved towards that goal, beginning with the removal of such aggravations as English-only federal cheques and moving on to make Ottawa a reasonably bilingual city, to spread Radio Canada – both radio and television – across the country, to nurture francophone power in the civil service, and to make such federal institutions as Air Canada, the RCMP and the armed forces function in both languages. Was it perfect? Hardly. Lise Payette still wasn't able, as she pointed out with some glee in our Montreal dialogue, to buy a *timbre-poste* in Kelowna, and I could still feel like an alien at the security desk at the *Maison Radio-Canada* in Montreal, trying, in my clumsy *joual*, to explain why I needed to get into a radio studio at six o'clock in the morning. On the other hand, it still seemed unnatural to hear the co-pilot of the flight between, say, Saskatoon and Regina, wrestling with the safety instructions in French, and it was frustrating for an executive of Petro-Canada in Calgary to have to wait until her report had been translated before she could release it. There was, to be sure, much that was both inefficient and silly about it, and sometimes defending its excesses against even the most temperate of its critics was not easy. As Peter Brimelow pointed out in his disdainful *The Patriot Game*, for example – to take just one instance I recalled from an earlier season of *Morningside* – by requiring that our prime ministers be bilingual we eliminate eighty-five per cent of the population from contention. But, dammit, it was all right; for all its flaws, it was us. It felt *good* to get on an Air Canada flight coming home from San Francisco and hear those French announce-ments, or to hear, on Canada Day, a choir from St. John's singing about the *terre de leurs aillieux*. By the turn of the decade, 228,000 non-Quebec students were enrolled in French immersion. We were getting there.

And then, even before the collapse of Meech Lake – and, it could be argued, one of the factors that led to the accord's collapse – it became evident that that had not been what Quebec wanted at all. What the nationalists aspired to was not a bilingual nation but a *unilingual* Quebec; what language the rest of the country spoke was of no consequence to them whatever.

The clarion was Bill 178, the language law that forbade the posting of signs in "languages other than French." To even the most sympathetic non-Quebeckers – among whom I had long counted myself, for what that's worth – 178 (and never mind the fact that Robert Bourassa, whose government wrote the bill, had promised better) seemed both unnecessary and outrageous. French, after all, was in more robust health in Quebec than it had been since the Conquest, and whatever threat did hang over it came not from its own anglophone citizenry (who had, in the years since the Quiet Revolution, become the most bilingual com-munity in Canada), but from the great wash of world – specifically American – culture. "*I* am not the problem," I remember barking at Gérald Godin, the poet in René Lévesque's Parti Québécois Cabinet, "Michael Jackson is the problem." In that context, some of the other apparently Draconian language laws of Quebec – even, for example, the restriction on English-language films until they were also available in French – could be at least understood. (Though my friend Bob Duncan, who made a film about Hugh MacLennan for the National Film Board and then couldn't show it in Quebec schools because his francophone colleagues didn't like it enough to have it translated, wouldn't agree.) But to make it an offence to put a for-sale sign on your own house in your own language? Or to call your bookstore a bookstore? Sorry. We didn't get it – any more than we got, a year or so later, the regulation that was proposed for Montreal separate schools (if later withdrawn) that would have prohibited "languages other than French" even in the corridors and school yards. In one poll, seventy-six per cent of Canadians said they opposed 178. Among the responses on *Morningside* that stuck in my mind was that of an intelligent and down-to-earth man named Dave Yager, the editor of an oil-patch magazine, who, in a panel we put together on a trip to Calgary, said forlornly, "Know what I can't understand, Peter? How come the law says we *have* to have signs here in both languages – on the Mountie cars, in the post office, all over Banff. But in Quebec, the law says you *can't* do that. It just doesn't make sense."

No, on the surface, it didn't. Struggling with it – with the fact that a province whose first elected *indépendantiste* government, in the seventies, had at least begun as a wellspring of social democracy had now imposed a quintessentially *un*democratic law – it was hard not to wrestle with the realization that there might exist, in French and English(-speaking) Canada, different ideas of the relative importance of collective and individual rights. As George Grant had reminded us in *Lament for a Nation*, but which, like so many of the insights in that remarkable work, we had apparently chosen either to ignore or to forget, "The French Canadians had entered Confederation not to protect the rights of the individual but the rights of a nation." So that in Quebec eyes, the rights of the collective to impose restrictions on – in this case – the use of language could be justified by its own right to survive. To the rest of us, particularly in the light of our proud new Charter of Rights and Freedoms, that simply wouldn't hold.

Was this the case? When I put it to Jacques Parizeau, the PQ leader who, perforce, supported Bourassa's law, he agreed. "Of course," he said, with the charming insouciance (and unaccented English) that so enrages many non-Quebeckers – and doesn't always sit too well in his own province. And when Bourassa himself, challenged to defend his law in the courts, chose not to argue its viability under the Canadian Charter but instead to say he would apply it "notwithstanding" the Charter – thereby employing, as some Canadians were wont to forget, a constitutional provision first asked for by two western provinces – he seemed to be underlining the difference in perceptions.

But if it *were* the case, did it not signify a gap between the two cultures greater even than their linguistic differences? Would admitting to it not also admit to a fundamental difference between political values? And if that difference did exist, could it, in the end, be reconciled in what we still wanted to call a single nation?

Reflecting on these questions, it was hard not to be aware of an inherent irony. Collectivity, after all, is perhaps the single characteristic of Canadian society that sets us most apart from our giant neighbour to the south. Even the two oft-quoted parallel triptychs of our founding documents, their "life, liberty and the pursuit of happiness," and our "peace, order and good government," serve to establish the differences. As the legal scholar Robert Martin wrote in an anthology called *After Meech Lake*, "At the centre of the U.S. project is the individual and at the centre of the individual's existence is the pursuit of material wealth." Canada, by contrast, is "a society which has a sense of its own organic nature and of the mutual rights and obligations of its members."

So much of what we have done has been defined by our willingness – our need, if you want – to huddle together against the cold. We have, as I (among others) have written elsewhere, learned how to pool our resources. We've made public institutions –railways, airlines, energy conglomerates, broadcasting networks – to do the work that private enterprise couldn't, or wouldn't, do. We've built a social safety network – medical care, unemployment insurance, family allowances, universal pensions – that has made certain that the least privileged among us have the same access to what we regard as rights and necessities as the richest. Lacking the kind of private fortunes that would have supported patronage of the arts, we've created a public pool, the Canada Council, seeding it (to quote myself again) from the death taxes of two rich old men, but sweetening it thereafter from the common purse. In classical terms, our political centre of gravity is – or has been – well to the left of centre. In nearly every aspect of our national life, in other words, we have acted collectively. So that one way to look at the rift between Quebec and the rest of us in the seasons of 1989 to 1991 was that Quebec, in the language law we all found so intolerable, was just being more Canadian than we were prepared to accept.

Weird, eh?

But it could break your heart.

IF MICHAEL JACKSON, that handy symbol of a homogenized continental culture, is Gérald Godin's problem, so, too, is he ours. In the late eighties, according to Rick Salutin, in the anthology *If You Love This Country*, eighty-five per cent of records and tapes sold in Canada were by "non-Canadian" artists. (As we do with "languages other than French" in the Quebec legislation, we know what that means, don't we?) Less than five per cent of the fare shown on Canadian theatrical movie screens was Canadian (and ninety-seven per cent of the profits from films left the country). Ninety-five per cent of the television drama available to English-speaking Canadians came from elsewhere, and seventy-seven per cent of the magazines. Canadian-owned publishers, who published eighty per cent of the books written by Canadians, accounted for only twenty per cent of the market in their own country. And so on and so on. There *is* a Canadian culture, but it is a tenuous one, still vulnerable in its own venue. It exists next door to the greatest popular culture the world has ever known, which flows over it across the world's most open border, and seeps into every gully and crevasse. Without help, it still can't quite stand on its own.

In the late eighties and early nineties, alas, many of the structures that protected it were coming down. Whatever one's feelings had been about the Free Trade Agreement with the U.S. – mine had been mixed, to be honest; I was intellectually willing to accept the need for wider markets, but instinctively opposed to being tied even more closely to our best friends – no one had argued it would *further* our cultural independence. But in theory at least, culture had been left out of the deal. Now, as the seasons represented in this book were drawing to a close, talks were beginning about a new agreement, this time tri-lateral, with Mexico included. In this round, the Americans wanted culture on the table. American magazine publishers, presumably, would like to see the end of Bill C-58, which disallows advertising in their Canadian editions as a Canadian business expense, and American broadcasters would like to be able to sell ads in their border stations to Canadian businesses without restriction – two areas where the Canadian cultural industries need protection against what is, in effect, dumping. Once again, the Conservatives proclaimed their determination to keep it off. "Culture is not negotiable," said Michael Wilson, the retiring minister of finance. But, the FTA aside (and the Baie Comeau policy on the ownership of publishing companies), the Tories' record as guardians of Canadian cultural institutions had not been an encouraging one. Under their aegis, the CBC budget had been hacked; magazines had lost their postal subsidies; funds to the Canada Council had been cut (in real terms, as economists say) and books and magazines had been subjected to the Goods and Services Tax, giving Canada – *Canada*, of all places – the dubious distinction of leading the Western world in the taxation of reading.

In many ways, the years of Tory rule had witnessed an acceleration of what could only be called the Americanization of Canada. Much of this trend was evident in the paring or the guillotining of distinctive institutions, from the CBC to VIA Rail. Others – Petro-Canada, our "window on the energy sector," and Air Canada, our national airline, to name only the two most prominent – began to move from the (Canadian) public sector and into the (American) private sector. The effects of free trade? During the election debate that led up to it, opponents had argued forcefully that the FTA, with its emphasis on a leaner, meaner, more competitive economy, would inevitably threaten the social safety network. And, clearly, there was pressure from the corporate world – to trim the costs of unemployment insurance, for example, or to look, at least, at user fees for medicare. Still, the network seemed to be holding – so far. In yet another twist of irony, the more stress there was exerted on Canadian medicare, the more Americans appeared to be looking at our system with interest and admiration – even though, in the early nineties, it was still true that while no political party in Canada stood far enough to the right to oppose medicare, no party in the U.S. stood far enough to the left to support it.

But in many other ways, the social fabric of Canada was changing. In almost every aspect of national life, from food banks to support of the arts, private capital and private resources were being called upon to provide services for which we had once relied on governments. This trend was sometimes difficult to substantiate; even in lean times, facing intolerable deficits, no government wanted to go to the people with a platform of cutting good works. And even amid the changes, government in Canada continued to outspend the private sector in what the charitable world calls "humanistic services" by a factor of thirty to one, far higher than the American ratio. But the trend was there. I could see it in the work I did for literacy. Though given (and grateful for, I should add) seed funding from the Literacy Secretariat of the Department of the Secretary of State, our golf tournaments still went hat in hand to the corporate community, looking for funds from breweries and energy companies and banks to help to teach people to read. Other good causes, perhaps not as fashionable as literacy, felt the same pinch. In some ways, of course, this was a healthy change. The private sector in Canada – and, indeed, Canadian individuals – have not been known for their generosity towards charity. American corporations, albeit with better tax advantages, give at four times the rate of their Canadian counterparts; private donors at three times. And easing the public sector out of good works may well have been what we ought to have done. But it was not the way we were used to doing things, not the *collective* way. It was a change, from the Canadian system to the American one. Now, when we huddled together against the cold, we were being asked, more and more, to bring our own overcoats.

Not all the currents in the tide of Americanization were so overtly political. Some were simply the ways of the world. We had become an urban society. By the mid-eighties, three out of four of us lived in towns and cities, thirty per cent in Toronto, Montreal or Vancouver alone. (A century ago eighty per cent of Canadians lived on farms.) Of those, sixty-two per cent lived in what sociologists call the *inner* cities. With those changes had come the plagues of the late twentieth century: filth in the gutters, hookers in the neighbourhoods, traffic gridlock, crack houses, hand-guns, gang wars – the sort of phenomena we had never thought were ours. In one poll taken in 1984, forty-four per cent of city dwellers said they didn't feel safe in their own neighbourhoods at night. In some ways, this may just have been perception – another function of the foreign domination of our magazines and television screens. Over the years, for example, I had sat in hotel rooms as far apart – and as remote from the violence of urban Canada – as Prince Rupert and Pangnirtung, watching, by satellite, the evening news from Detroit, the murder capital of the world, and wondering if I had figured out why so many Canadians believe street crime is so epidemic. But, for those of us in the cities, it was reality, too. As Allan Gregg and Michael Posner wrote in *The Big Picture*, "On the one hand, we believed we were more tolerant than Americans – that Canada was what President George Bush had in mind when he said he wanted to make the United States a kinder, gentler nation. On the other, the reported incidence of rape and violent assault, racism and illegal drug use had reached levels once associated with the inner ghettos of American cities."

Even among the political forces at work in the Americanization of Canada, not all could be blamed on Brian Mulroney, the boy who had sung at the knee of an American industrialist and the man who had added a presidential podium to the prime ministerial cavalcade. The most vital, in fact, may have dated back to Pierre Elliott Trudeau. This was our esteemed Charter itself, both a triumph of individual rights and an elevation of the power of the courts – and a shift therefore of the centre of political power. "Perhaps the most important step that Canada has taken to Americanize itself," wrote the American sociologist Seymour Martin Lipset in his definitive *Continental Divide*, " – far greater in its implications than the signing of the free trade treaty – has been the incorporation into its constitution of a bill of rights, the Charter of Rights and Freedoms, placing the power of the state under judicial restraint. Although the principles of parliamentary supremacy and consideration for group rights are retained, the Charter makes Canada a more individualistic and litigious culture, one that will place more stress on the enforcement of personal rights through adversary procedures rather than governmental adjudication. . . . By enacting the Charter, Canada has gone far toward joining the United States culturally." In *After Meech Lake*, Robert Martin went further. The Charter, he wrote, "has transformed our system of parliamentary government. It has led to a redefinition of what Canadian judges do and the way they do it. . . . Today our courts are awash with American jurisprudence. American decisions, American monographs, American journal articles are cited in profusion and discussed at agonizing length. One begins to wonder whether the judges of the Supreme Court of Canada still realize they live in a different country."

THE TENSIONS between French- and English-speaking Canada, the erosion of our distinctive institutions, the decline of life in the cities – these were not the only developments of 1989-91 that disturbed *Morningside*'s listeners, as they disturbed so many other Canadians. From the summer of 1990 on, with the confrontations at Oka and Kahnawake, it was no longer possible to ignore the plight of the native population of Canada.

For a nation that had prided itself on its compassion and decency, the sight of armed troops facing its own citizens across barbed-wire barricades was both traumatic and shocking. Perhaps it shouldn't have been. For two hundred years, Canada's treatment of its aboriginal peoples had not been one to be proud of. Although the Europeans had never set out to commit genocide on the people who had been here when they arrived (except, of course, for the Beothuk of Newfoundland), the diseases, drugs, warfare and depletion of resources that had been concomitant with their arrival had all but done the job for them. By the best accounts, there were about 350,000 people living in what we now call Canada when white settlement began. By 1867, the year of our Confederation, there were fewer than two hundred thousand. The trend continued downward well into the twentieth century, until, and with the help of – at last – improved medical services, it turned around. By the 1986 census, the total number of "Métis, Inuit and North American Indian" on the list of ethnic origins in Canadians was back up over seven hundred thousand, the sev-enth-largest group in the land, after British, French, Polish, German, Italian, Ukrainian and Dutch, but ahead, for example, of Scandinavian, Chinese and Jewish, and with – you may have noted the baby-boom figures in Pond Inlet – a birth rate that was right at the top.

Having refused to die, the first peoples of Canada also survived our attempts to assimilate them. We closeted them in a series of reserves and sent missionaries and government officials to try to teach them how to be like us. We took their children to residential schools and – I will ignore the growing number of revelations of physical and sexual assault in those schools – strapped them for speaking their own languages. By 1990, there were fifty-three original languages left in Canada. According to one of the government's own reports, only three had a chance to survive into the twenty-first century unless drastic measures were taken. Until 1960, we kept the vote from native Canadians unless they renounced all other rights, and insisted that their reserves be run under the watchful eyes of "Indian agents." But all our efforts failed. By the end of the 1980s, the native peoples of Canada were more aware of their own cultures, and more committed to preserve them, than they had been in the past two centuries. Even the moribund languages began to come back to life, in immer-sion schools on reserves, where, as a symbol of their determina-tion, teachers pasted words in Mohawk and T'lingit and Onandaga under the pictures of Dick and Jane. The native people of Canada wanted, as the drama at Oka and Kahnawake showed, to take power into their own hands. And stepping to the fore, as we were to see when the Assembly of First Nations met in Winnipeg in 1991 – with the media, for once, in full attendance – was a new generation of smart, tough, articulate and determined leaders.

Those leaders, to be sure, faced enormous challenges. In urban slums and remote reserves, far too many of their people lived in abject, Third-World poverty; rates of suicide, illiteracy, alcoholism, unemployment were among the worst in the country. And, to be fair, not all the problems were government imposed. But as Canada entered its one hundred and twenty-fifth summer as a nation, its first peoples had put themselves and their needs on the agenda. If armed confrontation had been part of the process, well, that was the way it was.

MY TRIP TO POND INLET, as I say, was not my first to the Canadian Arctic. I first went north of 60 in 1971, to Iqaluit, when it was still called Frobisher Bay (and still, unfortunately, had a liquor store). Since then I've been from Broughton Island to the Mackenzie Delta. I've been to the Northern Games in Tuktoyaktuk (where it was ninety degrees Fahrenheit, and I sweated so much the Inuvialuit thought I was sick) and to a fishing camp north of Coppermine. I've been ravaged by black flies and bitten by frost. I've ridden a dog sled up the Peel River out of Aklavik, with a man named Archie Headpoint, and snowmobiled across Trout Lake, not far from the Nahanni country, where I went to look at leg-hold traps. I've tasted muktuk, muskox and muskrat, reindeer and caribou, Arctic hare, Arctic char and (illegally) Arctic owl, and jackfish caught in a net by the father of Nellie Cournoyea, the Northwest Territory's minister of resources. I've been booed in the best bar in Inuvik, after the late-night talk show I hosted supplanted the cowboy movies on TV. I've tested my nerve in a small plane braking to a stop at the edge of a cliff in Arctic Red River and, in a wet suit, under the waters of Hidden Lake, thirty miles out of Yellowknife, where my cousin Wayne makes his living as a diver. I've walked the land and travelled the waters, and come to count many northern people among my friends.

But for all that, I'm still a southerner. No matter how many times I've visited it, the north remains for me more an *idea* than a place, and each time I go there is as the first time, at once a discovery and – as it began to come clear to me in Pond – a return.

I had, I realize now, two norths when I was young. One was the north of childhood summers, my grandparents' cottage at Lake Simcoe, fifty miles from Toronto, or Nagiwa, a boys' camp on the Severn River, not much farther, a north of spruce and tamarack, starlit nights and camp-fires. The other was in my mind, a north of howling winds and barren tundra, bold explorers and stoic natives. I knew it from books and newsreels and from – God bless it – the radio. And it, too, was real to me. When, delivering the Galt *Reporter* along the snowbound streets, running a trapline in my mind, I shouted a silent "gee," the chimerical dog team fanning out ahead of me turned right as surely as my stepfather's Olds-mobile coupe did when he turned the wheel. When I read the tales of Arctic adventures, I was *there*. As surely as the heroes of Foster Hewitt's hockey broadcasts or the words to "The Maple Leaf Forever," that north, where I had never been, was part of my consciousness.

Since then, I've expanded both my norths. The highway to Lake Simcoe gave way to the Quebec, North Shore and Labrador Railway, where I worked on a survey gang to help defray the costs of my first year at university; Camp Nagiwa to the Porcupine of Northern Ontario, where I served my newspaper apprentice-ship, first as a reporter on the Timmins *Daily Press* and, later, as the world's most callow weekly editor, in Kapuskasing. At *Mor-ningside*, as I've indicated – or *This Country in the Morning*, as it was then – my dog teams turned to flesh.

But along the way – and this is what became so clear in Pond – experience and imagination have merged; the two norths have become one. And that one is the land itself, with all its stretching, untrammelled, awesome beauty, a land like no other place on earth, that is ours, that shapes us and defines us and makes us who we are. So that to go there, even for the first time, is also to go home.

Know something? Canada, which we tend to think of as a thin ribbon of city lights stretched out along the forty-ninth parallel, is as high as it is wide. It's as far from Eureka, on Ellesmere Island, to Point Pelee in Ontario (which in fact is south of parts of California) as from Carbonear to Skidegate. The north is *enormous*. More than a third of our land mass lies above 60, and it's as varied – from mountains to deserts to icy archipelagos – as the rest of the country put together. If Lake Simcoe is "north" from Toronto, and Timmins from Lake Simcoe, then Churchill, which is more than twice as far as Timmins is from Toronto, must be *really* north. Yet at Churchill you are not even half-way there. If we are bounded by the United States to the south, the Pacific to the west and the Atlantic to the east, to the north there is only space. From the corner of Bloor and Spadina, if you wanted to and had five or six months to spare, you could walk to the North Pole.

NOT MANY OF US, of course, are so inclined. We flock (understandably) to Florida or Hawaii in the winters, and, in summer, venture scarcely farther than the nearest beach. Canadian kids – my own among them – who want to see the world start off in London or Paris or, from the west, Hong Kong. Our most beautiful wilderness seems to attract more people from abroad than from our own south. In the staggering mountain scenery of Auyuittuq National Park on Baffin Island – the fifth largest island in the world – you are as likely to run into someone from Copenhagen as from Kitchener (if you run into anyone at all), and the house in Yellowknife that features skylights for staring at the aurora borealis is usually full of wide-eyed Japanese.

Those who do go there are invariably moved. In the season of 1990-91, *Morningside* ran a series of panels celebrating various regional landscapes. (One, on the Prairies, forms the last chapter in this book.) From the north – we linked Nain, Goose Bay and Yellowknife – there was much talk of light ("The snow is like fine salt," said the artist K.M. Graham; "it picks up all the colours, all the pinks and mauves and blues, and as you're walking through it it's behind you, under you, in front of you . . . incredible") and of the aurora borealis itself ("I've seen the whole sky lit," said the print-maker Gilbert Hay in Nain). After that panel, I received a letter from Catherine Pigott, the young world traveller whose letters from Pakistan also appear in these pages, and who also, unlike so many of her contemporaries, has visited the Canadian Arctic. One night in Fort Good Hope in the Mackenzie Delta, Catherine wrote:

I'd been working late at the Adult Education Centre. When I finally stepped outside and turned to go up the hill, I saw a sky full of light, dancing streaks that performed against the last rays of the sunset. The colours were continuously transforming themselves, from brilliant purple to green to white, with shades I couldn't name in between. And they didn't just streak across the sky, they surrounded me; they danced around me in a circle.

The hood of my parka fell back as I gazed up. I'd been told by my students, who were trappers and wise in these things, that if I whistled, the lights would come down to me. I'd always wondered, could this be true? The lights were already very close. Perhaps my whistling would cause some change in the atmosphere and draw them closer. I puckered my lips to test the theory.

It wasn't easy. The cold had stiffened my skin and nothing but air came out when I whistled. I'd never been a great whistler, even at the best of times, but now, when I needed it, I couldn't find a note. Then, at last, a faint, faint whistle came forth. I looked up. No immediate response. I whistled again. The lights moved. Were they just dancing anyway or were they responding to my call? I didn't see anyone else out in the village. It was just me, my whistling, and the northern lights. They flickered and dipped, but they never did come right down and

touch me, as I'd been told they would. But I wasn't disappointed. They must have heard me. As soon as I stopped whistling, they faded, leaving only an afterglow.

Our neglect, I suppose, is forgivable. Travel to the north is uncon-
scionably expensive; it's cheaper to fly to Amsterdam from
Toronto than to Iqaluit; there are more flights from Vancouver to
Hawaii than to Whitehorse. In my own most honest moments,
indeed, I wonder if I'd have been smart enough to try to see the
Arctic myself if my work hadn't taken me there.

And yet, and yet. It is fifty-six years since Stephen Leacock
wrote the poignant words that appear in my epigraph here – not
long in the course of human history, but enough for the world to
have changed. Leacock would have taken the better part of a day
to get from Toronto to the boat-house on Lake Couchiching where
he wrote. Today, he could make it in an hour and a half. Today,
the trip he could only pine for from his summer home might very
well have become for him the kind of reality my own northern
pilgrimages have, through my good fortune, become for me. He
might, indeed – I would certainly have asked him – have joined us
in one of our golf tournaments, though the only account I've ever
heard of his playing involved more swigs than swings. But in the
end, I'd submit, it wouldn't have mattered very much. Imagination and reality *are* one. "To all of us," Leacock wrote in "I'll Stay
In Canada," "the vast unknown country of the North, reaching
away to the polar seas, supplies a peculiar mental background."

Whether or *not* we go there, in other words, the north is part
of all of us; it belongs to us and we belong to it.

THE FIRST GOLF TOURNAMENT for literacy I played in after Pond
Inlet was at the Briars, on Lake Simcoe, in Ontario – Stephen
Leacock's old stomping grounds, as it happens (he is buried in a
churchyard up the road, and the course itself is where he is said
to have played his own whisky-enhanced round), but also the
same neighbourhood as my grandparents' old cottage, and now

of the small house where I spend all my weekends and most of my summers. The Briars was where all the tournaments had started. In the summer of 1986, when I'd been at *Morningside* four years, Gill Howard and I – Gill and I live together – decided to gather a few friends and raise a few dollars for the cause of reading. Since then, they've grown exponentially. Counting Pond, which was our second game on the ice (we'd been to Yellowknife the year before), there would be eleven in 1991, from Victoria to Charlottetown, and more are planned for seasons to come. But the Briars, my own home course (I used to play with my grand-father there, and now do so with my sons), has remained special to me. In 1990, the tournament's fifth anniversary, Gill and I moved the party that used to be held at our place down the road to the Red Barn, a summer theatre that's served the area for forty years. The night before the tournament, under the guidance of Carole Warren, who had been *Morningside*'s entertainment pro-ducer, we took over the Barn's stage with some writers, singers and dancers to celebrate our success – and raise a few more dollars for the cause.

It was a lovely evening – like a village party, someone said, although it would be a lucky village whose citizens included W.O. Mitchell, Timothy Findley, June Callwood, Stuart McLean, Diane Francis, Veronica Tennant, Hagood Hardy, Tom Cochrane and Murray McLauchlan, to name but a few – and in 1991, even without the excuse of an anniversary, we decided to do it again, with different people. Carole had ended her first concert (if that's what it was) with a duet. Tom and Murray sang their "Let the Good Guys Win," and all of us left the theatre with a glow. This year she wanted something different. Although she had left *Mor-ningside* to take up life in the countryside, Carole, too, was feeling the tensions in the nation. She thought our evening at the Barn could be, at least in part, a response to them. "Let's end with 'O Canada,'" she said. "I don't care how corny it is, and we'll type up the words if nobody knows them. I just think we *need* it." I agreed, and we asked Tom Jackson, the tall and powerful native singer and actor who'd been in Toronto in *Dry Lips Oughta Move to Kapuskasing*, to lead it.

Once again, the evening went well. Cynthia Dale sang, with Pond Inlet still fresh in her mind, too, and the young jazz star, Holly Cole, the soprano Catherine Robbin and her husband, the bass John Dodington, sang too. Kenneth Welsh, Alison Gordon, Scott Young, Gale Garnett and some learners read. Margaret Illmann and Rex Harrington from the National Ballet risked their graceful bodies on the Barn's rough-hewn stage. Peter Mansbridge told a story, accompanied, via VCR, by Wendy Mesley. At one point, Bob Rae, looking drawn, came up to the piano, played and sang a hilarious song of his own, then said he needed someone to turn the pages for his next one. Out of the audience, looking fit, tanned and the *opposite* of drawn, came the man whose government Rae had defeated, David Peterson.

But when it came time for Carole's finale, we were in trouble. Tom Jackson, who'd gone home to Winnipeg after *Dry Lips*, was stranded in a hotel in Toronto. His luggage and – worse – his guitar had been lost in transit. We couldn't get him to the Barn on time. In desperation, I asked Murray McLauchlan, who was (as he had several times before) playing in the tournament and, indeed, had agreed to be our poet laureate – we always have a poet laureate – was in the hall.

"Can you take Tom's place?" I pleaded.

As Bob Rae and David Peterson left the stage to warm applause, Murray ambled out, guitar (Murray *always* has his guitar) at the ready.

"I hope this works," I said to Carole.

"Trust me,"she said.

And then Murray, as if he had been reading my mind – for I was still a long way from writing this – began to strum the chords of one of his own songs. Before he sang the first words, I knew what it was, and that *he* knew how much I liked it – he'd sung it on *Morningside* not long after it was written – and, in the summer of 1991, how appropriate it was. Murray sang:

Those A.Y. Jackson houses stand
In a sun like blood and rust.
When spring waters run
The blackflies come
Like a cloud of hungry dust.
Glass, steel towns huddle down
By the U.S. border signs.
That's the heart of the country
But the soul is out past the timberline.

Bush plane pilot rumbles out on floats
And then a flash of spray,
Twelve fuel drums, four Indian kids
And their mother fly, fly away.
Down in Toronto
Blue-suited commanders
Taxi flying hotels past the green marker signs.
That's the heart of the country
But the soul is out past the timberline.

Oh Canada,
I would have never believed it.
You got in my heart after all
You seem like such an endless place
In a world that's getting small.
No Canada ain't some cabinet man
In the Rideau Club
At election time.
Oh Canada is somewhere out there
Out past the timberline.

And then some of the stars and some of the Grievous Angels, who would play music on the first tee the next morning, and some of the learners and some of the people who had been with them went up on stage, and all the rest of us stood, too.

And *then* we sang "O Canada," and everyone joined in. We

sang so loudly, I think, that if they had been listening in Pond Inlet they might have heard us.

I DON'T KNOW the answers. I'm not even sure – yet – that I know all the questions, which, as a radio guy, I'm better at than I am at answers anyway.

I think they're there, though. I think there is a way out of the mess we've got ourselves into. (That *is* "got," by the way; it's Americans who say "gotten.") I don't imagine we'll ever be quite the same as we were before, but when I think about that I think of a golf story I know, in which a man is coming in from the eighteenth hole and someone asks him if he's played his usual game, and he answers, "I never do." "The way we were before," in other words, is really a whole lot of ways, and which ones you think – or thought – were important always depended on where you were, and what was weighing on your mind at the time.

For what it's worth, I think we need a victory now. Desperately. By "victory" I mean only something that goes right, something we can agree on, even if it's only the *process* by which we try to mend things and not – yet – the contents of a new deal. To use a sports term, we have to turn the momentum around. We have to get some people together to say, Look, we agree on *these* things, now maybe we can get down to what Lester Pearson used to call "expanding the common ground."

Even on process, there are a couple of things the rest of us could learn from the north. One is the way they turn to their elders. The elders – witness the way our golf party was welcomed to Baffin – are a part of life in the north; people listen to them. And when we're in a business as tricky as trying to write some new constitutional phrases, I'd argue, we need to hear, as I remember Dalton Camp saying on *Morningside*, from "people who've spent a lot of time thinking about such things."

I wish, too, that we would notice how the legislature of the Northwest Territories works. It is, believe it or not, non-partisan. Twenty-four people are elected from the constituencies on the basis of *their* ideas, not their parties', and then they get together in Yellowknife and choose the speaker and the government from among themselves the same way. There are some clumsy aspects to this system, to be sure (it's sometimes hard to know who you're mad at) but it works – without the kind of acrimonious, Question-Period wrestling that has so many of us so cheesed off with Ottawa. The government leader, or anyone else, is quite capable of saying, in mid-debate, Hey, that's a good idea; wish I'd thought of it. In Pond Inlet, I listened to Steven Kakfwi in one session explain his policy on a dicey matter of education and, in another, tell people how, if they didn't like it, they could circumvent it.

Furthermore, there are not two but *eight* official languages in the Northwest Territories legislature: Inuktitut, Chippewayan, North Slavey, South Slavey, Louchoux, Dogrib, English and (yes) French. The room where the councillors meet is rimmed by more glass boxes than the SkyDome. But that works, too.

Whatever the forum (and patently we're not going to remodel the whole parliamentary process), what we need most of all, I think, is a new kind of debate – or, perhaps better, discussion. Not another Spicer Commission (the "national enema," as one politician I know described it privately), but a discourse to which people would bring not only their emotions and their *partis pris* but a willingess to listen to the other side. The trouble with the free trade debate, for instance, which *could* have been an opportunity to settle some important questions, is that neither side was prepared to concede that the other side had some points. Every argument, every statistic we heard was offered to support an already established position. This time we simply have to do it the other way around. We have to do what we failed to do in the free trade debate and what we have neglected to do as we have watched the erosion of our institutions. We have to look at all the arguments first, as clearly and as calmly as we can. We have to set out first the principles we want to live by.

If we do that, I am convinced, we can move on. Bilingualism? Surely we can get rid of the awkward parts without throwing out the *bébé*. If Robert Bourassa can be persuaded – and I believe he can, for he is not an irrational man – that a retreat from the most Draconian measures of 178 would do wonders to defuse the atmosphere, then Dave Yager, equally surely, would recognize that those signs on the Mountie cars and in the parks really don't do any *harm*; they're kind of pleasant, in fact. If we can come to our senses about "distinct society" (does anyone in his right mind actually think Quebec *isn't* distinct?), then maybe – this is a big one, admittedly – the increasingly clear arguments that Quebec, as well as the rest of Canada, is better off economically within a confederation than without it, and that French in North America is more secure when it is shored up by all of Canada than it would be in an independent and isolated Quebec . . . maybe those arguments will sink home.

If they do, then surely we can – together – come to a proper accommodation between the rights of individuals on the one hand and George Grant's "rights of nations" on the other. This is, to be sure, tricky stuff, certainly more easily stated than negotiated. But if each side could begin by admitting that its own position wasn't absolute – if English-speaking Canadians would be prepared to recognize and respect Quebec's needs to shore up its language by societal action, and if Quebec would recognize the rights of English-speaking individuals within that society to live in and practise *their* language – then we would at least have a beginning.

Multi-culturalism? Surely the same principles apply. It probably *is* time, at least in government policy, to back off from the emphasis on differences that subsidized multi-culturalism implies and begin to work a lot harder at seeking the similarities – Mike Pearson's common ground. But backing off from the aggravations doesn't have to mean denying the values that have led to them. However dissatisfied we've become with some of its ramifications – a federal department devoted to its maintenance – we agree, do we not, that there is merit in the idea of a mosaic instead of a melting pot? And if we do, does it not then follow that the presence of Quebec in Canada is a fundament? So let's look carefully, eh? And along the way, let's keep the process going that has already started in our relationship with the First Nations. (And if we ever want to say "founding peoples" again, let's admit first that there were a lot of vital societies here before we "founded" anything.) On that issue, if Keith Spicer is to be believed ("For the vast majority of participants, the history of aboriginal and non-aboriginal relations in Canada is appalling . . . ") there is already consensus. We're ashamed of ourselves. We want to set things right. Let's get on with it.

Collectivity? Okay, some of the old institutions don't work any longer. No, we weren't riding the trains (though we might have if they'd been run a little differently). Maybe we don't need a public window on the energy industry, and maybe there are areas of humanistic works that can be better handled by the private sector. But the way to amend the system is not to slash at it indiscriminately until it loses its critical mass. The way to change it is to stand back for a minute and figure out what's really important to us, what we want to keep and what we are willing to let go.

We might start by trying to quantify some of the ideas we're re-examining. If there is a price in private wealth for the public benefits we have achieved for ourselves – and there is – let's at least try to figure out what it is. What does bilingualism *cost*, for example? (Not that much, I suspect.) Is the Canadian concept that if there's no work in Cape Breton, you send in public money so people can stay there until something turns up better – or more costly – than the American principle that if there's no work in Alabama, too bad, you can move to Chicago? How much does the social network *really* figure in our difficulties competing with other industrialized countries? What *can* we do to stem the flood of people who accept all of Canada's common benefits rushing south to buy their goods? Where do unions fit in? (We're much more heavily unionized than almost everyone we compete with.) And so on, once again, and so on. Maybe we even have to look at the very basic fact of our lives in North America: that it may be better to be rich in the United States but it is – or has been – a damned sight better to be poor here. Maybe, when we think about it, we'll want to temper that a bit.

But only maybe, and only temper it and only – I hope – a bit. We have a good thing going here, don't we? All we have to do now is figure out what we want to be when we grow up.

WHEN THE SUMMER THAT BEGAN for me in Pond Inlet was over, I would return, once again, to *Morningside*. In my tenth season, as in the nine that preceded it, I would have the privilege of talking with hundreds of the most interesting people in the country, and the pleasure, each morning, of reading the thoughts and responses of thousands more. I would travel more, too, as I had continued to travel through my summer hiatus, and see more of the land I am lucky enough to live in. Through it all, I knew, I would continue to think of the vast, lonely spaces that reached up above me, and I would wish that I could pucker up my lips and whistle down the northern lights for all of us to see.

– Peter Gzowski
Lake Simcoe, Ontario

Chris and Mark, Krista and Gail and (Among Others) the Incredible Shrinking Man

On the air, *Morningside* has what the producers unabashedly refer to as "friends of the program," who vary from such columnists as Richard Osler, who's been doing business with us as long as I've been host, or Stephen Lewis, the Tuesday-morning sage who kept in touch with us – and appeared on the radio–even during his term as ambassador to the United Nations, to such regular drop-ins as the ballerina Evelyn Hart or the singer, songwriter and poet Murray McLauchlan. They're all just people we count on. Over the years, some of our letter-writers have become old friends as well, and I look forward to their letters so much that, to Shelley's dismay (she likes to get her hands on it first and organize it for me to see in the morning), I often peruse the pile of mail that arrives each afternoon to see if any of them are there. With the same feeling, I thought it would be appropriate to begin this fourth collection of *Papers* with some of their contributions. So this first chapter is held together only by the fact that all its authors have been in at least one earlier *Papers*, and some – Krista Munroe, for instance – have been in them all. (She's in this one later on, as well, with her thoughts on tomatoes.)

If you know the earlier works, you'll recognize Krista as the young woman who fought back from Hodgkin's disease and gave birth to the remarkable Ben Longshot Munroe-McFee (in the spring of 1991 she topped that by having twins); Chris Czajkowski as the builder of her own log cabin in the wilds of British Columbia (as forecast in *The Latest Papers*, Chris *has* since published a book of her own – two, in fact); Mark Leier as the young labour historian who wrote first about a memorable meal, and whose adventures and thoughts we've since followed from Vancouver to St. John's and back again (Mark was on *Morningside* in the 1990-91 season, telling stories and singing songs from his book about the Wobblies); Gail Mackay as the happy chronicler of her own childhood and domestic adventures; Donna Cookson Martin as the Alberta mother and writer whose blindness seems to *open* horizons for her; and Dennis Kaye, of course, as the Incredible Shrinking Man. (Dennis has ALS.) Lindor Reynolds, who's now back in Winnipeg, used to write to us from the Virgin Islands – a member of the foreign correspondents' club that gives us three chapters this time around. Another member of the foreigners' club, Pat Cameron, was in Fiji. And Patrick McWade is . . . well, you've probably read (or heard) Patrick's letters before, but we thought this time you should also see him as the spritely cartoonist (he, too, now has a book of his own) whose decorated and decorative letters enliven the *Morningside* mailbag. As a matter of fact, after the longest and most solemn introduction in the history of the *Papers*, we thought you should meet him *first*.

✉ Through independent, grantless research, I have discovered a method of eradicating the problem of peanut butter stuck to the roof of one's mouth.

Like the paid researcher with half a peanut named after him, I too say, Don't get it there in the first place.

How? you ask.

You simply turn the bun or bread on which the sticky spread rests over and take a bite.

The peanut butter then sticks to your tongue and the back of your bottom front teeth.

Unsticking from these parts of the oral cavity is less of a problem.

✉ As well researched as Morningside is, and as hard-working your staff of subject studiers, one facet of the death of the record was omitted: reading the record.

Between the label and the last song is a nearly plain piece of record. The serial number is there.

But on some 45s and LPs are words. (I first started to look for these when I heard that Phil Spector resumed his practice of etching Phil + Ronnie from his early days onto the Beatles' *Let It Be* album he produced.)

There was the usual "Play loud" or "Fast side." George Harrison often had praise for Krishna.

But the most interesting I've seen so far are on Eagles' albums. *Hotel California* reads "Is it six o'clock yet?" on side one, and "V.O.L. is five piece live" on the other. *The Long Run* has "Never let your monster lay down" and "From the Polack who sailed north."

So far, though, nothing on CDs but a serial number.

One more piece of record-owner eccentricity cast aside and littering the highway of music technology. It blows along with the pops, statics and skips so rarely recycled.

All the rough edges are smoothed by the audio file.

✉ Whenever I buy a new book (or record; doesn't work as well with CDs), I smell it. As I read the book, I continue to smell it.

It drives my wife crazy. One day she noticed one of our kids do it. I was blamed.

Once someone haltingly asked, "Did I just see you *smell* that book?"

Whenever I'd walk into the old Book City on Yonge Street, my sensors felt we were inside a new book. My wife couldn't spend too long in that store because, dare I say, she couldn't stand the smell.

A nose by any other name would still smell.

✉ Today you pondered the name of the large hole in the 45.

Why must everything be named?

Did you know that there are names for that ridge between your upper lip and nose, those plastic things at the ends of shoe-laces, and the spot between the hole and the dirt from that hole?

Will it change the social life of your vocabulary to learn these names?

Jack Farr has *The Radio Show*, Robbie Robertson was in The Band, Renault built Le Car, and my sister's favourite brand of store-bought beer in B.C. is called Beer.

Are these all names?

Or did they become names?

✉ When our little girl was in grade one or two – I always forget how old the kids were (she's eight now) – we enrolled her in Brownies with her friends. And because we're surrounded by lakes, she and her brother continued in swimming lessons.

At one point my wife asked Baleigh, our kid, if she would like to join any of the other teams or activities that some of her friends were in.

She said no. She wanted to be able to take time off to be a kid. It sounded good to us.

Patrick McWade
Red Lake, Ontario

✉ Captain Bob longed (no, truthfully, I should say he *lusted*) for a big new boat, a boat where the hanging locker was bigger than an airline carry-on carton, and the Johnson 2.2 wasn't stored under the dinette.

"Okay," I said. There was little point in offering resistance. When Captain Bob sets his mind on something, he's like a coho after herring (actually a starfish on a rock is a better analogy).

So, we blew our brains out on a thirty-four-foot Uniflite, which came from Bullfrog (there is *too* a place called Bullfrog!) and named her *White Banner*.

Her real name (I'm so embarrassed about this) was *Happy Hooker*. I told our agent that the name (and the naked mermaid) had to go before the boat crossed the forty-ninth.

Marine tradition has it that it is unlucky to change a boat's name. The sign painter said he had never heard of that.

Now, *White Banner* is a translation, from the Gaelic, of the Mackay family rallying cry. My nephew, Ken, observed that it has probably more to do with survival and surrender – mine.

This boat still seems big to me. I'm surprised Canada Post hasn't issued us a postal code and started delivery.

I've had to modify my whole way of behaving now that we own her. For example, how do I acknowledge the cheering natives on the gas barge?

The presumption is, of course, that Captain Bob has a seat on the VSE, and people close to him address him as Don Something-or-Other.

Stuff for a big boat is expensive, and you have to have two of everything. We have two radios. This is in case the galley experiences an emergency, such as a shortage of Scotch, and wishes to notify the captain on channel sixteen.

We have a Mansfield head. A Mansfield head is a cross between a port-a-potty and a DC-10.

We also have a generator, which operates everything. I like the generator better than thirty-amp power. Before, I used to go up and down the coast tripping circuits and being followed by B.C. Hydro crews.

Now, *White Banner* doesn't have *everything*. She doesn't have a trash compactor. Well, she doesn't have a wide-screen TV, either, but Captain Bob is working on that.

Our regular boating buddies are not sure that they are going to like the generator, but if they make much more fuss about it, we're just going to go inside the cabin, close the door and turn up the air conditioner!

Gail Mackay
North Vancouver

✉ I woke up this morning to minus thirty-five temperatures. The weather station felt it was necessary to tell me this was "very cold." But they were wrong. This isn't very cold weather. This is the weather of myth, the sort of temperatures we'll brag about having survived. "Remember that spell before Christmas in '89? Damn, that was cold!" This is, of course, assuming we survive.

This is almost, I remind myself constantly, the apocryphal forty below. There's something perversely exciting about standing in a snowbank, attaching the jumper cables and praying to the battery gods in weather conditions that approach that mysterious low. Forty below. The temperature all Prairie mothers invoke when forcing their children to wrap itchy scarves across wet, snotty noses. Forty below. And we're almost there.

This is another item to add to the list of "why I'm grateful I work at home." I think this one comes right after "because I can wear my bathrobe to work" and before "because I hate office parties."

But the longing to return to the Caribbean fills my frozen self on days like today. I can't even claim it's a homesickness. I don't have to return to my beloved Montserrat. Give me Saint Croix again. Teleport me to Barbados. Hell, I could be happy in Hawaii when it's almost forty below here.

We returned to Winnipeg last summer. For almost two months, my family lived in my mother-in-law's basement. There were days I missed my Saint Croix chickens more than I could have thought possible.

We bought a house here as we do most other things – quickly, and without much forethought. It's a sufficient house, but it's not a home. We've been here over a year, something of a record in recent times. We've done all the things you're supposed to do to settle into a life. There are two cars and a truck outside. We have a pair of large, slobbery hounds. I'm free-lancing and doing well. My husband owns a home renovation company. His telephone rings as often as it needs to. And we have stuff. Oh, God, do we have stuff. A new couch. A computer. Clothes. And all manner of kitchen things that plug in and perform jobs I used to do by hand. Symbols, every one. Almost daily, I wonder where my fervent desire not to be swept up in North American consumerism went. I think I lost it on the furniture floor at the Bay.

But I have this sense of fighting fate. It's not unlike that feeling you have when you've quit smoking for the dozenth time. If I'm doing so well, how come I'm still thinking about it every day? Non-smokers don't congratulate themselves every day for not smoking, do they? People who have truly licked their need, shaken off their jones to live someplace a little warmer and a little wilder don't think about it every day. Do they?

Maybe they do. I don't know. I spent my twenties travelling, trying geographic cures for a variety of psychic ailments, meeting people and trying to live inside their worlds so I could understand mine a little bit better. And all roads lead back to Winnipeg. Where, eventually, everything will work out. If I'm willing to be humble, hunker down and just work here, most anything's possible. It's the trade-off for the winters, I think.

Katie has become a little Canadian. She's three this weekend and said "eh" for the first time yesterday. I resisted the temptation to wash her mouth out with soap. She's adapting, probably better than her mother is.

I can't go back to Montserrat, because Hurricane Hugo removed most of it. The rioting and looting on Saint Croix after the storm confirmed what we'd been trying to tell people about that island, about the danger of fencing in the poor people and making them watch while you buy souvenirs. I've got ambitions here, things I'd like to accomplish. Things that require staying put for more than a year.

But Bequia sure sounds appealing. An island even smaller than Montserrat. One where Katie could run barefoot. One where I could run barefoot.

We'll see.

Lindor Reynolds
Winnipeg

✉ I lived in Fiji for four years. After my return, there were many things I saw in Canada with fresh eyes.

If I may start with elemental observations about bathrooms. In Fiji we had two toilet models – the pit latrine and your basic pull-the-chain-and-flush variety. Here, there are buttons to push, handles to pull, things on the floor to step on, and all these flushing devices are arranged in varying places above, beside and around the toilet. You can't imagine the consternation of our five-year-old, valiantly trying to deal with creative sanitation. He was confronted by a tap whose knob had to be pushed down with both hands in order to get the water flowing. It stopped as soon as he let go to put his hands under the stream. His comment on this ingenious technical innovation was, "Boy, things are sure crazy in Canada."

And speaking of bathrooms, surely with all the variations on the theme of waste removal that are evident here, someone could come up with a way of providing warm toilet seats. After years in the tropics, the cold ceramic has given a whole new meaning to the term "bottom line." However, something I do appreciate every time I look at a sink is hot running water. If you are ever having trouble thinking of what to be grateful for, put hot water on your list.

I mentioned technology earlier. Compact discs have become an everyday phenomenon during our absence. They astonish me! They're shiny and small and sound so wonderful – if I can figure out the machine that makes them play. I turned on a television and video machine with what I thought was a CD remote. Then I couldn't change the channel – due to cable TV, none of the numbers on the buttons mean what they used to mean back in the days when one stood up, walked to the TV and turned the dial.

By the time I realized I had been vanquished by buttons, I was absorbed in the advertisements for long-distance telephones and nasal decongestants. There is no television in Fiji, which was pretty nice. The little TV I've watched here, usually by accident, has utterly convinced me that some of the most creative minds around are writing ads. Someone should tell those guys about the cold toilet seat problem – I'm sure they could come up with something.

If all this stuff can happen in four short years and confound a reasonably well-educated, marginally young person, what must it be like for elderly folks who have seen so much change in their lifetime? I'll tell you what it's like. My eighty-four-year-old grandmother told me in a few quick sentences how to use those bank machines that whir and click and spit money at you. When she demonstrated, she did it so fast (so that I wouldn't learn her personal identification number, she explained) that I needed a second lesson.

Other stuff I've noticed since returning: salt comes out of salt shakers, rather than becoming congealed in a sweating lump due to humidity. Butter never gets soft enough to spread easily. More importantly, despite being warned that Canadians have become even more reserved, I've found people to be friendly – they meet my gaze, return my smile and offer assistance. The other day I saw a guy on the highway signalling to another driver that her rear tire was soft. It's refreshing.

And winter. I figured we were crazy to leave the southern hemisphere summer for the northern winter. And truth to tell, I am often uncomfortably cold. But last week, the crisp cold cleared the skies of cloud and the sun shone glaringly bright on the white snow, glistening through diamonds of ice that clothed black trees. I had forgotten how beautiful it can be. I guess within this breast beats the heart of a native daughter. I just wish the blood it pumped through these shivering veins was a little thicker. None the less, it's good to be home.

Pat Cameron
Hamilton, Ontario

✉ Still dark. There is no moon and there is a haze over the stars, but they and the snow give enough light to see dim reflections from the islands on the new ice of the lake. It froze all at once, the whole lake, two days ago. It had been trying to for long enough. Every time the wind dropped, networks of crystals formed and the swells grew oily-looking, but then the wind would roar again and whip the waves to white-caps, driving bobbing rafts of broken ice to the far back corner of the lake. Then, two nights ago, it was calm: the wind came up again the following day, but the ice held. I had not intended to step on it, but as I chopped a hole for water I slipped and fell on it with a crash and it did not so much as crack.

I am leaving this morning for Nimpo as soon as it is light enough to see. My journals show me that, quite by coincidence, I started out on exactly the same date on the previous two years that I have been here. Last year the snow was ankle deep about the cabin, the year before there was none at all. But this year the deluges that ravaged so much of southern B.C. fell mostly as snow here, and already there are a packed thirty inches around the cabin, almost as much as the peak depth in early March last year. Something tells me it is going to be a long winter.

A few miles below me is another lake. If it is open, I have three river crossings to make, if frozen, only one shallow one at the lower end. The upper crossings are safe enough but waist deep, and if they are open I will have to strip off and wade, chopping a path through half-formed ice as I go. I carry an old pair of boots especially for the river crossings so that I will not damage numbed feet on rocks.

Did I tell you that I fell through some ice on my way out last March? I was on snow-shoes and sank to my shirt pockets. The dog thought it was a wonderful new game and skipped about delightedly. Fortunately both our packs were on a toboggan on good ice; equally fortunately the weather was warm so the dunk-ing was not serious. I had to put up with soggy felt liners for my snow-packs, though, for the remaining two days of my trip.

The two cabins I have been building here are finished – finally. This summer I had my first guests. I wasn't really ready for them, as some of the interior work was not yet complete and there were still brush piles outside that were not disposed of. I was very apprehensive: would my clients like the place? Would they find the lack of amenities and ruggedness of the country too uncom-fortable? Would I, who love solitude, be able to cope with having people here and entertaining them? I was amazed. Not only did my visitors enthuse most satisfactorily, but I found that I enjoyed them enormously. I took them into the mountains and showed them the panoramic views and spectacular alpine meadows, and they loved it. One man came unexpectedly; he had his own plane. He lives in Vancouver, which for me is a minimum three-day trip on foot and by bus (much longer in the winter, of course) but for him is only a two-hour flight from his door to mine. He'd flown up, with his wife and friends, to drop by for coffee, just as you or I might take a Sunday afternoon drive. He has since visited twice for longer stays.

So the two and a half years of single-mindedness and privations have paid off; the business has scrambled into being. Now that the snow has come and the tourists have gone, I am alone again and can at last throw myself into long-neglected projects: painting, spinning and weaving, and writing. I have been working on drawings and roughed out several chapters of a book. These will travel out with me today, rolled in a garbage bag and stuffed into a length of sewage pipe sealed with duct tape. I just hope they stay dry. I thought there must be few writers who treat their manuscripts so, but I have just read a biography of Grey Owl. His cabins were a lot less luxurious than mine and his trails no easier. I cannot help but feel a kinship with that man. We have both lived similar dreams. I think I can understand what drove him although I can't really explain it. He wrote, "When the morning star hangs on the edge of the black swamp to the east . . . I will be on my snow-shoe trail. Goodbye." Can city folk understand the depth of feeling in those words? Or what they mean to me as I, too, wait for the dawn?

Chris Czajkowski
Nimpo Lake, British Columbia

September 12, 1989

✉ I wrote you back in May about ALS or Lou Gehrig's disease. For the benefit of those who don't know what ALS is, a simple explanation goes like this. At the base of the brain there are motor neurons responsible for sending messages from the brain to various parts of the body. As these neurons die, you lose your ability to control your muscles, and in the end your ability to breathe. Because it is terminal, your priorities are drastically altered. Seeing your children graduate becomes an unlikely dream, and that honeymoon you thought you'd eventually have enough money for meets a similar fate.

Being one of the youngest people to contract ALS—thirty—I have a better chance than most to exceed the three- to five-year life expectancy. These figures, by the way, have recently been lowered to from six months to three years, so at a cocky thirty-four I feel a sense of duty to spout off for those who can't.

Since my last letter, the loss of strength has spread more noticeably to my speech, causing my palate to fall during conversation. This leaves me sounding kind of like Darth Vader with a harelip. Because I have to talk on one of those awful-sounding speaker phones, those who don't know me often think that I'm drunk. Mind you, this can be convenient at times because every once in a while I am. My legs have shown the most dramatic weakening since May, and because my arms have long since lost their usefulness, this is making a difficult situation even more difficult.

So that you might better grasp what it's like, try to imagine walking on a medium-sized pair of stilts. In the middle of each stilt imagine a hinge. Whatever you do, don't lean back! Now, to complete the picture, on the bottom of each stilt is affixed a small but very responsive spring. Needless to say, I walk like someone who can't decide if he's on a leisurely stroll or dancing to "La Bamba."

One evening a while back, I was heading for the bathroom and ended up in the bedroom. I was wobbling along, minding my own business, when suddenly, for reasons I can't explain, one of my stilts parted in the middle. The rest is history! I remember saying goodbye to myself in the mirror as I left the bathroom on an unscheduled flight. Thank God for walls. A couple of swan-like twirls later I landed spread-eagled and face down on top of our bedside table. As I lay there like some turtle with its shell on backwards, I heard this sarcastic voice inside me say, "And now for my next trick."

Within seconds my wife and daughters came to the rescue and helped me to my feet, but much later, after I'm sure everyone else was asleep, the decision was made to embark on that bureaucratic trail towards obtaining a wheelchair. The one I'm rumoured to be getting is four-wheel drive so I'm sure new adventures lie ahead. I'll keep you posted.

By the way, the broken rib I got that night is almost healed. Luckily it only hurts when I laugh.

January 16, 1990

✉ Me again! I got my wheelchair. It's electric and goes like hell. Day before yesterday was my first day out and around in ages. It was great! The kids tied their tricycle to the back of the chair, so with one daughter clinging to my seat, the other riding chariot-style on the trike and me playing Mario Andretti, we were off on the infamous "Q Cove Grand Prix." It's hard to explain how wonderful it felt to be the source of my children's fun again. The checkered flag finally fell when we rounded a particularly tricky corner at the end of the garden; stretching from our house to the garden fence and lying in the tall grass was our garden hose. Unfortunately, all good hoses have to come to an end and when this one did, I'd succeeded in momentarily tight-lining the tricycle in mid-air. I turned in time to see the strangest look come over number-1-daughter's face as she tried, mid-flight, to calculate the unavoidable gravity of the situation. The grass was not only tall but very wet, and as she lay sprawling and soaked, she looked up through crocodile tears and vowed never to forgive me. It was a good two hours before she did and was heard today asking when the weather would improve enough to take the wheelchair out again.

Since my last letter, the disease's progression has been somewhat slow in terms of strength loss but a physical appraisal of my body reveals a continuing loss of weight. My pelvis and shoulder bones protrude now so that my skin is beginning to look like it's been draped on. My face is sinking and my lower arms have become very thin. In short, I'm starting to look a lot like someone waiting to be freed from Auschwitz.

So that you don't think I've lost my sense of humour altogether, I've decided to close with a joke:

Question: How long does it take for a person with ALS to put in a light bulb?

Answer: I'll keep you posted.

April 16, 1990

✉ One year since my first letter and I'm still kicking. I suppose I'll have to check out pretty soon or you'll think I've been pulling your leg.

The pace of change in medicine is so rapid these days that I can't help but find it both amazing and at the same time troubling. We've come so far! A person can pour alcohol down their throat day after day, year after year and when the result is cirrhosis of the liver, a mountain of medical knowledge will instantly be shifted into gear. After voluntarily sucking in thousands of cigarettes, our cancer will be bombarded with a barrage of high-tech and incredibly expensive bells and whistles. Despite a huge social awareness campaign, those who can't resist buggering the rectums of others or puncturing themselves with shared needles will, when infected, not only tap into a monstrous lobbying force but become the beneficiaries of the most concerted research effort in history. So while safety nets spring up all around us and breakthroughs become commonplace, ALS remains on the scientific sidelines. One hundred years since ALS was identified and there still isn't even a known cause, let alone a treatment or cure.

I've been racking my brain for some means of attracting attention to our plight. The first idea is to get a friend to coat me in crude petroleum and leave me on a nearby public beach.

Failing this, I felt a cross-country walk might generate some interest. Sure, it's been done before, but not the way I plan. My arms aren't strong enough to propel a wheelchair and I can't hop,

56

but my wife timed me a few days back and I managed to shuffle across our living-room in thirty-five seconds flat. By my closest calculation, I could make it from St. John's to Vancouver in just under one hundred and nine years, give or take a decade. People could sponsor me by the inch and hey, we could call it the "man in slow-motion tour."

If all else fails, there's always good old-fashioned civil disobedience. I figure if a couple of hundred ALS spouses and relatives were to deposit their limp loved ones on the steps of the Parliament Buildings, who knows, maybe a few thousand pounds of fasciculating flesh would get someone's attention!

Sooner or later, things have to change, but for now I'd like to close by dedicating this letter to my wife who helps me eat, wash, stand up, sit down and everything in between, and to my two daughters who come running every time I mumble.

To sum things up, I wrote this short rhyme:

Some diseases take your brain,

Others take your brawn.

ALS just takes and takes and takes until you're gone.

September 17, 1990

✉ I know I said that I'd probably be history by now, and to be completely honest, I really didn't think I'd be writing again, but it's getting so you can't depend on anything any more. I thought that maybe I would die last spring but I just haven't been able to find the time. Take this morning, for example; the alarm went off and before you could say amyotrophic lateral sclerosis, my eyes were open again. It's a good thing, too, because I need them open to use some of the new gadgets I have, gadgets like a nifty voice aid.

Not being able to speak properly has been especially frustrating for me because I've always been a bit of a big-mouth, but an even greater disappointment was losing the ability to read.

Enter . . . my automatic page flipper, a sophisticated tool specifically designed to turn the pages of a book. And I used to think the space shuttle was advanced. Through a series of intricate guides, rollers and page holders, this moving mass of mechanical ingenuity successfully duplicates the dexterity of the human hand. It took no time to master, and being able to read again is, in every sense of the word, a gift. None the less, after spending so much of my working life at physically demanding jobs, I still find it incredible that I could so quickly be reduced to needing a machine just to move a piece of paper. When I couple mechanical godsends like these to the mobility that an electric wheelchair offers, life remains well worth living.

In fact, I have a whole new theory on life. The loss of an arm or leg often results in a transfer of strength to the remaining limbs, and they say that when you lose your sight or hearing, your remaining senses somehow become heightened. Similarly, when you have ALS and you're robbed of the ability to do anything, you gain the ability to appreciate everything.

A friend of ours named Graham died recently, leaving a wife and two young children. Like me, he was only in his thirties. The disease struck him with its usual merciless severity, taking him in just three years. On average, ALS has run its course and killed its victim in two and a half years, so I began to think that I, well into my fifth year, had been singled out for cruel and unusual punishment. I had even begun to look upon Graham's death, in secret, as a luxury that I was being denied. I could not have been more wrong. Unlike me, Graham and thousands like him have been taken so swiftly that there simply isn't time to adjust. The disease's spread is normally so rapid that for most ALSers and their families, just coping becomes all-consuming.

I suppose a similar outcome awaits me, too, but because the disease in my case has been slightly more lenient, I'm better able to absorb what is happening to me. If I am being granted time to face my own disintegration, squandering that time would be nothing less than an insult to people like Graham, who fought so hard.

Geese have begun their long flight south and as western leaves show their first signs of changing colour, it looks like I'm about to see another autumn. How long I hang around has become irrelevant. The important thing is, I'm actually looking forward to another spring.

The Incredible Shrinking Man
Dennis Kaye
Quathiaski Cove, British Columbia

✉ Annette and I have arrived safely in British Columbia. It is home to both of us, but after a year in Newfoundland, Vancouver has lost some of its attraction. Maybe in the one-hundred-kilometre-an-hour winds and horizontal snow (who from Vancouver would have believed such snow was possible!), we created a city that had roses in December. Maybe, on a Friday night with nowhere to go and no one to see, we conjured a picture of a city that never stopped, one with more restaurants and theatres and people than Paris. Or just maybe, maybe there was more to St. John's than we knew, and it got to us. We laughed at the slow pace of life there, but in Vancouver, things just seem hectic and exhausting. The bars here are too big, too glitzy. My body, positively fit by Newfoundland standards, is pudgy here. I show up at parties woefully underdressed, something that was impossible in St. John's. The arts world is utterly foreign, plays about people I don't know and never see in my day-to-day life, paintings about ideas and visions I have trouble understanding. Once it all made me feel cosmopolitan, even, on a good day, avant-garde. Now it all seems foreign and unreal. The humour, so sophisticated and clever, seems forced and brittle, and I keep remembering Codco and how they talked about my friends and neighbours in a way that was sharp and rude and honest and kindly. I miss Audrey and Allan, our next-door neighbours on Carter's Hill. We were there one day before Audrey sailed over with huge loaves of steaming fresh bread and Allan stuck his head in to bellow, "Hello dere, how da fuck are ye?" We've been in Vancouver – home –

three months and have yet to really talk with the people in the basement suite of the house we rent.

I was born in a small town, and my high-school graduation present to myself was to move to Vancouver. It really was my city, and I loved it. Ah, to be known and introduced as Mark, not "Jim and Margie's boy." I loved the fast people who talked so knowingly about metaphysics and literature and politics, the exotic foods, the sense of really understanding the world. I could barely stand to be reminded of my rural roots, and I knew that if forced to choose, I'd gladly trade all the trees in British Columbia for New York City.

I'm not so sure now. I miss The Rock, though so many things there made me frustrated and angry. People were good to us, even though they laughed at our accents ("too slow and nasal"). The food was terrible – too much salt cod and oil, too few vegetables – but meals were an occasion, just like they had been when I was growing up. The neighbours there, like those in my home town, couldn't discuss Hegel or Monet, but they knew things, and they cared about me, even when I acted like a jerk. They would help us if we needed it, and even when we didn't need it or want it. They weren't sophisticated, but they knew how to start my car when it stalled, and they knew what to do if I was sick. They would drive me crazy with half-baked schemes and bizarre political commentaries and a collection of prejudices that nearly included witch-burning, but they knew how to cure angst and melancholia with a boot in the arse and a spell of ice-fishing. Mind you, they didn't call it angst: it was "foolishness," usually brought on in my case through reading too many books.

I don't know what it all means. Maybe, with the pressures of working and writing a thesis, Annette and I are idealizing St. John's. Or maybe humans just aren't really designed to live in these wonderful chromed cities. Maybe it's all tied up with learning to see my parents as human beings with their own stories and wisdom and my home town as a good place to grow up in, rather than as a collection of half-wits all out to get me and turn me into one of them. I dunno.

Every morning in St. John's, the CBC would play two songs before its programming began, "O Canada" and "Ode to Newfoundland." We used to laugh so hard at the provincial (in every sense of the word) anthem, especially its chorus of "We love thee, we love thee, we love thee, Newfoundland." The parodies we made of that! But now, back in Vancouver, I understand, just a little, why they sing so proudly of that barren rock. Could I live there for a lifetime? Maybe not. But when I think of that odd little island, I miss it terribly.

Mark Leier
North Vancouver

November 15, 1989

✉ My father-in-law died of metastatic melanoma about an hour ago. Harold McFee, Hymie (that's what everyone called him), was one month short of his seventy-third birthday.

Hymie was a young man when he went to Italy in 1943. He was still a young man when he stepped on a mine in 1944. He said that every minute he lived after that day seemed like gravy to him. He seldom complained about personal discomfort, but sometimes the phantom pains were too much to ignore. He was a cheerful guinea pig when it came to testing new prostheses, and he was delighted when the newer artificial legs made golfing easier (he was addicted to golf and was pretty good for a guy with two legs, much less one!).

He believed in responsibility, duty, integrity and honesty and he practised those particular arts. He was also good at them. His long involvement in civic politics didn't compromise them, either . . . he left politics no richer than when he entered. He was a rare man.

When his cancer recurred, I spoke to him on the phone. He knew things looked pretty bad and I asked him what he was going to do – whether he'd take any more chemotherapy or not. He repeated what he'd told me seven years ago when I got cancer: "You do what you can and what you have to. Everything else looks after itself, one way or another." He didn't spend much time on the things he couldn't affect.

My son, Ben, and I went to see Hymie a couple of weeks ago. I wanted Hymie and Ben to know each other – we're so far away, they hadn't seen one another for more than two years. Ben was fascinated with Hymie's stump and wanted to know what "they" had done with the leg that used to be there. Hymie was very good-natured about the whole subject – and stayed good-natured even the fourteenth or fifteenth time.

Hymie didn't treat this whole business as a tragedy. It was more like something you lived, maybe you learned from – after all, it was life. Ben "trick or treated" Grampa Hymie, and like all real grandfathers, Hymie guessed right away what the costume was. He also was very impressed, like all real grandfathers are, by the accompanying sound effects. (Ben was loop-the-loop lightning – it's from a picture he saw in *Scientific American*. Not an easy thing to guess except for real grandfathers.)

Hymie didn't talk about the war much but he told us one story that I'll tell Ben some day. Hymie had managed, somehow, to get his hands on four bottles of wine and he intended to enjoy them – they were the first things approaching luxury that he'd seen in months. So he holed up in a barn, out of the rain, and began to savour the treat. A few hours later the party blew up. You see, the barn was the lone structure in that area, and the Allied artillery seemed to think that their duty involved blowing the barn to vapour. Which they were in the process of doing when Hymie boiled over. He hardly ever got really angry, but when he did, he apparently was quite impressive. When he told the story, he'd said that he "wasn't too concerned with getting killed himself, but he'd be goddamned before he let the bastards kill his wine!" He'd laughed when he said that . . . and no one could say "goddamn" the way Hymie could. Probably because he didn't say it very often.

He had a strong love of music and an equally strong faith. Although my own faith, in God at least, is missing, it never seemed out of place in him. It seemed right and natural because he made it so.

He was a private man, and a dignified one. And that's how he was when I last saw him. That's how I'll remember him. As for "dying the right way" – we could handle the situation worse than he did, but we'd be hard-pressed to do better.

January 1, 1990

✉ Ready for yet another instalment of "Passages in the Life of K. Munroe"?

Happy New Year! 1990! When I was little, I thought they'd have flying cars by now. Instead there's dioxin in the diet of the Inuit. This doesn't seem to be a technological advance, somehow.

My plan was to write you and wish you Happy New Year and tell you Longshot II (or should that be "the latest Longshot") was on the way. Up until the day before yesterday, he was. But on my wedding anniversary, I lost five pints of blood and my baby.

Everyone says it's better this way, that there was something wrong – the baby wasn't developing properly. Better now than later. Better at eleven weeks than at forty. I know they're right. But it feels awful.

Like anything else, we'll survive this. All these things build character, right? I feel like I've been subjected to major construction and I'm ready to dedicate the damned structure! But life is a work in progress – sometimes, though, it's such hard work.

Ben is unimpressed with the advent of a new decade. His is an alternative reality, though, full of Daffy Duck, John Prine, Winnie-the-Pooh, the Bungalo Boys and the Natural Hockey League, and Samson the Church Cat. It is an interesting reality, too, and I feel lucky to share even a small part of it.

He was impressed with Christmas, though. Ribbon candy, candy canes, Christmas cookies, taffy, lemon-drops – I'd forgotten how magical these things are. As far as presents go, he was content with opening his first one – a View-Master – and could hardly be induced to open anything else. (I remember loving my View-Master, too . . . I had the "Seven Wonders of the Ancient World" and the pictures amazed me.)

January 9, 1990

✉ It's taken a while to get back to this letter. It's been chinooking (Sorry. I really meant, it's very warm and the wind is shrieking like a member of the opposition) and I can almost walk a whole block. This *is* an accomplishment. Honest.

Ben and I will be going down to the train station to see the last passenger train through Medicine Hat. He has been a traveller on this train, and we often go down to see it. It has always been a great, exciting thing for him . . . and to tell the truth, for me, too. There's something about living next to the railway. When I was a kid, like every other kid, I put pennies on the track, put my ear to the rails and pretended I could tell when the train was coming, witnessed some of the fires caused in Nova Scotia summers by stuck brakes, and walked across trestles, terrified that the train would come before the trek was done. Ever notice how the ties are always just exactly the wrong distance apart for walking?

March 19, 1990

✉ Ben is great. He finally stopped being Batman (this is especially nice since he's stopped calling me "Bat Mother"). Unfortunately he is now a Teenage Mutant Ninja Turtle. He likes to pretend to be characters that always "win" – this is probably psychologically significant. It is definitely tiring. And marketing being what it is, it could also be financially draining (thank God Grampa was a Scotsman!).

We're both recovering from CMV mononucleosis. (I'm laughing as I write this. The state of my health is starting to sound a little like "A Letter from Camp": " . . . and they say we'll have some fun when it stops raining." Luckily, no ptomaine poisoning. Yet.) I asked Ben's doctor if Ben could still go to school and she said that there's no problem as long as lots of saliva wasn't changing mouths, as in French kissing. I promised to make Ben give up French kissing right away. (It's not polite to speculate on how I caught mono.)

For his part, Ben thinks this whole virus thing is wonderful. He's too tired to set the table, clean his room, wash the toilet – too tired to do anything but sit down and do monster mazes. I know *I'm* surprised!

Ben told me some of the things he really liked about grandparents. At grandparents' houses you can play with the bucksaw (I didn't think this was especially a highlight), you can throw real horseshoes, help build a fire in the fireplace, pull important things out of the garden (like onions) and not just insignificant things (like weeds). You can also feed the squirrels. At parents' houses, you have to set the table all the time. I offered to let Ben live at his grandparents' house (of course I didn't tell *them*) but Ben said he'd stay so that we'd have company. And when I told my mom and dad, they almost managed to hide their relief.

With these constant discussions about relative merits of different jobs, Ben is trying to wear me down, I'm sure. What do you say to your kids? "Do it or I'll kill you" doesn't work any more. I've never delivered, so Ben just laughs and says the police will come and get me if I kill him, and besides I won't kill him anyway . . . yak yak yak. Sigh.

December 2, 1990

✉ It's been almost a year! How are you? The last time I wrote, I was just getting over that awful miscarriage. At the time I wasn't sure I really wanted to experiment with pregnancy any more, given that a routine miscarriage turned into a life-threatening experience. I'd pretty much decided to take up knitting and crib-bage and leave all that other stuff to the young and sterile. At least, I had decided that until some crazed impulse possessed me – spring fever, maybe? – and we put the crib board away. (Don't we *ever* learn *anything*?!) The first week in September the home pregnancy test was positive. Since doctors only believe something once they've billed the government for it, the second week in September the test was confirmed.

I promptly faded away from all doctors, not wishing to jeopardize my health or the baby's. I resurfaced only to schedule an amniocentesis. You see, back when Ben was conceived, the statistics for post-chemotherapy, post-radiation therapy pregnancies were not very good, so we checked it out. When I requested another amnio, there were no questions asked, and last week I went to the Foothills Hospital in Calgary for an amnio for this kid.

It turns out that the statistics are much better now than they were nearly seven years ago, and it seems that Ben's "longshot-edness" (this *must* be a word) depends primarily on the failure of birth control and on the fact that I really didn't expect to survive long enough to ever get pregnant. This all leads up to the undeniable fact that the boys at the amnio clinic were surprised that I was scheduled for the procedure at all: I was healthy, I have no family history of genetic disease, and my last chemotherapy was more than two years ago.

They had one other concern. It seems that amniocentesis is a little riskier when it's done on twins, and thirty seconds before the ace M.D. walked into the room, the technician discovered that my expected one baby was, in fact, a most unexpected two babies.

My reaction has been mixed, to be polite. How could it be anything else? My husband's reaction was delayed by a few minutes: he had to pick himself up off the floor first. Ben said that twins were okay with him – well, hell, *he's* only *six*! Most everybody in my family said, "Congratulations. Glad it isn't me" or variations of same. That's pretty much what everyone says about twins, I'm beginning to discover. It's probably because twins happen once in a hundred pregnancies, and when people hear about the latest victims they pat themselves on the back, mop their brows in relief and think they're safe for ninety-nine more zaps.

So, aside from expanding at approximately the same rate as the universe, I'm fine. Ben is delightful. He still sings constantly, in two languages, thanks to school. He finally decided to colour this year, after resisting all of last year. He's like any other kid his age. He likes Ninja Turtles and Ghostbusters, although he's made up his own superhero – a guy called Biggest Bill of Them All – who makes the Turtles look like ninety-eight-pound-weakling heroes. Biggest Bill is a big blue tom-cat that lives on Earth-Io (because it has lots of volcanoes, just like Jupiter's moon, Io), and Ben has adapted all the songs (from the Turtles and Spider-Man, for example) to accommodate Biggest Bill's particular attributes. Ben tells me he's making a movie about Biggest, and he gives me details often. From everything he's told me, this Biggest character is one tough blue tom-cat! Ben has also discovered the joy of snow. We got two feet of it last weekend – the first real snowfall he's ever seen – and he flopped around like a stranded dolphin. He made angels and fell over again and again, just to prove that it didn't hurt, I guess. Ben is also telling people that his mother will "lay" twins in the spring (babies do come from eggs, right?). He is endlessly interesting, to me anyway. I really hope that the new babies don't take too much of my time away from Ben, but I'm not realistically counting on it.

Krista Munroe
Medicine Hat

September 21, 1989

✉ Born legally blind, I was integrated into the public school system back in 1954 before such a thing was even considered possible, let alone desirable. It came about, not so much because my parents believed in integration, but because they could not tolerate the prospect of sending a six-year-old from an isolated Alberta farm all the way to Brantford, Ontario, to the then nearest school for the blind. I wouldn't have been able to go home for Christmas. Yet the school board and superintendent were adamant that there was no place in the regular classroom for a blind student.

My mother, not to be dissuaded, ordered correspondence lessons and taught me herself. (She also taught my sighted younger sister, Sandra, who was not quite old enough to be eligible for school, so that she wouldn't disturb my work.) This was no small undertaking for a busy farm wife of twenty-five with only a grade ten education who was soon to find yet another baby on the way. There was no electricity, no running water, no telephone, no experts to give her encouragement or support. Yet with much patience, pain and perseverance on both our parts, Mum taught me, using what limited vision I had, to read ink print. When I was in grade two, a stroke of miraculous good fortune led us to discover a doctor in New York City who fitted me with special glasses—the only glasses I've ever found useful—which made reading somewhat easier.

In grade three, I went to school, and my sister went with me. The authorities were still highly doubtful. But the fact that I could read and was clearly gifted academically persuaded them to take the gamble and let me give the local school a try. While I could read, my useful vision was – and is – restricted to what I could bring within a few inches of my eyes. There were no resources, no teacher aides, no support systems, and I have to admire the courage and ingenuity of several wonderful teachers who rose to the occasion.

The real heroine – and victim – of the situation was my little sister, who was expected to be my constant companion and guide, to read the blackboard for me, to be, in other words, a seven-year-old teacher's aide. When I entered an essay contest in grade six, the teacher made Sandra re-copy my work because my handwriting would not be acceptable for the contest, and then she made Sandra do it again because she had not done it neatly enough the first time. I won first prize, and no one remembered to thank Sandra. The situation persisted until we went off to university in Edmonton and finally went our separate ways, not without considerable damage to our personal relationship.

Essentially, I made my own rules, and they were seldom questioned. I didn't want to play outside so I didn't play outside. I assumed I couldn't take physical education, and no one ever disputed that. Even at university, I announced that I wouldn't be able to manage the required laboratory science, so the dean waived the requirement.

I won the awards, basked in admiration and adulation, but I was terribly alone. I was the only blind person I knew, the only blind person anyone around me knew. I knew I had to set an example. I knew I dared not fail at anything. Succeeding was not enough. Whatever I did, I had to do it better than a sighted person could. The result has been many risks I've never taken, many things I've never tried.

My biggest fear was that all those people who admired me so much would discover, if they ever met another blind person, that I was really very ordinary, perhaps even a complete clod, and nothing special at all. More to the point, I was afraid that I would discover I was really very ordinary and nothing special at all.

I did have some sense of the problem, and when I was in junior high, I asked my parents to send me to a school for the blind. (By then Alberta students were being accepted at Jericho Hill School in Vancouver.) My parents were horrified. So was my CNIB case worker, the only resource person of any kind who had ever been available to us. Why, they all demanded, would I want to go to a school for the blind when I could manage so well in the world of the sighted?

And so I stayed in the world of the sighted. And I made it. But I made it at a price. Socially, I was admired, but not really accepted. I didn't date until my third year of university–I couldn't imagine that any guy would want to discuss anything with me beyond math marks. I was seen as a confidante, but not a friend you did things with. Academically, I could hold my own any-where, but I never danced or participated in sports. And I didn't learn to cook or sew on buttons or tie shoe-laces or swim because no one urged me to do those things or offered to give the time and attention to teach me, and I didn't have the courage, or the sense, to ask. (I've had to teach myself a lot of things as an adult, and I still haven't learned to dance or swim.)

I have another sister, Wendy, eight years younger, who, like me, is blind. She was integrated into the classroom from grade one–no questions asked. But, unlike me, she has never been able to see well enough to read ink print. Beginning in seventh grade, therefore, she was sent to a school for the blind for three years in order to learn Braille, mobility techniques and so on. (Yes, she also learned to dance and sew on buttons and swim – and she knew how she measured up in the world of the blind as well as the world of the sighted.) The separation from the family was difficult, but she returned far better adjusted than I had been at her age and well prepared to take on the challenges of regular high school and university.

One last thought – my four-year-old nephew almost died from sudden infant death syndrome at four months. Though revived, he suffered massive brain damage. He is tube-fed; he cannot sit up or control his body movements. He is totally blind and we can only hope that he may have some residual hearing. His parents and therapists have worked long and hard with him, and the progress has been heartbreakingly small. They try unfalteringly to see Nigel as his own little person, as an intrinsic part of their family. His parents cherish the dream that one day soon he will be wheeled in his own special chair by his own special aide with his own special program into the same grade one classroom where his older sisters and brother started school. We pray that day will come. But I wonder.

March 11, 1991

✉ I remember the year I was in grade seven, one of the most momentous years of my life. No, it was not momentous because it was the year I became a teenager or because it was the year I (finally) acquired my first monthly reminder of impending womanhood. It was momentous because that was the year I learned to type.

By the time I got to grade seven, I had been taught to read and even to print. But handwriting was another matter. Time and again the teacher would guide my hand, trying to get me to make the proper strokes in the proper direction in the proper order. But since I could not get close enough to see what the teacher was doing while she was actually doing it, I couldn't duplicate what she had done. Worse yet, I, like the rest of the class, was expected to use one of those old-fashioned straight pens that you had to keep dipping into the ink bottle. My nose and fingers were forever touching the paper and producing ink blots that would have been the envy of Rorschach. Still the teacher insisted that I should use that pen and take notes, and I obediently used that pen and took notes and got ink all over my fingers. Privately, however, I thought note-taking was a ridiculous waste of time. Even if I *had* been able to read my handwriting – and I never have been able to learn to read anyone's handwriting with any degree of comfort – reading anything took so long that I knew I would never have time to read anything more than once. It was obvious to me that, if I were to succeed in school, I would have to learn things at the first reading or at the first listening or not at all. Taking notes, legible or otherwise, seemed utterly irrelevant.

But the teacher insisted, and I complied. However, I came from a thrifty Alberta farm family where there wasn't much money.

Thus, when I reached the last page of my note scribbler, I would just turn back to the beginning and start writing on top of the work I'd already done. Needless to say, I was the despair of my teachers and my parents, too.

Then came grade seven, and one day during lunch hour, my teacher, Miss Cade, called me in from the playground. She didn't have to call me twice. Who wants to spend a lunch-hour outside in thigh-deep snow in minus-twenty-degree weather in Alberta in January?

Still, the tightness in Miss Cade's voice told me that once again she'd been struggling to read my notes on the wonderful process of photosynthesis.

"Now, Donna," she said in weary resignation, "it's time you learned to type."

For me, the sudden opportunity was an incredibly tantalizing proposition. After all, typing was not on the curriculum until grade nine.

Miss Cade sat me down in front of an old Royal manual type-writer and showed me how to position my fingers on the centre row of keys and how to access the rows immediately above and below.

That was the only typing lesson she ever gave me. That was the only typing lesson I ever needed. Within weeks I was typing notes on photosynthesis to Miss Cade's heart's content. I still didn't get around to reading them. But I typed them. More impor-tant to me, I could now write letters and stories, things I really wanted to do but never could before. I even entered writing contests and sometimes won. What's more, my classmates, who had never appreciated having to include me on the softball team, loved to have me type out their chain letters and the words to the latest Elvis and Buddy Holly songs.

Then came grade nine, and the rest of the kids started typing class. I had to take typing class, too, since our small school offered no other options.

I thought it would be a breeze. It was awful. All those endless drills seemed so pointless to me. Since I couldn't sit close enough to the book to read and type at the same time, I had to keep stopping to pick up the book to read the next line. The only way I could do a timed drill was to memorize the whole exercise first. I was sure my time could be better spent writing the essay on the significance of Alberta's oil resources that was due next Friday.

I could see no point in typing over and over again, "The quick brown fox jumped over the lazy dog." What I really wanted to do was write yet another letter to Punch Imlach to give him my advice on how to handle Frank Mahovlich. Surely, he wouldn't let Stafford Smythe sell Frank to Chicago for a million dollars – would he?

But the *coup de grâce* came when the typing teacher played a recording of "The Battle Hymn of the Republic" and instructed us to type to the rhythm of the march. Why in the world would I want to be able to compose a letter to Punch Imlach to the rhythm of "The Battle Hymn of the Republic"?

What all this comes down to is a very simple message. A child, or even an adult, can and will acquire any skill that his abilities will permit, if he has the basic tools he needs and, more important, if he believes he has a compelling reason for doing so. For truly effective learning to take place, the method is not what matters very much. It is the learner's motivation that counts. It was a terrible struggle for me to learn to read. I might never have done it if I hadn't, quite by fortunate accident, come upon some very special glasses when I was seven. But reading was something I wanted desperately to do, and once I had those glasses, I did the rest myself. Handwriting and note-making, on the other hand, just didn't make sense to me and weren't worth the effort. But typing opened a whole new world to me, and the method by which I was taught the skill of typing was of little significance.

Let me add just another couple of things. When Miss Cade taught me basic typewriter fingering, she neglected to teach me the top row, the row where the numbers are. Because I had little use for typing numbers (I had little use for things mathematical in general), I never learned that top row and always had to pause and fumble for the right key. Then, some twenty years later, for reasons that still baffle me, I found myself appointed treasurer of my church, and that meant not just one congregation, but five. Believe me, with that kind of motivation, it did not take me long to learn the numbers row on the typewriter.

Then computers entered my life – rather belatedly. I had assumed a computer wouldn't be for me. The eighty-column screen was just too difficult to read, and I hadn't learned to handle voice technology. Finally, however, I attended a seminar on computers for the blind. There I discovered a word-processing program that could print to the screen in forty columns and even larger.

"You buy the program," the instructor urged me, "and I'll teach you how to use it."

"And how much will you charge for teaching me?" I asked.

"Oh, I can do it for two hundred dollars a day," he told me generously.

I gave him a smile and bought the program and brought it home. First I read the manual. Then I booted the program. And then, in those occasional moments when I wasn't making peanut-butter sandwiches, kissing bruised knees, breast-feeding a hungry six-month-old or changing a soggy diaper, I learned to use my word-processing program. And I didn't have to pay that instructor one cent.

Donna Cookson Martin
Sedgewick, Alberta

The Monday Morning Poetry Club...

... isn't a club at all, of course. Its members are the poets *Morningside* has asked, in recent seasons, to drop in (one at a time) for a chat and a sample of what they've been up to. This was my idea, if I may say so (not *all* the good suggestions come from the producers); I happen to think Canadian poetry deserves a much wider audience than it usually gets, and I've learned, for instance, at the golf tournaments we hold for literacy, each of which features a "poet laureate," how popular fine poetry can be. But the person who brought it off was the producer Nancy Watson, who arranged nearly all our Monday sessions – bringing to radio, over the months, a remarkable variety of distinguished voices – and, when I asked her, put together this sampler of some of the work her guests had written and performed for us.

Maxine Tynes

High school teacher Maxine Tynes has been on sabbatical for six months, working on her second book of poetry, *Woman Talking*

Woman (Ragweed Press), and on a film based on one of her short stories. She writes eloquently about being black and being a woman, as well as more playful poems. This is one Maxine wrote lamenting the end of summer and the return to the classroom. She performed it on *Morningside* on Labour Day.

Hit That Rewind Button Back to the Dog Days of Summer (1990)

Sitting here
at the back end of summer
Halifax Harbour eclipsing my fate
I elastic my mind back
boomerang my time, my days to endless summer
endless summer
Yahoo this shout to echo
always echo
beach
beach shoes
sand and kelp between my toes
summer
and summer
and St. John River dreams.

Wanna be a rubber band
wanna be an elastic living memory of August
hot, hot, hotter than July
wanna slip into those Kodak snapshots
and be lolling again
under some big old tree
dropping its shade and its caterpillars all over me

wanna be that rubber band
wanna snap and boomerang me back
wanna hit that rewind button
back to the dog days of summer.

Patrick Lane

In his latest work, Patrick Lane of Saskatoon explores the relationship between fathers and children. In many ways, he felt as if he grew up without a father. His dad served in the Second World War and was killed in 1968 when a stray bullet fired by a former co-worker hit him in the heart. By looking at his relationship with his father, Patrick also examines the way he connects with his children.

He read this moving poem on *Morningside* in the fall.

Father

My father with his bright burst heart, the bullet
exploding in him like some gift the wind had given him,
fell from the sky he'd climbed to, the blood
rushing into him from his startled flesh
so that I imagine his heart a broken sail,
the centre suddenly torn and the strong wind rushing
through him, his blood taking him nowhere
at last, his body a whole vessel.

Who will I be,
I who am now as old as his death,
I who have never been a father to my own
lost children, who have left them
to shift in their worlds, their faces shining
in the bright bewilderment of their lives?

I have turned in my flesh,
rising to the night and the light of the candles
and stood among shadows that are only the stunned
wandering of moths, their burning wings bright sails
in the flickering light. It is here in the shadows
I try to imagine myself young again, a man
who can lift him from the sky,
take him down and hold him in my arms,
hold him against my mouth,

and with one free hand, stroke his wet red hair
away from his forehead and tell him it is all
right, that I have him, that the bullet
that streamed through the air toward him
was only the wind.
                    It did not want his death,
was only a bit of wind in the wrong place
tearing him apart. I want then the whole sails of his heart
beating against my chest. I want him smiling
up at me and saying something I can hear at last
instead of this silence, the sound of his voice,
my own children far away rocking in their lives,
his body next to mine, both of us still alive
and not falling, not falling,
the hurt heart dead at last.

Susan Musgrave

Susan Musgrave, from Sidney, British Columbia, is a poet, a columnist and a teacher. She's also a mother, and this poem was written after she found her six-year-old daughter weeping in bed. The children next door had told her that we all would die one day, and she wanted Susan to deny this. Susan felt that by saying yes, she'd make her daughter feel worse, so she did what she swore she wouldn't do to her children. She lied. This is a poem about belief, about being a mother and about her loss of innocence. This poem was published in *In the Small Hours of the Rain*, which won this year's bp Nichol Chapbook Award Reference West in Victoria.

One Evening, The Wind Rising, It Began

raining. I peeked out from behind the blinds
while the lights blinked and my mother went
from room to room in her silence, lighting
the few candles. Flowers on their drunken stems
were opening themselves like brides, and I tried
to explain to my daughter how she couldn't go out
and play any longer in that garden.

Tears fell like spring rain down her face
when I said I thought death might be something
we could return from as another life.
She didn't want to hear this and pushed me
away. She said she wanted to be herself,
always. She wanted me, too, to be who I am.

I have reached an age when even a spring
rain falling on the spring ground can make me
less of what I am. So I told her then what I've tried
to believe in my life, that we don't have to die,
ever. Victorious she turned to me, like the flowers
of this world, the brilliance sliding from her.

Richard Lemm

Richard Lemm grew up in Seattle, where he learned to love
baseball. He moved to Canada in 1967 to avoid fighting in Viet-
nam and has written eloquent poems about the futility of war.
Richard teaches Canadian and English literature at the University
of Prince Edward Island in Charlottetown and still loves baseball.
He's a member of the Wolfville Ridge Rats, a pick-up team of
Maritime writers, and has become a big Blue Jays fan. He helped
Morningside celebrate the play-offs by writing "The Sandlot."

The Sandlot

I

In the beginning was the wood
and the wood was from god
and god turned the wood into baseball bats
and said, "Kid, get good wood on the ball."

So I was on the sandlot every summer morning
and every schoolday afternoon in good weather.
My station in life: shortstop.
Because I loved that word
and the ball kicking up off rocks
into my glove and the double-plays
starting from me to Michael Moises to Duke Dupree
and the liners I'd dive for into the hole,
ripping the jeans my grandmother would patch once more.
A skinny kid, I had no home-run power,
couldn't bust the windows
of Mrs. Gadsby's house down the left-field line.
But I had the eye, drove the ball to the gaps
and stretched almost anything into a double.

So the voice said, "Kid, try out for Little League."
The neighbourhood team was the Italian Club,
Seattle's best, owned by Tomasa's Bakery.
Three hundred kids at try-out day.
Most of us like midget scarecrows
with a cap and glove stuck on.
The coaches tried a dozen kids at once
at each position. A man slapped a score of grounders
to the twelve of us bunched at short.
I was too polite, anxious, confused,
and froze. Not one ball reached me.
Then I got to bat, against the Club's
ace, O'Leary. I'd hit his fastballs
and curves before, on the lot. But now

I was paralyzed by coaches with clipboards,
the line-up of kids behind me, crowds of
fathers urging on their sons. I took three
swings, each a week late, and a man
yelled "Next!" And that was it.
Back to the sandlot, no longer a hotshot
hopeful, just the slickest of the ones
who didn't make the grass,
the uniforms of the Italian Club.

II
Thirty years later, Marea del Portilla, Cuba,
I'm with a hundred-plus Canadians at this small
remote resort beside a pleasant village.
One day I say to Miguel, "Why don't you try to
get some villagers together and I'll make up
a Canadian team." He laughs.
Everyone (male, that is)
plays in this baseball-mad country.

Since most of my team never played before
I ask for softball, slow-pitch. Again Miguel
laughs, and scratches his head. Slow
pitch? He finds a softball
in the nearest city, sixty miles away.
On Sunday the Canadians walk down the beach,
through the coconut palms and
at the village, blend with hundreds of Cubans
on bicycles, horseback and burro-cart
heading for the field. A rhumba band
plays in the tree-shade on a hill.
Dugouts of palm fronds cover galvanized tubs
full of block-ice and beer.

I'm at shortstop, and seeing the ball
off a Cuban's bat, I dive toward the hole,

one-hop the ball and on my knees
fire to the manager
of Kitchener's Baskin-Robbins at first base
who stretches for the out.

Our half of the third and an Edmonton doctor
risks her hands to bunt her way on,
loading the bases. I'm up next and
line the first pitch over second base.
Canadians 2, Cubans 0.
It doesn't end that way.

The Cubans have the bases loaded
in the fifth. Miguel pops one
into shallow centre. I back and collide
with a Red Cross instructor from New Brunswick,
two runs score, and then, like certain Blue Jays,
I throw stupidly and wildly to home.
In their half of the sixth our second baseman,
a broadcaster from Montreal, passes out
with heatstroke. The game is called.

In the bar that night, Cubans and Canadians dancing,
buying each other drinks, Miguel says,
"Ricardo, you make a fine beisebol player."
And I just say, "Gracias, Miguel, muchas gracias."

Roo Borson

"Superstar" is usually a term reserved for rock musicians, but at
least one critic used it to describe Roo Borson. She's considered
one of the best young poets in the country. Her work is lyrical
and evocative and often reflects her passion for the outdoors.
Although Roo lives in downtown Toronto, she spends much of
her time walking, both in the city and the country. She says the
rhythm of walking helps her capture a crucial moment in poetry.

Roo was a guest on *Morningside* in October, one of her favourite months. She charmed everyone with a poem about lowly footwear – rubber boots. (The poem was published by McClelland & Stewart.)

Rubber Boots

In Ontario, in autumn,
black and limp, with shining curves,
they are the only footwear for the fields.
All year they have lain in
fishy heaps at the back of closets
and now halls and entryways
are lined with them, pair by pair,
dripping onto newspaper,
upright, leaning drunkenly together, or toppled,
helpless as dull black beetles,
their legs in the air.
I remember the morning
Jane fell in love, in San Francisco,
with a pair,
glazed, brilliant as lemons
in the shop window.
But what shines in a wild Pacific storm
would leak within minutes
when the world turns to mud
and sucks at the heels
in Elora or Owen Sound.
A gash is an unhappy thing,
especially in black rubber,
when boots are cheap:
the kind thing is to carve
the toes like jack-o'-lanterns
and let them leer
unexpectedly in hallways.
Nothing mourns like a boot
for its lost mate.

You must fill it with water,
and flowers.
Unlike other shoes,
they never smell of possession.
They have mapped the sodden marsh,
trod on ice.
You step into them,
sound and seamless,
with a double pair of thick socks.
You enter the Ark.

Sheree Fitch

Sheree Fitch from Fredericton, New Brunswick, is probably best known for her irresistible children's poems. She's also a regular *Morningside* guest on Wednesday, when she gets together with Doris McCarthy (an artist in Toronto) and George Archer (an economist in Montreal) to talk about family dinners, monogamy and everything in between.

Last May, Sheree spent a couple of weeks in the ghetto of Belize City researching a book and performing her poetry. One of the children asked her to describe snow. She felt she hadn't really answered his question and wrote this poem in response. Sheree read it on *Morningside* just before Christmas and for three minutes made us all believe in miracles.

To Landy in Belize Who Said: "Tell Me About That Snow in Canada"

There are different kinds of snow, Landy . . .

Some mornings the sky is grey and close to the earth
There is a stillness; as if the day is holding its breath
Then, without you noticing when it begins
Snow falls in slow feathershapes
Settles on cheeks
Kisses your eyelids

"Hold out your tongue, for the taste of snow is white"

Then there are days the snow is splinter-sharp
Needlepoints in your skin
It sounds like small stones
Being thrown at the window

"Turn your back to the wind
And come in by the fire with me
We will sip hot chocolate
And eat cinnamon toast"

Frozen on the ground, the snow
Becomes a crust that shines beneath the moon
Like a new waxed floor

"Listen to it crunch
See how far we can walk in the moonlight
Before the snowcrust breaks and we sink through
To the softer snow below"

On a blue day when the air is peppermint clean
We go to the hill, waddle up a long slope
Dragging toboggans behind
This snow speaks, too
Squeaks a rubbery language beneath our feet

Then we ride down the hill
The wind scratching our cheeks
Until the ride is over too soon too soon

The snow that sticks
In white pebbles
To woollen mittens
Is the kind for making snowballs
or snowmen
Or tunnels

You can make a secret underworld
Play there all afternoon
Until indigo shadows fall across the yard
And it is time for supper

Then there is snow
That refuses to go
When the world turns warm again
Stubborn humps
Of mud splattered snow
Hiding from the heat
But the fingers of the sun find it finally
And rub the last of it away

Snow – sometimes like sugar frosting
Sometimes like wind-whipped waves of white
Sometimes designs like you find in dunes of sand
Sometimes the trace of bird feet

And the trees after a snow?
Branches wearing long white gloves

So there, Landy . . . .

I have tried to tell you of its taste and smell
Its sound and touch

But it is not much . . . .

Is it?

For I know what you want
Is to hold it in your own hand
And feel it melt to pearls of water
Until it is gone . . . .

I tell you what I will do:
This Christmas afternoon
I will take my sons
Out in the backyard
We will lie on our backs
Swish our arms
And make angels in the snow
Just for you

And will you be at the beach in Cay Caulker?
Please, then, take your mother by the hands
And just for us, make angels in the sand

On this day of miracles, remember
That the sun you see
Is the same sun we see
And that no two snowflakes are alike
No two snowflakes are alike

And this, too, is a miracle

Patricia Young

Patricia Young, who lives in Victoria, British Columbia, writes wonderful poems about detergent, game shows and playing the tooth fairy. Her work is both whimsical and poignant, as she chronicles her childhood memories and family life.

Patricia was a guest on *Morningside* soon after Rosemary Sexton, society columnist for the *Globe and Mail*, taught Peter Gzowski to waltz . . . on air. Patricia had just learned to waltz. "Saturday Night Dance at the Boy Scout Hall" is from *Those Were the Mermaid Days*, published by Ragweed Press.

Saturday Night Dance at the Boy Scout Hall

Fifteen years of yanking
each other this way
and that. This dance cannot
work with two wanting
to lead, neither knowing
the steps. As a boy
you came up for air, heard
your father say to the life-
guard the pool was half-decent.
Ah, the glorious indifference
of that word. You used it
to describe whatever you could:
a yo-yo, your sister's
beehive, later, the LSD bought
from a friend. Tonight we jerk
around this room avoiding the tried
and true couples who glide
to sublime blue music.
Like children, we stumble
and count, onetwothree,
onetwothree when suddenly
we've got it, this waltz
is half-decent! Surrounded
by wilderness murals we cling
to each other looking down
at our amazed feet.
And when we look up
the bear has a fish in its paw.
The owl and the deer
are watching.

Jan Conn

Jan Conn is both an accomplished biologist and a first-rate poet. She still calls Toronto home, but she's lived and worked around the world. Her third collection of poetry, *South of the Tudo Bem Cafe*, was written over five years in eight different countries. Jan combines family memories, travel and science in her work and through her vivid and detailed descriptions can take readers to exotic locales. "Letter Home After Living Six Months in Caracas" (published by Véhicule Press) was written while Jan was researching malaria-carrying mosquitoes in Venezuela.

Letter Home After Living Six Months in Caracas

I am at loose ends
waking from dreams of lost language,
stuttering in French and very bad Spanish.

Too many days with only the company
of books on Antarctica, a Japanese novel,
and the sad story of *The Wide Sargasso Sea*.

Too much fuel, not enough fire.

Right hemisphere to left hemisphere, do you read me?

Chile is "free"
but Nicaragua is a "threat."
Mexico vigorously denies AMNESTY reports.
Former president Lusinchi departs for Miami.
I go to study mosquitoes and malaria in La Lengüeta.

In Canada the leaves turn gold and amber and scarlet
and cinnamon
but here the poinsettias year round
bleed brilliantly.

One small apartment in San Bernardino (with balcony)
can contain the world
or reject it.

I'm living on black olives and salted almonds.

Surely this affects my poise?
Ma poésie?
The fragile internal balance of things?

There is no place to be calm in this city.
I'm the firefly caught in our field station in Guaquitas
blinking off/on, off/on.

Paul Horn is inside the Taj Mahal (lucky man).
I'm inside nothing, a bubble of air.

The sun penetrates in brief long lances
which I parry,
leaving me the clouds, a poor victory.

Is there anything the matter?

: a dying rat on the sidewalk yesterday, twitching,
surrounded by the purple slippers of bougainvillea;
my tiger oven-mitts bite down hungrily
not on antelopes but on air.

Ralph Gustafson

At eighty-two, Ralph Gustafson published his twenty-eighth book of poetry – a collection of playful philosophical musings on love, nature and the meaning of life. Many of the poems capture the beauty of North Hatley, Quebec, where he's lived for many years.

"One Has To Pretend Something Is Amused" is from Ralph's latest collection, *Shadows in the Grass*, published by McClelland & Stewart.

One Has To Pretend Something Is Amused

Death in a taxi going from here to there
Instead of staying put pursuing truth
In the kitchen or up in the attic or somewhere,
Perhaps making love or pulling up weeds
In the garden which is far safer and less trouble
Later on. However, one must be
In movement to sell goods and converse with the world.
Hazard is inevitable. Too bad if the heart
Gives out and the driver has to dispose
Of an unwanted corpse but he turned down the flag
On his meter and so must take a chance as well
On being responsible or not.

       On the whole it seems best not to make
A move. Though here again who can judge
When the kidneys and liver will shut down
Or in the statistically likely case I spoke of,
That of the arteries to the old pump? I wouldn't
Want to be alone in any case but probably
Will be, two loves and death
Never coinciding.

       A tip ready for old Charon poling
Your ghost across the river Styx would be
Appropriate. You know the Greek myth? Never
Mind. Take your earthly taxi to where
You are off to. Destiny will be as much amused,
Lack of understanding won't matter.

DECEMBER 6, 1989

In all the years I've worked at *Morningside*, no single event has brought as much mail as the massacre of fourteen woman engineering students at L'Ecole Polytechnique in Montreal – a tragedy that is now engraved on our memories by its date alone. I still remember my own first reaction: staring in uncomprehending horror at the black headline in the *Globe and Mail* that had clumped outside my apartment door. Just a short time earlier, as I recalled later on the radio, that door had seemed a safeguard, and I had smiled ruefully at the insistence of the woman I live with that it be locked at all times. Now, as of that bleak morning, the world had changed – for women, for us all.

At *Morningside*, we struggled over our coverage. On the seventh, we put together as best we could the stories of witnesses and survivors. But when the program was over, all of us found ourselves crammed into a corner of our ramshackle office, huddling together, still talking about the murders and their aftermath. Out of our own conversation, we began to build a panel for the following day, not of experts (unless Francine Pelletier, the Montreal feminist and *Morningside* regular who turned out to have been on the killer's hit list, so qualified), but of people – women *and* men – who could try to find some context in their own lives for what had happened.

In that discussion, as in so many similar conversations that must have taken place in offices and homes and other institutions in the days that followed December 6, no clear answers emerged. But all of us, I think, were made to deal with the questions the massacre posed: Were *all* men to blame? (Did men even have the right to grieve?) Or, if the insane act committed in Montreal was simply the product of one twisted soul, how did that soul get twisted? What went wrong? What could we have done to see it coming? To prevent it? And what could we do now to prevent it happening again?

In the mail that ensued – there were more than four hundred letters before the torrent died down, so many that at least one graduate student (in Ottawa) used them as the basis for her MA thesis – there were no simple answers, either. Many of them were variations on the themes in this small cross-section; others echoed and re-echoed our own desperate need just to talk about it.

Before I turn you over to this sampling, one thought that lingers – also, not surprisingly, from *Morningside*: A year after the Montreal massacre – on December 6, 1990 – our producer, Sheri Lecker, put together an hour of tribute. In that hour, Sheri made an electronic trip across the country, also on December 6, 1989. Relentlessly, she presented *other* stories of violence against women – including one case of spousal murder – that had occurred on that day, but that had not, until she took to the telephone and the mails, been reported.

And maybe *that's* the true lesson of the tragedy of L'Ecole.

⊠ I feel sadness for those who have been touched by the tragic events that occurred in Montreal this week, but until now, I felt very detached from it all. I felt that this tragedy should be seen as an isolated act of a madman and not as a commentary on society. I went so far as to express these views to my mother after we had been to a concert that evening. She had taken part in the memorial service in Toronto earlier that day and saw the incident from a different perspective: as being symptomatic of the greater problem facing women in society. I was so preoccupied with expounding my views that I did not hear what she was saying, and we parted, I to my home, my parents to theirs. It was not until later that night that I realized the monstrous blunder I had made, and what an absolutely insensitive boor I must have appeared to be. *My mother is an engineer.* Her name is Professor Ursula Franklin, and she has taught metallurgy and material sciences at the University of Toronto to graduate engineering students for decades. She has contributed to this society both as a woman and as a world-renowned scholar, and her opinions are greatly respected and sought-after. I was so absorbed in speaking my mind that I could not see how this situation had touched my mother, and I am shaken by the obvious "what if's." My mother is both an engineer and a feminist and she teaches in the largest university in the country. What if Marc Lépine had lived in Toronto? The class he might have sought out would have been her class, the name on his hit list would have been hers. Not only was I blind to her sadness, but I also was blind to the reality of the situation. I never was an insulated male bystander.

I have learned some valuable lessons from this. In my willingness to offer an opinion on what I thought was an isolated incident, I forgot to take into account the limitations of my perspective. It is not up to me to tell other people how to express their grief, nor can I begin to understand what it is like to be a feminist and to view this tragedy through a woman's eyes. I have no more self-righteous male indignation, and I feel profoundly ashamed for having felt that way. I only feel a deep overwhelming sadness. It certainly has radically changed the way I view women. I hope that in my case, through increased awareness, there will come better understanding.

Martin Franklin
Toronto

✉ I was on the U of T campus years ago. I married a U of T grad, raised the customary two children, one of each sex, worked hard at home to further my husband's career (at which he was very successful) and kept a large home. At many stages I thought of doing something more rewarding for me, but realized it would interfere with my ability to do business entertaining, or travel with my husband on his business trips, so put that aside and was happy to do what I could for the long-term goals of the family.

Today I am separated after twenty-nine years of marriage, left alone to learn at this late date how to place value on my own wishes and desires and fill my life without those for whom I had devoted my life.

Now I know that I had been deceived, lied to and cheated by a husband who wouldn't dream of using any of those behaviour patterns on any of his business associates. I am to blame in many ways. I was brought up to believe that my job was to support a man, to subjugate my wishes and even my thoughts to his, and I trusted him.

My story is so common, but isn't this part of the violence against women? It seems to be okay not to consider them. The golden rule doesn't seem necessary if applied to women. And the most damning realization of all is that still, so many of us think that men who are considerate of women, who show them the respect and understanding they show another man, are thought of as wimps. There are many women who feel this, too, and until recently, I was one. Society has to change a great deal yet before we are safe. If women still sound strident, perhaps it is not yet time for the pendulum to come back to centre.

Ruth Grunau
Ganges, British Columbia

✉ I don't believe this is a feminist or sexist issue. It is a case of one mentally ill individual who carried out an atrocious and senseless crime.

I do not deny that most violent crime here in Canada, and almost everywhere in the world, is carried out by men. This does not mean that all men are violent, nor that all men should be expected to take responsibility for the acts of one. That just doesn't make any sense to me. Nor do I believe that any woman should place blame on men in general. Blame should be assessed against the individual who did the deed.

It is only a matter of time before someone blames the man's mother for these murders. Maybe his father will be blamed, too. I feel it is wrong to blame someone other than the murderer for his crimes. It was his fault, not yours, not mine, not his parents', and not society's.

Let the living victims rest. The only guilty party is dead.

Catherine Povaschuk
Edmonton

✉ What does this terrible thing tell me about the world for which I must prepare my children, and about myself?

Marc Lépine refused to believe that he bore any responsibility for his disappointments in life. He found it convenient and liberating to blame everything on women, whom he equated with feminists – however he defined the term.

The refusal to be self-critical and to take personal responsibility is human and gender-free. The society in which I live, and in which my daughter and son must live, goes to great lengths to absolve people of personal responsibility. Do people drink to excess? Blame liquor advertising, peer pressure, chemical imbalances in the body. Do people sexually abuse children? Blame bad childhoods, celibacy – or the victims themselves. Do people use violence to get their way, or to make a statement? Blame movies, video games, pornography, social change or an extra Y chromosome. Never, never put the blame where it belongs: squarely on the drunkard, the child molester or the murderer.

In the past, we had the devil to blame for our downfalls; nowadays the triad of World, Flesh and Devil has been reduced to the dyad of World (read "society," "economic system," "peer group") and Flesh (read "genetic predisposition," "PMS," "chemical imbalance"). It's not our fault when something goes wrong; someone else must take the blame and suffer, because it's *not our fault!*

I'm not denying that there are social ills. There is poverty, and hunger, and neglect, and injustice, but these are institutionalized forms of individual action or lack of action. Either I as an individual person aid and abet a bad state of affairs because it suits me and it's someone else's fault, *or* I will say no, this will not go on, I will help put a stop to this because it is wrong, and because it is my responsibility.

When all the shock and reaction has faded away, there will still be fourteen murders and one suicide to remember from December 6, 1989.

There are many, many disappointed and unhappy people in the world, but not all of them kill. They choose either to take steps to change their lives, or to learn to live with what they cannot change.

Marc Lépine made a bad choice.

Perhaps, at the last, he realized this and judged himself accordingly. Too bad he couldn't have been less judgemental, and more honest. Please let me remember that lesson and live by it. "Peace on earth" begins with me.

Barbara J. Saylor
Regina

✉ Being male (and, now, once again feeling somewhat uncomfortable with that fact), I share a sense of shame and guilt, partly because of some of the comments and editorials and partly despite them.

I was angry about this. Angry that I should be made to feel guilty; angry because I did feel that way anyway. That somehow that day, because of this kind of event, I was guilty of something I was powerless to change – being male. What injustice that I could not too be allowed the outrage that others felt because of my gender.

But anger is what caused this tragedy in the first place, misplaced anger. I must remember this. We must all realize that the causes of this tragedy are anger, resentment, ignorance and fear. Out of these emotions, hatred found its seed in Marc Lépine.

I will not triumph the cause of "men" rightly or wrongly accused, nor of "women"; for that will only tend to segregate and diffuse our common cause. And that is the extinction of injustice itself. Not just violence; that is only one form of injustice of which there are many, many forms. Again fear, ignorance, anger are the causes.

I've since, reluctantly, come to accept the fact that I, as a person, am, by no doing of my own, associated with a group that has a rich history of inflicting grave injustices on others and that probably, despite my protests, this group will continue in this tradition for some time to come. I cannot escape it. I must take my share of the responsibility for being that part of humanity that is the male sex.

Helplessness and despair also have followed in the wake of this tragedy. The other night I was sitting in our living-room watching TV and for no particular reason, I began to cry. At the time I didn't know why, and my wife, concerned, cradled me there as I gently wept. I see now that in a small way Montreal was a part of those tears. But others have cried many more tears, and mine are insignificant in comparison.

Also, I realize that, through no fault of my own, I am part of a larger group who have inflicted great injustices on, yes, themselves. And for that also I have wept. All of us, as part of humanity, bear the responsibility of all the injustices contrived at the hands of one of our members. All of us must bear some responsibility for what happened in Montreal. We must not do as Marc Lépine that night, separate the men from the women.

There was another victim in Montreal that night that I have not heard anyone dare to mention yet, and this too is another injustice. But fear and anger have many hiding places and none of us is free of them. The mention that Marc Lépine was also no less tragic a victim than the other fourteen may outrage some. I cannot blame them. As I say, fear and anger have many hiding places. But none the less, Marc too was a victim of the event. Long before that he also was a victim of fear, ignorance, resentment and anger, mostly his own. He was unable to cope with the complexities that our society demands of our emotional make-up and as no one was there to do otherwise, he nurtured an already distorted view of the facts into his own nightmarish fantasy of revenge.

Please do not misunderstand me, I make no excuses for Marc Lépine. I condemn his actions to the last, but that does not change the fact that he was a victim. A member of our society and culture. He too had a shocked family who wept that day; a mother who once dreamed about the future of the baby boy she cradled in her arms. If he had won the Nobel Peace Prize we would have all fallen over ourselves with pride and run to shake his hand. We would be quick to share the credit that he was Canadian, that he was one of us.

Make no mistake! Marc Lépine was a victim, and he is not the only one. As sure as the sun rises, we breed them with alarming regularity. Look at the list of murders and the trail of broken lives over the past years. Allan Legere, Clifford Olson, and so on. And they're not just men. I read of a woman who strangled the life from her baby, horrifyingly, just the other day. That is not the point.

Society as culprit is not a new revelation, and some say no one could have predicted that kind of action in Marc Lépine. But when will we begin to act on the realization that we all have a stake in every human life that comes into this world? That society is no one else but us – you and me? That if we really feel the outrage that we profess about these events, we must all take responsibility for them and work to prevent them, not just stuff our courts, our prisons and our minds with the accused. We cannot hide behind the blame of others. It's not just men, or women, it's all of us. We each make the choices every day when we choose to ignore our fellows; when we ignore the homeless for the sake of real-estate speculation or the hitch-hiker at the side of the road. We play roulette, the Russian kind, and no one knows whose sons or daughters will be next to fall. Fourteen young, beautiful lives would have been saved if someone had started with Marc. How many more are now at risk?

Rick Wise
Sudbury, Ontario

✉ Today I am ashamed to be a man; one of my fellow *men* has chosen to vent his hatred of women by killing fourteen and wounding another seventeen. Some of my fellow citizens are in denial that the sex of the victims has any bearing.

Today I am ashamed to be a man; while the Montreal killings made headlines and history, at women's shelters, lawyers' offices, in the courts and hospitals across the country, it was business as usual with broken ribs, bruising, bleeding, fear and self-loathing. I am disgusted that violence is seen as the method of choice for solving problems, in international diplomacy, in sport, in movies, on television and in relationships.

Today I am ashamed to be a man; I lie to my daughter, telling her she can do anything she wants without explaining the price she will have to pay because of her sex. I don't tell her that she will probably earn sixty cents to her brother's dollar and that the difference in economic power may be the reason she will stay in a violent relationship. I fear for my son growing up in this society that condones violence by men on so many levels.

Today I am ashamed to be a man; because I too have laughed at misogynist humour and condoned by my silence degrading and humiliating remarks made about women in my presence; because I failed in my duty to protect those women in Montreal, across the country and in my own town from the death and violence that keeps so many subservient and afraid.

Today I am ashamed to be a man.

Howard Beye
Creston, British Columbia

✉ Women obviously have a lot to fear, and a lot to be angry about in our society. And, in their justified anger, they blamed society – as they have so often in the past. I think the reaction of these women was reflexive and, in my opinion, wrong.

Marc Lépine was a madman. His picking of women as his victims no more reflects society's attitudes towards women than the McDonald's massacre in 1984 reflects society's view of fast food. He was a pathologically troubled young man who needed a scape-goat for his failures in life. He as easily might have picked university professors or neo-Nazis or Jews or blacks, but he needed *some* group to blame his troubles on.

Since Marc Lépine did pick women, we witnessed the ultimate act of violence against women. But the reaction of the feminists, although understandable, is not only wrong but dangerous, as well. Most men, if they are anything like myself, are *not* going to accept any responsibility in his choice of targets. And they are going to resent being told that they should.

On top of that, some women's groups seem to have gone out of their way to alienate men in the wake of this national tragedy. At one vigil, a woman asked the men to segregate themselves. This was a grave mistake. First they blamed the men, then denied them a chance to grieve. In fact, the action could be interpreted as a denial that men *could* grieve.

Is it any wonder that feminism has acquired a dirty name lately? It seems to me that if feminists are ever going to change society, they have to start accepting men in the process.

And although I don't believe that Marc Lépine's actions reflect society's views towards women, the fear and anger felt by women at his actions obviously do. Men who thought that great strides had been made in equal rights must look at this fear and anger and wonder where these powerful emotions come from.

The answer is that no great strides have been taken – just the first few steps. We still have a long way to go.

David Shaw
Hamilton

✉ I am a mature student at the University of Guelph. I joined the march of remembrance organized by the university students. Later a commemoration was held, in what I have come to understand as the "Guelph style" – informal testimonials coming straight from the heart. The young women and men of the university, one following the other, rose to condemn a world that tolerates and fosters such violence against women, to demand gun control and a royal commission and to pledge to "mourn first, then work for change."

And this we did. For, so I am told, fifteen years a painting has hung in the graduate students' lounge. It is a painting of a nude woman, on a black background, passed out, thrown open and vulnerable, with a beer bottle in the foreground. It is a painting that bellows that women are volitionless pieces of meat to be abused and violated. For at least seven (and I would expect actually the full fifteen) years, women have been petitioning, requesting that the painting be taken down. The Graduate Students Union has been intransigent – it's not violent, it's art!

Today first mourning, then working for change, participants in the commemoration removed the painting from the graduate students' lounge. Of course, it seems we had only the right to mourn. We acted outside the rules by working for change. However the painting is down and many of us feel we have taken one small but very real step towards creating a world that says no to violence against women.

Heather Ross
Guelph, Ontario

✉ I am a Prairie man, age forty-three, husband, father of four, lover of sports, especially football, a die-hard Sask. Rider fan who will never forget the 1989 season, and newly emerging anti-sexist.

In our society, I was socialized to deny feelings, to endure pain without showing it, to strive to be among the "winners," to be "boss" of the family, to be the source of all knowledge, wisdom and power. I was taught always to "stand tall," which meant to be ruggedly independent and deny any need for support except, perhaps, within the confines of a marriage bed.

For a good deal of my life, I was all those things: competitive, successful, independent, patriarch of the family. As a result, my older children grew up with a largely absentee father. It was almost an imposition when I would come home on weekends and interrupt a single parent's relationship with her children.

My sole emotional support was my wife and a few women who had listening skills. Male friends were those whom I met on the "Field of Honour," whether it was work, golf, cribbage or Trivial Pursuit. We spoke of sports, politics or religion, the so-called taboo subjects, when, in reality, the taboo subject was how are you really feeling. To illustrate the point, in my youth and young adulthood, two male friends committed suicide. In both cases, it came as a real shock to me. I hadn't imagined that either man had such deeply rooted emotional problems.

My point of enlightenment came when I experienced my own emotional crisis. It is a long story but the point I want to make is that my socialization as a Canadian man ill-equipped me for it. Under severe stress at work, I had no support network. As a patriarch, I could not show my need for support except with my spouse, who also was under severe stress as a result.

It was in this period of personal crisis that I was led to question our society's norms for manhood. I recognized that I never really was a ruggedly independent John Wayne type, nor did I want to be. Like any other person, male or female, I have weaknesses and need for support in trying to survive in this complex and confusing age. I was greatly helped in my search for a new way of living by the work and support of feminist friends.

Today I am part of a men's support group in Saskatoon. We call ourselves the Aaron's Beard Collective. We meet monthly for story telling and support. We hardly ever talk of sports or politics, we're too busy learning what each other's personal journey is like and being good supportive listeners. If any of my new male friends are experiencing crises, I expect to hear about them and to give support. In return, I do not face my journey alone. It feels very good!

I recognize that for me the journey to becoming a new man and really living an anti-sexist life-style is just beginning. But with my family and with both intimate male and female friends to love and support me and I them, I celebrate that the journey has begun. I struggle with the reality that I still perform better when competing. But I take pride in my burgeoning house-husband skills. And I am not ashamed to weep in public.

This, at last, brings me to the tragedy that is the reason for my writing. When I heard the news of the massacre, I was not surprised but I was, none the less, shocked and sickened. It hurt to be a Canadian man that day!

In this pervasively misogynist society, it was only a matter of time before the violence daily perpetrated on women by men took on such a public face. I responded by calling my female friends and giving what support I could to them and by seeking support for myself from my like-minded male friends.

As we learn more about the murderer's life experiences as a battered child and as a loner incapable of relating to others, the pieces seem to fit. The misfortune of Marc Lépine, which partially explains if it does not justify his actions, is that he was born into a de-humanizing society that undervalues and victimizes women. He simply learned what our society taught him. As a victim himself, he then acted out the extreme of a continuum that begins with unequal pay for work of equal value, of exclusion of women from certain categories of work and positions of authority, and works its way down through emotional abuse, physical battering, rape and finally ends in mass murder.

Those who claim this massacre to have been the isolated act of an irrational and unbalanced man need to examine our society's attitudes and standards more carefully. I believe that sexism along with the growing racism in Canada are our two most serious social problems. As a man, I realize that the world will only change when we, men, own our responsibility for male violence against women and decide to work on changing ourselves.

Reverend Ray Purdie
Spiritwood, Saskatchewan

✉ I grew up in an extended family of loving men – father, uncles, grandfathers. I grew up believing that men were witty, supportive, patient and loving. That they would teach a little girl how to shingle a roof as cheerfully as they would teach a boy. That politics was open for discussion, and both sexes and all ages were welcome to state an opinion. That hugging was good, spanking was out and yelling only happened if the barn was on fire.

At university, I learned some of the mystery of physical love with a man as passionate and romantic as any I had met.

I was angry at the women's group on campus (strident lesbian man-haters) spreading their anger and peddling their lies about men. They just didn't know how to love!

My first real inkling that all was not well between men and women came when I worked in a factory with immigrant women. They told stories of their husbands' infidelities, abuse, abandonment and oppression. They had to hide money in order to have some for the children. They had to ask permission to join an organization, to go for a cup of coffee, to "borrow" the car.

That year, I was raped by a man I was dating. He said I wasn't loving enough so he had to take some action.

Even at that point, I still shied away from feminists. Until I met a woman who explained that feminism was about women telling the truth concerning women's lives. If that made men uncomfortable, so be it. But by telling the truth, rather than what we had been led to believe, we would discover who we are as women.

Since then, in a job where I work with people, I have heard with alarming regularity stories of violent physical and sexual abuse of women who are allowed no choice in the direction of their lives and women who are one husband away from poverty. We work together to speak the anger, to find the strength to heal and to shape a new destiny.

No, not all men are awful. I know many passionate and wonderful men. Unfortunately, we live in a society where the other kind of man – the one who gains strength by controlling the thoughts and actions of others – that man is alive and well. Maybe the thing that *he* needs to look at is the truth of *his* life. And women need to stop protecting him from doing it.

Anonymous

✉ In a flash I recalled something I'd long buried.

In a fit of anger during an argument, my father grabbed my mother. He wasn't listening to the pleas of his children to stop, so I ran out, ran across the street and knocked on a door. "My father's beating up my mother. Please help."

It was a woman who answered the door. She had on an apron. She looked over her shoulder at her husband, who stood there a few feet behind her. Something got communicated between the two and the door was closed in my face.

I was scared to knock at another door – all the houses in that neighbourhood looked alike and perhaps in my seven-year-old mind I thought I would receive the same treatment at them all. Anyway, I was worried about time passing, about my mother back in the kitchen, so I ran home again. The kitchen was empty. The big brown mixing bowl – the one that was used for everything, for cookies, bread–was smashed on the floor and our supper of mashed potatoes and fish and string beans was all over the floor.

"She's next door," my father said when he saw me.

In an apartment attached to our house, a large house that had been built long before the bungalows that surrounded it, I found my mother with the "career woman" who lived in the apartment. My mother was holding her arm in a funny way. It was broken. But the heat and terror of the discord were over. My mother comforted me before she called a doctor friend to come and take her to get the arm set.

My parents got divorced, went through years of struggle, but now, living separate lives in separate cities with all their marital strife long past, they are best friends, best friends who call one another, see one another, consult one another on matters of importance.

Though I do not consider my father to be an abusive father, when he was angered, his anger led him to strike out. The broken arm incident is the only time I know of in their marriage when there was physical abuse. I think it scared them both. My father is a much-respected man. He is known in this area for speaking up for the underdog. For probably forty years, he has been instrumental in organizing for better conditions for working men. There are hundreds, perhaps thousands, of his co-workers who would sing his praises. He is not an evil man. But he is, or was, one of those who didn't know the stopping point between anger and violence. His education and his society taught him nothing about the difference between anger and violence that arises as an action out of anger. And his enculturation included the conviction that women were not equal to men.

My father has had to learn the equality of the sexes in a long, hard struggle. If he knew as a young man that women were equal, that violence against women just wasn't a possibility, he would likely still be living with my mother, a woman whom he admires and loves and with whom he has more in common than perhaps with any other person now living.

How do we raise our sons?

Deirdre Kessler
Charlottetown

NOT THE LAST WORD, MAYBE, BUT CERTAINLY THE LONGEST

Morningside's listeners must be, as I've said elsewhere, the most literate radio audience in the world, and in the seasons this book encompasses, they continued their watch over our use (and sometimes misuse) of language.

✉ It is time to set the record straight about the old story of King Canute trying to hold the tide back.

Canute was annoyed. His all-too-rare morning stroll on the beach was being spoiled because a thane or abbot would approach him every five minutes with a supplication. "Corn is too dear, Sire, do something." "There is much crime in the towns, Sire, do something." "Your officials are on the take, Sire, do something."

Being economical of word and gesture, Canute placed his large English feet on the squishy edge of the seashore and issued his command for the tide to retreat. Of course it didn't, and of course most of the thanes and abbots missed the point.

That was irony. Irony is a kind of joke where at least one of those present doesn't catch on, or is presumed not to catch on. Thus Canute is the all-time champion ironist since millions of people have been missing his point over the centuries, taking him for a fool in the bargain.

I hope King Canute doesn't listen to the radio from the grave. He would find it most peculiar how the words "irony" or "ironic" turn up in almost every news item—instead of "funny," "strange," "paradoxical," or any of a dozen other words that would be better —especially since we are too busy being earnest to appreciate true irony. But that is another story . . .

Axel Harvey
La Macaza, Quebec

✉ I take umbrage at a remark I overheard—"the ides of April are past."

The Roman calendar, imported from the Greeks, was a totally illogical collection of terms and reckonings.

1. There were three fixed days: the calends (whence comes our word "calendar"), which always came on the *first* of every month.
2. Then came the nones, which usually fell on the *fifth* of the month.
3. Finally, there came the ides, which usually fell on the *thirteenth* of the month.

However, just to make things confusing,

. . . In March, July, October, May,
The nones fall on the seventh day . . .

This also pushed the ides to the fifteenth on these four months, including the notorious but *exceptional* ides of March.

Dates were then reckoned as so many days before the calends (or nones or ides) of the following month, though for some strange reason they included the first and last (actual calends, nones, et cetera) day. You had to know your March, July, October, May, or you would end up being two days out of phase in your date.

Jan Szymański
Ottawa

✉ I have a suggestion for the neutering of the English language.

It is a real problem to remember to double-gender personal pronouns; and embarrassing, when speaking, to have to back up and add "or she."

I would like to suggest the following neuter alternatives:

For: he/she: hesh
    her/his: shir
    her/him: herm
    herself/himself: hermself

Since we do not yet have a Ministry of Language, these new words could be introduced by writers and broadcasters and eventually receive the blessing of lexicographers. Perhaps these words might even find their way into future versions of the Bible.

I hope that hesh, who opens your morning mail, will put this on your desk.

Norman C. Reed
Tobermory, Ontario

✉ During the heady days of the mid-seventies, I was working on the staff of the Vancouver Status of Women and, as we were heart-and-soul-deep in creating a brave new world, we didn't stint at cleaning up the language while we were at it. With great good will, and quite a lot of tongue in cheek, we offered a solution: "peop" (pronounced "peep") as in "one *peop*," "two or more *people*." We rejected "one peep" or "two peop-peop" as being silly.

"Peop" is a most useful word, being both non-gender specific and easy to spell. In addition, it has a certain perky charm that can cut through the sexism of "businessman" and the pomposity of its non-sexist substitute "business executive" and give us "businesspeop." The words that we use to refer to people help shape how we regard those people. So, how approachable and friendly a "policepeop" seems. A "postpeop" would surely deliver our mail with cheerful reliability. You can almost anticipate the helpful smile of a "salespeop." A "repairpeop" will turn up on time. A "chairpeop" runs a meeting more efficiently than a "chairperson" and an "alderpeop" and a "councilpeop" are dedicated to the best interests of their constituents.

Those who object to wearing of fur and leather garments could insist on "peop-made" materials. Injured workers could apply for "workpeop compensation."

Our generous attempts at language reformation did not gain wide acceptance – well, okay, even within the VSW there were five, maybe six of us who were fluent in peop-speak. However, from time to time a scrap of graffiti would appear on a bulletin-board or wash-room mirror such as: "Schupeop wrote some good stuff" to be answered by: "I'm more into bluegrass myself. I love a good peopdolin."

So, to all those who meet the lame explanation "when man is used, woman is assumed to be included" with the rude wet raspberry that it deserves, I offer "peop." A modest word to be sure, but I think you'll be pleased with its spirit.

Jo Dunaway
Vancouver

✉ What is the equivalent of stick-handling in a woman's experience? What are the qualities and components of stick-handling that are similar to what I have experienced?

Being quick, deft, skilled, agile and aware come to mind, while balancing the knowledge of the skills and talents of your opponents. The only thing in my life that was comparable was putting dinner on the table in the evening when our four children were teenagers.

I remember needing to be quick and deft, draining vegetables, answering the phone and the doorbell, turning off the TV, getting one of the kids to feed the dog, balancing the music lessons, the practice, the hockey games, swimming teams, emotional teen love affairs and their food preferences and my husband's day at the office.

I'm not sure there is a word like stick-handling to capture the essence of all that juggling of skills, so perhaps it will have to do. What I do remember is that when I did manage it all, and when everyone was well fed and off on their evening activities, I sure wish I'd had someone to shout into the evening . . . She Scored!

Mufty Mathewson
Edmonton

✉ The word antidisestablishmentarianism does not appear in my 1959 edition of the *Shorter Oxford English Dictionary*; if it did, it would contain one letter less than floccinaucinihilipilification (I pronounce it floxy-nausi-nigh, hilly-pilly-fication), which is defined as the action or habit of estimating as worthless.

I therefore urge you to join me in regarding antidisestablishmentarianism's clearly unjustified claim to ultimate sesquipedality with the floccinaucinihilipilification it so richly deserves.

David Wyman
Toronto

✉ I note that one of your corresponding nit-pickers has attempted to dislodge antidisestablishmentarianism from its rightful pedestal as the longest word in the English language. The writer claimed that floxy-something-or-other noses out antidisestablishmentarianism by at least one letter.

That may be so, but remember that antidisestablishmentarianism is more than a political movement. To its adherents it is a state of mind, an attitude and manner known as antidisestablishmentarianismness.

For example, "The candidate for the Archbishop's job is noted for his unswerving antidisestablishmentarianismness."

This beats floxy by one.

Bob Richardson
Burlington, Ontario

✉ Since the English language has always esteemed it to be grammatically correct to permit the addition of prefixes and of suffixes to create words, not only of greater length but also of greater complexity, please permit me to add not only a further word, but perhaps also the final word on this subject and suggest to you that one may suffer an antidisestablishmentarianisationalistically and possibly correct or perhaps incorrect leaning, and may, in so suffering, inadvertently write what may–or may not–be the longest single sentence ever written in the mellifluous and ever-changing English language.

John Lockett
Winnipeg

✉ "Mortals who abide in vitreous edifices should not possess morbid propensities towards intertranscontinentalizationalized-antidisestablishmentarianizationalism."

Sort of just rolls off the tongue, doesn't it?

Glen Pearce
Cloyne, Ontario

✉ I used to live in Wales. One Welsh town, commonly referred to as Lan Fyer Pg, has fifty-eight letters and translates to: "Saint Mary's church by the white aspen over the whirlpool and Saint Tysylio's church by the red cave." The town is Llanfairpwllgwyngyllgogerychwyrndrobwllllantysyliogogogoch.

John A. Clarke
Toronto

✉ I teach English as a second language in Ottawa and I recently came across a good word in a book dealing with word stems. Try this on for size: pneumonoultramicroscopicsilicovolcanoconiosis.
Whew! Count 'em – forty-five letters! Does it win the prize?

Shirley Nelson
Ottawa

✉ I send along this cautionary note for people who can't spell:
Last but knot leased: don't trussed spell chequers; there knot as smart as ewe may have bin lead to bee leave.

Word-processing equipment and laser printers give people a false sense of mastery over the language by producing spell-checked documents that look good. As a result, anyone working with the written word will tell you, junky publications have multiplied, flabby language has proliferated, and typing skills have declined to the point of, well, have *you* ever printed an error-free document on the first try?

I'm not complaining – my services as an editor have never been in greater demand. All the same, flabby writing is often an indication of flabby thinking – when you can "write" as quickly as a word processor allows, you often don't have time to think through what you want to say (sorry this is so long, I didn't have time to write it shorter, and all that).

The fact that access to word processing is so easy doesn't mean that all of us are equally qualified to print everything we can generate on a screen. Just consider the direct mail that comes through your door.

All that paper! All that verbiage! All that time wasted! Enough! If we had to typeset by hand everything we publish, we'd think twice about wasting a single word – even a single letter or punctuation mark.

Even this letter has gone on far beyond what was needed to make the point I started with. Which only goes to demonstrate my point about word processors and verbal diarrhoea.

Kathryn Randle
Ottawa

NOW IF ONLY THERE WERE BLUE SNOW FLEAS

As in, of course, blue cows, which readers of *The Latest Morningside Papers* will recall.

This time – as with the blue cows – I simply told someone on the radio that I hadn't heard of the creatures he called snow fleas. And, in fact, had serious doubts about their existence. After all these years, you'd think I'd know better.

✉ It is surprising how many Canadians have not seen or heard of snow fleas. They are sometimes seen as a harbinger of spring, although it seems they can manifest themselves almost any time during the winter when the temperature reaches a certain point, about 3° to 5° C. At this point the surface of the snow becomes peppered with quadrillions (or googols) of these intriguing little critters, happily hippity-hopping hither and thither.

Last November – a rather unusual time – we had an outbreak of them. I don't think there was even any snow on the ground, but little puddles of water on our back porch were covered with a black scum following a warm spell and upon examination turned out to be an eruption (irruption?) of snow fleas.

Often when I go cross-country skiing in spring, the ski tracks are outlined in black by them. A few days ago, the whitewashed lower portion of our barn was covered with them (rather hard snow!) as they basked in the sun.

Don Hull
Bracebridge, Ontario

✉ Snow fleas are real, but they're not fleas; they just jump, and they don't bite.

Actually there are many things that live at about 0° C, including some that could reasonably be called ice worms. Many of these 0° C animals, some spiders for example, live under the snow where the temperature is near 0° C and come out on mild days, perhaps to avoid flooding. Some Antarctic fish are active at about −2° C, and many moths fly only on nights near freezing. Most of the moths cheat, running their flight muscles at around 3° C, but a few of them are actually cold. Both types overheat at what we would call comfortable temperatures.

Bruce Winterbon
Deep River, Ontario

✉ In early February my husband and I decided to venture out in the woods near our house for a walk. We had just suffered through a couple of days of snow and desperately felt the need for a fix of sunshine on this first sunny mild day for weeks. There is an old lumbering road close to my house that we frequently use for walks in spring, summer and fall but not being a winter enthusiast this was my first venture along it in snow. Our dog accompanied us, bounding several feet ahead. As we headed towards the house, I noticed these little black specks on the snow. When I drew my husband's attention to this, he looked at me in amazement. "You've never seen a snow flea before?"

"No. What's a snow flea?"

He showed them to me and when I continued to express a combination of surprise and disbelief his response was, "Weren't you ever told as a kid not to eat the snow?"

"Well, of course," I replied. "All children are told that, but that had nothing to do with snow fleas."

"Sure it did," he said. "My grandparents always told me not to eat the snow, it has bugs in it."

Well, that was news to me. All children have been warned not to eat the snow, it's dirty, but I had never heard anyone claim that it had bugs in it.

Jill Lounsberry
Salisbury, New Brunswick

✉ For the past few years I have been a teaching assistant for a third-year ecology course at Carleton University in Ottawa and one of my duties (and, as I see it, pleasures) is to accompany the instructor and students on several outdoor field excursions that are part of the laboratory component of the course. These take place in January and February when the temperatures are mostly in the sub-zero range. We talk about how local organisms, including birds, mammals and insects, adapt to winter. And of course, we look for evidence of activity: rabbit and squirrel footprints, mouse tunnels in the snow, insects overwintering in a dormant state under bark or in crevices, Black-capped Chickadees and Downy Woodpeckers actively feeding despite the cold. And every year we look for our favourite winter organism – the snow flea.

First we whet the students' appetites by telling them how this remarkable insect hops about on the surface of the snow, stark naked, in the middle of winter. (Would you do that?) Then we look for them. The snow fleas are not always accommodating, but sometimes we are lucky. A good place to search is around the base of trees, where the snow softens on a sunny winter day and melts back a bit from the dark trunk, providing a route to the surface. Snow fleas look very much like little black specks of dirt or bark on the snow. They are less than two millimetres long, black and rather slim. Peer closely at those specks of dirt. If any of them move, you have found snow fleas.

Snow fleas are not really fleas at all, but actually belong to an order of tiny wingless insects called springtails (or *Collembolans*, depending on how scientific you are feeling). They make their living as scavengers in leaf litter on the forest floor, do not bite and are related to other types of springtails often found on the surface of ponds and streams. Their common name probably comes from their size and impressive jumping ability, but unlike the true flea, they don't use their legs to jump. Instead, each snow flea carries beneath its body a long forked appendage called a furcula. When the insect is sitting still, the furcula is bent under and forward and is held in place by a kind of clasp. When the clasp is released, the furcula snaps back, and the snow flea is propelled through the air for some distance, often up to ten centimetres, which is quite impressive when you consider this is about fifty times its own length.

Two questions come to mind when considering the antics of these tiny creatures. First, why do they frolic about in the middle of winter when other insects are safely insulated beneath the snow surface, or underground, or protected by vegetation? Second, how do they manage, not only to survive, but to remain active at such low temperatures?

You will never guess the answer to the first question. Rumour has it that they come up to the surface of the snow to mate! What we are witnessing may be a kind of snow flea orgy on ice.

As to how they resist the cold, there are a couple of hypotheses. Insects are, of course, cold-blooded and depend on the environment for maintaining their body temperature. Snow flea sorties tend to happen on sunny days. The black colour of the insects' bodies helps them absorb the warming rays and increase their temperature above that of the surrounding air. In addition, many insects protect themselves from freezing by producing chemicals akin to antifreeze. However, most remain inactive despite this protection. The ability of the snow flea to frolic in the snow is indeed to be wondered at.

Is there something uniquely Canadian about this attitude to the climate? This appreciation of sun on a cold winter day? I like to think so. Gilles Vigneault said, "*Mon pays, c'est l'hiver.*" Whether Québécois or not, this is something we share. So here's to the snow flea and here's to us, hardy northerners all.

Kringen Henein
Ottawa

✉ Below is an illustration of a typical springtail (Order *Collembola*) to which the infamous snow flea *Hypogastrura nivicola* is closely related.

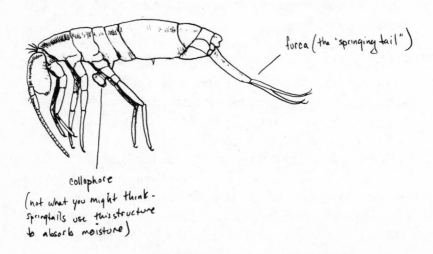

furca (the "springing tail")

collophore
(not what you might think -
springtails use this structure
to absorb moisture)

Heather Proctor
Mississauga, Ontario

✉ I have a 35 mm slide of *yellow* snow fleas. I took it three years ago on the trail to Chester Lake in the Kananaskis country west of Calgary.

Some snow was left on the trail and here and there were patches of what looked like yellow spray paint. Only when I examined a piece of icy snow did I see that the yellow was moving.

"Don't eat yellow snow" takes on a new meaning!

Jeffrey Perkins
Calgary

✉ "Snowfire" can be seen usually only if an early morning or late afternoon reddish sun is seen through the swirls of windblown loose snow. Usually the coppery-coloured sun must be low, near the horizon, and the observer's sightline must be close to or below the surface of the snow-covered area.

An observance of snowfire is usually serendipitous, as mine have been, but probably can be sought out in all snowy areas when and where all appropriate circumstances and conditions coincide.

I suppose one would have to be a bit of a romantic to appreciate this rarely mentioned phenomenon; otherwise it is thought of as just one more annoyance of wintry weather.

Arthur Reid
Toronto

✉ See your snow fleas and raise you one. Nice as it is to hear that these inconspicuous little guys demonstrate that insect life is out there in the Great White North in winter, it's nicer yet to see butterflies. That's right, butterflies!

Karen McIntosh and I were up to our beloved Algonquin Park for a weekend of snowshoeing and searching for Whiskeyjack nests. Whiskeyjacks, or better yet, Canada Jays, are those remarkable birds with the unfortunately bland official name of Gray Jay that store food in great quantity all summer and fall, then use this bounty to support themselves and their nestlings through a late-winter nesting in the famine days of March and April. If they survive, this gives the young a real leg up on setting up their own household. Whiskeyjacks are furiously building nests now and some are even incubating eggs. Now there's a sign of spring for you!

Anyway, back to the butterfly. As we drove along the highway in the park after prolonged snowshoeing across knee-deep snow pack and waist-deep drifts in silent, frozen northern woods, what we took to be a dried-up leaf fluttered across the road and bounced off the hood of our van. When this "leaf" hit the road, however, it continued to flutter. Most un-leaf like, to be sure. Not quite believing it, we drove back and were astonished to find a living, breathing butterfly – a Milbert's Tortoiseshell, to be exact. The animal was in perfect shape to look at, though the collision damaged it in unseen ways and it soon expired. This lovely little black, brown and orange butterfly with a wing span of about two inches had its brief winter fling and untimely end on the sixteenth of March. This was a week before the start of spring according to the calendar and many weeks before that by any ecological measure.

The Milbert's Tortoiseshell is a member of the anglewing group of butterflies, which overwinter as adults. The more familiar Mourningcloak – a large, blackish butterfly with a broad, pale yellow band on its wing margins – is often the first butterfly of the year to be seen. So it's not all that surprising that we would see one of these butterflies early in the year . . . but with snow on the ground?

Daniel F. Brunton
Ottawa

MORLEY CALLAGHAN AND NORTHROP FRYE

Two great Canadian men of letters died during the period covered by this collection of letters – within months of each other, as it turned out, and both in Toronto. As had been the case following the deaths of Margaret Laurence and Elizabeth Smart (*The New Morningside Papers*), listeners found the program a fitting place to salute their memories.

✉ I was struck by Morley Callaghan's comment that if artists are to be able to continue to create throughout their lives, they have to keep seeing life from a new angle; that life is like a crystal that artists must always be giving a little turn in order to see some new facet of experience. Suddenly I remembered that the many-faceted crystal a friend had given me several years ago was still lying in its box in my dresser drawer. While Morley's words still echoed in my head, I hung the crystal in my study window where it now flashes in the sun as it turns, flinging scores of rainbows round the room. It's going to remind me of Morley and his advice every time I look at it, every time I give it his "artist's little turn."

Norm Esdon
Kingston, Ontario

✉ This Northrop Frye story concerns neither his literary theories nor his reading of the Bible, but I like to recall it nevertheless.

I do not remember the exact context of the remark, but it was made to one of those crowded post-war classes at Victoria College of which I was a member. Dismissing some idea with which he was in disagreement, Professor Frye said that it was "not worth a dam," and then, as if to cushion the shock caused by such a phrase on the lips of an ordained United Church minister in the forties, he added, "which is a small Indian coin worth about half a cent." After class I consulted the dictionary, and of course he was right: "DAM, n. Name of a small Indian coin of slight value – 'not worth a *dam*'." The word, then, spelled like that and used in such a context had nothing profane or blasphemous about it. I thought immediately of *Gone With the Wind* and of Rhett Butler's farewell to Scarlett O'Hara. If Margaret Mitchell had known what Northrop Frye knew, Rhett would have said, "My dear, I don't give a dam" – without a final *n*. And if David Selznick and his attorneys and the Hays Office and its attorneys had known what Northrop Frye knew, there need never have been the brou-haha there was about the filming of that final scene between Clark Gable and Vivien Leigh.

Fred Farr
Thornhill, Ontario

124

✉ In 1965 I was a first-year student in English Lang. & Lit. at Vic and fortunate enough to be in Northrop Frye's Shakespeare course. I knew even then that I was privileged to be part of his lectures and the tutorial sessions that followed. (Incidentally, our tutorial leader, exciting and impressive in his own right, was a young graduate student named Dennis Lee.)

At any rate, it was a course I did not skip for any reason. In fact, I must have made a point of arriving at Frye's class uncharacteristically early because, in my memory, I am always sitting in a front-row seat, mesmerized by his quiet erudition (delivered in that "step back, step forward" lecture style). It was impossible to take adequate notes. Usually, I started each class with the best of intentions, but soon settled for scribbling the occasional word or phrase while I listened instead. I remember straining so hard to follow the connections Frye seemed to make so effortlessly as his thoughts ranged from one Shakespearean play to another, and from Blake to the Bible, that I was breathless at the end of the hour.

Those are my recollections of Frye the scholar – I have another one of Northrop Frye, the person, due to an encounter I had with him outside class.

During that first year, I lived in Annesley Hall, one of Victoria College's residences for women, and a Victorian place it was indeed. Among the many quaint and curious regulations and customs we were expected to adhere to, perhaps none was more quaint and more curious than the compulsory Sunday "tea with the Dean." Every Sunday, two or three of us hapless students were chosen to attend a Tea with Vic's Dean of Women. I think it was in January when my name came up on the dreaded "Dean's List," which was posted on the Annesley bulletin board. There was no way out of it. You could trade places, and I probably had, with someone else once or possibly even twice and thus postpone the agony, but eventually it had to be faced.

I arrived in Annesley's drawing-room on the appointed day, more or less suitably attired in a clean, white blouse and a cheap, ill-fitting, black wool skirt – probably the only one I had. I was acutely self-conscious and uncomfortable.

The Tea was a formal affair, complete with silver tea service, tiny sandwiches and a printed program of the events to follow. Genteel, lady-like deportment was definitely the order of the day. There was at least some hope of anonymity; I counted a dozen people there: the Dean, a don or two, we students and assorted other guests. The guest of honour that day was Northrop Frye. Yet that was a fact I scarcely noticed, so caught up was I in feeling out-of-place, rustic and plump in the ugly, hated black skirt.

My sense of alienation must have been obvious to at least one person. At a certain point in the afternoon, when the tea had been served and everyone was more or less settled in, I was able to take up a place of refuge beside the piano, in the "back row," so to speak. All eyes were turned towards the Dean, who was making polite conversation about something.

Then, out of the corner of my eye, I noticed something Northrop Frye was doing on the other side of the piano. Could he be – yes, he was – folding the program into a paper airplane! Almost before I knew what was happening, he shot the paper airplane across the gleaming, black surface of the piano to me! I quickly picked it up – I didn't have the nerve to shoot it back. But when I looked at him, there was a twinkle in his eye and the hint of a smile on his face – kind of a naughty smile at that. I smiled back. And that was the end of it – just a small private joke. But what a breath of fresh air it blew into that stuffy room! A *real* social (i.e., human) act amid all the artificial social manners on display there that day.

After twenty-five years, I can still see that airplane sliding across the piano to me, can still feel my shock, can see the twinkle in his eye – and it still makes me smile.

Mary Upper
North Bay, Ontario

✉ I am sitting here, weeping at the news of the passing of Northrop Frye. I'd like to share a story that only the hundred and twenty people who took his Principles of Literary Symbolism graduate course in 1973 might remember, since it will show another side of this remarkable, witty, profoundly decent human being.

About half-way through that wonderful course, a potentially horrible thing happened. It was during one of Dr. Frye's daring pauses – when he'd ask for questions and wait for up to ten minutes of excruciating silence, until someone finally dared raise his or her hand.

Well, this time one fellow waved his hand and stood up. His question was quite dreadful and self-damning: it showed that the young man had not read that week's reading, nor Dr. Frye's notes, nor any of his books.

The entire class turned from the unfortunate student back to the front of the class, expecting this wise, inspired man to destroy the questioner. What else could he do? We all imagined that Professor Frye would mortify the student, shame him before his peers, cut him to ribbons, Cuisinart him with his own foolish words.

Professor Frye – then in his early sixties – paused for about a minute. He cleared his throat, stared warmly at the hapless student and said, "You know, that's really a fine question, but I think it needs to be rephrased somewhat before I can give it the reply it deserves."

Dr. Frye then took the stupid question, twisted it inside out until it made sense, answered it generously and returned to his lecturing.

And some hundred and twenty graduate students of English let out a collective sigh of admiration and awe. There was an explosion of shock – and love.

What a lesson he taught us then! You know, I fibbed before, when I began my letter by saying that only those students present on that cold Toronto afternoon nearly two decades ago would know this story.

I've told this anecdote whenever I lectured on ethics and morals, in countless talks across the United States and Canada. I remind my audiences – who always burst into smiles of pleasure and joy when I share it – that Professor Northrop Frye taught me a lesson that day on how to teach, how to be kind – how to live – that has sustained me throughout my life.

The death of Professor Frye is one of the greatest losses this country – this world – has sustained, during this century. But his life, and his teaching, and the way he taught, are among the greatest gifts our country has given the world. May he rest in peace.

Allan Gould
Toronto

✉ I can't help thinking how rich, in a different way, a portrait of Dr. Frye might be if it came from some people who, until recently, had daily or weekly contact with him at his place of work. Their memories cover so much time and, so often, entail conversations or Frye "bon mots" of a nature not necessarily remembered by university presidents and other famous people. What a shame not to have sent someone with a tape recorder into Victoria or Massey College in search of some of our funny, moving, affectionate and awe-filled memories. Some of us might have reminded Margaret Atwood of the time, not so long ago, when Dr. Frye introduced her to the Victoria College/U of T Convocation, which she then addressed. Dr. Frye said of her, "Margaret Atwood has been called a great Canadian author. She has been called a great woman author. She has been called a great Toronto author. But Margaret Atwood, like the CN Tower, is a free-standing structure and doesn't need any of those supporting qualifiers."

Frank Collins
Toronto

✉ At Morley Callaghan's last book launch, for *A Wild Old Man on the Road*, Barry Callaghan, who had co-ordinated the event at Toronto's Bistingo restaurant, had elected, for reasons best known to himself, to seat *me* next to Dr. Frye. Now, I am a "responsive" speaker with strangers. It is also known that Northrop Frye was a deeply shy man, not given to chat. So, after "hello," we both fell to sort of staring straight ahead. People kept stopping by, saying, "Hello, Professor Frye," "Good evening, Professor Frye." The cultural hero beside me on the banquette seat got to looking, as I saw out of the corner of my eye, sadder and sadder. Sympathy prompted speech. "You get 'Professor Frye-ed' a lot" (the MacKenzie Brothers will be pleased to note that I think I concluded this deep philosophical inquiry with "eh?"). "Yes," he replied with soft weariness, "constantly." I felt I could help. "Want to make it stop?" For the first time, the good doctor looked me directly in the eye. "Oh yes." From my Tasteful Little Evening Bag, I extracted an item I carry with me always: a bright red clown nose (it stops fights, ends silent sulking, de-machoes crude guys in the street and stops rotten kids from screaming in Loblaws). I held the little red ball in the palm of my hand. "Put this on." He looked at it, considering. "You think?" "Mmm." He put it on. "Does it look silly?" I produced a small mirror and held it up. "Yes," I said quietly, "of course." Dr. Frye smiled at his image and, leaving the shiny red nose in place, commenced eating his *poulet quelque chose*. Someone came by, grinned broadly and said, "Hi Norrie!" Five or six "Hi Norrie"-ers later, Doctor Frye, smiling shyly, asked, "Um . . . may I . . . keep it?" "Sure," I replied, "I've got lots." After that, we did have a fine conversation on the clown tradition in different cultures. He remained in the nose for the rest of the evening.

Northrop Frye was mercifully taken before the commencement of a stupid, technology-driven war that I'm certain he would've loathed on every level. I hope he took the nose. And I'm equally certain that the gods and angels where the good doctor now resides are now, all their bright red noses firmly in place, having a wonderful discussion of the clown tradition in different religions, with one of the world's finest theological scholars, Canada's own "Norrie."

Gale Garnett
Toronto

FOREIGN AFFAIRS I: CORRESPONDENTS WITHOUT TRENCH COATS

Actually, this could be "Foreign Affairs VI or VII," since the practice of including in these anthologies some of the letters we get from temporarily expatriate Canadians all over the world began with the original *Morningside Papers*, and has continued to flourish. Now, Shelley Ambrose, who handles this department of the program in addition to all the work she does as my assistant and who put this chapter together, receives nearly a letter a day from abroad – sometimes on old-fashioned, flimsy air-mail paper, but, increasingly nowadays, by fax.

In spite of the speed with which they're sometimes sent, the letters that work best for us are seldom about what journalists call news, or even current affairs. They're just about life in other countries, as seen and lived by Canadians. To wit:

Tamale, Northern Region, Ghana

✉ The orphanage in Tamale is, quite literally, at the end of the road. You follow a series of rutted paths out of town until they suddenly end unceremoniously in front of a collection of skeletal buildings. Left-overs from colonial times. As the car motor dies, the sound of children's voices can be heard coming from one of the buildings.

They're singing. "The people on the bus go bump, bump, bump, all through the town." Karen Leslie gets out of the car, chattering away to herself about all the things she has forgotten to bring. It doesn't look to me that she has forgotten anything but the kitchen sink. She scoops up a heavy bundle of newspapers, outdated issues of Canada's national newspaper, to be exact, and a tub of home-made paste for the children. Over her shoulder is a red sports bag full of crayons, books and children's scissors she bought in Eaton's when she was home on vacation last month. A thermos of drinking water dangles from one hand, because there is no water in the orphanage except what the children fetch in buckets from suspicious sources. In the other hand she clutches a bouquet of flowers from her own garden. "Something colourful for the children to look at," she says.

I can imagine Karen, dressed in the same summery blue skirt and white blouse, heading off to a day-care centre in Canada. Back home in Huntsville, Karen is a teacher of day-care workers, a mother and a grandmother. She came to Africa only a year ago, for the first time. Her husband, Ted, thought it would be an interesting experience to work for Ghana's national electricity company for a couple of years, a kind of exchange program with Ontario Hydro. It took Karen two months to find herself two jobs, one here at the orphanage, another at a newly opened day-care centre, the first of its kind in northern Ghana.

Unlike the dozens and dozens of foreign development workers who are in town in the name of bilateral aid with large salaries and healthy fringe benefits, Karen does her jobs voluntarily. No one pays her a penny or supplies her with materials or transportation. Only the lack of supplies seems to bother her. As I follow her into the orphanage, I can't help but think about so many of the other expatriate wives I've met in Africa, who can idle away years moaning about their slovenly houseboys and the lack of good washing-powder. Karen's days are filled with other things.

There are teddy bears to sew, stories to type out, games to prepare and training programs for the kindergarten workers.

She approaches the orphanage "school" as though this were nothing new to her at all. There are no doors or windows, and the corrugated tin roof has been mangled over the years by tremendous wind storms. It glints in the sun like a piece of angry sculpture in downtown North America. Florence, the teacher who spends her mornings with the forty or so children in the orphanage school, asks the children if they are glad to see Mrs. Leslie, who has been away in Canada.

They rise and shout, "Yes."

"I'm glad to see you, too," Karen says, then giggles, and starts digging into her red sports bag. She hands me an old seed catalogue and a pair of scissors and asks me to start cutting out pictures of flowers for the children to paste onto old Canadian news stories in the *Globe and Mail*, which is torn into sheets, one per child.

While they're waiting for the pictures, the children continue their song. "The wheels on the bus go round and round. Round and round." Karen stops handing out crayons long enough to dip once more into her red bag of tricks and produces triumphantly a picture of a bus to show the children what they are singing about. Few of them speak English, so the words to the songs they are taught don't mean much to them. They squint at the photograph as it is passed from one pair of eager hands to another.

The older children are left with Florence, who commands them to be silent while they're working on their individual pieces of artwork. Karen leads the younger ones outside, talking away to them as though they understood her. One toddler who can barely walk clings to her skirt for support. Florence shouts at a small girl, whose legs are shaped like flippers, to follow along. She drags herself along using her hands, following Karen, who is leading the children in search of stones, which she then piles up and wets down with her drinking water, to make them shine.

"You've got to be inventive," she says, laughing. "You can do a lot with very little. But I've never worked with *nothing* before!"

An hour later, after leading the children through elephant walks and some new songs about seeds growing, she leaves them gluing and pasting and colouring and says it's time to visit the babies in the other section of the orphanage, a long, squat building that resembles a prison more than anything else.

The women who tend the infants ask Karen all about her visit to Canada. They proudly show her the newest addition to the family of infants in the orphanage, a three-week-old baby boy, whose mother died in childbirth. Fathers often bring babies to the orphanage if they are the progeny of deceased mothers. Something to do with good and bad omens and spirits that no one here likes to tangle with.

There are five babies lying unmoving on a blanket on the floor. One of them, bone thin, looks to me as though he's dying. Karen exclaims that he has improved. She kneels beside him on the floor, playing little piggies on his tiny fingers, and whispers, "Seybou, I was worried about you all the time I was away." She lets him play with the bracelets on her arm and murmurs that she's got to bring some more tin-can rattles for them. Something, anything for stimulation. She's gentle with her advice to the orphanage workers, merely suggesting that they spend more time playing with the babies, helping them to sit up, checking the supplies of milk powder. She's so natural that it looks as though she's been working under these conditions for years.

The rest of the Canadian development contingent in Tamale, and there are a dozen of them here, don't even know who Karen is, or if they do, they don't take much interest in her work. They live in a fairly closed world of meetings and reports and clubhouse soirées. They speak a special language, the jargon of the development "expert," phrases like top-down or bottom-up approach, or participatory development and sustainability, the words that fill volumes and volumes of studies the Canadians have carried out here in the past decade, in theory, to develop the Northern Region. Millions of Canadian tax dollars go into Tamale every year for massive projects that produce little, other than more vehicles and reports and confusion at all levels. While Karen quietly and modestly, without a single cent of support from anyone except herself and her husband, goes cheerfully about her business, giving kids a couple of years of her time and opening up their minds.

✉ Last summer when I was home in Canada for a holiday, I did some long overdue house cleaning. This involved digging through closets, drawers and mouse-eaten boxes and pulling out piece after piece of out-of-date and out-of-shape clothing. I stuffed it all in three green garbage bags. These bags sat around for a while, getting in the way and blocking doors until finally I went in search of a disposal bin. I eventually found this receptacle at a supermarket, in a lonely corner of a parking lot as big as PEI. The bin was already buried deep in similar bags, and I added mine to the pile and drove off. I felt very pleased with myself.

I don't know what happened to the clothing. Perhaps it wound up in the drawers of some needy or environmentally conscious Canadian. But our continent can't begin to absorb what it throws away.

Africa can, though.

The markets in West Africa are overflowing with second-hand clothing from the developed world. Here in Ghana these clothes are called *broniwawu*, which means "dead white man."

I asked Ama, a Ghanaian friend, why the second-hand clothing has such a sordid name.

"Because," she answered, "it is hard to imagine that anyone who wasn't dead would ever part with such good clothing." Then she laughed.

I used to avoid the second-hand clothing stalls in the Tamale market. There was something about all that worn linen and slightly musty-smelling clothing piled high on rickety tables that bothered me. Pawing through cast-offs destined for the poor struck me as unseemly for someone who, weeks earlier, had been throwing away equally good clothing.

135

But then one day a young man managed to trap me with a pair of OshKosh overalls. I was striding purposefully through the market on a quest for oranges at the time. I had just threaded past a herd of dried and smoked cow heads and hooves and was picking my way on tiptoe over small fetid streams of human waste when the vendor leapt in front of me, blocking my path.

"You want to buy, madame?" he asked, holding up the pint-sized blue jeans with a triumphant smile. "Good for your small boy," he announced.

I stopped and fingered the overalls. There was a bit of wear on the knees. We discussed the price. He was firm – I couldn't have them for less than two hundred cedis, about a dollar.

I pretended to be contemplating the price – part of the game of haggling – and happened to glance up at a stall hung with T-shirts only to find myself being stared down by Michael Jackson. His finely sculpted – if faded – visage gazed out across the market from a dozen black T-shirts. Looking around the market at the number of times that same face appeared, it would have been easy to believe that Michael Jackson was the patron saint of Tamale. He, or Mickey Mouse. Even the Ninja Turtles are there. The second-hand market in Tamale offers a stroll down the – short – memory lane of our own pop culture.

The array of T-shirts reads like a what's what and who's who in North American institutions. Universities, breweries, pop stars, rock concerts, gas stations, fast-food huts and fun runs were all represented. One shirt was advertising in large red letters a ten-kilometre run sponsored by the British Columbia Dairy Foundation. Another expressed love for the city of Toronto. Ironically, most of the people buying and wearing these T-shirts are unable to read. For them there is no irony.

"You buy, madame?" repeated the young man. He waved the overalls in my face.

I bought. The OshKosh overalls went into my basket, and the quest for oranges was put on hold.

I moved to the next stand, which dealt in swim wear – and was hung with brassieres. The swimming suits were piled unceremoniously on top of a rickety table, and I dug through them feeling decidedly like a happy Woolco shopper at dollar forty-nine day. There was excited chatter as I held one up for sizing. The man behind the counter told me this was an *undergarment*. Swimming is virtually unknown in Tamale, outside a lone pool in the military camp. Beside me three young women were trying on steel-girder brassieres over their blouses.

The next stall was loaded with ski jackets. In spite of the heat, they are a popular item with progressive young men in town. In Tamale the temperature usually hovers in the mid- to upper thirties. Fashion – even second hand – knows no logic.

There was also an Edmonton Oilers sweat-shirt, but the colours had run badly. I wondered who had washed it, and who had worn it before it started out on its voyage to Africa.

In fact it is not easy to trace the path this second-hand clothing takes to get to such out-of-the-way places as the Tamale market. Wholesalers bring the stuff in by the shipload; the bales are unpacked and sorted in enormous warehouses, and the long chain of distribution begins. The day a truckload arrives in the Tamale market, it is quickly and loudly sorted for distribution. The dapper men who operate roadside stalls take the best clothes, which they iron and hang up in open-air displays that stretch for kilometres. Young boys head out for a daily round of door-to-door peddling, a few T-shirts dangling from their arms. The rest – the shoes, belts, purses, socks, dresses, coats, slacks – are piled in mounds on the roadsides or in market stalls. The local people go through these heaps of ragged, rumpled clothing as though they were tailings of a gold mine. Second-hand clothing is big business, a way of life here.

Is this the famous "trickle-down" theory at work?

It is not that Ghana does not have its own locally made textiles and clothes. It does, but this is mostly traditional dress – elaborate hand-woven smocks and batiks and colourful prints. More and more this ancestral clothing is something worn only at traditional ceremonies. Frippery is far cheaper. And a polyester suit for a dollar is much more durable than a suit made of hand-spun cotton.

Economics aside, there is also the aesthetic problem frippery creates. Those who can afford the choice items turn themselves out in fine style with these cast-offs. But for the vast majority, the clothing looks exactly like what it is – something someone in another richer land discarded. It is not unusual to see a woman heading off to market dressed in an off-colour slip or a nightgown. I have trouble having a serious conversation with a young man who is wearing a fun-fur hat and a pair of wildly striped pyjamas.

I voiced my lofty complaints to a Ghanaian friend recently, suggesting that there was something intrinsically wrong with one continent dressing itself in the rejected styles and clothing of another.

"It may not be right," he said rather hotly. "But you cannot stop the second-hand market now. If you did, there would be a lot of people walking around here naked. We need our *broniwawu*, the dead white man."

✉ I think it was in grade four that we covered "Africa" in our social studies class. The fictional African boy we read about was Bunga, and he lived in a picturesque little village in the rain forest. The village consisted of mud houses with thatch roofs and was surrounded by leafy banana trees.

That textbook has undoubtedly long since been withdrawn from the curriculum. It was probably hopelessly inaccurate and pedagogically out of date.

But I loved it and the Rousseauist picture it painted of that tranquil and self-sufficient African community. I had all but forgotten this mental image of Africa until I happened this week to make a journey and find myself in Rome, Bethlehem and BBC. Rome, Bethlehem and BBC are *villages*. I suspect they represent a Ghana, an Africa, which for the most part has gone the way of that social studies book, out of date and out of style.

They are fishing villages on the edge of the Black Volta River in northern Ghana. They are not accessible by road, not shown on any map, and they are, as a result, an aeon away from civilization as we know it.

To get to them, you have first to find an interpreter, preferably someone with connections, who can negotiate for a boat in the river port of Buipe. Through friends, I found Wilson Yakubu. He knew Jonas, who knew Dartey, who owns a "flying boat" (an engine boat) called *No Play*. The alternative, Wilson told me, was a "paddle canoe." "But in one of the paddle canoes, we'd be travelling all day," he said, "and as for your safety . . . " He then flashed me one of those big grins that make completed sentences superfluous.

Wilson negotiated a price for the river journey with Jonas and Dartey. It would be expensive. *No Play* had just been fitted with a new twenty-five-horsepower Yamaha outboard motor and was in good condition – that is, its weathered wooden bottom kept out more water than it allowed in. The negotiations took two hours and spanned six languages. There were: Ewe, Twi, Ada, Gonja, pidgin English – and occasionally some formal English I recognized.

When we set off from Buipe we were ten in the boat: two on the motor, two on the bailing can, four who just came along for the ride, Wilson and myself.

I was the only passenger with luggage. I had: a camera (which stopped working about the time the boat motor started), insect repellent, a folding camp bed with mosquito net, two flashlights, sun cream with a protection factor of thirty-six, twenty-five litres of cold water, a portable water filter, a change of clothes, two novels, Resoquin in case of a sudden attack of malaria, assorted first-aid equipment and a large sun hat.

The breeze on the river, after the rancid heat on the polluted Buipe shore, was wonderful. But I had little time to savour the trip. Wilson watched me struggling (unsuccessfully) to repair the camera, applying sun screen and taking inventory of my supplies in the event of an unforeseen catastrophe, then suddenly burst into laughter. "You whites," he said, howling, "you try to be wiser than God." He began to examine all the gadgets and provisions I had brought along, showing them around to amuse his fellow passengers.

Two hours into the journey we passed Bethlehem, a collection of mud huts perched on a treed cliff above the river. Then came Rome, which looked much the same. Finally, we arrived at the village Wilson told me was called BBC. There we decided to go ashore.

When our "flying boat" slid onto the beach and the modern roar of the engine died, there was nothing but stillness. A few thatch roofs were visible over the rise, behind neat rows of cassava plants. Silk-cotton trees and enormous brown termite nests dwarfed the man-made dwellings. There were no crowds of curious children running to mob the white intruder, no garbage in sight, nothing, in fact, except a few canoes pulled onto the beach and some blue fishing nets laid out on the shore.

I followed Wilson and his entourage up a narrow path to the chief's house. There, under a thatch roof, women and naked children were sitting down to a communal bowl of yams. Fish were laid out over clay fireplaces, for smoking. The most striking thing about the village was its cleanliness, its order, the silence – not at all the Africa I have come to know over the years in more accessible and more "modern" and "developed" communities. The women glanced up as though they had been expecting us, offered some muted greetings and continued their lunch. Under an adjacent thatch awning sat the chief of BBC. Benches and cups of water were immediately produced for the visitors. The chief, through two translations, impassively welcomed us to BBC. His wife sat off to one side with a bemused expression on her face. I looked for an excuse to explain my uncalled-for intrusion into his peaceful compound and then asked why fishing villages in this remote part of the country had named themselves after foreign cities and famous broadcasting corporations. He said quite simply, "We liked the names. BBC. Rome. Bethlehem." The names and the nylon fishing nets appeared to be the only things the villages had borrowed from this century. They had water, food and their own rhythms – which followed the sun, the seasons and the natural cycle of life and death.

140

His daughter, about nine and naked, was unable to take her eyes off me. She had never seen a white person before. Eventually, I offered her a balloon, which Wilson blew up – since no one else in the village had any idea what it was.

It was at that minute that I felt I had stepped into my grade four social studies book. I felt I had made a mistake offering the balloon to the girl. It would be blown up once, and it would probably break, disappointing everyone. Then it would become the first piece of litter in an otherwise pristine village. What did they need of me and my silly trinkets?

When we left BBC, it was already dusk. Our brand-new Yamaha motor quit just about the time the sun dropped abruptly below a horizon of river and scraggy savannah trees. As we drifted in darkness down the Black Volta, at the mercy of faulty technology and river currents, we could just catch the dark shapes of paddle canoes overtaking us, on their way up the river to Buipe. In that river, at night, I wondered who was moving backwards.

Joan Baxter

New Zealand

✉ The *Rainbow Warrior* is under full sail this morning. Huge blue sails billow majestically above her green hull. On the jib sail, a large white peace dove is stitched in place, on the bow, a painted rainbow. As I sit at the computer in our little office on board, the smell of coffee wafts out from the galley; breakfast dishes clatter in the sink. Sleepy faces emerge from their cabins. Outside, an albatross wings silently by. The ship rocks gently, belying the atmosphere of anticipation on board.

It is four and a half years to the day after the bombing of the first *Rainbow Warrior* by the French Intelligence. And three months since I boarded as ship's doctor and deck-hand in New York. Now both she and I are embarking on our first environmental campaign. Greenpeace wants to put a stop to drift-net fishing, a technique whereby ships set walls of invisible net fifteen metres deep and up to seventy kilometres long that kill indiscriminately. It is estimated that fifty thousand kilometres of net are set daily the world over.

We are seeking Japanese and Taiwanese drift-net fishing boats in the Tasman Sea between New Zealand and Australia. We know where to look, but it's a big ocean out there. Nevertheless we expect to make contact any hour or any day. Then all our preparations will pay off.

And what diverse preparations there have been. We are a ship's crew of a dozen–captain, mates, radio operator, carpenter, cooks, doctor and engineers. For the campaign, our numbers have swelled to thirty: professional divers, underwater photographers and film makers, Greenpeace drift-net campaigners and the press have joined our effort. All told, we represent ten countries, from Japan and the Solomon Islands to Canada, New Zealand and the Netherlands.

Our days are a frenzy of activity. The new crew needs to learn safety procedures; we have fire drills and abandon-ship and man-overboard drills. We are perfecting our ability to launch and handle our Zodiacs, the hallmark of a Greenpeace action. Strategy meetings hold clear Greenpeace's commitment to non-violence. Communication with the outside world is constant; our ability to tell the story that no one could otherwise hear is paramount. The photographers and divers are down in the hold fine-tuning their equipment so that we can document the marine life trapped in the nets.

Yesterday, we spent hours amongst a pod of sperm whales. Their massive black bodies moved so easily through the water. At times it seemed they were sleeping just below the surface, floating quietly. Then sprays of water came swooshing from their blow-holes. In a moment they would dive for the depths to feed, showing their tail as if saying goodbye. Sadly, their presence confirms our fears. Drift-nets are being set every night across the migration path of these great animals. We know huge quantities of albacore tuna are taken by the drift-nets; that after all is their purpose. Some regional fisheries scientists say that at this rate, the South Pacific tuna stock will collapse within a few years. But what of the incidental catch? We fear for dolphins, for whales, for other fish and for turtles. And for birds who dive into the nets and are drowned by the thousands.

Last night, as the sun set golden purple and I was doing some last-minute deck work before dark, a friend shouted, "Hey! A dolphin!" Sure enough, just a few metres away, a dolphin rode our bow wave, frolicking, leaping! It is good to pause, to breathe this salt air and to be reminded of why we are here.

✉ The last few days have been hectic. Radio transmissions revealed that we were within a hundred miles of the Japanese drift-net fleet. At first they were able to evade us. We'd see a Japanese ship steaming towards us. They'd get within waving distance. "It's a three-masted schooner," we'd hear them say on their radio. "Does it have a rainbow?" their patrol vessel would question. Then came the instructions not to set any drift-nets while we were within sight. A small victory, but not one that enables us to document the catch in the nets as we had hoped.

So, we dropped away. By monitoring the air waves, we were able to establish the drift-netters' evening positions. Under cover of dark we approach. Now we've been working every night to document the catches in as great a length of drift-net as possible – a total of one hundred and eighty kilometres so far. But, some-how, we never managed to have a photographer in the right place at the right time to show the world that these vast curtains of net take not only albacore tuna – the target species – but also dolphins, sharks and almost everything else that swims into them.

Last night, four of us set out in a Zodiac to count the catch being hauled onto a Japanese drift-net boat. Within five minutes, we were galvanized into action when two adult dolphins were hauled up fin to fin. To our amazement, the fishermen, who had greeted our arrival alongside their ship with smiles and waves, seemed nonplussed by our cameras. They casually threw the dead dolphins overboard in full view.

Just before 4:00 A.M., many kilometres of net and one dead shark later, a baby dolphin was pulled from the sea. The fisherman turned and dropped the body right by us – it floated! We all hung over the sides of the inflatable, grabbing at the small carcass. And suddenly, there I was, holding this streamlined body the size of a small toddler with smooth grey and white patterned skin.

"We need some photographs," said our photographer to the much-subdued group. Back to work – or so I thought. As I picked up my clipboard to continue recording the take in the net, a great smear of dolphin blood ran off my hand across the page. Suddenly the tears came, hot and silent. I felt so sad – nauseated and sad.

As I marked down the data through blurry eyes, the photographer noticed my face. Very professionally, she said: "Silvia, I think we should take a few more shots. Do you mind?" And so I again held the wee beast on my lap, gazing at its graceful lines.

Knowing that there are more than a thousand such drift-net ships operating in the Pacific, and that each ship is estimated to kill 1.7 dolphins a day during the fishing season, and that that works out to more than two hundred thousand dolphins per year, it would have been easy to get angry. But as we returned our gaze to the deck of the drift-netter, the fisherman came to the rails and shrugged his shoulders kindly, as if to say, "But what can we do?" It was good to be reminded that these people are simply wage workers, not policy makers.

And so we continued our work. By 5:30 A.M., the sun had nosed its way over the horizon and we had seen twenty-five kilometres of net go by – just half of this one ship's set for the night.

Silvia Schriever

144

Uganda

✉ Crossing into Uganda from Kenya brought back memories. In 1981 I was escorted to this border from Kampala by four members of the Uganda police. Status: *persona non grata*. The Obote government had lost patience with my reports on the BBC each evening – a litany of military atrocity, famine and high-level corruption. That ride to the border nine years ago offered a pretty clear vision of the state of the nation. The highway itself was a cruel and exhausting trial. Years of neglect and heavy traffic had left the pavement cratered like a war zone. We swerved and bounced our way along for five and a half hours, past sugar and tea estates overgrown with weeds, past towns and villages filled with shuttered windows and palpable fear, past military roadblocks manned by surly privates who gave substance to the fear. Uganda, in 1981, was not a happy place.

And frankly, there's still not much cause for joy. But at least there are signs of improvement. The highway has been redone. Fields of sugar cane are being tended, and the lush green tea estates are back in business. In the swampy clay soil of the valleys near Kampala, dozens of local brickworks are busy. There is new construction everywhere. I'm impressed by little things. We drove to a friend's house in Kampala one evening and passed people in the streets out for a stroll. After dark . . . in Kampala. Nine years ago, the only people who left home after dark were soldiers and thieves, and often those two categories overlapped. Uganda doesn't hit the headlines as often as it did when the PR genius of Idi Amin was hard at work. Peace and quiet don't make very good copy. When Uganda does make the news these days, chances are the subject is AIDS.

Words like *disaster* and *tragedy* are the stuff of everyday headlines. The aggregates – the tens, even hundreds of thousands who die from AIDS – have lost their power to shock. Many of my former class-mates and friends are gone. *Many* – there's another aggregate. Too often this past few weeks, it's been like this: "Where's your brother Henry these days?" A silent shake of the head.

Nobody bothers to mention the cause of death unless it was something other than AIDS.

For two decades, killers with guns stalked the streets. Now, the killer has no face. It courses through the veins of who knows whom. Scarcely a family here has not had a piece of its heart torn out. There are posters all around urging people to "love carefully," and many people seem to have taken it to heart. Though here – as in North America – there is visible backsliding. One friend told me, "Yes, we're very conscious about AIDS . . . until the sun goes down."

Most people here haven't given much thought to what AIDS could mean for Uganda's future. It's a vision that's too horrific to grasp. If you go beyond the individual tragedies – the children without parents, the husbands without wives, the empty seats in a circle of friends – beyond that one can already see villages where a generation has been wiped out. Grandparents who've earned their rest are toiling in the fields to feed, clothe and educate six-year-olds whose parents are gone. Shift that scenario from a few remote villages, imagine it across the country and into the cities, and you wonder who will grow the crops to feed the survivors, who will be there to teach in the schools or run the factories. How, you wonder, can today's leaders do any sensible planning when no one knows whom AIDS will leave behind.

And so, like people everywhere, Ugandans concentrate on the here and now. And even with all the signs of economic improve- ment here, life is still very hard. Putting food on the table, finding money for the kids' school fees, simply getting back and forth to work each day – these are full-time occupations for most Ugandans.

My old alma mater, Kampala's Makerere University, has a motto: "Build for the future." Somehow, despite all the odds, Ugandans are doing that again. Doing it with energy and intelli- gence and remarkable good humour.

Tanzania

✉ Does the name John Williamson ring a bell? I suspect not. He was big news in the late forties and early fifties, a rich, good-looking bachelor with a penchant for privacy, an Ottawa Valley kid who went to McGill, marched to his own drummer and struck it rich. And what – you may ask – does this have to do with Tanzania? Well, this is where Williamson found his wealth, and, more important in 1990, this is where he left most of it, too.

The township of Mwadui sits in the middle of a huge dry plateau south of Lake Victoria. Until 1940, the outside world had little reason to be interested in the Shinyanga plains. It seemed there was nothing here but miles of overused grazing land. But John Williamson – Jack to his friends – thought otherwise. For three years he'd been prospecting in Shinyanga, living hand to mouth, convinced he was on the right track. In March 1940, beneath the dusty black cotton at a place called Mwadui, the obsessive young geologist from Montreal found what he was looking for: diamonds.

Lots and lots of diamonds.

By the late forties, Dr. John Williamson had become something of a media star. He was the little guy who made it the hard way. He'd suffered disease, privation and no small amount of ridicule during his search. The papers called him "the richest bachelor in the world," and it may have been true. He was reclusive, eccentric and sometimes downright pugnacious in his dealings with the world outside Mwadui.

In the early fifties, his apparent willingness and ability to go it alone caused worry and corners of real fear in the tightly organized diamond industry. For newspaper editors, he was great copy.

Williamson died in 1958. He was just fifty-two years old. Throat cancer. And, for the world beyond east Africa, that was pretty well the end of the Williamson story.

But at Mwadui in 1990, his name hasn't been forgotten. Drive past the small white sign, which still says Williamson Diamonds Ltd., and suddenly you're on a smoothly paved road. A few hundred metres farther along, and you've left the sparse brown plains for the shade of tall green trees along avenues of well-built houses. Mwadui is a company town, built by a man who wanted a home and a mine he could be proud of. Williamson died more than thirty years ago, but you can still detect the pride among employees of the company today. They live, by Tanzanian standards, a privileged life. The plumbing and electricity are reliable, the schools still offer a good education to employees' children, you can buy fresh milk from the company dairy and vegetables from the company farm at prices better than the open market can offer.

On Sunday afternoon one of the managers took me out for a beer. We drove about five miles to the edge of the property and relaxed with a couple of cold ones on the verandah of the company sailing club. Ducks swam in the man-made lake in front of us, the biggest body of year-round water on this parched African prairie.

True, Mwadui isn't what it was in the fifties. The golf course is overgrown and the swimming pool is empty. Most of the houses and office buildings could use a coat of paint. On the mine site itself the physical plant shows signs of age and neglect. Equipment lies idle for lack of spare parts.

Talking to the people who run the mine, you get the sense that they're waiting and hoping, with no real idea of what the future may hold.

The diamond ground is just about exhausted. The company doesn't produce enough wealth to justify new investment either in mining equipment or in the township itself.

If Mwadui were in Canada, one of two things would happen. Either the government would step in with huge subsidies, or Mwadui would become a ghost town. Here, the first option isn't available, and the second is unthinkable. Mwadui represents something rare and valuable for Tanzania. It is a critical mass of physical and intellectual resources unrivalled in the country.

One remarkable Canadian laid the groundwork here. Who will preserve and enhance that legacy? I wonder.

Cam Morton

Zaire

✉ We were warned before we came to Dungu, in north-eastern Zaire, that we were going to be very isolated and deprived of many material comforts. Before coming here, though, we lived on Savary Island – a tiny sand dune on the west coast, where the full-time population was twenty, and we made our own electricity.

Dungu has a population of about fifteen thousand, three markets, a cathedral as well as several churches, five elementary schools and two high schools. We occasionally have hydro power, but the river is often too high or too low for the turbines. For much of the year, we have three hours of self-generated power in the evening. There are almost no imported goods or food, so we are dependent on local farmers and hunters. The diet is a bit monotonous but nutritious – rice, a variety of tropical fruits and wild meat, including antelope and boar.

There is also a small "ex-pat" community here – a Canadian carpenter, a Belgian accountant, some clergy. Mostly, though, our friends are the Zairois. Their life is hard and unrelenting. Few have the luxury of thinking beyond enough food and firewood for the day. They live in small, round mud huts with straw roofs. No one has running water or electricity. None the less, everyone is immaculately clean and as well-dressed as their meagre means allow.

Education and health care are privileges, not rights. Only half of the children go to elementary school, and only seven per cent graduate. Sometimes there is not a single girl in the graduating class. Women do the bulk of the work in the fields – and everywhere else, for that matter – so sending a girl to school is a great burden on the family. Many of the boys in grade eleven or twelve are already married, their brides in the fields hoeing rice and beans. For a girl, of course, marriage means the end of her studies. A full year's school – fees, exercise books, pens and uniform – costs about twenty-five dollars, the equivalent of a month's wages for most workers.

Hospital care also costs money – effectively denying it to the bulk of the population. Our hospital is a crumbling brick and concrete building left over from the time of the Belgians. It has occasional electricity, antiquated equipment, a scarcity of virtually everything, two dedicated Zairois doctors and a number of locally trained nurses. Patients must provide their own support staff. Usually a family member comes to wash the bed linen and prepare and serve the meals. The courtyard of the hospital is covered with freshly laundered sheets drying on the grass, and there is the smell of charcoal braziers as rice and beans are cooked.

When we came to Dungu, I was prepared for the hot and humid climate, the culture and the need to speak French. The greatest surprise was landing in the fifteenth century. Aside from the Jeeps driven by the missionaries and our own plane, there is no hint of the twentieth century here. It makes me laugh when I hear the words "information age." There is no television here. We have one of the very few radios (short-wave, of course); there are no newspapers, magazines or books. Mail is sent with travellers – there is no post office. Ninety-nine per cent of the people walk. There are few bicycles, and most people have never had a ride in a vehicle.

As it did five hundred years ago, the Catholic church does everything and is practically the only employer. The clergy run the schools and the hospital and the organization my husband and I work for and provide the only entertainment in town. There are no movie-houses, ice rinks or swimming pools. The river looks very inviting on a forty-degree day, but occasional crocodiles are sighted so . . . Instead, hundreds of people crowd the cathedral for each mass and for special events like Christmas, Easter or ordinations. Hundreds more people stand outside listening to the service, which can last up to four hours. While the people love the pageantry and ritual – which is very Africanized here; the priest and altar boys wear locally made clothes and dance on the altar, and all the hymns are indigenous – and they come in droves, they are never buried in the church. Apparently, burial and the link with ancestors is too important to be left to a "new" religion.

And while many people are baptized, there are very few "church" marriages. This is because of the *dot*, the opposite of a dowry. Women are commodities – sold by the parents, bought by the husband, usually at impossibly high prices. Since the husband cannot pay the *dot* when the young couple start living together, and because he doesn't *want* to pay the *dot* until he has proof of fertility in the form of a live child, the church cannot perform a marriage ceremony. The newly-weds are, in fact, not free to consent to the union. The bride is still owned by her family, and children can be claimed by her family until the *dot* is paid.

We had a tragic reminder of this a while ago when a young woman died in childbirth, along with her child. The next day, her family arrived to prevent the burial of the two bodies until the *dot* was paid in full. The grief-stricken husband frantically borrowed money from all and sundry so that he could bury the rapidly decomposing bodies.

There are many stories here, some sad and others full of courage. There are also many kindnesses and much generosity and a lot of humour. I have laughed more in the past year than in the previous forty-seven, I think. Perhaps because death is always so close and illness, particularly malaria, so prevalent, the Zairois always have time to laugh.

✉ Life in the steaming jungle goes on. Since this is semester exam week in Dungu, I'm taking advantage of the break to come to Bangadi, half an hour's flight from Dungu, to stay with a small group of Québécois *frères*. Bangadi is much more *en brousse* than Dungu, with a smaller population – about ten thousand. Antelope are often shot right in the village, and even an occasional lion is seen. While the farmers in Dungu try to guard their harvest against the two-ton hippos that come out of the river at night to feed, here I saw evidence of baboons who like to eat a little and destroy much more. A farmer told me that he had left his two little boys in the field playing the *tam tams* (drums) to frighten away the monkeys. One of the boys turned around in mid-melody to see half a dozen monkeys watching him attentively. They seemed more interested in learning to play than they were frightened by the noise.

The collapse of the economy here means that there are no imported goods at all. And the state of the roads is so bad that it has been months since a truck arrived. Our plane provides the only link, bringing local mail and some supplies from Dungu and Isiro.

And like all of Haut Zaire, the land must support not only its own people, but a growing flood of Sudanese refugees. I talked to a number of them this morning as they washed their clothes in a muddy little stream. There were perhaps fifteen hundred in Bangadi a month ago. Now there are only six hundred, and they are planning to leave. Many have left to search for other family members, lost during the flight from the Sudan. There is talk of a UN refugee camp to be set up in Haut Zaire, but to date nothing has been done.

In late November, the Sudanese Liberation People's Army took several southern towns in the Sudan and warned the people to leave before the government forces began shelling. Zaire was the nearest border. People left with all the possessions they could carry, but their load was considerably lightened by the time they entered Zaire. The border guards relieved them of money, watches, radios, even shoes. Several thousand walked 285 kilometres through the bush to get to Dungu, selling clothes and bedding to buy food *en route*. By the time they arrived, they were penniless and hungry.

The mission in Dungu provides daily rations and shelter. As well, several hundred refugee families were taken into the homes of the Zairois. It is humbling to see people living in mud huts eking out a living from their fields and living on rice and beans taking in strangers and sharing what they have. In most cases they can't even communicate, since the Sudanese speak Arabic and English and the Zarois speak Lingala or French.

152

When I went to talk to the refugees in Dungu about a week ago, a number of people were gathered around a metal trunk set upon the grass under the shade of a large acacia tree. "Our dispensary," they told me. It was filled with aspirin, chloroquine (an anti-malaria drug), rehydration kits and bandages. The trunk was a gift from the Franciscan sisters and seemed pathetically little, but of course it was more than they had and was deeply appreciated. It was also greatly needed. There were a number of people suffering from malaria and children who had dysentery. The refugees were right beside the Uele River, and the temptation was great, especially for children, to drink the water, rather than packing it half a kilometre from the nearest pump. Unfortunately the muddy flow contained a variety of diseases and parasites.

About six hundred Sudanese are housed here in *le château*. It is a large crumbling brick monument to folly. In the 1940s a Belgian engineer was sent to Dungu to construct a two-lane bridge across the conjunction of the Uele and Dungu rivers. Far from Brussels, deep in the jungle, he apparently gave way to delusions of grandeur. He constructed a single-lane bridge and, with the rest of the money, bricks and labour, he built a *château* worthy of a French baron. The entrance to the grounds is a brick archway, and a circular driveway through the spacious grounds under the shade of the leafy trees takes you past numerous outbuildings for servants and livestock to the *château* itself. There are fireplaces faced with colourful European tiles, innumerable rooms with views of the river and window seats lacking only maidens with long flowing hair, embroidery in hand. But there are also dangerous holes in the floors, missing stairs and no window panes, so that in a storm sheets of rain cascade into the building. Unfortunately for the engineer, his superiors came from Europe to check on his progress and he was sent home before he moved into his dream. To my knowledge, the housing of refugees is the first good use to which it has been put.

The people sleep on grass mats they have woven and placed on the flaking cement floors, huddled together without sheets or blankets. Once a week the mission hands out rations of rice and beans and cooking oil. I talked to a woman who was peeling sweet potatoes and she told me that her husband had managed to find a little work cleaning up a yard, and they had some extra food. Almost all the refugees actively sought work, but it's very difficult. The Zairois economy has fallen so precipitously that there is less and less opportunity. I talked to a young man who was very worried about his asthmatic two-year-old son. "He needs a blanket, he's so cold at night," he told me. The grass was spread with drying clothes and men sat in the shade discussing their limited options.

There were a number of school teachers amongst the refugees, and they talked about the possibility of resuming classes, even in the open air with no books or pencils. Several people asked if it were possible for me to get seeds from Canada. They asked if I had any English-language magazines they could read and were interested in news of the Gulf War. I wondered what the future would bring as the dry season continued and the food became scarcer. It is now estimated that there are more than one hundred thousand refugees in Zaire, twenty-five thousand in our diocese of Dungu-Doruma. The world is spending fifty million dollars a day in the Gulf, and these people have no blankets for their children. If you think about it too long, your whole world goes out of focus.

✉ It's been an exciting week in this little village in the middle of Africa. Dungu had its first ever public military trial. With thousands of Sudanese refugees, the government decided to send in a special group of soldiers to maintain order. The result has been just the opposite. The soldiers extorted money and food from the population, beat several men, including a local shopkeeper, stabbed one woman and broke the ribs of another, and worst of all, shot a young man in the back when he tried to protect his sister from a soldier's unwelcome advances. After this last incident, the local commandant wisely removed all his men's weapons, both rifles and knives, and put the men under a dusk-to-dawn curfew. Then the military made an unprecedented political decision. The military trial of the seven miscreants would be in Dungu and would be public.

Monday, March 25, the appointed day, turned out to be the second consecutive day of a *brume sèche* or dry fog, a peculiarity of the dry season, which seemed to be the tail end of a sandstorm on the faraway Sahara. One could look at the palm trees in the distance with their leafy tassels shrouded in mist and think of damp winter days on the Pacific coast. But instead it was close to forty degrees, and the shrouded sun looked white and merciless and cruel.

The trial took place at the Okapi Hotel, a dilapidated brick building across from the equally dilapidated police station. The five judges were sitting at a long table set up on the broken cement terrace of the hotel. Cheap bright green table-cloths with puckered hems covered the table. There were some two hundred spectators, all standing and pressing forward to hear and see the proceedings. In front of the judges were thirty chairs, all occupied by soldiers with ancient rifles casually slung over their shoulders. There were other soldiers standing at attention beside the judges or slouched against the walls. If they were expecting a riot, they certainly had the numbers and the artillery to quell it.

The first soldier to testify was a man who had badly beaten a young man in Dungu. He held the mike with a visibly trembling hand and explained that he had had a lot of *arak* (the native home brew, made from cassava) to drink and had gone to see his woman, Sylvie, and she had left the impromptu party with another man, causing him to kick his rival in the rear end. Unfortunately the rival fell and was concussed. The victim then testified, but made little sense, and after several sentences, the judges called his brother forward. The brother stated that the soldier had repeatedly kicked the victim in the head with his heavy army-issue boots and had rendered the boy insensible. His mind was still damaged.

The judge asked the soldier if he were married to Sylvie. No, he admitted, Sylvie was a concubine, he had a wife and children in his own village. "Well," said the judge (illogically, I thought), "you had no right to become jealous over a woman to whom you weren't legally married." He gave the soldier five years, a fine of twenty-thousand zaires (someone told me that the amount had been set long before inflation had eaten it down to a mere five dollars), and noted that his family was required to pay for his food in prison.

I expected to feel ripples of tension, both from the spectators and from the soldiers, but all I could discern was absolute attention. There wasn't a sound, not a cough or a shuffling of feet, during all the long hours. The soldier who had shot and wounded a woman in Bangadi was given ten years, a soldier who had stolen some goods from a shop in Dungu and then roughed up the shopkeeper when he complained drew five years, and the soldier who fatally shot the youth in Dungu was given life imprisonment. This was theatre of the type that few of us will ever see. After all, there had been seething resentment against these soldiers for years when they extorted money from people, took food from the basins on top of women's heads after they had walked miles from their fields, stolen their bicycles, and almost everyone knew at least one of the victims. It was no wonder they paid attention to the proceedings.

All in all, I was suitably impressed. If justice was not only to be done, but to be seen to be done, the trial seemed to have accomplished its purpose in showing the people that the military hierarchy were determined to discipline their man. I was impressed until the next morning, at least, when our neighbour, Mado, came for coffee and said cynically, "It was probably all a farce, and they'll be jailed for a few weeks, and then sent off to do duty in another province."

Perhaps I had just witnessed my first "show" trial.

Heather Allen

Bamako, Mali

✉ I came to Africa to shock myself out of my Eurocentricity. To think of time as something other than money and to learn that a good story doesn't have to include sex and violence. I had arranged to stay with other expatriots whom I expected would help me ease my way into the local culture. I was wrong.

The first time I heard a Quebecker call the main street that runs through Bamako "St. Catherine Street" I shuddered with embarrassment. Isn't a good visitor supposed to respect the customs of his host? I couldn't be sure, but I didn't think renaming the main street qualified. Yet here was a Canadian diplomat on a multi-year posting doing his best to make Bamako a little Montreal.

Bamako is nothing like Montreal. It is the capital of Mali, a land-locked French West African country slightly larger than Ontario. It is half Sahara, half Sahel and all sweltering heat.

The Canadian government considers it one of the most unpleasant places on earth in which to be posted. Yet ex-pats, like the previously mentioned Quebecker, are everywhere. They are a speckled band of exiles, diplomats and development workers who have left home for adventure, money or moral gratification.

The Canadian community in Bamako is especially large and lively. They meet every Friday for lunch, every second Saturday for a dinner and dance and monthly for the women's night out and men's poker game. There are also never-ending dinner parties, tennis matches, lunches by the pool and outings. I've never had such a busy social life. Nor have I ever spent so much time talking about Parizeau and Pierre Berton. All the gatherings seem designed to make you forget you are in Africa.

A typical ex-pat event took place last weekend. The Canadian embassy personnel and staff challenged the U.S. embassy personnel and staff to a soccer match. It was held in the Omnisport Pavilion at the edge of town. The arena is built at the foot of the cliffs that forcefully demark Bamako city limits. The unfortunate result is that area shepherds bring their goats down from the parched plateau to graze on the relatively lush playing field. When games begin, the herders grudgingly move their flocks to the upper bleachers where they sulk for the duration of the match.

The goats could probably have fielded a better team than the Canadians. A handful of pudgy, middle-aged bureaucrats (who used to play quite a bit of hockey) and not nearly enough fit Malian guards and clerks walked onto the pitch accompanied by chants of "Let's go Canada, let's go!" Meanwhile, at the other end of the grounds, young marines dressed in matching shimmering silver team shirts joined fit Malian guards and clerks in trotting out onto the field and posing for team pictures. An act copied by the Canadians as soon as someone found a camera.

The people who undoubtedly enjoyed the game most were the thirty or so Bamakois in the stands. They were there only because someone forgot to tell them that the Bamako league semi-finals had been transferred to another stadium. I don't think they had laughed so hard in a very long time. Those forty-five minutes probably did more towards dismantling the vestiges of fear and respect left over from colonialism than ten years of CIDA projects. That positive outcome was almost nullified by the behaviour of the daughter of a Canadian diplomat. The seventeen-year-old blond wanted to leave the match early but she couldn't remember who her driver was. She spent half an hour methodically going from one black spectator to another plaintively asking, "*Est-tu mon chauffeur?*"

We lost.

The international community in Mali doesn't spend all its time trying to outmanoeuvre itself while the locals look on wishing they would either field a better team or get off the pitch. Between the cocktail parties and Robert Charleboix Appreciation Society meetings, actual work does get done. Some projects are dismal failures – the French installed millions of dollars worth of solar panels up near Tombouctou. Ten minutes after they were turned on, they melted in the Saharan sun. The successes tend to be on a more modest scale. Every week for the past fifteen years, Suzanne, a Québécoise, has gone into the bush to teach one woman in every village she can reach basic hygiene. Dana, a London School of Economics educated American, has spent two years showing farmers how to set up co-operatives to buy and maintain water pumps for irrigation. It is these individuals who are making a difference in Africa.

The work is tedious and slow. Many will not see large-scale results in their lifetime. If it takes regular hockey scores, Ginette Reno and the mirage of St. Catherine Street to keep them sane, so be it. The casual visitor like I will have to find their own way to the world of African culture.

Alexandra, South Africa

✉ If you stay at a certain level of society here in South Africa, everything seems exactly like back home. The food stalls are on the ground floor of the mall, *Star Trek* is on the weekend and teenagers are on the phone. The only major difference is that the liberal intellectuals have slightly more African art in their living-rooms.

Then there are the other levels. A week before all the violence started, I went with Gerty, the maid, to visit Alexandra, one of the oldest townships in South Africa. We travelled by *combi*, the fourteen-seat mini-buses that constitute a secondary public transit system for blacks. The city buses don't go near the townships. The driver let us off at the wrong spot and we had a thirty-minute walk through the centre of Alex. The township, or location, is built along opposing slopes of a valley. Along the floor of the valley is what looks like a dried river bed, but is actually a trench that collects the refuse that washes down the slopes at every rain.

The trench also serves to divide Alex into the appallingly poor section, replete with aluminum lean-tos, illicit beer halls and work-ers' hostels, and the simply lower-class section with tiny detached houses, front yards and pet dogs. We walked through the appallingly poor section, where all the violence has been, over the bridge across the trench and to Gerty's uncle's detached bungalow.

I was incredibly well received during the first part of the walk. Residents were astonished to see me. Once the glare from my skin ceased to blind them, they shouted out greetings.

Gerty's uncle's house was just like any other working-class house in the Western world. The living-room: orangey-brown, flower print, velour upholstered, matching couch and chairs, plastic covering optional. Impeccably clean, genuine plywood, imitation mahogany coffee table with ceramic ashtray and copy of *Cosmo*. Above the couch, a beige, elaborately framed, faded print of an oil painting of a rocky coastline. In the corner by the window with the floor-length light brown curtains, a copper plant stand holding a ferny thing. Scattered here and there about the room, incredibly welcoming inhabitants. George, the uncle, was sitting on the couch holding a beer, and Elaine, the aunt, was in the kitchen preparing us food.

As always when a South African meets a foreigner for the first time, we talked politics. George asked me what I thought of his country. As always when talking politics with a South African I've never met, I gave a vague, liberal answer. George listened. When I stopped, he took over.

"I don't think South Africa should have a black president for another twenty to thirty years." He tossed it off casually. "We just don't have the leadership experience yet. It would be a disaster for all South Africans."

He continued along the same lines, pointing out the inability of Mandela and Buthelezi to control their own supporters, let alone those hostile to them. I boggled. Had a white told me the same thing, I would have branded him a racist and not bothered paying him much attention. But what to do when a black man in Alex says those things and his wife, sitting behind a sewing machine doing piece work, periodically nods in agreement?

As dusk fell and the barrel fires started being lit on the other side of the trench, George called on a friend with an ancient, beat-up Mercedes to drive us home. Gerty and I got into the car and

160

Lucky, the driver, asked me what I thought of South Africa. Out came my vaguely liberal answer, sounding a bit battered. He cut me short. "Me, I'm a De Klerk man." And he drove us back to the white suburbs.

Cleo Paskal

Leningrad

✉ It's the first official day of rationing in Leningrad and the whole city is abuzz with rumours and speculation. Will the coupons actually guarantee availability of food? For the past few days, people have been receiving their coupons, ten in all for one month: for one and a half kilograms of meat, one kilo of sausage, ten eggs, half a kilo of butter, a quarter kilo of oil, half a kilo of flour, one kilo of cereal or macaroni per person per month. How well could the average Canadian make out on such quantities for a month?

Nevzorov, the popular television broadcaster and producer of the nightly news show here called *Six Hundred Seconds*, made waves when he claimed on air the other evening that the amount being rationed is actually less than was allotted during Leningrad's infamous wartime blockade, when well over half a million people perished from starvation.

Gifts from the miraculous West still excite people. Germany is sending food packages to the elderly and the invalids, which are gratefully received. Yesterday a German concession began selling pints of imported draught beer and sausages for roubles, and a hearty line-up of people waited patiently in the damp cold to sample the fare. Usually such delicacies are available only in hard – not Soviet or "wooden" – currency.

Most people struggle to survive with a kind of doleful listless-ness and disillusionment. Unfortunately this applies to young and old alike. It's only by coming to know people closely that one can gauge the real extent of despair here. Totalitarianism has left its marks. And most people remain removed from politics of any kind.

It is only a tiny minority who have the energy and optimism required to fight for change.

I've been spending time with an old friend. I remember eight years ago, long evenings over dark, Georgian wine and tables of food. We laughed at the inconsistencies and absurdities of Soviet life. Then, Olga and her best friend had just finished university. They dreamt, somewhat unrealistically, of travel to the West, perhaps even emigration. Her friend has now emigrated, marrying a German. Olga remains here working as a German translator. Her family's apartment is undergoing repairs and is full of sawdust, refuse and broken furniture.

We drink in the kitchen now, under a bare light bulb – usually cheap vodka instead of Georgian wine. The table is barer – lots of macaroni but no meat. Olga's mother, who I remember as a chatty and eccentric woman, is now a confirmed alcoholic and has twice attempted suicide. She looks thin; her eyebrows are heavily painted, and her smile is forced. Olga's father, a writer and dreamy-eyed intellectual, wanders around the cramped apartment in a patched dressing-gown, trying to stimulate capitalism in Russia by making imaginary business deals with Azerbaijani entrepreneurs. He asks me, *me* of all people, why bread has disappeared from the shelves over the past week. Then he wonders if I know of anyone in Canada who would like to buy, or invest in, a Soviet brick factory.

Olga says he's not all there any more. She worries about both her parents, but is also angered by their childishness and embittered by the futility of her own position. There is not too much heroic about her. She believes in nothing, least of all the future.

✉ In the despotic tsarist Russia of a hundred or so years ago, liberal reformers dreamed of bringing about meaningful reform through the performance of so-called "small deeds." Perhaps a century later, Soviet Russia, with its dying villages and totalitarian power structure, can only be fundamentally reformed through millions upon millions of such small deeds. An old friend has recently convinced me of this.

I have just returned from visiting Igor. I knew Igor nine years ago in Moscow, when he was finishing his degree in geology and I in history as a foreign student. From a working-class family in the textile factory town of Orekhovo-Zuyevo, about one hundred and twenty kilometres from Moscow, Igor was bright, serious and ambitious; he dreamed of travel to exotic places – hence his interest in geology. Like few others of his generation, he was honest *and* patriotic, miraculously maintaining a decency and integrity about himself, which was not entirely in keeping with socialist morality and education.

Although Igor was officially banned from mixing with foreigners, he risked my company and we would take long walks through Moscow's streets and parks, discussing in hushed tones everything from the meaning of Russian history to our own life plans. He was curious to know my opinions, but maintained a firm belief in the Soviet system. When I cursed the whole Soviet experiment, he replied that yes, somewhere, something may have gone wrong – Brezhnev was no shining example of a leader . . . but *Lenin* – there was a genius, a seeker of truth, a light to humanity.

When we parted in the spring of 1982, Igor was off to work in the gold mines of faraway Uzbekistan. Nine years later, we still correspond. Family interests figure most in our letters. I knew that Igor had returned to his native parts, married a local village girl and was a proud new father. I was surprised to learn that he had given up a geology career to work as a dyer in a local factory. When Igor invited me to visit his village and new family, I readily assented.

As my train pulled into the station, I did not recognize the smiling face waving at me from the platform. On closer inspection, I remembered the friendly blue eyes, but could not get over the sunken cheeks, deep-set wrinkles and greying, balding head of hair. As Igor presented me with a bouquet of red carnations, he joked, "You see, you were right – look at what socialism does to young men – it ages us prematurely!" Then he revealed a bit to me about the years spent in Uzbekistan – the corruption, brutality and violence – and he told me how relieved he was to be back "home" in Russia.

Igor's village, Drovoseki, is like thousands of other Russian villages – sleepy, rutted and ramshackle. All the inhabitants still draw water in metal buckets from the local well (Igor with a six-month-old infant hauls water eighteen times a day!), and there are scary reports that the well water is heavily polluted by pesticides. Igor's mother-in-law's house, where he lives with his wife and baby, is a large two-room wooden cottage, painted a cheerful green but sadly in need of basic repair. Igor has tried countless times to obtain hard-to-procure building supplies from the local village soviet, but only met bureaucratic obstacles. Like all the other dozens of homes in the village, Igor's has electricity, but no running water or indoor plumbing. This, in a village only one hundred and fifty kilometres from the centre of Moscow!

Two buildings stand out from the others in Drovoseki, both made of brick. One is a solid white one-storey structure, built single-handedly by one villager through savings accumulated over decades from the revenue received from two dairy cows. Another is a much more imposing two-storey red brick house, belonging to the chairman of the local *sovkhoz* or state farm. While the enterprising villager is highly respected by his neighbours, the *sovkhoz* chairman is widely detested. "Until all the Communists are gone – every last one – such parasites will flaunt themselves in our village," says Igor's next-door neighbour.

Igor, like all his neighbours, works hard – six days a week at his factory job (most villagers hold factory jobs or work on the railways nearby), and then after hours, doing domestic duties and trying to feed his family from a tired and meagre patch of land. He misses the intellectual challenge of geology but has cheerfully resigned himself to life's new challenges – there are no jobs here for geologists anyway, and even if there were, the pay is not sufficient to survive on. Igor excitedly showed off his garden and potato field to me (they are not really his nor his mother-in-law's, since the state owns all the land). They were still covered in deep snow under the warm spring sun.

"It's a godsend to have this land during such a time – perestroika – it has literally fed our whole family during the last year – but you know – our crop yield is so pitiful and the quality of the vegetables so poor! None of us could believe the beautiful potatoes harvested by some Dutch farmers not far from here, who were rented some land last year to experiment with." Then Igor asked me for seeds of all kinds – could I send them? Maybe, just maybe – Canadian seeds could help bring the abused Russian soil back to life. Meanwhile, he and Elizaveta Pavlovna, his mother-in-law, plan to get some chickens in the spring, since eggs are almost unobtainable in the shops. "But what shall we feed them?" Igor queried. "I just don't know." Elizaveta Pavlovna, at the age of fifty-five, goes off every second day to work a fifteen-hour shift repairing broken railway ties – a difficult life for an older woman. Although obviously a strong woman, she confessed to me in tears one evening she feared for the future of her new little granddaughter. "We work and work and work – and there is *nothing* to show for it. What about the little ones?"

The village as a whole received me royally, as a special guest, right down to the tipsy letter carrier, Auntie Tiesia. I learned that they are as hostile towards Gorbachev as are their intelligentsia counterparts in the cities. Most plan to vote no in the upcoming referendum, not an anti-union vote, but a protest vote against Gorbachev's politics. Yeltsin, so far at least, is believed and trusted by all of them. Again, according to Igor, the biggest problem is the villagers' passivity – they look to Yeltsin as though he *can* and *will* change everything. Instead, Igor says, they must cease once and for all their long-suffering forbearance, they must rely on themselves and quit looking to someone else higher up to take care of them.

What a change the last decade has wrought in Igor! Despite his measured wisdom about life, he has not totally succumbed to the all-encompassing pessimism of almost everyone I know in the city.

He knows bad times are ahead – he is trying to prepare for them – but he is simply too busy with his endless small tasks to worry too much.

It was sad taking leave of Igor and his family. As I left on the dark, cold evening to catch a Moscow train, Elizaveta Pavlovna, in typical Russian fashion, thrust a package of carefully prepared food – green apples, brown bread and sausage – into my hands and hugged me robustly. "Thank you . . . thank you for visiting us. Thank you for overlooking and forgiving us our poverty."

Slipping and sliding beside me along the icy patches of uneven road, Igor looked up at the starry sky and mused, "Who knows? Maybe, just maybe, if you come to visit us again nine years from now, this road might be fixed. We could walk along a smooth road. Even *that* – such a small thing – would be a big improvement for us. After all, we must start somewhere, mustn't we?"

Patricia Patchet-Golubev

Thought for Food

Morningside listeners – including, apparently, the premier of Prince Edward Island – love cooking almost as much as their host likes talking about it. Sometimes, as with scalloped potatoes, we all do it together, swapping recipes as we go. On other occasions, we just toss out a recipe for, say, rice pudding, and see what happens.

✉ Here I sit with a cup of newly perked coffee, the spring sun coming through the window, the first wild sweet pea of the season peeking at me from the jar the kids put it in, my garden half planted, and my mouth is watering for some Atlantic dulse. It is all of thirty years – I was a child of about ten, I think – when our neighbour brought us a treat – dulse. He would be romantically referred to as "an Irish immigrant" but to us he was just Bob. Where and why he obtained the dulse I don't recall – perhaps some of his family in the old country sent it to him. But there it was, clumsily wrapped in old brown paper. He opened the package – I remember his hands trembled a bit – and proudly displayed his prize – a large handful of a purplish-brown stuff that looked like the weeds in the sloughs that we cut for hay and smelled like the

167

dried, salted herring my Norwegian father bought us each winter. Bob assured us it was good for us and tasted heavenly and promptly stuffed a generous hunk into his mouth. A typical, sceptical ten-year-old, I lifted a pinch of the stuff. It felt leathery but smooth and was not unlike chewing tobacco, only coarser. When Bob said, "No, it wasn't washed," I was ready to throw it out but Mom was game and I finally ate a tiny piece, too. (I checked to be sure there was no sand or sea shells stuck to it!)

Dulse is habit-forming. Unlike our refined snacks that dissolve on contact with the tongue, dulse can be chewed and chewed. Not quite as long as wheat gum, mind you, but certainly long enough to satisfy a kid. We grew to love the stuff. The salty taste, the sweet undertones, the velvety feel on our tongues.

Bob brought us dulse once a year for several years. Then he moved away and the years rolled by. I haven't seen, smelled or tasted the stuff for years, but the thought of it makes my mouth water still.

Wendy Caldwell
Ceylon, Saskatchewan

✉ In my youth – I was born in the dim, distant 1920s on Vancouver Island – all people with discretion ate Gravenstein apples, and if they didn't have a tree of their own they cultivated a friendship with someone who did.

Recently I found a plan of my father's orchard tucked into the pages of *The Culture of Fruit and Vegetables* by Sutton and Sons, 1908. I learned that Father planted two Gravenstein apples, one in 1916 and another in 1920. Other varieties included Blenheim Orange, Cox Orange Pippin, Jonathan, Northern Spy, Wagner, and Duchess of Oldenburg – all in 1914. Then there was an Alexander and a McIntosh that went in after he returned from the war in 1919.

By the time I was old enough to bite into anything and remember it, all but two of those trees had gone to the great apple orchard in the sky. The survivors were the Jonathan and the Gravenstein – both good eaters. The former was an excellent keeper but the Gravenstein wasn't too bad at keeping, either. They never went fozzy. I believe both these trees are still extant. Later we planted a King, which developed water core and tasted like fresh pine-apple; and a Melba, which is early and makes pink apple sauce. But for eating raw, nothing exceeds a Gravenstein. As a child I was a connoisseur of apples and would devour six to eight a day, and I was pretty discriminating – such inferior types as Red or Golden Delicious or Winter Banana might be considered suitable pig food – if I didn't like the pig very much.

Monica Oldham
Victoria

✉ Gravensteins are grown still in this area of the West Koote-nays at the north end of Kootenay Lake in south-east British Columbia. The Red Gravenstein is considered to be kind of bogus. As one of the old-timers said, "When they put the colour in, they bumped the flavour out." The local Kaslo Gravenstein, named after the town of Kaslo, is yellow with a red blush and/or stripes and a particular but indescribable combination of sweetness, crunch, tang and juice. It was known far and wide in the trade. One of the old orchardists here told me of his last large shipment of Kaslo Gravenstein, which left in 1956 on the *Moyie*, a steam-powered stern wheeler, going down Kootenay Lake to the railhead and then on to faraway New York City. When the *Moyie* was beached in 1957, the orchard industry at this end of the lake died with it, to be revived in a small way in the seventies as road transportation improved. Even now I occasionally get calls from faraway places for the Kaslo Gravenstein.

Dave Putt
Argenta, British Columbia

✉ Many people in this narrow coastal valley consider Bella Coola to be Canada's Gravenstein capital. Gravensteins were a favourite of the original Norwegian settlers, and the first trees arrived here early in this century. At one point, boxes of Gravensteins from Bella Coola were shipped by the hundreds to the thriving mill town of Ocean Falls and the salmon cannery at Namu each fall by boat.

Nowadays, only remnant populations exist there, and many of the old orchards of Bella Coola have been cut down. But there are still Gravenstein trees in this valley. I've successfully grafted scions from some of the oldest remaining trees and grow some of the newer red-sport Gravensteins as well.

More than twenty varieties of Gravenstein exist, and in my experience they are all quite distinctive.

Kevin O'Neill
Bella Coola, British Columbia

✉ I started messing around with spices and herbs this year, both growing and drying, and I have a cabinet full of home-grown mints and thymes, as well as the exotic cinnamon, cloves and cardamom. It is very soothing to fuss about with them, either when cooking or making sachets and pot-pourris.

A word on nutmeg – when I first arrived at the University of Toronto in September 1972, I received a "survival kit" about sex and drugs on campus. In the section on hallucinogens was a mention of nutmeg, with a warning that there had been one death from nutmeg overdose. A high enough dose to give you a kick could also poison you.

Here is a herbal cold remedy–it was described to me as "Ukrainian penicillin." Cut a clove of garlic in half and eat it, washing it down with a shot of vodka. (I believe the cutting is partly to release the juice and partly to make it easier to swallow the garlic.)

I can't remember if it worked, but it certainly kept people far enough away from me that I did not spread the cold!

Elizabeth Creith
Elmvale, Ontario

✉ Some years ago when I was on a trip to the Blood Indian reserve near Lethbridge, Alberta, I was introduced to prairie oysters.

The ingredients are soda crackers, ketchup and butter.

I was told that one went into a restaurant and ordered a bowl of soup. With the soup came crackers and the little squares of butter. There was always a bottle of ketchup on the table.

You took the soda crackers, built a little wall of butter around the sides of the cracker, filled in the space with ketchup and . . . down the hatch!

I believe this practice started in Depression days.

I don't know whether it's still in vogue.

John Grimshaw
Campbellville, Ontario

Elizabeth Baird, of *Canadian Living* magazine, started us on rice pudding, with this recipe:

✉ What I love about rice pudding is its creaminess. And this comes from slow cooking in plenty of milk, either the old-fashioned way in the top of a double boiler – guaranteed no scorching or boil-overs – or simmered in a large heavy saucepan with lots of stirring. Fancy up a bowl with raisins, cinnamon and nutmeg, or ginger and orange, or apricots and orange – or whatever strikes your fancy.

½ cup short grain rice, Italian recommended
¼ cup granulated sugar
¼ teaspoon nutmeg
pinch salt
2½ cups (approximately) milk
½ cup raisins
1 tablespoon butter
1 teaspoon vanilla
cinnamon

In a large heavy-bottomed saucepan, stir together the rice, sugar, nutmeg, salt and milk. Cover and over very low heat bring to a simmer. Simmer very gently, stirring often, for 20 minutes. Add raisins and cook for 5 to 10 minutes longer or until rice is tender and the milk is thickened and creamy. Stir in butter and vanilla. Add more milk, if desired, for an even creamier pudding.

If serving immediately, spoon into bowls and sprinkle with cinnamon. If serving later, transfer to an airtight container and pour in about ⅓ cup more milk to keep the surface moist. Let cool, cover and refrigerate. Stir milk into the pudding before serving. Makes 4 servings.

Variation: Orange Ginger or Orange Apricot Rice Pudding: Make rice pudding according to the method above. Instead of the nutmeg, use 1½ teaspoons coarsely grated orange rind, and instead of the raisins, add either 1 tablespoon chopped crystallized ginger or ½ cup thinly sliced dried apricots. Omit the vanilla and cinnamon.

Toasted Almond Rice Pudding: Top any of the versions above with 2 tablespoons toasted slivered almonds just before serving.

Elizabeth Baird
Toronto

✉ I spent the first five years or so of our marriage searching for the recipe for the Perfect Rice Pudding my husband remembered from his childhood. I tried every recipe I came across, some starting from raw rice, some from cooked rice. Some came close, some were awful, but at last I was able to consolidate the best points into *the* Rice Pudding.

¾ cup rice (short grain)
5 to 6 cups milk
¼ teaspoon salt
3 eggs
¼ to ½ cup sugar (brown or white)
1 teaspoon vanilla
½ cup raisins

Cook rice, milk and salt in top of double boiler about 1 hour. Beat eggs and sugar. Stir some of pudding into eggs and stir all back into the pudding with the vanilla and raisins. Stir well (the heat of the pudding cooks the eggs). Chill.

This makes lots of pudding to feed a family of five.

Now, mind you, had you asked me for the recipe for genuine rice pudding *before* my marriage I would have voted for the kind *my* mother used to make. Milk, rice and a little sugar were baked *slowly* in the oven. As the brown, tasty crust forms, it is stirred into the pudding two or three times, giving it a lovely caramelized flavour. Eggs do not enter into it. About once every five years I succumb and make *that* kind.

Margaret Pointing
Mississauga, Ontario

✉ I know when I am served a rice-based dish for supper that a creamy, mouth-watering rice pudding made from left-overs will follow shortly thereafter. Similarly, I look forward to bread pudding made from bread that has gone stale; banana bread made from the fruit that has spoiled; and my own personal favourite –

macaroni pudding–made from left-over pasta, milk, a pat of butter (Granny would have frowned on artificial substitutes) and a pinch of nutmeg. Ah! Ambrosia!

My wife has more than a dozen cookbooks, but when I see her thumbing through the small, blue, spiral-bound notebook that has been passed down from generation to generation, my salivary glands go into spontaneous, rapturous spasm. My granny could have told the world a thing or two about taste and economy!

Gary Brannon
Kitchener, Ontario

✉ With declared war overseas and sometimes seemingly unde-clared war in Canada, how reassuring it is to retreat in memory to the warmth and comfort of a big porridge bowl of rice pudding.

For me, rice pudding was a twice-a-week-at-least dessert at Granny's big house right next door to our smaller one back on the farm in the early fifties. True, my mother, like the good daughter-in-law she was, learned to make rice pudding, too – her survival as a central Alberta farmer's wife depended on it. But she never got the recipe quite right. She kept trying to dress it up with big, plump raisins or even almonds. She never seemed to get the idea that the only thing that belongs in a rice pudding is rice.

Granny made rice pudding every wash-day, and the thick, creamy delight was always baking in the oven of the old coal-and-wood cook-stove by eight o'clock in the morning. That way it would be ready to serve for dinner, the major meal of the day, which always occurred promptly at twelve noon. This, mind you, was back in that idyllic time of housewifery before electricity and before indoor plumbing, when dessert was on the menu twice a day every day and was eaten and enjoyed to the last morsel without the slightest pang of guilt. Today, at our house, we never have dessert with family meals, and sometimes not even when company comes. And I don't even have the excuse that I have a full-time job (unless you call raising five kids a full-time job).

174

Whatever would Granny say if she could see her beloved grand-daughter now?

Granny's rice pudding was made in her biggest, deepest ceramic pudding basin with Delta short grain rice – the only rice on the grocery store shelf. A cup of rice, two quart sealers of fresh-from-the-cow milk, a generous half cup of sugar, a little cinnamon and nutmeg and a capful of vanilla, and the dish was ready for the oven. The pudding baked all morning in the oven, while on top of the stove, a huge pot of beef stew shared the cooking space with the big rusty old wash boiler, where the dirtiest clothes were boiled and bleached and water was heated for the washing machine. The washing machine was an incredibly noisy gasoline-engined contraption, which had been pulled with two square laundry tubs into the middle of the kitchen floor. I kept my dis-tance from that washing machine, having been darkly warned that if my fingers ever came within a laundry tub's distance of the washer's mighty wringer, they would end up squashed flatter than Grand-dad's socks.

Instead I hovered near the oven, which Granny would open every half hour or so to stir the pudding. An unstirred pudding would take its revenge by boiling all over the oven and filling the house with the smell of scorched milk.

At last, after three or four stirrings and half a dozen wash loads – start with the whites, then the lights and work your way to the darkest and dirtiest overalls – it was time for dinner. I dutifully ate the beef stew and boiled potatoes, always peeled and cooked to semi-mush – Granny hadn't heard about preserving vitamins – and then the pudding. If I had been an especially good five-year-old, and naturally Granny thought I always was, I would be allowed to very carefully dip the serving spoon into the pudding basin, breaking through the tough skin that had formed on top. That skin, all browned and just a little bit burned, was even better than the soft, sweet, milk-swollen rice beneath. And Granny would always let me have a second dish.

Granny and Grand-dad are gone now. The old farmhouse has been moved to town and modernized, and the coal-and-wood cook-stove and gasoline washing machine haven't been seen in thirty-five years. But I still dream of finding again that rice pudding.

I've ordered it in restaurants, but the finest chefs just don't know how to make it. Either it arrives as a square of disgusting baked custard or as a thoroughly unacceptable top-of-the-stove imitation. And almost invariably it is sullied with raisins. I feel the same disappointment I felt when I went to England, expecting to drink wonderful tea, just like Granny made only better, steeped from loose leaves in an earthenware or china pot. Instead, I found tepid water in a one-cup metal pot with a tea-bag tossed on a saucer.

I guess the only way to get my perfect rice pudding is to make it myself. And I do make it once in a while. Of course, it isn't quite like Granny's. I don't have Granny's pudding basin, and I have to use my self-cleaning electric oven. (A microwave just won't do the job.) And in order to justify using so much energy for one decadent dessert, I have to cook a roast along with it. It has to be served for supper – who would have time to eat a roast beef dinner for lunch?

But this afternoon, that inimitable aroma of baking rice pudding fills my kitchen. I can almost smell the hot wash water and the bleach. And did I hear Granny warning me one more time away from that wringer? Oops, I think it's time to give that pudding another stir.

Donna Cookson Martin
Sedgewick, Alberta

✉ In a letter, my great-grandfather, Captain Thomas Waters, mentioned his mother's Christmas pudding. This recipe has been handed down and used by each generation of our family.

English Plum Pudding

If you wish to make the pudding in which everyone delights,
Of six pretty new-laid eggs you must take the yolks and
 whites.
Beat them well up together till they thoroughly combine
And be sure you chop the suet up particularly fine.
Take a pound of well-stoned raisins and a pound of currants
 dried,
A pound of pounded sugar, and some candied peel beside.
Beat it all up well together with a pound of wheaten flour
And let it stand and settle for a quarter of an hour.
Then tie the mixture in a cloth and put it in a pot,
Some people like the water cold and some prefer it hot.
Although I do not know which of these two plans I ought to
 praise,
I know it ought to boil an hour for every pound it weighs.
If I were Queen of France, or, still better, Pope of Rome,
I would have a Christmas Pudding every day I dined at home.
All the world should have a piece, and if any did remain,
Next morning for my breakfast I would have it fried again.

Elizabeth Evans
Regina

**And then the premier of Prince Edward Island gave us
his most famous recipe:**

✉ In order to have a good Caesar salad, preparation should
commence at least five hours before serving.
This recipe should satisfy six persons.

 1. Four to five slices of home-made bread. Cube the bread
into crouton-sized bites. Melt plenty of butter in a large frying
pan and dump the croutons in the butter and allow to crisp at
low heat. More butter may have to be added during the process.
The more butter, the better!

2. Crush 4 cloves of garlic into a medium-sized bowl.

3. Once the croutons are crisp, mix them in with the crushed garlic.

4. Add olive oil to the level of the top of the croutons and mix thoroughly so that the garlic is spread evenly through the croutons and oil. Cover the mixture and let sit until salad is prepared.

5. Wash 2 romaine lettuces thoroughly and dry leaves individually. Tear leaves by hand into a large salad bowl. Add lots of lemon. When you think you have enough lemon, add that much more again.

6. Add pepper. Add Parmesan cheese. The rule for Parmesan cheese is to put in a sufficient quantity so that you are satisfied that you have put too much in – then double the amount.

7. Add the mixture of croutons, garlic and olive oil. Add salt to taste.

8. Perhaps add Worcestershire sauce, anchovies.

9. Add 2 egg yolks. Mix thoroughly into salad.

10. Toss salad thoroughly. Serve immediately.

P.S. A generous portion of chopped-up bacon should also be added.

Joe Ghiz
Charlottetown

✉ Here's a low-fat crouton recipe:

Butter each piece of bread (preferably whole-wheat), stack them up and carve the pile into 1-inch squares. Spread cubes on a greased cookie sheet (use olive oil – 1 tablespoon – just to wet the sheet) and bake at 250°C, and stir around until crisp. They're great that way and healthier! Olive oil is fine (it's a mono-unsaturate) but use butter sparingly. (I hate margarine and won't use it.) Must have the taste of butter or I won't eat.

But at our age, swimming in fried butter ain't a good idea, especially if we smoke!

Gretchen Grinnell
Toronto

And one of my favourite radio hosts did the same with scalloped potatoes:

✉ Peel and thinly slice 6 medium-sized potatoes. Peel and thinly slice 3 large onions. Cut up one squash or turnip into 1-inch cubes, boil till soft and mash. In a buttered casserole (oven-proof) set a layer of potato. Salt and pepper. Dot with butter or margarine. Cover this layer with onion. Follow with second layer of potato. Salt, pepper and dot with butter. Next layer is turnip. Keep this order of layering until casserole is full but finish with potato. Pour 1 cup of milk over everything. Bake 1 hour in 375° oven – covered for 45 minutes, uncovered for 15.

Max Ferguson
Toronto

✉ *This* is how you make scalloped potatoes:

  4 cups peeled potatoes, sliced thin (less than ¼ inch)
  2 cups medium white sauce (4 tablespoons butter, 4 tablespoons flour, 2 cups milk, salt, pepper)
  1 cup onions, very thinly sliced in rings
  paprika

Rinse sliced potatoes briefly in cold water; drain. Drop into boiling water. Parboil 8 to 10 minutes; drain.
  Meanwhile, make white sauce.
  In buttered casserole (preferably one made by a Saskatchewan potter), layer half potato and onion slices alternately; pour on

half the sauce. Repeat with remaining potatoes, onions and sauce. Sprinkle top lightly with paprika. Bake uncovered at 350° for 45 minutes.

This is not my mother's recipe. She made them with the dabs of butter and the sprinkles of flour. Having watched her, I used to make them that way, too.

But twenty years ago, when my husband and I inadvertently found ourselves saddled with what used to be called "role reversal," he decided one day to make scalloped potatoes.

Having never watched his mother do it, he looked it up in a book . . . an old *Good Housekeeping* cookbook circa the early forties. As above, with a few minor modifications – we added the paprika. But then, I tend to add paprika to a lot of things; I suspect that in their wanderings from Spain to the Russian *shtetl*, some of my ancestors spent a little time in Hungary and Romania.

Ours uses a couple of saucepans and a baking dish. Big deal. It's richly yummy old-fashioned "comfort food" at its best.

Lora Burke
Regina

✉ Rowan-berries, as they are called in England, *Vogelbeeren* or bird berries, as they are called in Germany, mountain ash berries as they are called here, are from the family of apples (*Sorbus aucuparia, S. americana, S. decora*).

Most children are told not to eat them, as they are poisonous. But my cookbook lists them as the fruit containing more vitamin C than rose-hips, which have twenty-eight times as much as oranges.

For the birds they are the food bank. The birds eat them here in Central Alberta generally immediately following a severe cold snap.

Mountain ash berries, like rose-hips, can be picked until Christmas; they should have at least one good frost.

It took me many years to find a suitable recipe, which I would like to share.

Mountain Ash Jam

5½ cups mountain ash berries
2¾ cups sugar
one average-sized apple cut into pieces
juice of 1 lemon

Add a little water and boil until it gels.

Since I have a sweet tooth, I add more apple and sugar.

Bernd Hartmann
Red Deer, Alberta

✉ Fiddleheads are to be treasured! Thanks to my friend Carol Marino (photographer extraordinaire), I've been able to pick them these last two years (in a spot not to be revealed!).

My personal favourite way to eat them is: Boiled until tender and cooled, then served cold with thin slices of purple onion and red pepper; tossed with toasted sesame seeds, olive oil, red vinegar and a few generous drops of sesame oil. A delicacy, and a delight. Sea horse tail salad!

Elissa Gallander
Toronto

✉ I have been forever grateful to a friend's mother, who showed me a very simple method of making hollandaise. (She was a good friend of Mme. Benoit, and perhaps it was Mme. Benoit who taught her.)

We have made this at the cottage on the fireplace, and our son at a very early age learned to make it as well. This goes to prove how very easy it is!

It's best made in a small enamelled iron saucepan. I use an egg yolk, about a tablespoon or less of lemon juice, and about a half a cup or more of butter. (I don't measure.) Place ingredients in saucepan and heat very slowly on low. Stir with a rubber spatula as the butter begins to soften. The important thing is to not allow the sauce to become too hot. The test is to be able to put your hand on the bottom of the pan at all times.

If the sauce is allowed to get too hot, it will curdle. It usually can be saved by sprinkling about half a teaspoon of cold water into the sauce and beating briefly with a wire whisk.

As soon as the sauce thickens, it is ready and can be held by setting in a bowl of water at "bathtub" temperature (not too hot). Change water as necessary to keep warm. Makes about three-quarters of a cup of sauce.

Phyllis Ketcheson
Toronto

✉ I won a five-dollar bet with my Mock Apple Pie years ago. Two friends of my husband were boasting how great their taste buds were. No one could fool them.

I made them a bet of five dollars that they could not tell me what kind of pie I served them.

One guy took me up on it, and we made a date.

When I served him the pieces of pie, he was pretty good. He detected that I had nutmeg in one, cinnamon in the other. Also, after much tasting, he came up with the cream of tartar I had put in.

Then I asked, "Do you like them?" His answer was: he did not care much for nutmeg in apple pie. But they were both very good.

He could not believe it when I told him what kind of pie I had served him. He asked me for the recipe and said he would have his wife make it before he would pay.

A couple of days later he came over to the house and handed me five dollars.

182

Mock Apple Pie

1. Line 9-inch pie plate with bottom crust.
2. Boil together for 2 to 3 minutes:
    1½ cups water
    1½ cups sugar (white or brown)
    1½ teaspoons cream of tartar
3. Set aside to cool.
4. On unbaked pie crust, place 12 salted crackers broken in quarters.
5. Pour cooled liquid over crackers.
6. Dot with 1 teaspoon butter.
7. Sprinkle over ingredients 1 teaspoon of nutmeg or cinnamon.
8. Cover with top crust.
9. Bake at 400° for 35 to 40 minutes or until top crust is golden brown.

Irene Kettle
Terrace Bay, Ontario

✉ Here is the no-work streamlined method for roasting a turkey, in tune with today's hectic times.

Remove a frozen turkey from your freezer the night before the feast. With a knife, spread it generously with shortening all over except its back. Cover it loosely with a large piece of foil wrap and put it in the roasting pan. (It's as hard as a rock, and it won't hurt it to sit overnight in a cool place.)

At an appropriate time the next day, put it in a regular oven at 300° to 325° F and roast it at time-and-a-half per pound owing to its being frozen.

Test at prescribed time by jabbing the thing with a fork. No basting is necessary. It will brown beautifully under the foil wrap.

As for the dressing, gravy and cranberry sauce, they can all be done days before the festive occasion. A good dry dressing (with savoury) can be made in huge amounts and stored in the freezer to be reconstituted, at the last moment, in the microwave oven. The bulk of the gravy can be made from chicken broth and saved juices from stews and pot roasts. This can be frozen and reconstituted on the stove or in the microwave. Add to this, at the end, the juice from the newly roasted turkey. That's all!

I know that gourmets, health-nuts and fuss-cooks will remonstrate that the dressing has no flavour unless passed through the bird, that it's safer to eat birds that were started from the thawed state rather than the frozen, and that the meat is less succulent when started from the latter state. I suggest the blindfold test on two dinners done by the two different methods.

It's a kind of freedom to graduate from the thawing, stuffing, trussing and gravy panicking that I went through when I was first married. And although I do not pride myself on being a great cook like my husband, I do get some compliments on my turkey dinners.

Frances Gammon
Fredericton

✉ In the grocery store, I always wasted too much time going up and down the bread aisle trying to choose the "right" bread. My mother learned to bake bread from our elderly next-door neighbour, and it was delicious! As a young bride, I decided that I would attempt the feat with only the help of a recipe book, and with no instruction from my mother. A whole day later, with only one small banana-bread-sized loaf to show for my hours of effort, I conceded that perhaps I *could* learn from my mother! She taught me well, and I make my own bread all the time, only buying the occasional loaf over the years. I have revised my mother's technique slightly in that I have learned that one can stretch out the process of baking bread over a whole day or one can fit it into a three-hour period. Bread baking does not have to be a painful task.

The following recipe is to make two loaves of bread.

184

1 teaspoon sugar
¼ cup lukewarm water
1 tablespoon dry yeast (or 1 package)
2 tablespoons white sugar
2 teaspoons salt
2 tablespoons shortening
1 cup milk (skim is fine)
1 cup warm water
6 to 8 cups all-purpose flour

In a small bowl, dissolve 1 teaspoon sugar in lukewarm water. Sprinkle yeast over and let stand 10 minutes.

Into a very large bowl, measure the sugar, salt and shortening. Scald the milk and add to sugar, stirring until shortening is melted. Add water, then add yeast mixture.

Begin adding flour ½ cup at a time until dough is stiff enough to knead. Knead for about 10 minutes, or until you have a smooth, satiny ball.

Place in an oiled bowl, cover with waxed paper and let rise until doubled, about 1 hour.

Punch dough down; shape into two loaves and place in oiled tins. Cover with waxed paper. Let rise till doubled, about 1 hour.

Bake at 350° for 30 to 35 minutes. Cool on wire racks.

Variations:
Cheese and Onion Bread – After first rising, roll dough out. Sprinkle ½ cup grated cheese and 1 tablespoon onion soup mix on dough, then roll to form a loaf.

Cinnamon Buns – Spread rolled-out dough with ⅓ cup softened butter; sprinkle with ½ cup brown sugar, 2 teaspoons cinnamon, ½ cup raisins and ¼ cup chopped walnuts or pecans.

Roll up as before. Cut cylinder into 1-inch pieces. Place in a buttered 8-by-8-inch pan, let rise for an hour, then bake at 350° for 15 to 20 minutes.

Madge Skinner
Sudbury, Ontario

✉ I make my own bread, and I cannot *imagine* how anyone could spread out the process for six hours, unless, of course, they were making a huge batch.

It takes me about three hours, made up as follows:

Proving yeast, assembling ingredients, mixing – 15 minutes
Kneading – 10 minutes
First rising – 45 minutes
Knocking down, kneading, shaping – 10 minutes
Second rising – 45 minutes
Cooking – 45 minutes
Total: 2 hours 50 minutes.

Furthermore, at the second rising I can pop it into the refrigerator, go away for as long as necessary (I have gone up to four hours), come back, heat the oven and pop in the loaf – no problem.

No need for added ingredients!

I am told it can be refrigerated all night and cooked in the morning, but have not tried this.

People seem to keep solving non-existent problems.

Eleanor Haydock
Vancouver

✉ I remember a poem from an old Women's Institute cookbook.

Ode to a Crust of Bread

I found a little crust of bread
That must not go to waste,
So, by a famous recipe
I seasoned it to taste;
I used six eggs, a pint of cream
Some citron and some spice,
Two lemons, dates and raisins
And a brimming cup of rice
It took a lot of things, I know.

(That's how the cookbook read)
And no one cared for it – but oh,
I saved that crust of bread!

Barbara Dalby
Lantzville, British Columbia

✉ Socrates Soup (also called Hobo Soup or Recession Barter and Trade)

Sauté some onions, minced celery, garlic
Season to taste
Chop potatoes, cabbage, carrots
Add a can of tomatoes and some spring water.
Bring to a boil. Simmer 45 minutes. Eat some, freeze the rest.
Add anything into this – parsley, leek, beans. Do not use tap water, though, as it has chlorine.

Katannya Kiernan
Vancouver

✉   *Bush vs. Broccoli*

George Bush was feeling fretful
He stamped his foot and fumed
"No broccoli, no broccoli
It will not be consumed!

"My mother made me eat it
And other veggies green
But now that I am President
No one can be that mean!

"So take the broccoli off my 'plane
Take it off my plate.
I'll never eat that stuff again
That veggie which I hate!

"Now I'm in the Oval Office
I can eat my favourite food
So remove old Ronnie's jelly beans
They don't improve my mood.

"As long as I am President
I'll indulge my every whim
Let's outlaw nasty broccoli
I'll go out on a limb

"And when I next address the Nation
I'll ban all broccoli
All transgressors stand accused
Of flagrant treachery.

"So anyone growing broccoli
(And, Babs dear, don't you dare)
Will be tried by jury and condemned
To death by electric chair!"

Patricia Black
London, Ontario

✉ *Broccoli*

Broccoli is green and bushy,
it looks good – it's fun to eat.
When Mom says I have to have some,
I don't tell – I think it's neat.
I like it raw
it looks like trees
I like it cooked
with lots of cheese
good in salads
good in dips
eat the stalks
then eat the tips

But Mom will never know I like it.
She won't even have a clue.
'Cause I'll just fork food 'round my plate
then put some in my mouth – and chew.

Diane E. Salmon
Sardis, British Columbia

✉ Re: Canada Needs Broccoli:

Broccoli – bleah!

Dave Pimm
Ottawa

WAR MEMOIRS, 1991

The first are mine, as you'll see. I started taking notes at home on the evening the war in the Persian Gulf broke out. I typed them out the next morning, in the midst of the flurry of activity at the *Morningside* office, and read them on the air.

Most of the producers had been on the phone most of that first night, and, by the time I arrived, about 4:00 A.M., they were in full flight. They stayed in that mode through the early days of the war, running on adrenaline, as we went live to all time zones, broadcasting for seven straight hours a day. But as the war wore on, and some of the frustration that shows through my own journals mounted–frustration at the need to rely on so much "official" coverage – we returned to our normal schedule, going live to the Atlantic provinces and cycling the tapes through the rest of the country, interrupting ourselves only when there were real developments to report.

So, too, do my notes–"the war memoirs of an arm-chair correspondent," as I dared to call them – slow down. When the war ended, I found I had nothing to say. My journals just stopped. My emotions were too mixed. Even now, months after the Allies have pulled out, with the Americans still celebrating the ferocious success of Desert Storm and Stormin' Norman Schwarzkopf videos on sale at my own local emporium, but with the tragedy of the Kurdish refugees fresh in our minds, the villainous Saddam Hussein still in power and Kuwait still a mockery of democracy, the judgement of history has yet to be rendered. But these journals – I have resisted the temptation to second guess myself – were my own notes on the run, during a time that shook us all.

And, again as you'll see, I was not the only distant observer keeping a diary – or writing letters about how I felt about the war.

Volume 1

January 16, 6:50 P.M.: I cannot believe that my own first act is to order in some food. But, just a few minutes after the boss has called me at home to put me on red alert (I am a notorious evening napper) and – along with King Hussein of Jordan, I am to learn later, and Dick Cheney, the American secretary of defence – I have settled down in front of CNN, I dial out for barbecued chicken wings, buffalo chips and coleslaw. A long evening lies ahead. I am disturbed, worried, more than a little fearful. In honesty, I never did believe they'd do it. When the bulletin seeped into *As It Happens*, which had been playing softly as I dozed in the bedroom – saying the *Iraqis* appeared to have been firing – I *still* thought (all right, hoped) they were wrong. Even when Patsy called – she was at a friend's house. . . . But no, now it's clear. This is it. And I'm phoning out for chicken wings. Chris Waddell, who was in this morning for the business column, talked in the office about a family he knew who'd settled in Tuesday midnight, when the deadline expired, turning on their TV and waiting for the start of hostilities, like the Super Bowl. War at 12. We laughed. But now I'm doing the same.

7:10 P.M.: It doesn't seem to have sunk in yet. I have taken a quick trip downstairs to stock up on mineral water and cigarettes. When I say to a couple in the elevator, "Bad, eh?" they think I'm talking about the weather. But in the lobby, the concierge beckons me over. He sits all day looking at his own bank of television sets – the sauna, the back entrance, the parking garage, but no CNN. The look of anguish on his face tells me what he wants to know from me.

Across the street, I notice that the only other customer in the convenience store looks Semitic – as in Arab. I want to talk to him, ask him how his reaction might differ from mine. But I hurry back to the TV. Does war mean this as well? That we begin to look at strangers differently?

Back upstairs, there is a message on the phone from my son the apprentice newspaperman. He is running copy for one of the Toronto dailies – probably, in this electronic age, the last genera-tion to have to do this. He has called to confirm the news. He sounds grim, but full of energy. News people – even apprentices – have mixed emotion to bad news. It is bad, awful, but – let's face it – it's exhilarating, too. Two hours later, still at home. Gill has come back from Winnipeg. She is slumped in despair. On the plane, she says, she and her companions had been laughing at the pilot's voice – like Woger Wabbit's, she says. But then, just over the Lakehead, he broke the news of war over the PA. In her own words, she teared up. On the way downtown, her cab had to avoid University Avenue, clogged by demonstrators. "I don't even know what side they were on," she says.

She joins me at the television. As if explaining the characters in a favourite series, I catch her up on the extraordinary reports from the Al Rasheed hotel, by CNN's trio of Peter Arnett, John Holliman and Bernard – or Bernie, as we have learned to call him – Shaw. At the moment, they are taking turns hiding under a bed, in case the Iraqis – who, one assumes, are also listening to their reports – sweep the room, and one will be left to carry on. At 9:22, Arnett tells us – still well before dawn in Baghdad – a rooster crows, presumably fooled by the lights of war.

These three, surely, are the first memorable correspondents to emerge in this televised war–or, more frequently, televised at one remove; we have still not seen pictures of actual conflict. We have still seen no one die. And, along with many of their colleagues at safer vantage points–no anchor anywhere shows more poise than Peter Mansbridge–they are distinguishing themselves tonight. But, in a curious way, I still can't help longing for some of the old guys, whose voices I know from distant memory or archival radio tapes. Without benefit of pictures, they could simply *describe* better.

11:00 P.M.: The news flows on. The impressions begin to distill. It is still hard to believe that these first hours have been as triumphant for the good guys – the television still vacillates between U.S. and UN in describing them–as the spokespeople are saying.

Reluctantly, I leave for the bedroom. The radio is still playing. Just before eleven, when I will drift off to fitful sleep, I hear Michael Enright, talking to a bar in Esquimault, meet, by remarkable coincidence, Gordon, the sailor son of Dennis McIvor, the hockey scout and peace activist whom Michael has interviewed at the top of *As It Happens* just a couple of nights earlier.

Like everyone else, I hope this thing is over before Gordon has to go.

Volume 2

Thursday, January 17: As happens occasionally for different reasons, most of them involving insomnia or work I ought to have done the night before, I was up this morning even before the *Globe and Mail* arrived. The television was on when I heard the thump outside my apartment door and the retreating footsteps down the corridor. But as has *never* happened before, I didn't respond. I simply sat where I was, transfixed by the images on the screen, while the paper, with its now-stale headlines–Allies Bomb Baghdad, said the *Globe*, in interesting contrast to *USA Today*, which said *U.S. Bombs Baghdad* in the same size type – lay outside, unread.

I still can't get over how much this is a television war. Even here, at *Morningside*, we have wheeled a console into the middle of the office – its sound blares as I write these notes – and the producers' custom of briefing me for the day's interviews with thoughtful memos backed by files of clippings and print-outs from the wire services has given way, in many cases, to quick verbal summaries of what has just been on the ubiquitous CNN. Quickly, the correspondents and the anchors – the trench-coated Charles Jaco in Saudi Arabia, bearded Wolf Blitzer at the Pentagon, Linda Scherzer in Jerusalem, pearls on a black sweater while the war swirls around her – are emerging as new stars.

And yet, dammit, we are not *seeing* the war. We're seeing generals moving their pointers over maps, pilots with jaws like Dick Tracy's, missiles smoking their way into the skies, more maps, charts, peace demonstrators, empty streets, angry Arabs, endless images of a smiling Saddam Hussein (how many from the files, one wonders) and, to be fair, tension, anxiety and even fear on the faces of the people who are talking to us. But those missiles are *landing*; the bombs are crunching. People – the phrase "absolute minimum of casualties" is beginning to grate on my ears – are dying. And we are not seeing *that* on TV.

Later today – Wednesday afternoon – I actually hear someone use the word "euphoria" to describe reaction to the progress of the war.

7:24 P.M.: There will be no euphoria now. As word comes through that the missiles have hit Israel, we watch in dread as a bureau chief in Tel Aviv – CNN's again – gropes with his gas mask. From home base, an anchor wonders what we'd hear if the bureau chief – his name is Larry Register – opens the window.

But when Register, passing his ear-piece to a colleague while he slips the eerie mask over his face, talks about the window being taped shut, the anchor, realizing his error, tells him urgently to forget it.

At home, I find myself barking at the screen. "Tell him to get the hell out of there," I say.

9:23 P.M.: Is this becoming normal television fare? The war fades from the screen and, one after the other, I watch commercials for Freedent ("moistens your mouth"), for Extra-Strength Tylenol Gelcaps (would Larry Register like one now, I wonder), for cruises on a line that proudly calls its ships Love Boats and uses Gavin MacLeod to shill for them (television being used to sell television) and something called the Easy Glider, on which, before my eyes, in time-lapse photography, a man loses seventy-five pounds.

Now, back to Tel Aviv.

Day three. This morning, actually, as once again I await the *Globe and Mail*. On CBS – I am beginning to prefer its more reflective coverage to the fever of CNN, which now has little to add – the co-anchors, Susan Spencer and Charles Osgood, who stammer almost as much as I do, are chatting up a correspondent in London named Dan Raviv. Raviv, apparently, young and handsome, has written a couple of books about terrorists. Susan Spencer, asking a question, says, "Forgive my ignorance of the international terrorist community . . . but . . ."

Bemusement makes me miss Raviv's answer.

"The international terrorist *community*?"

Do they all live in the same neighbourhood? Do they hold conventions? Have a newsletter? Wink knowingly at each other as they pass at airports?

The word "community," I realize, is constantly being asked to carry more freight than it can bear these days. The black community, the arts community, the homosexual community. Maybe the whole *world* can be described by Joe Clark's now outdated "community of communities." But the international *terrorists*?

The first casualty of war is truth, people are reminding us. Maybe the second is language. As in "decimate," which in fact means to take a tithe or to kill one in every ten, or "euphoria" over the "absolute minimum of casualties," which to my mind, at least, would be zero.

Volume 3

Saturday, January 19, late at night: The numbers may be wrong here (I have not been taking notes), but this is how the joke goes: The Japanese have promised to pay $9 billion as their part of the cost of the war, but so far they've only sent in about $1.3 billion. Pause. President Bush has given them a deadline of February 1 to come up with the rest.

At home, we scarcely need the punch line explained to us. George Bush issuing a deadline now has a new and dreadful meaning.

Here's another: How many Iraqis does it take to change a light bulb? Answer: None–they're not turning the lights on any more.

This is Day Four of the war that became real on Wednesday evening, and I am watching *Saturday Night Live* on NBC. These are, to my knowledge, the first Gulf jokes on television. At least in the part of his monologue that I watched on Friday night, Johnny Carson, who is usually a good barometer of what Main Street America is willing to laugh at, assiduously avoided the war. Is this the limit, I wonder. Four days before you can make jokes?

Sunday morning: I am listening to Elizabeth Gray's documentary on Israel's countdown to war and remembering, as I do, Elizabeth's call to *Morningside* on Friday – evening in Jerusalem but still morning in the Canadian west, where we are going live. We were just past the preliminaries of our chat when an alarm went off behind her. "I have to go," she said, "they're knocking on the door." My heart beat faster. Elizabeth – Liz Binks, she was, when I first met her–and I have known each other for thirty-five years, and the fear in her voice brings the war home to me in a particularly chilling way. This war scares me. A few days ago, before the hostilities broke into the open, Bud Whiteye, a Vietnam veteran who worked at *Morningside* for a while – he is at CBC Windsor now–dropped in for a visit. We talked about fear among soldiers. "Maybe when you're waiting," Bud said. "When the fighting starts, you're too busy to be scared." Maybe it's the same even working on the radio. You can get so caught up in the transoceanic links and trying to sort out the details of strategy and technology – exactly what *kind* of chemicals are there in chemical warheads? – that you forget the underlying horror of what you are reporting.

In her documentary, Elizabeth goes to a disco in Jerusalem where, on the eve of war, they are holding an "end-of-the-world party." The humour in here – not mine, I assure you, since about the last place I'd like to spend my last night on earth is in a disco – is a long way from the jokes on *Saturday Night Live*: defiant, black, grim. The same streak, I suppose, that has given American culture so much of its best night-club and broadcasting comedy. But the jokes on SNL are a braggart's jokes. There may be an ironic tone to what the young comedians of that often outrageously cheeky show are saying, but it's lost on me. They're not turning the lights on in Iran any more, eh? No. Because we're bombing them. A story in the *Globe and Mail* on Monday morning from Baghdad describes "the burning wreckage of a civilian bus."

Gill visited her nephews on Sunday afternoon, aged four and seven. One of their uncles – a brother of their American mother – is leaving for the Gulf. The television was on. A Nike commercial. "Just go for it." "I don't want them to go for it," said Daniel, four. "I don't want Uncle Cy to get killed." She asked Daniel's older brother about the other pictures on the television, the war pictures. He seemed reluctant to talk about it, she reported later. But then he said, "My dad can get to the Master level."

The Master level is a term for Nintendo games.

The wall-to-wall television reportage is winding down – as, indeed, is our own open-ended coverage. There are, simply, not enough developments to justify the hours and hours of time. Sometimes, punching through the channels on television, I'm not sure whether I'm watching news or fiction – one street demonstration I pause to look at turns out to be part of a drama. It's all blending together. Many of what appear to be news clips are, in fact, replays of old stories. CNN now brings us a recap – the war in pictures – just footage of the eerily beautiful tracer paths over Baghdad, the roiling flame of an oil refinery, the incomprehensible video games of the war-plane's bomb-sights. America pauses for football, with stars and stripes in the stands and yellow bands on the players' arms. Should events in the Middle East warrant, we're told, the telecast will be interrupted. But both play-off games make it to the end, with war catch-ups at half-time. When the second game is over, and the players, some of whom have knelt in prayer to aid the flight of a last-minute field-goal attempt, have gone to their dressing rooms, we go back to Dan Rather at the news centre. "What a game," Dan says, before turning to news of the war.

Volume 4

Tuesday, January 22, afternoon: More years ago than I care to remember, I wrote about television for *Maclean's* magazine. For reasons unimportant here, I used a pseudonym, Strabo, the squinter, and one of the programs I squinted at was the then new American sitcom *Hogan's Heroes*. You probably remember this program: set in a German POW camp – the camp was German, not the POWs – with Werner Klemperer as a kind of comic-opera Nazi colonel, Klink; John Banner as the ineffectual and somehow lovable Sergeant Schultz; Bob Crane as Hogan; and a cast of prisoners of whom I can now remember only Richard Dawson, who went on to become the kissing host of *Family Feud*. As Strabo, I said I found the show appalling, and that it was in unforgivable bad taste to try to make comedy of a situation that, in real life, had been so horrible.

In the back of my mind as I wrote my scathing review were the experiences of an uncle of mine who had *been* a prisoner of war. My uncle – his name was Ernest Madden – was a terrific guy. He'd been a junior office worker at Imperial Oil before the war, had signed up with the artillery and had become a Forward Observation Officer – a FOO, as he delighted in remembering. One story he used to tell was about crouching in a trench, observing the impact of the Canadian shells flying over his head – that's what FOOs did – and of watching an armed German soldier, not aware of his presence, hunker down in the same trench, yards away. He could, of course, have shot him, but – this never surprised me about Ernest – chose not to. I don't know if this was when he was taken prisoner or not, but most of his other stories were about the camp. Some of them involved ingenuity – they used to make cooking utensils out of tin cans, he told us, and concoct a kind of porridge from the crumbs of soda crackers – and about the bonds among the prisoners, many of whom remained Ernest's friends until his death a couple of years ago. But far more involved dysentery – epidemic in the POW camps of World War Two – and hardship. He and his buddies were almost always sick, worn out, miserable. I did not recall him quoting any boffo lines from lovable sergeants, and I said so in *Maclean's*.

After the column was published, Ernest called me. "Gee," he said, "I kind of *like Hogan's Heroes*."

I am thinking about that now, Tuesday afternoon – that and several other old stories that have come to mind in the early days of the new war. I have just been talking with an old friend who now lives on Prince Edward Island. We were doing other business, but before he hung up he mentioned both the cold he had been hearing in my voice the last week or so – it's better now, I think – and the strain as I have talked about the war. "My son's the same," he said. "He wasn't in the last one, either." I remembered that he (the father) had been, and he said his own experience had been largely confined to England, where he had met his wife, but she, he said, had been raised in Manchester; her childhood neighbourhood had been bombed mercilessly, and her family had had to move on Christmas Eve to escape the bombs. "She used to wonder," my friend said, "what all the fuss was about." I think about Linda Epstein, too, the young woman from Halifax who now lives in Jerusalem and whom I've been talking to from time to time during the crisis. Today, I'm told, Tuesday (I should perhaps note that I wrote this passage before the missile hit Tel Aviv), Linda spent the morning having her legs waxed.

Or, to come much closer to home, my own daughter. She – her name is Alison – set off for Czechoslovakia last June, mostly to teach English. Since then, she has been talking to young Europeans who grew up Communist and now have to cope with the new world. She has been recording their conversations and transcribing them. It's fascinating stuff, and Alison is making a book out of it, travelling all over the formerly Communist world. Early this month she took off for, of all places, Riga, in Latvia, and – this may be another reason there has been strain in my voice – I have been worried sick by the news from there. Then, this morning, when I came to work, there was a fax from her, which said, cheerily (and among other things), "I'm alive and well despite the unstable situation," and went on to complain, mildly, that the kids in Latvia are, in her words, "distressingly shy and unreliable about keeping dates."

The point of all this – I am learning some things in keeping these notes, even if no one else is – is that I am beginning to wonder if the people who are close to wars or even those who are actually in them don't have a different perspective from those of us lucky enough to miss them, who are left at home to wring our hands.

Don't get me wrong. I do not mean to suggest war is pleasant, or to send some hypocritical message to people whose loved ones' lives or freedoms are on the line. I learned only today that the pleasant commissionaire who helps to guard our front door against invaders, his chest bedecked with a veteran's honours, has a nephew flying combat missions in the Gulf, and I saw the concern on his face as he passed this information on to me, and, even as the war rages, I am reminded that many of the strongest warnings against it came from people – soldiers – who know what war is like. To suggest they like it, I think – though I'm sure there are exceptions – would be as foolish as to say the nurses and doctors in emergency wards like traffic accidents or appendicitis. But the people who are closer to things than I am seem to be better at accepting them and at getting on with their business. I wonder what they know that I do not.

Volume 5

Monday morning, January 28, day 13 of the war: Along with some 118 million Americans and who knows how many others around the globe, I spent more time yesterday than I ought to have watching Super Bowl XXV. (They're going to be sorry they started this Roman numeral thing when they get to, say, thirty-eight, aren't they?) All the way through it – and even taking into account Whitney Houston's stirring rendition of the national anthem, with the crowd roaring its support behind her, or the parade of soldiers' and sailors' children (not many of them black) who appeared at half-time . . . all of which, for even the most dispassionate observer, brought a lump to the throat – even taking all that into account, it was hard not to reflect on how flimsy are the analogies between sport and war of the late twentieth century. Some of the differences, of course, are obvious. People die in wars and get their wind knocked out in football games. Athletes – certainly professional athletes – do what they do for money and are quite capable, if the price is right, of changing sides between seasons. And so on.

But some of the other differences, I think, are growing clearer as the war in the Persian Gulf wears on, and it was hard not to think of them yesterday. For one thing, watching the Bills vs. the Giants, you could *see* everything that happened in great detail. The drama of the Giants' long, gallant march to a touchdown to close the second half, or the heartbreak of Buffalo's last-ditch field-goal attempt that was just a touch beyond their kicker's ability. In the war we're trying to find some patterns in, for all the hours it consumes on television and the time and space it occupies on radio and in the press, we are still getting second-hand accounts. We don't *know* what is happening. If this war were a football game, it would be being played somewhere over the hill, and every once in a while, the coaches of the side for which we were cheering would come back and say: we're winning; we *think* we're ahead by about two touchdowns, but we can't actually tell you the score yet; take our word for it. The other side, meantime, remaining tight-lipped, would not even admit to being behind and would claim, if not a touchdown, then a field goal or two of their own.

A far more significant difference is that football games are played within well-drawn limits, not only the lines at the edge of the field, but the carefully measured seconds on the clock. When the game began yesterday, each team had a clear objective. When the clock ran out, when that field-goal attempt went wide and short, we knew who had won. The Giants would get the rings and the big cheques. The Bills would go home again and start planning for another year.

In the Middle East, one wishes it were so simple. At the risk of seeming to miss the points made by so many experts – including some who have appeared on *Morningside* – I find myself now, thirteen days into this war, less certain about what will be defined as a victory for the coalition than I thought I was when it began. UN resolution 678, as I understand it – the premise for so much of what has happened since – both condemned Saddam Hussein's invasion of Kuwait and called for his withdrawal. Unless he complied, the rest of the world would move him out. But now – or so it seems – we are after much more than that. No one has spelled this out, as far as I know, but the feeling one gets is that that is now the objective: crush him. The more atrociously he behaves, of course – that's atrocious as in atrocities – the more just that objective becomes: A leader who hurls missiles at non-combatants, with no possible military advantage, who brutalizes his prisoners, who lets loose environmental horrors, must be more than pushed back, he must be destroyed. And yet, I can't help thinking, that was not the goal when the contest began. And after that has been accomplished, it seems increasingly clear, no one knows what will happen. Unlike an athletic contest, the war in the Gulf will *not* be over when it's over.

I wish my head were clearer about all this. I began setting down these notes on the morning after the war broke out, and this is only their fifth instalment. But it must be clear already how much my feelings and responses have vacillated. From the beginning, I've noted all my own reservations, my doubts, and it bothers me, as it must bother people whose similar reservations have led them to more all-out opposition than I can muster, that saying such things aloud is sometimes taken as lack of support for the men and women on our side. As may have been clear in my exchange with Peter Worthington last week, I am offended by this inference – by the suggestion that, whatever I feel about the pursuit of this war, I do not want the side we are on to win it. If it was a bad idea to start all this two weeks ago – and I am still not certain – then it has not become a good idea in retrospect. But however we got here, the battle has been joined. We must get on with it, with all our might – at least to the point where Hussein will admit he has lost and agree to some negotiated settlement. Like everyone else, I hope victory comes soon.

But that does not mean I am a fan of this war. I am a football fan. And that, as Super Bowl XXV reminded us, is a very different matter.

Volume 6

This is part six – or volume six, as I've been saying – of the little series of musings I've been calling "the war memoirs of an arm-chair correspondent," and though it follows the format of the first five pieces, in that it was sparked by something that took place yesterday, it's also a departure, in that it really *is* a memoir, about a time long past.

Where I was yesterday, day twenty of the Gulf War, was in what I still call Galt, where I spent my childhood, but which the rest of the world now calls Cambridge, Ontario, population about eighty thousand – four times and more what it was when I was a kid. Right away, when you drive off the 401 and head down what

I still want to call the Hespeler Road, you can see how much the town – maybe the country – has changed. Highway 24, as it is, is one long shopping mall, an apparently endless reach of fast-food outlets – there are forty-eight places to eat along that stretch, someone told me – Color Your Worlds, Pet-eramas, Midas Mufflers, Muffler Mans, Speedy Muffler Kings, that make it virtually indistinguishable from cities of the same size in Alberta or New Brunswick or, for that matter, Idaho. The only name that marked the city at all, it seemed to me, was Bennett Motors, out there amid the malls now; Cammie Bennett was in my class at Dickson School.

Dickson School, as it happens, is where I was headed. I went there from grade one to grade eight. For reading week, they'd asked me to come back. On the way to the school, over the bridge to Grand Avenue, up the hill at St. Andrew's, I reflected that this was, so far as I could remember, the first event in my life that took me back to a place where I had actually been fifty years ago, half a century.

Even when I was there, Dickson, which bears the name of one of Galt's Scots founders, was an old school: solid granite blocks, carved from the nearby quarries in the nineteenth century, two sedate stories overlooking a gravelled yard (two yards in my day, one for boys, one for girls) across the street from the cenotaph honouring the Galt dead of World War One; those from the second war were yet to be counted. Inside, I could not get over how little has been changed – except, of course, for the fact that the teachers were younger than I and had first names, and the rows of ink-welled desks had given way to open concepts and, where I think Miss Durward used to have her grade threes, there is now a French class – Dickson goes up to grade five only now – where le professeur was occupé. The rooms, which I had feared would look dark and Victorian, were instead bright and cheery, high-ceilinged, airy. They don't build schools like they used to, I thought, as I made my way past Pop Collins's picture – principal, 1931-1957 – and to the teachers' lounge upstairs.

On the wall were some old class photos. As would anyone else, I sought out mine and, to my amazement, was able to rhyme off without thinking the names of the boys in the row beside me: Donnie Engel, Louis Neibel, Bill Reid, Donny McIntosh, Dick Bradbeer, Geoff Johnstone and, sure enough, Cammie Bennett. I have lost touch with them all.

We were ten when that picture was taken. It was 1944. As I gazed at the row of friends and classmates, a thousand memories tumbled through my mind: games of scrub and British Bulldog in the gravelled schoolyard, marbles and soakers in the spring, Mr. McInnis saying he could stick-handle through our whole hockey team backwards and Billy Parkinson saying no, sir, you couldn't, you'd put yourself offside, Valentine notes to Georgina Scroggins, the smell of wet wool in the cloakrooms, cleaning the brushes on the fire escape, singing in the massed choirs on Victoria Day at Dickson Park, figuring out chess with Danny VanSickle – who plays bass with the Philadelphia Symphony, I think – Miss Zavitz's grade two, Christmas concerts, VE day when we wove crêpe paper through the spokes of our bike wheels – I in Dickson's blue and gold – and rode downtown and. . . .

Wait.

It had not occurred to me until that memory, although, of course, I knew it all along.

Canada had been at war all those years. From the time I started in grade one until just before I was getting ready to move on to high school, Galt was a wartime city. The war's presence was real, too. WRENS trained in Galt – women of the navy – and airmen from all over the Empire flew Harvard trainers over Dickson Park. Some of the fathers of the boys in that first row were overseas with the HLI – Galt's own Highland Light Infantry, the city's pride. There were war bonds (war savings certificates for kids), Victory gardens, rationing. We collected milkweed pods for the war effort – I am still not sure why – and the silver paper from our parents' cigarette packs. We learned to tell crooked-wing Stukas from Messerschmitts and Hurricanes from Spitfires and played games where the bad guys were dirty Japs or Nazis who said *Ach Himmel* and called their opponents *schweinhunds*. And, when the war was over, we decorated our bikes and rode down the hill to Queen's Park Crescent and cheered.

But the truth was, as the sequence of my memory showed, the war was just another part of our childhood, a fact of life. We could, really, not remember a time before it started. It wasn't awful, and it certainly wasn't good; it just *was*. We had no doubts who would win it and never for a moment considered that there might have been an alternative to our fathers' fighting it.

When I left the teachers' lounge, I went down to meet with some of the kids at Dickson now – among them, possibly, a grand-child or two of someone I'd played British Bulldog with so long ago. I read to them from Michael Kusugak's wonderful *Baseball Bats for Christmas*. They asked me some smart questions, none about war.

Later, driving back out past the fast-food restaurants, I thought about those kids, and about the pictures that are now on their television screens every night, and wondered whether for them, too, Canada at war might become just another fact of life.

–PG

✉ Tuesday, January 15, 1991

The countdown is on. The UN deadline is at midnight tonight. In one eleventh grade English class, we are playing "Poetry Pub-lisher": I have distributed three short poems with the poets' names removed and instructed the students to reach a group consensus about which poem would be most worth publishing. As in most of my poetry lessons, I try to avoid anticipating what they will choose. My unstated objective is simply to get *them* to ask the same questions about style and form and purpose that literary critics have been asking since Aristotle. The discussion proceeds uneventfully for about ten minutes until someone makes the point that a poem that "meant" one thing to the poet when it was written may take on new meaning at different times and with different people. The reader-response-theorist voices in my head give a small cheer, and I ask Laura if she will read to the class the poem she had shown to me earlier in the day. She agrees, but before she can begin, Melanie, who is usually quiet and polite, blurts out, "It's not about the war, is it? I really can't take any more of that."

Laura's poem is, in fact, "about the war." That is, while it was written many years ago, Laura has told me that for her it speaks in a very direct way to the thoughts and feelings aroused by the growing tension in the Persian Gulf. Laura has been reluctant to read poems in class. Her private observations about this poem and the turn of the immediate discussion are a serendipity I cannot resist; I am excited by the potential of this "teachable moment."

But Melanie is not just being rude. As Laura reads, I watch Melanie's face and the other sixteen-year-old faces before me. What I see is fear. Confusion. Pain. Laura finishes reading. There is a momentary pause. And then my teachable moment changes shape. With an energy they usually save for planning the weekend, my students hurl questions at me: What does it mean if Canada goes to war? Why are we going along with the Americans? How does the UN operate? What if nuclear weapons are employed? And the big question: Can we be drafted in Canada? The poetry lesson is abandoned.

I'm not so old myself. I share with my students the fact that in my lifetime my country has never gone to war. I struggle to remember details from long-forgotten classes in Canadian history and political science. I have no answers for these new questions. This is not like poetry; I cannot turn the questions back to my students. I can only validate their fear and try to share what hope I do have.

Melanie says, "At least now Remembrance Day will mean something."

Wednesday, January 16

6:05 P.M., Central Standard Time. James works Wednesday nights, so I've just finished my solitary feast of left-overs. I am

207

brushing my teeth when the radio announcer interrupts with the formal announcement: "The liberation of Kuwait has begun." I am appalled by the rhetoric of this statement. The fact that I am brushing my teeth at this precise moment makes me think of a poem by T.S. Eliot. For the rest of the evening, I divide my attention between the uncharacteristically frantic voices on CBC radio and the poetry of Eliot, Auden, Yeats. . . . I find myself understanding things in these poems that I had not previously. I come across an old favourite, written on the eve of another war – Yeats's "Lapis Lazuli," written in 1939.

Thursday, January 17
I have decided to present a formal lesson on "Lapis Lazuli" to all three grade eleven English classes. I need to do this because of what this poem says to me about history, perspective and hope. I need to do this for me, and for Melanie. In the first class, I fight back tears as I talk. As the day progresses, I grow steadier and more sure of what I want to say. We don't discuss the poem. I talk, and then I ask for a silent, written response. Some of my students thank me, but to others this is just a boring lecture about a poem that doesn't really appeal to them. I value their honesty. I didn't like this poem the first time I read it, either. Melanie's class is the last one of the day. When I finish speaking, a tall, athletic young man at the back of the room is weeping. Melanie writes:

No Title Deserved

There's a sickness
It's in my heart
It sits in my stomach
It churns my emotions

There's a sickness
It makes you feel helpless
It weakens your strength
It cuts off your power

Why so alone, do I feel?
I'm not the only one with it.
There's no explanation
But only the fear

There's a sickness
It turns your day into night
It swallows your pride
It intrudes in your future

This sickness, it lives
It's forced by the power of greed
And the power of illusion
The illusion of one mind
Who can change our lives forever.

At a suppertime meeting of the Humanities Committee we are arguing about marking spelling and grammar in student essays. Someone interrupts with news: Iraq has bombed Israel. Like my poetry lesson, the meeting dissolves. Later in the evening I am at home, watching the late news. On the screen flashes the image of a family waiting in their gas masks, in their sealed room. The father, I presume, is holding the video camera. The mother is adjusting her child's gas mask. On the right-hand side of the screen is what looks like a cross between a playpen and an oxygen tent. It looks, actually, the way the portable crib that my friend assembled in my spare room when I looked after her daughter would look if you wrapped it in Saran Wrap. Inside is a small baby, curled up in sleep, dressed in fuzzy pink sleepers. I have to leave the room, because this image distresses me so intensely that I do not want to look at it. But I have seen it, and I continue to see it.

Friday, January 18
In Melanie's English class we have a relaxed, informal hour of perusing poetry books in search of poems for the anthologies they are working on. One of these students is Israeli; his parents live in Jerusalem. I tell him I was thinking about him last night. I want to say other things, but I don't know what.

Saturday, January 19

On the radio CBC journalists are talking to "experts" about the psychological effects of the media's treatment of this war. Ask Melanie, I think wearily. Ask me. As the radio drones on, analysing the analysis of the war, I am flipping through a journal in search of fuel for our interrupted argument on marking essays.

The journal contains impassioned letters about why writing teachers should or should not write. As I skim these, I think about becoming aware. I think about my collection of notebooks containing bits of things that I meant to write but lost the energy and inspiration to continue. I think of Yeats, near the end of his own life, on the eve of another war, reflecting on his delicate carving, and penning a perspective on tragedy that would offer hope to a young high school English teacher generations away. I think of Melanie. I think about the rhetoric of war, and of babies who are too small to wear gas masks. And I write.

I will give this story to Melanie.

Anna Beauchamp
Winnipeg

✉ Today is January 26, 1991, Saturday; it is the tenth day of the war. A week ago, I was at a retreat for women from church. Instead of meeting in a luxury hotel in the Black Forest, as we all had looked forward to, we met huddled in the staff room of the Canadian West End School. The juxtaposition of singing praises to Jesus with joy and being guarded by soldiers circling the school was a sombre reminder of spiritual and physical battles. It was the first time I had ever been to a church function with armed guards. It is said that Canadians are not accustomed to armed patrols, i.e., a police presence; well, it is a skin-pinch reality. I am used to the green-clad, C-7 rifle-carrying, youngish soldiers now, since this has been the scene since Monday, January 14, when we were put on a security exercise. On Thursday, the first day of the war with Iraq, the exercise was no longer; it had become the real thing. At present, I look over the past week and wonder at my reaction – I have gone from being consumed by the horrific happenings to being complacent and taking the security precautions in stride. At odd moments I pray, and I do mean pray, for peace and the safety of the Canadian community here in Lahr. Indeed, I live in interesting times.

On January 17, I was reading the eighteenth chapter of Luke, which relates Jesus telling His disciples that He will suffer. How fitting, how eerie. I talked with my neighbour about the outbreak of war, and for the rest of the morning I was a magnet to the radio. In the afternoon I had to go to the Kaserne. (The Canadians have two compounds in Lahr: the airfield, which contains the hospital and the airport, and the Kaserne, which has various office buildings, schools and the headquarters for Canadian Forces Europe.) Outside the gate to the Kaserne were German peaceniks, demonstrating by holding white sheets with the words: SAGT NEIN ZUM KRIEG – say no to war. Some were singing, sitting in a circle; some were being carried off by the German police. There were four paddy-green German Polizei vans. Inside the gate, I showed my identification and walked on, past two APC – Armoured Personnel Carriers – and three armed soldiers. For me their presence was both frightening and comforting; after all, they were only doing their job of protecting us. There were armed guards on the school buses and around the PMQ – Private Married Quarters, the apartments set aside for military members and their dependants. "Dependant" is the controversial term given for spouses and children of the military personnel. After my commitment on the Kaserne, I walked home, passing another school, Gutenberg, again with C-7 rifle-, backpack-, radio-carrying, youngish soldiers. I said hello and pondered what a lonely, boring job that is. I became more aware of my observation skills.

On January 20, 1991, Sunday, I attended the Stiftskirche, a pre-Reformation sandstone Gothic church that the Canadians share with the German Protestant community. The sentry detail was one man and one woman, unarmed. I smiled as I entered the vestibule, noting no visible rifles on the guards, but nonetheless some protection presence. Again such a juxtaposition of spiritual peace and physical battle.

During the week I have walked around Lahr, a town of approximately thirty-nine thousand plus the ten thousand Canadians stationed here. The market area, the Markstrasse, reveals no difference; business goes on . . . as usual. From the balconies hang anti-war slogans. The signs to Canadian schools, offices, post office and radio station are masked with camouflage tape. I have got accustomed to the guards passing by my PMQ on both sides of the street, each soldier with his rifle and radio. I say hello and continue on my way towards home, home sweet, peaceful home. As well, I have got used to the modified life-style. On CFN – Canadian Forces Network Radio–we are instructed to think *security*. Large gatherings of Canadians in public places are discouraged, and, therefore, events have been cancelled, re-scheduled or re-located. Travelling is restricted, so I have changed my list of exotic spots to visit. And yes, the radio news has become more important to me. Because I have no television, I have savoured the radio the years I have lived in Germany. I hover above the wireless with my cup of steamy tea, remembering scenes of World War Two families clustered, listening to the inspiring statements of Churchill. Now I understand.

On the news I heard of more Scud missiles hitting Israel, and the damage and loss of lives. I pray; I am amazed by the restraint of the Jewish nation. I pray for peace in Jerusalem, for their and for my strength amidst adversity. We have had three bomb scares on the Canadian compound. The last one was yesterday, Friday, January 25. It was a hoax, but still a very real possibility in this current war of being a target for terrorism. It is something I never dreamed of happening to me. It has. Indeed, it has.

Joan Bond
Lahr, Germany

212

✉ *The Front Page*

Usually I like to see
familiar names
in
print

though just now I'd rather
sit with Dusty in his garden
with his wife and kids, have
a party, nibble on vegetable sticks
drink wine and eat quiche

or play cards Tuesday night with
Roger and Laura
try to guess who will win
the most
pennies

go to the pub with David
razz him about being a zoomie, playing
golf all day at work

only Dusty's name is now news
commander of the ships in the Gulf
floating

and David in his jet, a fighter
holds a sign "Hi, Mom"
full page colour from Qatar

in the rain I lift my umbrella
see Roger in uniform holding his baby
front page

I want them to stop jumping out at me
it was better when they were anonymous

in war time
it is dangerous to have your face
portrayed by newsprint dots
since what if
ink on paper ends out being
the last
trace

Eleanore Schönmaier
Ketch Harbour, Nova Scotia

✉ My husband's mother, Madelyn Fibronia Cutsey, was born in Mosul, Iraq, in 1901. Iraq was still called Mesopotamia at that time. Mosul, also called Al Mawsil, is on the banks of the Tigris River and across the river from the ruins of the ancient city of Nineveh. Madelyn was of Kurdish stock; her grandparents were born in Turkey and Mesopotamia. Her family were Catholics, members of an ancient Christian church dating from the early centuries A.D. The family name in Arabic translates to mean "one who has made a pilgrimage to the Holy Land." Madelyn's father, Yousif, was the major-domo of the bishop's palace in Mosul and was a master pastry chef. Her mother, Aziza, was the second wife to widowed Yousif, age thirty-two, who had two sons. This was an arranged marriage, and Aziza was only sixteen in 1901 when Madelyn, her eldest child, was born.

Yousif and Aziza must have seen trouble ahead for Kurdish Catholics in Mesopotamia. Perhaps they also felt the early rumblings of war over Turkey. The couple planned a new life in Canada. Yousif (changed to Joseph) went on ahead of his wife and daughter and two sons to Fort William, Ontario, to work for the CPR. His family name was altered to the Roman alphabet to be roughly phonetically equivalent to the Arabic. In 1905 (or 1906) Aziza (changed to Anne) and Madelyn, aged four or five, followed. Madelyn recalled the arduous trip with her mother and other women and children by stage-coach through the Middle

East and Europe to Marseilles. The family had converted its modest belongings to gold and jewels for the voyage. The stage-coach was robbed by highwaymen who took the gold and jewellery. They were, however, uninjured and still able to board ship in Marseilles, sail to Canada and then proceed by train to the Lakehead.

Four more children, three sons and a daughter, were born to Joseph and Anne in Fort William. The family became very Canadian, setting aside their Arabic language and customs. The Mesopotamian and Turkish heritage was remembered mainly in a few special recipes. Anne ran a neighbourhood grocery and confectionery.

Madelyn, whose middle name was Fibronia, was known as Fib to her family and friends. Fib attended normal school and became an elementary school teacher. She taught in Saskatchewan in the 1920s and early 1930s. She often told us of going off to school on horseback. She loved to dance and considered herself a "flapper." In the early 1930s, Fib's father was an unfortunate bystander in a labour scuffle and was struck over the head with a stick. He died of his injuries. Fib was called back to the Lakehead to help her family cope. She taught for the Fort William Separate School Board. Fib married Douglas in 1937 and her only child, Robert, was born in 1940.

The Iraqi/Turkish genetic heritage is quite evident in Robert and his four children (now aged nineteen to twenty-six, two sons and two daughters). With their dark wavy hair and dark eyes, they look strikingly like the young people of the Middle East we are seeing more and more on our televisions.

Until August of 1990, the distant Iraqi connection was considered an exotic gloss on an otherwise stolid English, Irish and Scottish background. Our family still has many cousins in Iraq and the Middle East. They are of the professional class, mainly engineers and academics. Their sons are probably in Iraq's armed forces; they are all in a war zone under great danger. We have lost contact long ago with the Iraqis but exchange Christmas cards with a cousin in the United Arab Emirates. He had tracked us down several years ago when trying to emigrate to Canada. One of the Ontario cousins visited Baghdad in 1989 and was grandly entertained by the Iraqi cousins.

In early August 1990, when Iraq overran Kuwait, the Iraqi connection took on a different and darker meaning for us. We half-kidded my mother-in-law that it was a good thing she got out of Iraq when she did. She seemed quite distressed by it all. Later in August, she suffered a major stroke and died five weeks later, three months short of her eighty-ninth birthday. We are grateful she isn't around to see the terrible war raging over the land of her birth. Perhaps she has made another timely escape.

Anne Adams
Vancouver

✉ I had gone to prayer meeting at our church where I am the pianist for the service. I had played a prelude and our pastor stood up and told us that he had just heard that we had launched missiles at Baghdad. I guess I can't tell you after all how I felt, not really. But I just put my head in my hands and started to sob. I think I admire people who can control their emotions. I know that every-body there felt awful but I was the only one to burst into loud, gasping sobs. Of course, I was the only one there who had a son in a bomber crew.

My first thought was that there is now no hope for peace. I felt such anguish for the loss of life that I knew would be the next news. Then I thought of Marlin. Missiles aren't bombs, I kept thinking. But I knew that bombs would be close behind them. I knew Marlin would be involved. We knew on the morning of the sixteenth that Marlin's crew had been relocated, possibly to Egypt, possibly to Turkey. We knew that the planes were moved into easier striking distance.

Throughout the service, I continued to struggle with my tears, mostly unsuccessfully. Finally we sang one last song before we went to prayer. I knew I had to go home but as the congregation gathered in small groups to pray, the great gulping sobs overwhelmed me again and I put my head down on the piano and cried my heart out. Arms tried to comfort me but I cried till I was calm again.

When I finally did get home, I cried still more. I cried till my head ached and my eyes were swollen. My husband called and said I would not be at work today. I teach first graders. I knew that the chance of getting through the day without dissolving into tears was very slim. Early this morning I went to the school and brought home some work that I could do to catch up at home. I've made myself do it but it has been very hard work because my thoughts are constantly with my son and every bit of news plays havoc in my heart. My life has become one constant prayer.

I still cry. My eyes hurt and still the tears come. I have a crying hangover, and still the tears flood. When it's time to write to Marlin today, what do I tell him? Does it matter if I write? Will they be getting mail now? What does he want to hear from me?

We have another son, Dan, who is also in the Air Force. A civil engineer, he is now stationed at Altus, Oklahoma. He called last night, his voice filled with dreadful awe. While he knows more about the military situation because he is in the Air Force, there are things he doesn't know. We all think of Marlin and feel better because we can talk to each other.

Talking to loved ones and friends is what helps me keep going. I know I have to go back to school tomorrow. I need to be around people. They may feel uncomfortable to see me cry but at a time like this, tears are necessary.

Another thing I want to do is cook. I am not eating much but I think about food a lot. Then it seems to stick in my throat. But I think about comfort foods and I ask myself, "Should I go ahead and make a batch of fudge? Will I really want to eat it?" I don't know.

So far I just do what I have to do, trying to keep my eyes on God and trust Him to be there for all of us in this terrible tragedy. I try not to give in to the black despair that crowds me. Today I fight the tears, but I know I'll cry again.

Nancy Klingensmith
Corry, Pennsylvania

✉ After hearing of the outbreak of war, I felt a sick, plummeting sensation in my stomach – as if I'd just said something hurtful and it was too late to take it back. My feelings were directed outward, towards the powerful and power-hungry men waging war "on my behalf" – those who were, and are, even as I write, putting at risk all that I believe in and everyone I care for.

Returning home late this evening, I descended into the cavernous Toronto subway. Buskers on the subway system here are so tightly controlled that they are almost non-existent. So, when I heard a clarinet echoing down the platform, I was especially curious. The clarinetist in question was obviously an unlicenced musical vigilante. He was dressed in an ankle-length denim coat, dark glasses and big winter boots, and I could almost imagine him furtively secreting his instrument away should a subway official chance to hear the unauthorized playing.

The tune was jazz, totally improvised – the floating, diving, spinning kind of music that makes me feel like I'm rounding the top of a Ferris wheel, over and over again. I stood on the platform nearby, transfixed, listening with my eyes closed. When I looked up again, there was another man standing a few feet from the clarinetist, swaying and jerking to the wind-like rise and fall of the music. Just the three of us stood there together, without speaking.

When the subway came, the dancing man left, and, at the next train, I regretfully did the same. Over the silent rumble of the moving car, I realized that that musical interlude had been the first time since the beginning of the war that horror and brutality hadn't been smouldering underneath all my thoughts. I will probably never see the two men again. But I thank them both, for reminding me what peace really means, and why I must continue to work towards that goal. May it be soon.

Erica Martin
Toronto

✉ *Post Christmas Sales – Edmonton, January 14, 1991*

There are,
so we are bluntly told,
in words
now bellicose and bold,
but two
remaining days to shop
before
the time civilities all stop
and war
consumes the Gulf.

The signs
in every shop and store
speak words
of commerce, not of war,
announcing
EVERYTHING MUST GO!
OUR PRICES/SLASHED!
though shoppers seem to know
a January sale
engulfs consumers

every year
when trade in goods is slow,
and slush
on city streets replaces snow.
The crowds move,
heads bent, quickly by
in sunshine,
heedless of the headlined cry
from coinboxed
papers that are scarcely read

announcing,
when the deadline passes
talks will cease

replaced by sound of guns and noiseless poisoned gases.
Missiles, tanks
will in Wagnerian cannonade
begin the overture
to what may be the last Crusade.
The Holy Land? Ha!
The name's ironic or mistaken.

An arm'ed camp
now God and sanity forsaken
prepares in haste
and hate for death and conflagration.
Thoughtless
of the day after tomorrow,
a handsome boy
consumed by joy, untouched by hate or sorrow
deserts
his post and leaves the shop

embracing
as he does, a slender girl,
he lifts her
with a kiss and half a twirl.
His lips
brush her soft hair, and in her ear
he whispers
news I cannot help but hear.
Oh, how I wish
that I had missed it

but it seems
this boy, not yet a man's enlisted,
signed up,
determined, and intent to leave this world,
a promising career,
his caring pretty girl,

to take up arms
against an enemy he doesn't know,
and leave
a clearance sale where EVERYTHING MUST GO!

John Bayly
Yellowknife

✉ Last Wednesday, after one or two morbidly fascinating days in front of the TV, I went from room to room, turning off all the radios, getting rid of newspapers and finally shutting off the TV. Dishes and laundry were piled up everywhere because I couldn't settle down to doing anything. I got out an old accordion I bought at a garage sale last summer and played the thing all morning. Inept as I am with this instrument, I made myself sit and play it, made myself learn a song. I had to focus to do it and it felt great.

I am two months away from turning forty. All my life practically, I've lived in the shadow of nuclear war. I remember as a child, going to bed the night of the Cuban missile crisis, hearing Norman DePoe on the CBC news, thinking the world was going to blow up and I'd be dead in the morning. This isn't a nuclear conflagration by any means, but why do I have all the same feelings now as I did when I was a kid?

I don't want to get into any discussions about what should or shouldn't be done, who's the bad guy, none of it. How did we fall into this so quickly? would be the better question.

So tomorrow, I'll dig out my seed catalogues and start planning my garden layout for spring, and I'll try hard to ignore this heavy feeling in my chest. Then I think I'll take the dog and the kids out on a walk, just look at the sky and the mountains and try to forget about what's going on across the world. I just don't know what else to do.

Jean Mathes
Revelstoke, British Columbia

✉ I was a post-war baby but my older brother was born in 1938. I remember my mother telling me that he always insisted on his sandwich being cut so that there would be a rounded end and a square end (in other words, not diagonally). He would pretend that one half was Britain and the other half was Germany (I don't know which was which). The eating of the sandwich was taken very seriously, being sure that Germany was finished off before Britain.

My brother is now the rear-admiral of the Canadian Navy on the Pacific Coast. I can't begin to imagine the pressures and responsibilities that he will be facing in the months to come. Oh for a simpler time – when the inevitable triumph of good over evil was secured by the last bite of a sandwich.

Carol Aubé
Barrie, Ontario

✉ In the summer of 1939, people with vans full of small, squarish cardboard boxes and bits of string interrupted our sunny day at a village school in the north of England. Harried teachers, parents and Ministry of Defence officials fitted us with L, M and S gas masks – mostly S.

Suddenly released from boring geography – much of which, we were too young to realize, was about to become obsolete – my class gloried in an extra recess.

Then came our turn: "Hold the straps with your thumbs, children, hook your chin into the bottom part, and then pull the straps over your head. When you take it off, you *must* pull the straps forward over your head. Never get hold of the cylinder – that's right, the tin bit – and pull the mask upwards off your face. Why not? Because you mustn't, that's why not." (I suspect it would have stretched the rubber and spoiled the fit.)

So you put the mask on at real recess, against all admonitions that it was not a toy, and shouted soundlessly at your friends, and ran round and round with outstretched arms, blowing hard to see who could make the rudest sound as the air forced out past your cheeks. And you crashed into each other, because the day was hot and the celluloid eyepiece steamed up in no time.

You took the mask proudly home and, with the importance of a nine-year-old, remembered to take it, together with the banana sandwich and Oxo cube, when setting off for school the next morning.

But it soon became a bore. Teachers kept telling you not to kick it, not to put frogs and stuff in the box with it, not to sit on it or remove its thick rubber band in attempts to discover what was in the tin part. Wearing it in the smoke of a garden rubbish fire "just to test it" also turned out to be taboo.

In an act of outstanding courage, a "big boy" gathered an audience in the boys' toilets and actually opened his mask's cylinder with pliers and a can opener. The result was disappointing. He found only a jumbled mess of felt pads and wire mesh and a shower of black granules; none of it of any apparent value. Nor, any longer, was the gask mask, but the hero didn't care.

Soon, the cardboard boxes wore out, and we were given cylindrical metal cans and new pieces of string. They had a cloth lining to protect the masks, and heaven knows these needed protection. My own survived a fall from a bus window at forty miles an hour. My name was scratched in the pale yellow paint of the kit, and some kind person found the scattered apparatus and returned it, to the relief of distraught parents who were, by now, reduced to the "you'd just better hope Hitler doesn't launch a gas attack today" stage.

My last clear memory of gas masks falls in the early forties, when a crew of Air Raid Precautions people showed up at my grammar school and let off real tear gas bombs in the school yard. We joyfully ran around in our masks, ignoring burning necks where the skin was exposed, trapping in our canisters as much as we could of the tear gas to take home for Mom to smell.

Mom didn't particularly enjoy it and, as time went on, we got somewhat sick of it ourselves. Despite tearing out and throwing away the cloth linings, our cans and masks reeked forever after of the sickly-sweet gas.

Forever after? For as long as we carried them. There is no

memory of the time we gave up on them, but certainly by 1943 I no longer had mine.

A mental picture of those times returned to me a dozen years ago on the island of Guernsey when, exploring a deserted eighteenth-century cottage, I came across the empty cardboard box of a long-lost rubber gas mask. Inside the lid were the printed instructions under the heading "Ministry of (gnawed hole)." Mice had made a home of one of silly man's best laid plans.

Michael Burn
Calgary

✉ In the day I have a good time, because we have no school. But at night! I've already gotten so used to attacks, even though we've only had two conventional attacks and two false alarms. I have a regular program for every time.

The siren wakes us up, usually it's between 1:00 and 4:00 A.M. I get up, groan, say some bad words, put on my slippers, grab a book and a wet rag I have ready and leave the room. I close the door and under the door I put the wet rag so that if it's a chemical attack and gas comes into my room, it can't get to the rest of the house. We all go into my parents' room, which we've sealed, and close the door. I put on my gas mask and a jacket, socks, shoes and plastic gloves and if I'm ready first I seal the door with tape and put a wet rag underneath. Then we all listen to the radio.

The first time, on Thursday night, or Friday morning if you like, at 2:00, my mother woke up from the siren and came to wake me up, because I didn't have it programmed into my head yet to wake up when the siren went. We all went into the room. I was shaking, I thought the end of the world had come. I could hardly put on my gas mask! The whole time we sat waiting for the radio to say we could leave, I was thinking about all of you and thinking about writing to you. If I'd written you right after that attack you would have thought that we were probably dead by now, because I was so scared!

224

Seven people were hurt lightly in that attack, and five old people died. One from a heart attack, and the rest from suffocating because they forgot to take the cover off the filter of their gas masks and were living alone so no one could tell them. The whole of Friday I couldn't stop thinking about it. Also, two Arab parents killed their little girl because they were shaking her so much to force her to get her gas mask on. I'm also trying to stop thinking about that.

The whole of Shabbat we left the radio on. On Friday night there was a siren at about 9:00 P.M., and we stayed in the closed room for about half an hour, and then they said on the radio it had been a false alarm. On Thursday we had been in the room for three hours! Then again on Friday night after we finally got to sleep, at 4:00 A.M., there was another alarm and again we had to go into the sealed room and put on our gas masks, and after forty minutes they said that again it was a false alarm. By then we were exhausted and went straight to sleep again. At 7:00 A.M. again we heard the siren, and again we dashed into the room, put on the gas masks and listened to the radio. This time it was real. When they found out it was a conventional attack and not a gas attack, they told us to stay in the sealed room but we could take off the gas masks, because a sealed room also helps in a conventional attack. At last at eight something, we could leave the room and we went back to bed, but I couldn't fall asleep.

So now it's Saturday evening, and I'm exhausted, and I'll bet we'll have another interesting night tonight! On the radio they said that ten more people had been hurt very lightly last night, only a scratch or something, and they're all out of hospital except one. Another old man had a heart attack and died. So many people died, and it wasn't directly because of the bombs! Also, I forgot to write that some more people are in hospital because on the first night, Thursday, the radio hadn't known that it was conventional and not gas, and the people were so scared that they got the symptoms of someone who had been hurt by nerve gas, their eyes were watering and they were throwing up, so they injected themselves with the atrophin injection, and since they hadn't been hurt by gas, the atrophin had a very bad effect on them. This concludes all the people that were hurt, and I hope there won't be any more tonight.

It's so weird, I never think that it's possible that I could be hurt. It just can't happen! In all the books we had read before the first attack, it said that people get very nervous and panic and I couldn't understand how people can lose control like that. Now I understand. I have never been so scared in my whole life like I was on Thursday night. Now I can already laugh. I only mind the attacks because they're nuisances and I'm tired. But then it was horrible, my eyes were watering and I thought maybe I should inject myself with the atrophin, but my mother said not to. Lucky for me, I didn't!

My mother was great throughout both nights, if she was panicky she didn't show it. My father is away at the army, right where the bombs were thrown, but he phoned us and he's all right.

I'm sorry I've written so depressingly, because actually I'm not at all depressed, and though I haven't been out all Thursday and Friday because the radio said not to, today me and the boys played on the porch for an hour and a half the game David and Daniel played with them and the ball. Another thing I've been doing these past few prison days is trying, I repeat, trying, to crochet a *kipah*. I would have saved it for Rafi but I think it's a bit too creative for his (or anybody's) taste. It's full of holes because I do it while watching TV so every time an exciting part comes on TV I forget about the *kipah* and let a stitch get lost. It's shaped like a skirt. Maybe I'll give it to my neighbours who have a little girl. Maybe she can use it as a skirt for her Barbie dolls.

I finished *Gone with the Wind*, and the book the Cashmans gave me a long time ago. On Thursday I went, at the risk of my life, to my friend's house to borrow some books. I was so bored! Now I have five books, I've already read two and a half. I hope we're allowed out again soon because when I finish the rest of the books I'm going to be desperate! I dreamt last night of shapes falling down on me, and even though I had my gas mask on, it couldn't protect me from them. It was scary.

By the way, I just heard on the radio that the person that hadn't been let out of the hospital yet is out. Isn't that great?

The only good thing about this war, except of course missing school, is the way Israel is uniting. My mother told me that every war this happens and afterward everyone becomes their old sour selves. But I won't believe that. There is such a feeling of everyone being brothers and sisters. Everyone cares about everyone else. And if someone dies there is a feeling of loss. On the nights of the attacks, there was this guy who was talking on the radio, trying to calm people down, there are special phone numbers for people who have questions, or for old people living by themselves who just want to talk to someone. On TV at the time of the attack they show old and new hits, and the music is very relaxing. Also, it's a good feeling to know that for once, other countries are backing us up.

Bracha Zornberg
Jerusalem

✉ I am an elementary school bus driver and a university student. As I expected, the children were excited this morning. I've discovered that many of the older boys (on my bus that's ages ten to thirteen) who normally sit at the back of the bus sit in the front whenever anything important happens. Important at this age can be the Al Iafrate trade or the outbreak of war in the Persian Gulf. The pattern continues with them talking about the event much louder than they would normally discuss anything. I've learned that this is my signal to enter the conversation.

Today the boys were giddy with excitement. I understand how they felt; several times last night as I watched the CNN reporters in Baghdad, who were unquestionably heady with the events they watched out their hotel windows, I too caught myself overwhelmed with the alleged success of the program of strategic bombing. I let the boys go on a little longer than I normally do. It was when they started imitating the sounds of video games and suggesting that none of the allies were or would be killed that I interjected.

At this point I trudged out that old truism – that the first casualty of war is the truth. I then pointed out that, in war, people on *both* sides *always* get killed. I predicted that on the news they would undoubtedly hear of fatalities on both sides and that they would probably see the bodies of dead children in Iraq. Maybe I crossed the Rubicon of what is appropriate. Nevertheless, they were quiet, and not just at the front of the bus – they were all quiet.

A number of the younger ones asked me if their parents and they themselves would get bombs dropped on them. I wanted to be Santa Claus and promise them that wouldn't happen. Instead, I told them that I was sure, as I am, that that would not happen and that Iraq was far, far away. Of course, some of these children have visited family in Europe, while others come from Hong Kong and even South America. They know that nothing is far, far away.

I have two runs every morning and the second was a photocopy of the first. On my way back to the storage yard I wondered if the truth wasn't just a little too tough. I rationalized that they were probably better off prepared. I still remember watching Walter Cronkite during the Vietnam war and how I used to look to Mother every time they showed something awful for the confirmation of its truth.

After I parked the bus, I walked down the aisle in my normal hunt for any forgotten mittens, lunches or – God forbid – sleeping children. I was shocked by what I saw on the windows. It's been damp lately in Southern Ontario and windows have been fogged up for days. Carved out of the fog on at least a dozen windows at the back of the bus were peace signs.

David Sandiford
Aurora, Ontario

The Fallen

Ironing Great-Aunt Nellie's pillowslips
I am caught between pleasure in using them
and doubt that I should.

I've only brought them out
after all this time.
If I wear them out,
no one will ever see
the great C in satin stitch
for her husband's family name,
and the scallops of crochetwork
ending in points
which it took me a while to see
formed hearts.

Grandma walked me over to Aunt Nellie's
a few times, when I was little.
She was a small woman, as Grandma was
and I became,
and seemed lost in the doorway of her big house.

At long last, Uncle Rob asked Grandma
to come and help him decide
about committing her.
She wouldn't leave the bathroom,
and she would eat only porridge.

It was then thirty-six years
since their only child
Robbie Cash, Dad's cousin,
had been killed in the Great War.
She had never gone out of the house again.

It was a war begun like this one:
meant to last "only a few weeks,"
or months, "at worst."

When Nellie's house was broken up,
among other things
I received an unused set of dishes –
my sister Bobbie some rolls of fine shirting
never made up.
One by one, I managed to break
every one of the dishes.
All but the celery dish.
I was a young mother,
nervous and rushing.

I hold the softened crocheted hearts
of Nellie's pillowslips;
I run my fingers along
the little oval parlour table.
I see her placing her fingers
on the edge of it
to hold on
to contain the new knowledge
that would not be contained
that blew heart and mind outwards
and left the small, aproned body
among the fallen.

Lorraine Fairley
Shelburne, Ontario

✉ I've been thinking a lot lately about how different the Gulf War must seem to me because I'm living in Northern Ireland. My memories of the war won't be the same as those of my friends and family at home.

I've heard people talk about how they will always remember where they were or what they were doing when certain things happened, like when John F. Kennedy was shot. I know that I was at a cottage on Georgian Bay, for instance, when the first men landed on the moon. My brother spent the better part of the day putting tin foil on the end of the aerial of our black and white TV in just the right way to improve the reception.

I was walking through the television department of an Eaton's store when the Challenger space shuttle blew up.

I imagine the Gulf War started much differently for me than it did for people in Canada. In one of those freak coincidences, the power went out on our street about an hour before the bombing of Iraq started. I was listening to Radio Canada International on a portable short-wave radio. *As It Happens* was the only thing that stayed on while we scrambled in the dark to find candles. The electricity board told us the problem couldn't be fixed until morning, so we took our candles and went to bed mumbling about how this would never happen in Canada.

So I didn't hear about the war at dinner time or on the evening news. When I heard about the bombing, it had been going on for hours. I was still half asleep in bed. The news of the fighting was made more dramatic by the fact that my husband and I listened to the reports by candle-light. We sat with the portable radio on the bed between us. We couldn't put the kettle on to make tea, and toast was out of the question, so we took our bowls of cereal to bed and ate our Weetabix with the covers pulled up around us. Without electricity we didn't have any heat, either.

As if that wasn't enough, later that morning a car went down the street with a man shouting in a strong Belfast accent over a loudspeaker. I had no idea what he was saying. The mystery was cleared up when I turned on the kitchen tap and got a terrible chugging sound. There was no water. I suppose they had to turn it off to dig up the power lines across the street.

There are also things about the war that apply specifically to Northern Ireland that I think I'll always remember. On the morning war broke out, I listened to an interview with Ian Paisley, the outspoken Protestant leader of the Democratic Unionist Party. He said he didn't know what to say to people who had relatives in the Gulf. It was the first time I've heard him at a loss for words.

Later, at Westminster, Mr. Paisley and another MP from Northern Ireland rose in the House to express their support for the Gulf

War. The Tory MP who spoke after them asked the prime minister to pledge that Britain would not stop fighting until Saddam Hussein left Northern Ireland. His slip of the tongue drew laughter and heckles.

Opinion on the war, like most things here, I suppose, is complicated by religion. The Pope after all has called for peace. But there's a new piece of graffiti on the Protestant Shankill Road. "Well done lads, operation Desert Storm," it says.

Living in Northern Ireland has also made me think about the amount of television coverage given to the Gulf War. When the fighting first broke out, the BBC and the independent network cancelled their regular programs and ran continuous Gulf news. But after a few days, people got tired of all the coverage. They complained to the networks in record numbers. Soon the Australian soap operas that are so popular here were back on the air twice a day.

There has been a lot of talk about how long support for the war will last. The public, some say, will get fed up if the war is too long. You only have to look to Northern Ireland to find out what happens when fighting drags on. The soldiers here aren't followed around by television crews with hook-ups and satellite telephones. There are no special hourly news updates on this fighting. It's old news. Only incidents such as the recent attack on the British Cabinet and the bombs in the train stations in London put the conflict back on the front pages of newspapers and remind the world that the problems here haven't gone away.

Lately I've been wondering how the British soldiers here feel with the conflict in the Gulf always on the news. Are they glad they're not in the desert? Or are they disappointed that they're over here while other soldiers are praised for their skill and bravery every night on TV?

I guess what I'll remember most about the start of the Gulf War is how I watched the world become engrossed in a new conflict while living amid an old conflict that the rest of the world is tired of.

Elizabeth Church
Belfast, Ireland

STRICTLY PERSONAL

Although such public events as the Montreal massacre and our coverage of them account for a large percentage of the hundred or so letters that come to *Morningside* every day (there's also a big batch we call "requests for information" - people who want to know what song that was we played in the second hour on Thursday, or what book it was whose title and author I mumbled on Friday), a lot, including some of the most memorable, come for no apparent reason at all.

Except, of course, that over the years the program has become a good place to tell your story.

Some of the contents of this chapter - certainly Vanessa Kramer's moving journal, which she sent us after we presented an hour on breast cancer - are in response to subjects we did on the radio. But most of them, I think, just arrived in the mail: people's lives, and what they wanted us to know about them.

✉ My husband likes to tease me about talking Italian in my sleep. When I doze off in front of the television some nights, he claims

I mumble away in Italian. One night, while he was watching *The National* (which doesn't air here in Yellowknife until 11:00 P.M.), he heard me say "*chiudi la luce*," which means "close the light" when translated literally into English. He doesn't understand Italian, but he noted the phrase and repeated it to me when I woke up. Was I surprised, since never before had he been able to offer anything as proof when I'd ask, "Okay, then, if I dream in Italian, what do I say?"

The only time I speak Italian these days is when I speak to my mother on the telephone, usually about once a week. I think Italian, like Spanish, is a faster languge than English, so I feel we really get our money's worth when we converse in Italian. And, of course, it's my mother's mother tongue; her English has come a long way, but she's more articulate in Italian – more precise.

It's nothing less than a phenomenon for someone like me to get caught dreaming in Italian. I was born in Canada, not far from a steel scrap-yard in downtown Hamilton, Ontario. My first words were in Italian, and I remember struggling to try to understand the kindergarten teacher when I was five years old. But since then, you could say I've been completely immersed in the English language – in high school, university, work and play. I even speak English to my father, who is from the old country! And over the years, especially since I moved north, I've distanced myself from the Italo-Canadian community. So why, then, do I continue to dream in Italian?

I can only conclude that I dream in Italian because I'm more expressive in Italian. My dreams are more colourful in Italian, more profound. And perhaps when I dream, I think of home. It's hard for me to think of southern Ontario without thinking of all the Italians who live there. Quite frankly, some of the things some of them are experiencing right now are fodder for the worst kinds of dreams – nightmares.

If I were to write about the Italian community in Canada from personal experience and observation, I think I would end up writing about power struggles, generation clashes, depression, separation, physical and mental abuse, rigidity and pretences. I want to write about these things one day, although I'm scared of opening wounds. The truth can be shocking.

I am thankful, however, that my mother taught me to speak and write Italian (not dialect, but proper Italian). And I find it interesting that, for whatever reason, when I'm alone with my thoughts my thoughts are in Italian.

Edi Casimirri
Yellowknife

✉ The young pilot I was promised to arrived in England on my nineteenth birthday, during the Battle of Britain. He came home again in 1942 to train fighter pilots in Canada, and we were married. Unfortunately my husband had a fatal heart attack when he was only forty-eight, so he will never grow old, like me.

In 1942 when I was a twenty-year-old bride, my new husband's first posting was to Dartmouth, Nova Scotia. He went ahead to find a place to live. I was to meet another Air Force wife in Toronto and we would travel down together.

We met at Union Station. She was one of the two most beautiful women I have ever seen, and in those days I wasn't bad looking either. We travelled to Montreal, then had to change trains for the trip down east. When we found our assigned coach and entered it, there was no one on board except a clutch of young new naval officers on their way to Halifax! They immediately went in to a huddle.

As soon as the train began to roll, one of them approached, greeted us and asked if we would like a drink. I had my mouth open to say, "No, thank you" (we hadn't been introduced) when my travelling companion said, "Yes, thank you – that would be very nice." Well, I bowed to her mature judgement, she being an older woman of twenty-four years.

The trip was most pleasant. We ate our meals together and had an enjoyable time. There were many toasts to "the bride of three weeks" (me).

We arrived in Halifax and said goodbye to these young men, then went and greeted our husbands.

We ran into some of this group one night at a supper dance, and that was the last we saw of them. I often wonder how many, if any, survived the war. I wish I had told them that I would always remember them fondly, because I shall.

Adeline Thompson
Mississauga, Ontario

✉ I'm trying to find a new rhythm to my life. This December I'll be forty-six, and in just eighteen years I'll be sixty-four, a number that holds some kind of magic for us old Beatles fans. I want a rhythm that allows me to enjoy what's left of my life. For instance, I just rediscovered my sense of smell this summer when we drove across Alberta and Saskatchewan, and now I want to get out and smell the world every day.

This year I'm teaching at a different elementary school. After nine years, I decided I wanted not only a change, but also less teaching time, so I went to half-time. I'm in the classroom for two and a half hours a day, but spend twice as much time planning, and several hours a week at meetings. This nets me about three hundred dollars a week. I plan to spend all the rest of my precious time doing the things I've put aside for the past nine years. This summer I bought a computer so that I could write every afternoon. So far, all I've written is letters. (This is one of them.) This afternoon when I came home, I weeded the front flower-beds and raked the lawn. It was a pleasure to be out there, working in the sunshine, smelling the earth. As I exchanged a few friendly words with the letter carrier who was speeding up our block, I felt we were fellow conspirators, both of us enjoying the kind of employ-ment that allows us to spend part of our lives outside in the sunshine.

Every day at four-thirty I pick my husband up from work and we go for a delicious hour's walk along the ocean. We congratulate ourselves for having decided to move to Victoria seventeen years ago. We had absolutely no idea what a lucky move it was. We usually use part of our alone time to talk over problems, like his possible career change, or our family concerns, like my healthy but aging mother and our two children, aged nineteen and fourteen. Our nineteen-year-old son is a major concern these days. He has a girl-friend and, against our explicit request to the contrary, has her stay overnight at times. Now, we're a little angry and quite confused about what to do. I was married at nineteen, divorced at twenty-two, had a couple of "meaningful relationships" in the late sixties. (I still exchange Christmas cards with one of these men. The other one joined the Hare Krishna movement.) I had my son and then married his father two years later, when I was really sure I wanted to be married again. So who am I to judge, right? Well, I'm the mother, that's who. And I want both my children to get the idea that casual sex isn't okay, especially in these days of AIDS. And I want my fourteen-year-old to have good role models. But our son's monogamous, isn't he? She's his only girl-friend for the past year. Yes, but his parents make the rules. He should move out if he can't follow the rules of the house, shouldn't he? But how can he move out? We want him to go to school, jobs are hard to find, and he just can't afford to leave. Around and around our conversations go, with no clear solutions.

And so I go on with my life, trying to find a comfortable rhythm, achieve some kind of peace and meet my obligations.

I can smell the earthy garden out there. Autumn calls to me through my open window. I still have to pick the tomatoes and scarlet runners, I tell myself, but I'd be happy just smelling the earth.

Amber Harvey
Victoria

✉ About three weeks ago I enjoyed a weekend away for the first time since I was married. I booked it alone, and I did not care if it rained or snowed. I just wanted to be alone, totally – no husband, no children, no friends, no anyone, for that matter, just alone! I've been craving this time away for years, and it was wonderful! The trouble is, it wasn't long enough, and I don't know when I will be able to do it again.

I was single for years and lived alone for most of that time. I enjoyed it but know what it is like to come home to an empty apartment and cook gourmet dinners for one. I, too, was governed by a biological clock that finally rang the alarm around age thirty. I married, not for romantic reasons, but for practical ones. We shared similar values, he seemed responsible, kind and interested in family life. I went from having so much time to myself that I didn't know what to do with it to so little I nearly went crazy. I went from total control over my life to a life that can be best described as totally out of control.

Am I happy? Well, maybe not blissfully, though I have my moments, but I think I'm doing okay. There are times when I can relate to the women who choose to be single mothers, and there are times when I'm glad to have a traditional marriage. There are times when I would love to be single again without children. However, I think I've learned something through all this: if we are to learn and grow within ourselves, we must learn to enjoy what we have when we have it. The phrase I heard the most when my children were very young was, "Enjoy them while they are young, soon they will be teenagers." And all too soon I will face the joy and pain of an empty nest. This is all part of the process of life. "A mirage is a beautiful thing but does not provide the real camel with the real water to cross the real desert."

Linda Smith
Delta, British Columbia

238

✉ In 1983, at age fifty-eight, after thirty-six years of marriage, I left my home and husband to find out who I was. For those thirty-six years, I was my husband's and five children's servant, mom, nurse, teacher, social worker, driver, cook, et cetera. I had no time for me. I often longed for one day all to myself. That never happened. And when the children left, my husband took over their space. I don't blame him. I also fell into the role. One day I said, Who am I? What do I want to do? Am I up to doing it myself? Well, old lady, if you are going to do it, it's now or never. If you don't make your move, then shut up. So I packed my bag and ran away from home. I did not discuss it with my husband. I phoned him from Vancouver to tell him that I had left for good. I was afraid if I told him face to face, he would talk me out of it.

I arrived in Toronto to live with my daughter. Lucky me to have a child who would support me. I got a job, and I've had a great time. I'm not sure as to who I am. It's nice to make my own decisions: to purchase my own car with my earnings; to get my own credit card; to quit my job and go to work for two years in Africa. Now I am retired and still having a ball.

When I was living with my daughter, she reversed our roles – she assumed the mom's role. On my job, I often worked late and came home about ten-thirty at night. One evening we decided to have a beer after work. I came home after eleven-thirty. My daughter was waiting up for me and very agitated. She said, "Where were you?" I said, "I went out for a beer." She said, "Well, you could have phoned." By this time we both saw the scene for what it was. We had a good laugh, and I got my independence.

Josie Hjorleifson
Duncan, British Columbia

239

✉ Thursday, March 29

I reach for the taps and turn them on. The water floods from the shower head in a steady stream into the bath-tub. I step in and begin to soap myself. I am thinking about the tasks I have to do that day. But there is something else. Something lurking in the back of my mind that perhaps I have forgotten to do. I stand for a while watching the steam disperse in the cold air outside among the branches of the white pine.

I dry myself on the towel. I can no longer see my reflection in the mirror, it is so thick with steam. As I pull on my dressing-gown, my mind retrieves the thing it could not remember in the shower.

I walk into the bedroom, into the soft light of the early-morning sun. I lie down on the bed and place my finger on the thing I was trying to recall. My fingertips seek it out immediately, a small tightly drawn-together lump of cells in my right breast just to one side of the nipple. I probe around it until the skin under which it is buried becomes sore to the touch. I look at the shadows of the pine boughs moving on the ceiling. And I know that I have dreamt doing this the night before.

I get up off the bed and walk into the living-room to the phone. There are three different shades of purple on the African violets on the shelf by the window. I study them closely while I wait for my doctor's office to answer. I notice how saturated with colour each petal is and how diffuse the green of the leaves is by comparison, embedded in the soft hairy surface. The secretary answers. I ask her what to do.

✉ Thursday, April 12

I am ushered into a large office, the windows of which overlook the city and the river and the distant hills dotted in isolation on the flat land. The surgeon gets up from his chair and crosses the room to greet me. We shake hands and I sit in one of the chairs grouped around a conference table.

I tell him I have been referred by my doctor because I have a lump in my breast. We embark on the usual questions about my family history of cancer. I invoke the memory of my maternal aunt who had breast cancer in her forties. Clearly this is deemed relevant information, and as he records it solemnly on my chart, I imagine my aunt to be present in the room, sitting in the empty chair beside me. She looks bemused and detached, making light of our guilt by association. Next, I mention my maternal grand-mother who died at the age of eighty of some kind of cancer I'm not sure about. The doctor smiles, asking me to repeat the age. My grandmother stands uncertainly at the door, but my aunt and I wave her away, confident that eighty is a respectable age to have cancer and that she will be spared from having to join the guilty circle.

"Well, let's have a look at it, shall we?" he says, leading the way to the examination room. My relatives drop quickly from my mind as I prepare to face what comes next. I enter the room with a growing sense of aloneness.

It is not hard for him to find the lump. "The first thing we can do is to aspirate it with a needle," he says, turning away from me to find one in the cabinet on the wall. The needle looks very thin and very long.

"This doesn't usually hurt and it only takes a few seconds," he says. "If the needle draws out fluid, we can all go home because it will mean it's a cyst and it'll disappear once it's drained." He seeks out the lump again, his fingers deftly measuring its position under the skin, then there is a reassuring pause of gathering concentration before the needle is plunged quickly and with no hesitation into the breast. It draws out nothing. There is only the slight breath of air from the syringe.

"Well, whatever it is, it will have to come out," he says philo-sophically. "We'll have to do a biopsy, to diagnose it correctly."

We discuss timetables, shapes of incisions, types of anaesthetic and procedures for out-patient admission to the hospital. I can tell he is taking note of the way I handle the situation, trying to judge how deep my surface calm may go and how to impart difficult information if it should become necessary. I judge he has a capacity to allow uncertainty to ebb and flow through the conversation, and I notice he shows a concern devoid of pity or moral judgement.

✉ Wednesday, April 18

I am lying on a narrow bed in a long, deserted hospital corridor. I have been here since 7:30 A.M. It is now mid-morning. The nurse in the out-patient admitting room said the orderly would come from surgery to get me once they were ready to do the biopsy. It is growing cold. The book I read with partial attention seems more and more irrelevant as the minutes drag by. Occasionally people pass by in the corridor.

A tall green-clad figure appears at the far end of the corridor from the elevators and begins to walk briskly towards me. A surgical mask is draped loosely around his neck. My surgeon has come to see if I am in the lineup. We chat briefly. He says I'm next. I assure him I'm ready.

The waiting begins to take its toll. Then an orderly hoves into view. The nurse hovers, pointing me out as the next to go. Solemnly, the orderly begins to push my bed towards the elevator. I feel very cold suddenly and try to rearrange the sheet to cover my arms and feet. We enter an elevator full of people in street clothes. I sharpen the wryness of my humour to ward off their stares. The doors open again and I am wheeled into the waiting area adjacent to the operating room. Around me I can hear the rustle of wrapped feet as people in green move about the corridors. Eventually they come out in twos and threes with clipboards. There is a flurry of activity and then I am left alone to wait again.

Above my head on the wall is a round convex mirror in which I can see myself reflected within the room and the corridors. I watch it in fascination as if I see myself in a crystal ball. As if what is happening is a dream. The bed moves suddenly and I enter a space full of bright light as if the ceiling were filled with a cluster of round mirrors, each brilliantly lit.

I am lifted onto the operating table. The anaesthetist takes my outstretched hand and begins to swab it with something cold. The veins, they say, are hard to find. I explain that it is because I got so cold in the corridor. They move to try the other hand while someone else places monitoring electrodes on my shoulders. Even before they put me out, I know I am losing my sense of time. I feel as if I am being trussed and placed in limbo. The anaesthetists have finally succeeded; I can feel the steady drip of fluid into my vein. It is as if I am entering a cave deep within the earth and my body is being pressed into a rock wall glistening across its surface with icy cold water. Beyond the wall is the roar of a vast ocean, and I will have to trust the rock not to give way and plunge me over the brink into a surging darkness.

Someone hovers behind me, murmuring about oxygen and placing a rubber mask over my nose and mouth. I can hear my breath struggling for life in the cool brittle flood of air under the harsh crystal light. I can hear the echoes of consciousness fading all around me until the room is full of the invasive rush of a void. I hear it wash over me until I can hear no more.

A VOICE IS CALLING my name. It comes again, this time joined by a second one of different pitch. They are insistent. With great effort, I manage to open my eyes, and I see a large room full of beds and sleeping people. Again they call. This time I hold my eyes open and see the two women in white uniforms leaning on the metal railings around my bed. They want to know how I'm feeling. Perhaps it is the power of suggestion for I am suddenly engulfed by an overwhelming wave of nausea. They produce a white enamel kidney bowl, then they move away from the bed.

Haltingly I construct a bridge across the gap back to the operating room and the biopsy. I try to see into the gap, try to see if it is malignant or benign. But deep down, I know why no one has yet answered the question that hangs in the air. I realize I am still very cold, and I manage to call to a nurse, who brings a white blanket that is hot and comforting. I feel safer nestled under its bulk, safe enough to sleep again.

Someone leans heavily on the railing of the bed, and I wake again to find my doctor looking down with intent at the bulge of my feet under the bedclothes. He looks exhausted. And I think, let's not discuss all this now, let's wait.

"It turned out to be more complicated than we expected," he says, still looking at my feet. He pauses then goes on to talk about the elastic bandage around my chest and how I'll have to come in to his office to have it removed tomorrow morning and that I should phone his secretary to arrange a time. I nod. We have managed to arrange the first step of the new sequence.

When he has gone, I move cautiously in the bed. It had not occurred to me that I was wearing a bandage. Now I imagine that it constricts my breathing. I drift off to sleep again.

The nurses are leaning on the railing while an orderly moves around preparing to move the bed to the out-patient recovery room. Something in the way they lean reminds me of looking at livestock on a farm. How many times have I leaned just like that on a railing discussing the looks of a new-born calf with my father. I realize they are rallying around to see me off. They pat me on the shoulders and tell me to go home and not do anything. Just go to bed, they say, and don't listen to the kids or to anyone. I just need to rest, they say. I already know it isn't going to be that simple.

✉ Thursday, April 19

I go to my doctor's office to have the bandage removed. I sit in the waiting-room. The room is full of people, and they all turn to look at me as I enter. Presently the door to the inner office opens and someone emerges. Our heads swivel to examine them. I am called in next.

The bandage is removed easily. It feels good to get rid of its constricting pressure. The doctor says the incision is healing well and he covers it with a small plaster. I finish dressing and join him in his office.

He leans back in his chair, searching for a comfortable position, knowing that in a situation like this there is none. I watch him, wondering how many times he has had to be the bringer of bad tidings. I can feel part of myself standing coldly apart saying, So this is what it's like, is it? This is what it's like to be told you have a life-threatening disease. The pause in the conversation seems to go on a long time. I look out into the cold sunshine and begin to count the hills in the distance. His voice brings me abruptly back to the room.

"What we found," he is saying, "is a change within the cells of the ducts that we removed." He hesitates, looking up at the ceiling, then rises from his chair to check the door to the office. He finds it slightly ajar and pushes it firmly closed before returning to his chair. He begins to speak again but I interrupt.

"Is what you found considered cancer?" I ask.

"Yes," he says, looking directly at me across the room. "But in its very early stages." He seems relieved that I have used the word cancer, and I understand that his hesitation was not the weight of the news but how to word it.

"Sometimes," he says, "I have had to treat patients with this disease and never once say the word cancer to them."

He goes on to explain the various stages of breast cancer and says that although nothing can be certain until the pathologist's report is in, it would seem that I have stage one cancer. It remains inside the duct where it has grown and has not yet moved away from there. "I suppose," I say, "if I have to have cancer, I'm lucky to have discovered it at this early stage."

He nods but then adds, "People will probably want to tell you that but no one is lucky to get cancer and you will be marked because of it. You have to realize it's your disease," he says. "It isn't mine or anyone else's. It's yours to decide how to deal with and how to live with. We are here to help you make choices in the treatments, and we can't really talk about those until we get the pathologist's report." We sit in silence again until I venture to break it.

"I think it's like going through a one-way door," I say cautiously. "Once on the other side I can't return and I have to look around to see what's there, where I am, and then I have to decide what to do."

We arrange our next appointment, then I leave. In the corridor, I walk straight to a bank of phones and call my next of kin.

✉ Monday, April 23

We are meeting in the same room. My doctor is holding the pathologist's report, and the look of concern on his face is unmistakable. I can feel my cautious optimism slipping away, and I begin to brace myself for the news. The pathologist has found evidence that the cancer is beyond stage one and is in fact invasive, having already moved out from the ducts.

"We also don't have clean margins on the sample," he continues. "That means there is some still left in there. Most likely we will have to do another operation, a lumpectomy we call it, where we remove only the tissues around the tumor. And we may have to remove some lymph nodes in order to find out if the cancer has spread that far."

He goes on to describe the "tumor board" that meets to advise on treatments and says that once the operation is done, we can discuss further procedures if they are necessary. Radiotherapy, chemotherapy, adjunct therapy. Each word is a weight that seems impossible to carry. We begin to discuss each in turn, trying to lighten them with information. I am worried about the effect an operation would have on my arm.

"I had thought," I say, hesitating. I was going to say "in my old age," but I change it. "In my later years, I would still be able to clamber over rocks on the beach. And I don't want to go on with all this right away. I need time to get my head around it. Time to accept it."

We work through the possibilities, the unpredictabilities and the time frames. As I leave the office, I ask the secretary for the number of the cancer support group. She watches me write down the information, then she leans towards me. "Good luck," she says softly.

Later I walk in the garden trying to get my numbed mind to think, but instead it notices the unfurling leaves against the brilliant blue sky and tells me it doesn't want to leave all this yet. And I kneel in the grass and cry.

✉ Friday, April 27

I have come to the woods, walking slowly, the fatigue of the anaesthetic still within me. I need to touch the scars and dry rot on the living trees and see that the dead ones still stand. I tread carefully among the red trilliums seeking out fallen birch logs spongy with decay inside their dry white skins. As I walk home, I see someone I know approaching in the distance, walking her dog. My heart sinks. I can't face telling her I have cancer. I'm not up to seeing the curious mixture of pity, fear and distance that may cross her face. Not now, later perhaps. Instead, she has news for me.

"Have you heard? They're going to log the woods," she says. "Well not log, they're going to tidy it up. Take out the dead trees."

"Why?" I ask incredulously.

"Oh, something about insurance." She laughs. "The owner doesn't want a dead tree to fall on passers-by and kill them. Are you okay? You look tired."

"I'm fine," I say, looking at the ground.

And I walk down the hill through suburbia with its carefully kept lawns and renovated houses, wondering where I fit into this society that has no tolerance for decay and so little time for death.

"Don't move," she says.

I am lying on a stretcher beneath a simulator, my right arm drawn up over my shoulder, my hand resting on a cold metal rod. I'm here to begin radiotherapy after an operation they consider bodes well, having shown clean margins and non-infected lymph nodes. Although I do not like this nuclear technology, I feel I cannot ignore the statistics, I cannot bet against the odds. The room is dark around me; a red light gleams in the ceiling overhead. A technician moves about busily, mapping my right breast.

In the face of the machine is a glass square etched with a grid of lines, straight and right-angled. The aperture moves closer, closing in on the surface of my skin, shining a beam of light that casts a shadow of the etched matrix onto my breast. She adjusts the angles.

"Just don't move," she repeats as she moves around double-checking the digital read-outs on the machine. It clicks and whirrs around me, photographing the angles, aligning itself over where the tumor had been. Finally satisfied, the angles judged, the boundaries defined, the contours worked out, she leans over me, tracing the shadow matrix onto my skin with thick red indelible ink. For good measure and added permanence, she pricks in four tattoo marks. The lines feel icy cold as the ink dries into the pores. Is it my life or my death that is now targeted?

"Try not to wash the lines off," she tells me as I climb off the stretcher and begin to pull on the old clothes they had advised I wear. "It's good you're wearing old clothes, the red ink stains cloth really easily."

When I finish dressing, she shows me the map she has drawn of my breast, explaining how the lead line she used across its surface allowed her to trace the contour of the nipple onto the page. It looks to me like a contour map of a landscape. As if we are in a war room planning for aerial bombing. A series of clinical strikes calculated not to kill all the healthy cells during the procedure.

✉ Tuesday, July 3

I walk into a well-lit room filled with a radiotherapy machine. It looks huge and complex and intimidating. By contrast, the technicians are open and friendly and reassuring. I follow their directions as well as I can as they manoeuvre me on the stretcher to a position between the outstretched arms of the machine. They tell me they want to check the alignment to see if it corresponds to the map of my breast. They set to work, calling out numbers, moving the stretcher and the machine to match the precise measurements. Eventually I can feel myself relax with the caring concern of the technicians. They are making all this possible for me.

They run a series of photographs, then they say the alignment is perfect and they will now give the first treatment. Immediately I feel the tension rush back into my limbs as they instruct me to hold my position, then they leave the room, closing the heavy door behind them. The sound echoes around the room, then there is silence before the machine is turned on. Its loud, incessant buzzing fills every corner of my brain, and I find the effort to stay still for forty seconds almost impossible, but I can feel nothing of the accelerated radioactive particles passing through my breast. The technicians are full of reassurance. They begin to adjust everything for treatment from the reverse angle. The machine seems to execute a cumbersome yet precise move to centre me in the gap through which the energy passes. But I am more relaxed now, for I have found something to focus on.

"What's that?" I ask, moving my eyes towards a hole in the ceiling.

They all look up as if they had never seen the ceiling before.

"We don't know," one answers. "We think it's part of a renovation that isn't finished yet."

As they work, I keep my eyes on the hole and I know that in the next five weeks of treatment, my mind will be slipping across its threshold, treading softly into the darkness beyond.

✉ Tuesday, August 7

The treatment is over. I am exhausted but have very few of the other possible side-effects. I am being examined by a doctor who is pleased with the results. She is pleased for me. "You know," she says cheerfully, "seventy per cent of the women in your condition are cured." She smiles at me, inviting my response. I am grateful for all they have done, but somewhere deep inside me a voice screams: "No more statistics, let me live and die on my own!"

But I am too exhausted to respond to either voice, and I know the word "cured" does not describe the way I feel.

Vanessa Kramer
St. Bruno, Quebec

✉ About breast cancer: I have been there – twice. In most discussions of this subject, the positive side is missing.

"Positive?" you ask. "Breast cancer?!"

Yes. I can think of three things.

1. I am alive!! (That's very positive.)
2. The funny things that happen – and they do.
3. My gratitude to the doctors who made Number 1 possible.

1. There are, of course, very dark periods, but once the operation was over and the pathology report positive, there was a whole new joy in living. I had faced death and would never again take life for granted. Waking up in the morning, I would say, "Wow! I'm alive!" Things looked better, smelled better, tasted better, and my children were handsomer.

2. Funny things? How about the morning when the dog got my prosthesis and took off up the street. I went after him at full pelt in my pink nightgown, while my two daughters stood in the doorway and laughed until they collapsed.

Shopping for my prosthesis had its moments, too.

3. I have lived to see my children grow up and to know my grandchildren because of the skill and diligence of two caring doctors. How can anyone adequately express gratitude for that?
P.S. Mammograms – pfftt!

Evelyn Lea
Winnipeg

✉ I am at the lake today, sitting at a picnic table, watching the light filter through the leaves, listening to the squirrels chittering, and thinking. My world seemed to revolve around goals and deadlines. But today I have none. For months, we have been looking forward to the marriage of our one and only daughter. And now that occasion has passed. For years (twenty to be exact) I've worked as a general duty nurse, and now I've laid that aside. I need new goals and horizons. And so today I've been taking into account my abilities, thinking, summing up, laying new plans.

As I was thinking I realized each member of our family is entering a new stage in life. Our youngest son is a-tingle with excitement and dread. He enters high school this fall. Our oldest son leaves home to take a course in welding. He yearns for independence and yet says over and over how much he'll miss home, porridge for breakfast, old friends, clean socks. Our daughter enters a new marriage, a new part-time job, a new year at a different university.

My husband, several years my senior, is planning for retirement. And I am leaving my familiar, fulfilling position of mother-home-maker-nurse. What's ahead? I don't know.

Many times I've thought New Year's would be better cele-brated on Labour Day weekend. So many roles change at that time when summer wanes, school's back in session, and at our little hospital young nurses start a new career. I always look forward to the day after Labour Day and a return to familiar routine. And so I sit here resting, summing up, reaching out to something new.

I haven't been to town yet to post this, so I'll add a postscript. No, I haven't settled the question of "What next?" But I had a moving experience that touched upon the question.

It was necessary to drive to the next farm early in the morning. Fog lingered thickly in the lowlands. If I drove too quickly, I was soon lost in a thick blanket. But if I drove moderately, the fog seemed to thin just enough to let me see what I had to see (about three lengths of the car). And I got to my destination without any trouble.

I am a person who likes to know what's ahead, miles ahead. And often I'm so concentrated on my goal, I miss out on the here and now. But if I slow down just a little, I know I will see and understand what I need to know and understand today. And I'll get there fine, I know.

Noreen Aarrestad
Debden, Saskatchewan

✉ I can't sign this, because my husband and I listen to your broadcast every morning on the way to work, but I thought you might like to hear from the wife of the man who talked about his history of wife-beating. My husband is not really that man, but he shares with him all the traits that combine to make a man strike out at his wife. Controlling is the word that best sums it up.

My husband – let's call him David – is not a beer-drinking Hell's Angel. He is a professional. In fact, we both earn six-digit salaries. We live in an elegant area in Toronto in a house that was paid off some time ago.

David was always the boss. Because he was the pragmatic one and was trained to earn us a good living, he convinced me that I should allow him to run the entire show, even to little details like how the dishwasher should be loaded (really!). As Mrs. Wimp, I allowed these statements of his assertion, passing them off as idiosyncrasies.

Get to the point, you say. Are you a battered wife? No, not really battered. There were three instances where physical violence occurred. Two were slaps, the other a neck twist. But mostly David's bullying was psychological. Head games. Nastiness towards me in front of other people. Put-downs. Inconsideration like keeping me waiting for hours for dinner without even a phone call, even on our anniversary. Little things that can often add up to a divorce.

Then, a strange thing happened. David lost his job. In a panic, I took one. David got another one right away, but I kept mine. After a few years, I began to do very well in my field. Then even better. Once my salary hit fifty thousand dollars a year, I made it very clear to David that I no longer needed him. The children were getting older, and the struggle to keep us together as a family was no longer relevant.

As a well-regarded, well-paid professional, I was no longer willing to put up with the kind of nonsense I had taken when I was a housewife begging for the wherewithal to buy something for the house or for myself. For the first time in my life, I had a little money, and I had control of it. David, still in awe of the fact that such a stupid idiot as I could have gotten anywhere beyond my kitchen, was strangely silent.

He began to change. With his growing respect, our marriage began to renew itself. We did love each other, after all. And as there were many things we enjoyed doing together, we worked it out. Today, we get along pretty well. We still disagree on many things, but by and large, it is a pretty okay relationship. And there is no physical violence.

Happily ever after, you ask? Well, not quite. If you think about it, what I was forced to do in order to have a good life with my husband was to earn my dignity and his respect – with money. And I think that's what this is all about. Control is another word for power in a relationship. Men usually earn more. They feel that as the bread-winners they are automatically entitled to a position of power in the household. For men who are sure of themselves, this isn't usually a problem. For a bully, it's a heyday.

I am something of a workaholic now. Subconsciously, I fear that if I lose my job in this recession, my relationship will revert back to its former malaise. I am also quite miserly with money now, squirrelling spare funds away in a secret account – just in case the worst happens and David rises like a phoenix to reclaim his former position in my life, gloating as he does because I've blown it, and I really am the idiot he used to say I was. I will at least have something to fall back on.

The fact that our relationship is held together by such fragile threads as my monetary situation is a sad commentary on society. I was lucky. I was bright and well-educated. I could escape the hell of being the object of a bully and even keep my marriage together. Less fortunate women cannot, and I empathize with them. Because I understand the frustration and agony they are feeling.

I think that this message should be emblazoned on every girls' locker-room in every high school:

"You are a fool in this day and age to expect any man to support you. You are a fool to let any man dominate you. Get an education, get a job. Take control and responsibility for your own life. Do it now while you still can. You'll be very sorry later if you don't."

I will sign myself,

Susan

✉ I am twenty-six and have finally found peace with the outside of my body. During my teen years and my early twenties, I was slim and was able to dress any way I wanted. I was also frequently depressed, drank very heavily, tried various drugs and smoked cigarettes. My self-image was lousy, and I wasted "the best years of my life" hating my form and my mind.

But I came out of those times, and now I exercise every day, my heart and lungs are strong and I'm about six kilos "over-weight." I'm happy, healthy, and my husband thinks I'm beautiful.

Sometimes I long for the petite person I used to be, but I would rather be round and content than bony and miserable.

Clara Bayliss-Collier
Valcartier Village, Quebec

✉ When I was eight years old, my father, a union organizer in the forties and fifties, was blacklisted, accused of communist activities. It meant no work – with a vengeance. My mother, then in her forties, had twin boys that spring – premature, and in pre-medicare times you can imagine the devastating costs for their care. I was hungry that year, hungry when I got up, hungry when I went to school, hungry when I went to sleep. In November I was asked to leave school because I only had boys' clothes to wear – hand-me-downs from a neighbour. I could come back, they said, when I dressed like a young lady.

The week before Christmas, the power and gas were disconnected. We ate soup made from carrots, potatoes, cabbage and grain meant to feed chickens, cooked on our wood garbage burner. Even as an eight-year-old, I knew the kind of hunger we had was nothing compared to people in India and Africa. I don't think we could have died in our middle-class Vancouver suburb. But I do know that the pain of hunger is intensified and brutal when you live in the midst of plenty. As Christmas preparations increased, I felt more and more isolated, excluded, set apart. I felt a deep, abiding hunger for more than food. Christmas Eve day came, grey and full of the bleak sleety rain of a west-coast winter. Two women, strangers, struggled up our driveway, loaded down with bags. They left before my mother answered the door. The porch was full of groceries – milk, butter, bread, cheese and Christmas oranges. We never knew who they were, and after that day, pride being what it was, we never spoke of them again. But I'm forty-five years old, and I remember them well.

Since then I've crafted a life of joy and independence, if not of financial security. Several years ago, living in Victoria, my son and I were walking up the street, once more in west-coast sleet and rain. It was just before Christmas and we were, as usual, counting our pennies to see if we'd have enough for all our festive treats, juggling these against the necessities. A young man stepped in front of me, very pale and carrying an old sleeping bag, and asked for spare change – not unusual in downtown Victoria. No, I said, and walked on. Something hit me like a physical blow about a block later. I left my son and walked back to find the young man. I gave him some of our Christmas luxury money – folded into a small square and tucked into his hand. It wasn't much, only ten dollars, but as I turned away, I saw the look of hopelessness turn into amazement and then joy. Well, said the rational part of my mind, Judith, you are a fool, you know he's just going up the street to the King's Hotel and spend it on drink or drugs. You've taken what belongs to your family and spent it on a frivolous romantic impulse. As I was lecturing myself on gullibility and sensible charity, I noticed the young man with the sleeping bag walking quickly up the opposite side of the street, heading straight for the King's. Well, let this be a lesson, said the rational Judith. To really rub it in, I decided to follow him. Just before the King's, he turned into a corner grocery store. I watched through the window, through the poinsettias and the stand-up Santas. I watched him buy milk, butter, bread, cheese and Christmas oranges.

Now, I have no idea how that young man arrived on the street in Victoria, nor will I ever have any real grasp of the events that led my family to a dark and hungry December. But I do know that charity cannot be treated as an RRSP. There is no best-investment way to give, no way to insure value for our dollar. Like the Magi, these three, the two older women struggling up the driveway and the young man with the sleeping bag, gave me, and continue to give me, wonderful gifts – the reminder that love and charity come most truly and abundantly from an open and unjudgemental heart.

Judith MacKenzie
Nelson, British Columbia

✉ I am one of the no doubt tens of thousands who are looking forward to relief of some kind when the calendar flips over this Sunday night and the damned eighties are over.

I am old enough (hell, it's no secret, I'm thirty-seven) to have protested the war in Vietnam, run an underground newspaper and assaulted my body with drugs in numbers and sorts that now make me tremble. I split to "Van" hitch-hiking in the summer of 1970, then again to California in 1973 in a VW bus (not flower-painted, however). I survived the idiotic late seventies by ignoring them. On the eve of the eighties, just like now, I hoped for something better. So much for that hope.

By now, everyone I went to school with has divided themselves into two groups – deadbeats and yuppies. While I admit that I am a deadbeat, I did have a couple of flings with yuppiedom. For example, in late 1986, I bought myself a custom-made leather jacket and a top-of-the-line Sony Walkman. In the winter of 1986-87, I went on a hideously expensive Caribbean holiday. All because I thought I deserved it – the yuppie justification chant.

I came to my senses, horrified. My friends, fellow deadbeats all, kindly pointed out that I was not in any real danger since I have lived in the same apartment for eleven years (rent-controlled, ho, ho), do not own a car of any kind or a garment with animals, polo players or somebody else's name on it. When I pointed to the Cartier watch on my wrist, they reminded me that it was given to me by a former boy-friend, who really wasn't any worse than the rest of my former boy-friends except he had more money, and that I had had to be restrained from throwing it, the watch, into Lake Ontario in a stressful moment.

So all right, materially, I seemed to be safe from yuppiedom. But the worst was yet to come. For ten years, I had been supporting myself as a free-lance writer, not, alas, of things Important or Weighty, but rather of such things as video scripts demonstrating how to avoid cutting one's foot off with a chain-saw and peppy employee newsletters in which I showed my superior prose style by restricting myself to only one exclamation point per page.

I was getting deeply bored. Given an assignment to write a full-page newspaper ad for a luxury condominium, I combed the Saturday *Star* for every nauseating, meaningless adjective used in those things and worked every single one into less than two hundred and fifty words. I showed this masterpiece to my deadbeat friends in high glee. "They'll never ask me to write one of these again," I said. Wrong. The client loved it. I finally cracked when asked to think up names for eight different styles of houses in a new "prestige" development in King City. "Something horsey," the client suggested. I quit.

By then I had met what I thought was a like-minded woman in a similar line of work. "Why not," we said, "do it ourselves? Direct client contact. Total control. Reduce the bull level by a notch or two out there in the hyped-up world of business communications." In late 1988, we went after corporate Canada, or at least, until one of us could afford a car, the parts accessible by public transit.

I am sorry to have to report that the three-piecers in boardrooms think a woman making a pitch for business who also makes a mild joke or two in the process is either stupid or weird or both. It didn't take me long to realize that they are right. It *is* both stupid and weird to make jokes in boardrooms. Apparently, I also made the mistake of banning words like "concept development," "idea marketing" and "marketing positioning" from my proposals and even my speech. They found my haircuts unsettling, but since I was the one who gave the electric hair clippers to my sister, I figured the least I could do was let her practise on me. The business was not a success.

Now, on the eve of the nineties, I am unemployed. But I'm hopeful. Maybe in the nineties, writers of condo ads won't have to bankrupt their thesauruses to satisfy greedy, illiterate developers. Maybe directors of human resources will realize that many employees can tolerate more than eight words to a page with fewer than six exclamation points. Maybe well-meaning safety organizations will realize they don't really need to spend two hundred thousand dollars on a half-hour video to help people recognize the perils of chain-saws. Maybe youngish self-employed females will be able to make jokes in boardrooms. Maybe then I'll be able to go back into a business that is often challenging and sometimes fun.

What do you think?

Francesca Scalzo
Toronto

✉ Joy to me means having my son home, alive, and reasonably well. Sometime in October – I'm unsure of the date; October and most of November are just a blur of days – sometime in October, I commented on the bitter irony of being surrounded by the promotions of AIDS Awareness Week while our son lay dying from the effects of the most recent attack on his shattered immune system.

But our son did not die. Some miracle of love, prayer, strength of will and determination – assisted by the necessary medical procedures, once they were implemented – combined to effect a quite remarkable recovery from an infection that ought to have proved fatal. This recovery surprised a number of people and stunned one doom-and-gloom neurologist who had solemnly pronounced an imminent demise. The look on his face while watching the patient he had given up for dead doggedly traversing the corridors in his wheeled chair was almost worth the weeks-long ordeal.

Soon we were able to venture outside the hospital, to a nearby park for an hour, or just to sit in the sun on fine days. By month's end, travel was feasible. An inter-hospital transfer was arranged by the social services department, and on October 31 we flew home. What a wonderful treat for Hallowe'en. What a welcoming committee of friends and family met our plane.

By December 20, our son was well enough to be discharged from the hospital, and we took him home to await the gathering of the entire family – the first time since Christmas 1982 that we would all be together at the same time. We celebrated a truly joyous and thankful Christmas this year. My husband was a king in the pageant at our church, his fourth year in that role. I was given the privilege of reading a passage based on Isaiah, and I must admit that when I spoke of resurrection and new life, the emotion was too much for me, my voice grew unsteady for a few moments – thus embarrassing our younger daughter once again. That's a bad habit I have.

I've kept a journal of those trying days and events when we struggled for our son's life – as much for my own sanity as anything, but also with the idea that through our experience we might at some time be of help to others who must face this ordeal. We don't know what the future holds, or just how much future we'll have together. It is unlikely that our son can survive another major infection. This was his third AIDS-related illness. Even miracles must be measured, and surely we've received our portion. For now it is enough to have him with us, where I can be sure he's well nourished and obtaining sufficient rest. He grows stronger daily, is regaining some of the weight he lost and looks well. He received treatment at our community hospital and is looking forward to the spring when he hopes to be able to resume working.

I thank God for every new day. The joy in my heart knows no bounds.

Mary Grant
Tisdale, Saskatchewan

THE GREAT TOMATO CRISIS – AND HOW TO COPE WITH IT

Everyone who's ever grown tomatoes (even Krista Munroe, as you'll see) knows the feeling. Suddenly, you've got more tomatoes than you ever thought possible. Trouble is, so has everyone else you know.

✉ Years ago, my late father taught me to eat tomatoes as a fruit – with cream and sugar (or honey drizzled over the sliced tomatoes). Since eating is believing, go and try some for yourself. Obviously, this is not for those who are concerned about cholesterol, but fortunately, both my father and I were born before they had invented cholesterol.

Vernon L. Dutton
Winnipeg

✉ When I first planted tomatoes in Medicine Hat, I knew that they were a fragile crop and I wanted to get a high enough yield so that we could make real tomato sauce. So I planted thirteen plants. I got ninety pounds of juicy tomatoes. I had sauce in every glass jar in the house. I gave away bagfuls and my friends would start conversations with, "No, I can't use any more tomatoes . . . ." I ate tomato everything. I got sick of tomato *anything*.

The next year I smartened up. I only planted seven plants, figuring that I could probably handle half the previous year's yield. I don't know what happened – maybe a tomato bomb went off in the back yard – but that year we got a hundred and twenty-five pounds of tomatoes. Every bowl in the house was full. Garbage bags were stuffed. Every flat surface contained ripening tomatoes. There were boxes full under every table full of tomatoes. I think my friends moved, since I was unable to contact any of them.

This year, I suggested to my husband that we not plant tomatoes at all. Seemed reasonable to me. That way we could use up the frozen tomatoes from the last few years and make room in our freezer for meat, or ice cream, or anything else at all for a change. But all the colour drained out of his face. While his hands shook, he explained some basic mathematical laws about inverse relationships. If thirteen plants gave ninety pounds, and seven plants gave one hundred and twenty-five pounds, then it was possible that no plants would yield an infinite number of tomatoes (isn't this science stuff wonderful?). So this year we planted five plants. We had never tried Roma tomatoes before and we thought the yield would be lower than Beefsteak or Early Girl plants gave.

We were wrong.

I have read salsa recipes that sound lovely, but they only use four tomatoes. I have enough tomatoes to make salsa for Central Africa. And hot sauce recipes – twenty tomatoes? I scoff! I could make hot sauce for the House of Commons (except that I think it's a shame to feed that bunch). A recipe that uses ten *pounds* is getting up to the right order of magnitude, though, and there may be hope yet.

Now, would you know anyone who has recipes for green peppers? I have fifty-three of the damn things, and once again all my so-called friends are on extended vacations. I love green peppers as long as they're not stuffed. And I'm not crazy about spending any time in the kitchen when I'm not drinking coffee and doing the crossword – so these recipes have to be simple and quick. But if you can help, I'd be grateful.

I'm going to stop now. I've got to start doing something with the tomatoes.

Krista Munroe
Medicine Hat

✉ For peeling one needs a pot with enough boiling water that each of the fruits can be completely dunked in. I use either of the parts of a double boiler, because that is narrow and high, for water and energy economy. This works best because with boiling water it is an in-and-out procedure. I spear each tomato on a barbecue fork: in and out. The fork seems to be enough to make the skin split spontaneously and come off without anything more than just that skin. The tomato stays cold and smooth.

The tomatoes are done one at a time. Peeling can be done after each one has been dunked. As a rule, I spear at the end with the little green rosette; that way the other end is not damaged and can be used for decorative use of the tomato. Since the end with the stem is often a bit under-ripe, it is important to have that deep boiling water for complete submersion. This goes too for less ripe tomatoes. Just count: in, one, two, out.

R.G. Aalders
Alexandria, Ontario

✉ I love tomatoes. In fact, if I had my druthers, I'd probably live on fresh tomato sandwiches and black licorice! At this time of year, when tomatoes are at their best, I love to eat them as one would an apple. I also like to freeze cooked tomatoes for later use in spaghetti and meat loaves, but I do this in the easiest way possible. And that is:

Remove skins from about twenty ripe tomatoes. Cut into quarters or if large into eighths. Peel about three large onions. Chop. Place tomatoes and onions in large pot. Cook until onions are transparent. Place this mixture in bottles or plastic containers. Store in the freezer for winter use.

To make spaghetti sauce, remove tomato-onion mix from freezer. Defrost in microwave. Place in frying pan or pot with one can tomato paste. Heat. Add oregano, meat, hot peppers, whatever, and there you have a tasty sauce.

Anne Fairley
Winnipeg

✉ The simplest thing to do with excess tomatoes is to wash them, dry them (so they won't stick together in one big glob) and put them in a plastic bag in the freezer. They do lose their fresh texture, but you still have the nice fresh-from-the-garden taste and can put bits and pieces in a salad or you can add them still frozen to a soup or stew as it is cooking. The skins just seem to disappear among the other veggies.

Mary's Tomato Soup

14 pounds tomatoes, peeled and cut up
1 cup sugar
7 large onions, chopped
3 tablespoons salt
½ pound butter
8 tablespoons flour or 4 tablespoons cornstarch

Boil tomatoes, onions, sugar and salt until soft. Purée in blender. Use a little to mix with the flour to a thin paste. Bring the rest to a boil again, stir in the butter and the flour paste and cook a few minutes more. Cool and freeze in one-meal-sized portions. Makes 24 to 28 cups. To serve, heat and add 150 mL milk to

500 mL soup. Also good thawed and served cold with a bit of yoghurt.

Margaret Pointing
Mississauga, Ontario

✉ I know a recipe for the delightful old Provençal standby, *Rata-touille*. The beauty of this dish is that it can be served hot or cold and freezes excellently. The addition of a little cooked fish or cooked ground meat makes a fast and absurdly easy one-dish meal for days when you are pressed for time.

Another beauty of this splendid dish is that the quantities are not critical. If you like lots of garlic, put in lots.

Ratatouille

Enough olive oil to cover the bottom of a large pot
2 chopped onions
1 chopped green pepper
1 medium chopped eggplant and 1 medium chopped zucchini (no need to peel them) or, if one of the zucchinis in your garden has somehow hidden itself under the leaves and grown to monstrous size, use that on its own
2 crushed garlic cloves
6 to 8 peeled chopped tomatoes

Wilt the onion and green pepper in the oil, but do not let them brown. Add the eggplant, zucchini and garlic and stir till they are coated with the oil. Add the tomatoes and stir till everything is well mixed. Bring to a boil and simmer gently, uncovered, till most of the moisture has evaporated and the mixture is yummily thick. Stir occasionally. At this point, I like to add a handful of sliced mushrooms, which only take a couple of minutes to cook.

And there you are. *Bon appetit.*

Alice Sinclair
Kleinburg, Ontario

⊠ Here's how I make my tomatoes for winter storage. I used to take the skins off, but now all the experts preach pulp so I leave them on. Just take off any spots, put the tomatoes in a big pot (I do about four quarts a day as mine ripen), boil for one minute and put into sterile jars – no salt, no sugar, just tomatoes, and they taste like fresh ones in the winter – lovely when I want a sauce.

Gladys Lewis
Guelph, Ontario

⊠ Green Tomato Chutney

3 pounds tomatoes
3 pounds apples
3 pounds onions
1 pound sultanas
2 quarts vinegar
4 ounces dry mustard
1½ pounds moist sugar
2 tablespoons salt
1 teaspoon cayenne pepper
2 teaspoons white pepper

Skin tomatoes and peel and core apples, then chop them up finely with the onions. Place in preserving pan with the sultanas and 1½ quarts of vinegar and boil until quite soft. Then mix the rest of the vinegar with the mustard and add to the tomatoes with the sugar, salt and peppers. Boil until the mixture will set like a jam. Pour into warm, dry jars and screw down the tops at once.

Ripe Tomato Chutney

3 pounds ripe tomatoes
3 pounds peeled and cored apples
1½ pounds sultanas

266

1½ pounds raisins
2 pounds small onions
2 pounds brown sugar
16 chilies
2 teaspoons cayenne pepper
4 teaspoons salt
24 cloves
1 pint vinegar

Place the tomatoes in hot water and remove skins. Chop up finely the tomatoes, apples, raisins and onions. Put all the ingredients except the vinegar into a pan and simmer half an hour. Add the vinegar and simmer 3 hours. Pour mixture into warm, dry jars and cover at once.

A word of explanation:

Moist sugar – use brown
Sultanas – white raisins
Raisins – use the dark raisins

Don't forget to stir. The aroma when this is cooking is (to my mind) much better than the hot tomato smell when you are making straight sauce.

Peggy Swift
Sarnia, Ontario

✉ Uncooked Tomato Relish

18 large red tomatoes
7 large onions
1 head celery
½ cup salt
2 cups vinegar
6 cups sugar
2 sweet red peppers

2 sweet green peppers
1 ounce mustard seed

Peel tomatoes and cut fine. (Scald tomatoes and plunge in cold water to help remove skins.) Cut onions and celery. Add salt. Let stand overnight. Drain for 2 to 3 hours in the morning, then add vinegar and sugar. Cut peppers fine and add with mustard seed. Leave rest of day. Stir occasionally. Bottle.

Connie Clark
Fredericton

✉ As an organic gardener of many years' standing, I found myself wondering how to deal with a glut of tomatoes at the end of the season knowing that in a few short weeks' time fresh tomatoes would be unavailable. Invariably I ended up with a few red tomatoes that would last a short time only, frozen ones that could not be used in salads and green ones wrapped in newspaper or on window sills that ended up in such a stinking mess, if not religiously checked daily, that the whole operation seemed counterproductive.

Three years ago I was so mad about an early upcoming frost that I decided to try an experiment. I dug up all my tomato plants and took them into the basement where I hung them upside down on nails in the overhead joists. Some tomatoes were red but the majority were green. It worked! Although I lost a few due to mildew, the majority slowly ripened on the plant despite the fact that the plant itself withered away. We enjoyed fresh-tasting tomatoes right around to early March, believe it or not. Admittedly, during the latter period, the tomatoes took on a wrinkled appearance, but the main thing was that they tasted good and sweet. I have followed this practice ever since.

Should any one like to try this, I have three tips found from experience. 1: After dealing with ripe tomatoes that had obeyed the law of gravity and mashed themselves onto the concrete floor, I learned that a plastic sheet suspended below the plants was advisable. 2: The best variety I have found to date is the Sweet 100, which are about one to two inches in diameter. 3: Bring them in *before* the first frost!

George Bowhay
Georgetown, Ontario

✉ I come from a ranch and forty-five or fifty years ago we had a big root cellar in which we kept all our vegetables – tons of potatoes, carrots, beets and turnips. Our cabbages we hung up by the roots and they were still good for coleslaw in the spring. The tomatoes we hung up by the roots, and they were fresh until at least January. The temperature in the root cellar – which was underground with double doors – was thirty-four to thirty-six degrees. I'm sure many other people in the Cariboo did this years before that.

Sonia Cornwall
150 Mile House, British Columbia

✉ The first summer my husband and I set up house, we planted, of course, tomatoes. At the end of the season, we had a large number of green tomatoes. My mother-in-law had heard that if the tomatoes were individually wrapped in newspaper and placed in a cool, dark spot they would ripen on their own.

So, we wrapped tomatoes. We wrapped *dozens* of tomatoes. We then placed them in our fruit cellar to ripen. A couple of months later, having thought they'd take quite some time to fully ripen, we trekked downstairs to harvest our crop of juicy, red tomatoes. We unwrapped one tomato only to find an empty ball of newspaper and a small pile of dust. The next unwrapped "tomato" was also empty, but it contained a few dried seeds. At this point I accused my husband of sneaking down and removing all the green tomatoes from their wrappers (something, I might add, I still wouldn't put past him!). Having denied this, he proceeded to demonstrate that it would be next to impossible to create these perfect little balls of newspaper, let alone dusty ones.

We continued to open all the little balls of newspaper, but alas, we didn't have tomatoes in our salad that night!

Betty Goodfellow
Burlington, Ontario

FOREIGN AFFAIRS II:
CATHERINE IN PAKISTAN

Catherine Pigott is a young journalist from Oakville, Ontario, with an interest in feminist issues. She was working on the Kingston (also Ontario) *Whig-Standard* when she got a hankering to see the world. Specifically, she wanted to see Pakistan, and how its woman leader, Benazir Bhutto, was making out. She applied for – and received – a grant.

When the original object of her curiosity was deposed, Catherine found herself deeply engrossed in Pakistani society, and from time to time over the next year or so she sat down to write us about it.

October 4

✉ Several months ago, I left a quiet eastern Ontario news-room where I had worked as a reporter for two years and came to Pakistan to write for an English daily called *The Muslim.*

In Pakistan's one-year-old democracy, most young journalists are doing real political reporting for the first time. Their prose may be awkward and sometimes partisan, but there's enthusiasm in it, and a sense of discovery. I've spent my initial weeks just trying to get my pen around the hyphenated Islamic names of politicians and parties.

My first glimpse of *The Muslim* office was a bit of a let-down. I guess I was expecting a prominent downtown building, with *The Muslim* engraved in stone over the door. It is, after all, the capital's leading daily. But on my first day of work, I almost missed the place. It's crammed into a small office above the Muslim Commercial Bank, on the edge of a bazaar that specializes in Bata shoes and bicycle repairs.

The first thing I noticed about the news-room was the number of human beings in that small space. Apart from sub-editors, proof-readers and pasters, there are the peons – professional errand-runners. It seems as if every full-time employee has his or her own peon, who sits nearby and waits for orders to bring tea or take messages.

Here, the process of putting out a daily involves a lot more people and more paper. The news desk is buried under scrolls of newsprint that roll in from bureaus and wire services. The piles are held down by paperweights so the ceiling fans won't blow them away.

Sub-editors scratch and scribble through each story. When they're not busy, they talk politics or read the Oxford dictionary. *The Muslim* may be published in English, but for everyone who works here, English is their third or fourth language. English has prestige, though, because the British used it to train Pakistan's élite. And the more flowery, the better. Crimes are "heinous" and criminals "ruthless." My unadorned, journalism-school prose pales in comparison. When I submitted what I thought was a colour piece on a Benazir Bhutto rally, an editor asked me, "Why do you write like a child?"

Many of the people handling copy at *The Muslim* aren't functional in English. On their tea-breaks, they'll happily pick up a spicy Urdu tabloid, *Oor-do*, written in Persian script.

Like every paper, *The Muslim* has its share of characters. My stories are proofed by a man who's descended from a Sufi saint.

He insists on reading every story out loud in a droning voice that rises like a prayer over the news-room.

In another corner, Mustapha Jaffery monitors the short-wave radio to see if BBC or Radio Moscow has news that we don't. But Mustapha is frustrated in his job. They installed new lighting six months ago, and since then all he can pick up is static. It's a waste of his linguistic and reporting talents, he told me. But he's almost blind, and he needs the work.

He's been with the paper since it was launched in 1979 by reporters who'd been sacked from other papers for their outspokenness. The country was under martial law. For more than a year, the government withheld official permission to publish, but the owner put the paper out anyway – without a mast-head, *and* without the government advertising that most papers survive on.

I'm still trying to figure out where we stand in this new democracy. Our editor is a close friend and advisor to Prime Minister Benazir Bhutto. But the owner is the secretary of the Islamic coalition that wants to bring Bhutto's government down. There's an uneasy stand-off between the two. The paper is a pastiche of opposing views, allegations and counter-allegations. Pakistanis agonize over their political past and present as few countries do. The homogeneity of General Zia's military rule is gone, and the press is getting used to the mayhem.

Finally, I have to keep reminding myself that I'm in a country where the literacy rate is below twenty-five per cent and dropping. The English press reaches no more than one in a hundred people. We write for Islamabad's élite "chattering classes," who thrive on politics. But many poor and rural Pakistanis who need basic information the most still aren't getting it. That's a challenge that goes far beyond what *The Muslim* can do.

November 5

✉ Nilt Village, Northern Areas: I had never seen a mountain breathe, until I came here. Raka Poshi, the twenty-five-thousand-foot peak that crowns the Hindu Kush range, appears to exhale cloud, like steamy breath in winter. The people who live by the mountain call it "Dumani," which means "mother of clouds." They believe that their mountain is, in an undefined way, alive, inhabited by a spirit hierarchy. The purest gods are female and live on the highest, whitest peaks. Animal spirits live lower down. Witches and demons dwell in the deep gorges.

The highway that brought me here connects Pakistan to China, twisting through the Himalayas, the Karakorams and the Pamirs. It follows an ancient silk route through an utterly silkless place of stubborn stone houses and people whose limbs are rock-hard from climbing.

I stayed with Akbar Hussain and his family in the village of Nilt, a place blessed with the rare gift of clean water. It flows down from the glaciers and fans out in an intricate network of streams to irrigate the terraced fields.

I awoke at five the first morning and heard babies crying in every compound. The smells of wood and smoke were in my nostrils. It was Eid, the day when Muslims celebrate the feast of sacrifice. The men all went to the mosque to pray. The women stayed behind. They were not allowed to defile such holy places. I watched them work. They wore shawls draped over their heads and tucked under their chins like wimples. They asked me to cover my head also, but the cloth kept slipping to my shoulders. All day, the young wives moved between the stream, the cooking fire and the store-room. In the cooler hours, they worked in the fields. At night, they slept in their clothes on straw mats, with children heaped between them.

It was summer, and the wheat grew like thick, matted hair. Apricots and mulberries fell from the trees. Akbar took me to visit some neighbours, and the women fed me bowls of fruit, fresh goat cheese and sweet tea. We sat in an orchard. "You have a land of plenty," I said to Akbar. "No," he answered. "This is a land of just enough."

I asked an old woman how many children she had given birth to. Fifteen, she said. Only one had lived. As we spoke, a pregnant woman walked by on her way to the well. She looked like a teenager. They told me her first baby died. No one knew why. Polio, perhaps, or a seizure. Akbar's sister mimicked the baby's death, clenching her fists and rolling her eyes. The women thought this was hilarious, though most of them had lost infants of their own. The pregnant mother smiled weakly and turned away.

Lyla, a mother of six, said that her baby daughter was killed by the Sobayan, a witch. Akbar shook his head apologetically. "She is very simple. She is not educated," he said, as if I should ignore her. But I wanted to speak to this woman who had raised six children in such unadorned isolation – and survived. Doctors and Western drugs were still remote. Lyla used herbs. If her baby became weak and sick, she held it under a wild rose-bush, which is considered a sacred tree.

Lyla brightened when I asked about her fifteen-year-old daughter, Hina. "She will live a better life," she said. "She's studied up to grade four." Lyla wanted her daughter to continue her education, but the girl was engaged, which meant all authority over her was transferred to the future husband's family.

Girls here are seen as an economic drain until they marry and produce sons. Most parents in this village used to think their daughters could learn all they needed to at home. Then, twenty years ago, the highway was built. Some villagers, like Akbar, began to travel south to the cities to work and have families. They no longer accepted a community that failed to teach its women. Akbar led the campaign for a girls' school. He was not unopposed. One of the village mullahs warned fathers that if girls learned to write, they would write letters to boys, and that could only lead to moral corruption. It would destroy society. His views made an impact, but support for the school won out. Classes started in the community hall last year, and now the government has promised a new building.

On my second night in Nilt, we celebrated Hina's engagement. She was betrothed to Bisharat, Akbar's nephew. A college boy. The wedding was still two years away, but the marriage contract had been settled that morning between Akbar and Hina's father. Akbar swore on the Koran that his nephew would protect the bride and give her everything she needed. His family set aside the sum of five hundred dollars for her, to be left untouched until she asked for it – which few brides ever do. Hina's father pledged that she would be an obedient and loyal wife. The two families were already related, and the bond strengthened the clan.

We walked by moonlight to Hina's house. There was Akbar, me, assorted children and a cousin who carried a suitcase full of bridal gifts on his head. The groom's mother brought the most precious gift of all: butter wrapped in beech bark. It had been buried under the apple tree for more than a year, awaiting a special occasion. We ate it with unleavened bread. It tasted smooth but bitter, like blue cheese.

Tradition demanded that Hina stay out of sight during the quiet celebrations. Bisharat was silent and shy while his new father-in-law spoke of the grandsons he hoped were to come. Akbar proudly opened the suitcase and out spilled shiny fabrics, glass bangles and plastic shoes. The women leaned forward, touching the gifts and nodding their approval. Hina's father stood up just beyond the flow of the kerosene lamp. "I am not a wealthy man," he said. "Neither am I strong. I give you everything I have. Please take care of it." The groom's mother embraced him.

Akbar translated for me and then shared the story of his first marriage. He spoke quietly. He'd been married at the age of eight to a one-year-old cousin. He remembered bitterly how the musicians danced around him and his infant bride. Akbar was twenty-one when he divorced her. Now, fifteen years later, he had a wife he loved and was the head of his family. His nephew's marriage represented a healing, he said. A new beginning. The couple will probably move away from this primitive place, as Akbar has done, and settle in the city, where they will dream of returning.

April 19

✉ I went to the shrine of a Muslim saint recently, where I met a wild-eyed worshipper. He threw his head back and started to sway and chant in Urdu. "Kings come and kings go," he wailed. "It's Allah's will."

Pakistan is a fascinating place to be if you want to meet retired kings. They handed over their princely states and kingdoms to the Pakistan government several decades ago, persuaded by a mixture of threats, bribes and brute force. Now their lives consist of socializing and trying to protect what they have left.

The most eccentric and reclusive of the monarchs I've met is the Khan of Kalat, who lives in Baluchistan. He's the Sardar of Sardars, the King of Kings, which means he is officially the boss of all sub-kings and tribal chiefs in the province. He presides over the Grand Councils that settle disputes between leaders and tribes.

Some people told me he has no real power any more, that his subjects are more interested in getting good jobs in Karachi and the Gulf states. But others say he can still raise ten thousand armed men at the snap of his fingers.

I went to see His Highness the Khan at his house in Quetta, Baluchistan's capital. One of his drivers came to pick me up in a car with tinted windows. A turbaned bodyguard with an AK-47 sub-machine-gun sat in the front seat, listening to heavy-metal music.

The Khan's family has a few enemies, even within its own ranks. His sons wear guns like jewellery. The oldest, Suleman, is heir to the throne. He was badly shot up in Karachi six months ago by thugs who work for his first cousin. He survived and vowed revenge.

"Your own cousin tried to kill you?" I asked. He said they had a feud and he was proud to have started it. He planned to wipe out that whole branch of the family – even if it meant killing his father's sister. "My father won't like it," he said. "He doesn't like violence. But he has to support me. I'm his son."

The present Khan certainly didn't impress me as a martial figure thirsting for battle. He's about fifty and is as wide as he is tall. He is immaculately groomed, with a close-cropped beard and spectacles. And he loves to talk.

He seemed remarkably contented, for a king without a kingdom.

Material things don't matter, he told me. The former state of Khalat once covered all the mountains and deserts of Baluchistan – which is nearly half of Pakistan. It had its own parliament and constitution and proclaimed independence at the time of partition. But the Pakistan army soon crushed the insurrection. Baluch tribesmen still dream of their own country, and the Khan waits to see if they will want him to be king again.

He was depressed about the lack of unity among his people, who design their houses like forts so they can shoot at each other. No wonder he didn't go out much.

His son Faisal took us to the family palace in the village of Kalat. He drove a bullet-proof Land Rover and kept his favourite machine-gun beside him. Clearly, material things mattered more to Faisal than to his father. He waved his arm out the window at a hostile landscape, dotted with nomads and camel caravans. "All this was ours," he said. "But the government took it." Their 1.3 million acres of land was gradually whittled down to 150,000 acres.

The palace was built by the previous Khan to resemble a steam-ship. It has decks, railings and even portholes. It looks wonderfully odd floating in the middle of the desert behind high mud walls. The rooms are filled with regimental silver and photographs of past Khans. Eight thousand saddles, once used by their private armies, are locked in a store-room, in a part of the palace now said to be haunted. The servants shook their heads when I asked about the decline of the empire. They brought out the old state flag and posed for a picture, holding up their guns.

Kalat rule lasted more than three centuries, but people in the area don't expect much from it any more. In the last election, the Khan's two brothers ran for national and provincial seats. They both lost, and a religious leader won. I guess the voters felt that Allah could offer them more.

The Khan himself predicts that the power of kings and chiefs in Baluchistan will soon be wiped out. He has left the militancy and violence to his sons and has retreated from the world. He spends hours reading the Koran and mixing herbs into medicine in his workshop.

His voice became excited as he told me how he sends servants to the mountains to pick plants for his herbal experiments. He said he has found what everyone else is still searching for: a cure for AIDS. He's been working on it for two years. I asked if he'd tried it out on anyone. The answer was no. His son Suleman was shocked that I would question the King of King's discovery. "He's my father and he knows these things. He has the cure." I was silenced. The Khan went on to discuss his remedies for jaundice, diabetes and haemorrhoids, which he hopes to distribute worldwide.

Tribal delegations still visit the Khan and ask him to join politics or at least make public statements. But the poverty of his province and the corruption of politics have defeated him. He told me: "I can't do anything for my people. What would I have for them but words?"

When I think of the Khan, I remember Prospero from Shakespeare's play *The Tempest*. Both men were robbed of their dukedoms. Both turned to books, herbs and spiritualism. Both lived in exile. But Prospero used his art to get his kingdom back. I don't think the Khan's art is strong enough to fight change in modern Pakistan.

May 20

✉ I've always felt a sense of claustrophobia when I see veiled women. I wonder if they feel trapped under all that fabric. Sometimes I see them in the markets in Rawalpindi, but generally they avoid public places. They believe that Allah wants them to stay at home, where the only men they see are their closest relatives.

One afternoon, though, I saw something extraordinary on Murree Road: A tiny, veiled woman driving a Toyota was jockeying fearlessly with a transport truck for road space. The letter L for "learner" was taped on her back windshield, but she drove like a pro. This was my first glimpse of Mrs. Amtul Mirza Awan, founder and owner of Asra Ladies' Driving School.

Months later a mutual friend introduced us. Mrs. Awan agreed to give me a lesson. It was hot – forty-two degrees centigrade. Mrs. Awan was teaching eight hours a day, without air-conditioning.

It took hours to find her place. I pounded on the door, hoping my knock would be heard over the din of all the little industries on her street. A hand with crimson fingernails beckoned me in. Mrs. Awan was wedged between the wall and the door, so no one could see her. She hadn't had time to cover her face.

She hugged me as if she knew me. I marvelled that, in spite of the heat and the fact that she had to hide her face from the world, she was powdered and coiffed. She backcombed her hair to an impressive height, but even then, she was barely five feet tall.

Her business was born of necessity. She told me she spent years looking after her sick parents. When her father died, she was past what is considered a marriageable age for a woman. She found herself single and poor. She worked as a typist but couldn't stand being trapped in an office all day. "What I really wanted," she said, "was my own business."

Mrs. Awan was born in Iran and raised in Iraq, where she took driving lessons. Her family moved to Pakistan in 1973, and she noticed there were no driving schools, at least none for women. Here, she thought, was her niche. In the past twelve years, she's taught more than two thousand women to brave traffic most North Americans would find terrifying. Now it was my turn.

Mrs. Awan put on a black full-length coat over her pants and tunic. By the time she finished buttoning it, the perspiration was streaming down her face. She threw a cape over her head and tied it tightly under her chin. Her deep red lips disappeared as she pulled a black veil across her nose and mouth, bandit style. "Sometimes people laugh at me driving in this *burqa*," she said. "I don't care. It's not difficult to drive in." She has worn it since she was twelve.

When I met her '74 Toyota Corolla, my heart sank. It had been repeatedly soldered, which gave it a very uneven texture. The front end visibly sagged. It looked chewed up and spat out, like a dog that's seen one fight too many. "Asra Motor Institute" was written on the back. *Asra*, Mrs. Awan said, means *journey* – the prophet Muhammad's night journey through the sky. She was proud of the name.

I told her I'd never driven in Pakistan, never driven a standard car and never driven on the left side of the road. She didn't flinch. I started the car.

She'd warned me there is no mercy for the slowpoke. Punjabi drivers practise "offensive driving" religiously. There's no margin for error; no one assesses risk. It's not unusual for a bus to overtake a bus that's overtaking another bus, three abreast on the road. You must be ready to swerve at any time to avoid death.

Mrs. Awan's hand was possessively over mine on the gear shift. She'd kicked off her high heels to work the brake and clutch on her side of the car. I remember her voice like an incantation: "Clutch, clutch, clutch, clutch . . . take it easy, take it easy . . . let it go, let it go . . . "

She was in control, sweating profusely but determined we should live. Twice she wrestled the steering wheel out of my hands. The car creaked and groaned at every seam. I kept asking what gear we were in and feeling tense, dazed and fearful. Packs of taxis and motorcycles carrying whole families careened past us. Drivers used their horns incessantly to communicate or ward off enemies.

In Pakistan, women still aren't welcome behind the wheel. "The men do not want us to drive on their roads," Mrs. Awan told me. She's been known to yell at truck drivers and fight traffic fines in the courts.

Her students, who are often inexperienced and frightened, learn from her. "When they come to me, they become bold," she told me proudly. She believed her work was life-changing. "When a woman drives a car," she said, "she can do so much. Without driving skills, she is helpless – she is without hands." Mrs. Awan is chipping away at age-old barriers, and it doesn't go unnoticed. "Some people do not like me," she admitted. "They say I am spoiling their women."

When the lesson ended, Mrs. Awan touched her forehead to

the dash and whispered, "Thank God." Then she rushed inside to prepare food for me and her husband. She married ten years ago. Her husband spied her in a used-car showroom and sent his brother to negotiate a match. He's not a well man. Her earnings support them both. But she accepts this. After all, the Koran says a woman should have a husband to protect and look after her.

Marriage hasn't fulfilled all her dreams, though. She wanted to be a doctor, then a pilot, but her parents wouldn't consider so much education for a girl. She peeled off her veil and sat down near me. "You know," she said, "I was very active and bold as a child. If there was a high tree where no child would go, I would go to the top of that tree, just to show them it was nothing. I was an adventurer."

Then she turned and disappeared into the kitchen.

Catherine Pigott

THE MORNINGSIDE
BIRD-WATCH

Enough said.
 Unless, of course, you're a raven.

✉ I remember the process by which I became a "birder." This
was not as easy as it may sound.

My conversion was done partly out of self-defence, since Kelly,
my husband, used to spend most of the weekends in the spring
and summer banding birds with his friend Stuart Houston. Early
in our relationship, I arrived in Saskatoon for a visit, was whisked
away from the airport and given fifteen minutes to change before
departing on an owl-banding expedition. I later discovered the
original plan had been to leave directly from the airport.

After Kelly and I became engaged, Stuart decreed that I had to
pass the Pelican Test before the wedding could proceed. No one
can say they have met all the requirements of being a birder until
they survive the Pelican Weekend.

Imagine my delight at the prospect of awakening at two in the
morning to make the trek to the pelican colony. The sunrise was
beautiful. We watched it from the middle of a quagmire of Sas-

katchewan gumbo while we tried to coax our vehicle back onto more solid mud.

By five o'clock I was standing on the shore of the lake. I still had not seen a bird. There was, however, an abundance of large winged creatures buzzing around my head, delighted at the prospect of breakfast.

After an uneventful trip across a lake in a canoe, I finally saw my first birds. As we approached an island, thousands of gulls swarmed into the air, squawking because they had been disturbed so early in the day. I was quickly dispatched to run after baby gulls. The chicks were not thrilled with this. They excreted and/or regurgitated their breakfast all over my hands while their parents dive-bombed me.

Six hundred Ring-bills and Californias were banded, then we moved on to the pelicans. The gulls had not wanted to be banded, but they did not protest nearly as much as the baby pelicans! When we pulled an individual from the closely packed "pod," they protested vehemently from both ends of their bodies. I had been warned it would be a smelly day.

Permission was granted for the wedding to proceed. Since then, Kelly and I have spent many pleasant weekends trekking across Saskatchewan with the Houstons. My advice to anyone setting out to pass the Pelican Test is to remember to wear a hat.

Cathy Tomlinson-Wylie
Munster, Ontario

✉ I look forward each year to several days in May at Point Pelee, scouring the beaches, trees and bushes for warblers, Indigo Buntings and (hope springs eternal . . .) Scissor-tailed Flycatchers.

We who journey to Pelee every spring for the migration have as many field marks, in our own way, as the birds we go to see. Hanging from our necks are the requisite binoculars – how else can you distinguish a Long-billed Dowitcher from a Short-billed Dowitcher? Although, to be honest, binoculars don't really help all that much with dowitchers. Also decorating the chest is a camera with lens of almost obscene length. How else can you get that magazine-cover-quality close-up? The truly dedicated bird watchers also carry over their shoulder a spotting scope on a tripod that can be set up pretty darned fast when the cry is heard, "Laughing Gull, just to the right of that piece of driftwood."

Now for our clothing. Let it never be said that birders are not image conscious. We just have our own style, a sort of uniform oddity: multi-pocketed pants and vests (how else can we carry field guides and extra camera lenses?) and slouch hats to shade our eyes. The migration hits its peak in May, but it's quite common to see people in ski jackets, warm-up pants, winter hats and gloves. Most experienced birders also carry a knapsack with rain gear in it and probably a thermos of hot coffee.

Birders also use words in their own way. If a birder stops and stares intently into the bushes with binoculars for more than about twenty seconds, someone will come up and say, "What have you got?" The verb "get" takes on new meaning among birders – it replaces "see" but has the added ego-nourishment that comes from being the *first* to spot the Kentucky Warbler and the first to report it to the visitor centre staff.

I sometimes think the fun of Point Pelee in the spring is as much in our experiences as in the returning birds. For example, how many times in your life would you stop and ask for directions to a town's sewage lagoon if you weren't chasing down birds?

Well, in Comber, near Point Pelee, the corner-gas-station attendant has had so many inquiries for directions to the sewage lagoon that he took one look at us and began to intone, like a recorded announcement: "Take the first street to the right, go about a block. Take the gravel road straight ahead, then veer to the right, past the tile and cement company, and you're there." *Fifty* cars were in the Comber sewage lagoon parking lot! (There were also lots of birds, including a Parula Warbler – good bird.)

Birding is a competitive but sharing activity – you want to be the first to see and identify the "good" bird, but it's important that someone else (preferably not a mate, who might be suspected of bias) share and confirm your sightings. You all stand poised, binoculars ready to snap into position at the merest hint of motion in the tangle. Suddenly, someone says in a hushed, excited whisper, "There, just above the stump, the one to the left with the bit of moss on it." All eyes, all binoculars train on the spot, and a chorus of "I've got it" echoes throughout the woods. Now comes breathy admiration, then exclamations of delight and wonder at the vibrant, exquisite coloration of such a tiny, elusive bird. It's like finding rubies or emeralds in a gravel bed.

A brief moment, then a flutter and streak, and the Golden-wing is gone. Lists come out, and small ticks of satisfaction mark the sighting. A most satisfying moment, but it lasts only until a faint cry is heard across the forest – "Black-throated Blue" – and the eager group of birders embarks upon its own migration.

Samm MacKay
Waterloo, Ontario

✉ I have a friend who maintains a Mountain Bluebird trail, and he despises the English Sparrow because they decimated the bluebird population soon after they arrived in Alberta.

Each year in early spring, he visits his bluebird boxes south of Lethbridge and makes whatever repairs are necessary. When the bluebird couples have arrived, my friend makes periodic visits to see how they are faring.

One summer day he checked the nest box and noted that the baby bluebirds were healthy and would probably be ready to fly away in a couple of days. He returned to the box a few days later to find that English Sparrows had chased off the parents, ripped the heads off the baby bluebirds, chucked the bodies out and taken over the nest.

My friend the avid sparrow hater now has a sparrow trap in his back yard. It's a large cage, and sparrows are lured in by grain and water but they cannot figure how to get out. He disposes of the sparrows in a humane manner (usually the garbage-bag-and-tailpipe method). In his back yard where only sparrows used to shriek, he has warblers and other native birds nesting.

My next-door neighbour has a tile roof, which acts as a condominium for sparrows in spring. When they are hungry, the birds come and feast on goodies in my garden. I'm thinking about making a sparrow trap myself. I hope God won't see the sparrows fall and will just hear the native songbirds that fly in to take their place.

Debby Gregorash
Coaldale, Alberta

✉ I don't care for starlings and feel fortunate that we see no more than two or three a year on our property. Still, I decided some years ago that these are interesting birds. I have been fooled by a lovely song into going to the window in search of a "respectable" bird only to find a starling the only bird in sight. I remember twenty years ago when I lived in Guelph often looking out the kitchen window on a blustery morning to see starlings lined up around the top of my neighbour's chimney looking quite toasty. There was a pear tree in our back garden. Not caring much for pears, we picked only a few, and many dozens of pears were left on the tree. To my astonishment, the starlings came and ate all the pears but left the cores hanging there, creating a surrealistic picture indeed!

April Steele
Maberly, Ontario

✉ I once spent a few years in Prince Rupert, where the wolf and the raven figure prominently. On the Prince Rupert golf course, I heard a most remarkable noise made by a raven. We were walking from the tenth green to the eleventh tee when I heard one call. I looked up and saw it sitting on the top of a tall tree overlooking the tee, and probably most of the course. When it called again, I was able to hear it clearly. It made the sound of a golf club swinging and hitting a ball, followed by cackling laughter. Swish, plock, cackle.

You can imagine what it had seen.

If you've ever played Rupert, you may recall sliding around in the red-mud rough, searching under dripping bushes and wondering if your ball went in the window of the half-buried Chrysler hulking there.

Maybe that's what the raven finds so funny.

R.J. Bowering
Vernon, British Columbia

✉ Last spring a raven chose to spend a good deal of its time loitering around our barnyard. We soon dubbed it "our raven" and assumed that it had moved in because we were gentle folk who had a nice place with a variety of birds, wild and domesticated. The large, lustrous-black bird with the big beak spent a lot of its time on a pile of white limestone or on a nearby fence post. It was a solitary bird, but apparently quite happy.

We have two geese, and we rather hoped that they were goose and gander. The two of them made a nest out of old down and hay in the barnyard, near the limestone pile. They fussed around the nest, and we assumed that, in the manner of geese, there would soon be a dozen eggs or so in the nest. But when we peeked under the hay to count the hidden eggs, to our surprise there was only one. A couple of days later, there was still only one. Call us slow, but it took us a while to connect a sleek, clinging raven to a shortage of goose eggs. Our suspicions were soon confirmed. I saw a goose leave the nest; the raven appeared, uncovered the egg and flew with the heavy object to a nearby field, where it promptly ate the egg.

After our innocence was lost, we competed with the raven for goose eggs and most days managed to get at least one.

Robert and Wendy Snefjellå
Bancroft, Ontario

✉ *The Ravens of Fort McMurray*

In Fort McMurray, Alberta,
When it's forty below
The ravens eat.

They jump on the lids of garbage cans
And jump on the lids of garbage cans
And jump on the lids of garbage cans
Till the lids come off.
Then they eat.

People who don't like mess
Tape the lids to their garbage cans.
Does this bother the ravens?
Hardly at all.

In Fort McMurray, Alberta,
The town is divided into districts
And each district has its garbage picked up
On a different day.

The ravens know this.
And they know Tuesday from Wednesday.
They are never wrong.

Each morning when the garbage trucks go out
They are met by a black cloud
Of ravens
Who know the right time
Who know the right place.

In Fort McMurray, Alberta,
When it's forty below
The ravens eat.

Merna Summers
Edmonton

✉ In Faro, in the Yukon, the street lights operate on some sort of light-sensitive system. When the lights go off for a while on a winter afternoon, the ravens perch on top of them and stretch their wings down over the light bulbs and make them come on again. I have seen three of them lined up behind each other with their wings spread down to keep the lights on, presumably for the warmth.

They only do this when the lights go out, and they always make them come on again. This is not an intelligent bird?

Dorothy Tattrie
Kimberley, British Columbia

✉ One fairly unproductive day, when there were not many salmon or striped bass running, I was enjoying the sun while lounging in a chair outside our ramshackle fishing cabin on the Saint John River, in New Brunswick. It was a typical Maritimes summer day except it wasn't raining, and I was thinking about pulling my net out in order to take a swim over at the Mactaquac Headpond. I was suddenly assaulted by the high-pitched screech of a black-feathered joker bird, who was situated, as usual, on top of one of the big beech trees that surround our landing. Startled, I lost the co-ordination required to maintain the precarious balance of my chair and fell heels over head into the sand.

I proceeded to undertake a vigorous missile assault on my antagonist, intending to do it physical harm. It was out of reach on its lofty perch, where it continued to voice its displeasure with my lazy attitude. With my failure weighing heavily on my mind, and the sand in my long hair, I decided to get into my canoe and retrieve my net.

My mood was further ripened after I paddled several hundred feet out to my net only to find it in a great tangle of driftwood, dead eels and heavy iron objects. I could still hear the raven's call, and it kept me boiling.

While I was untangling the net, I saw my uncle's car coming

down the hill to our landing. My uncle got out of the car and shouted some unintelligible message to me, then held up a white plastic grocery bag. Immediately I recognized it as my lunch. He walked over to the fallen chair, righted it, set my lunch on it and before I could holler to let him know I needed help, he hopped into his car and drove away.

Thanks, I thought.

I went right back to work on the net. My objective was to finish the job then paddle to the landing and haul net, ropes, anchors, paddles and canoe up above the high-water mark, then enjoy my lunch before I went for a much-needed swim.

Thirty minutes later, as I neared the shore line, I realized that I had not heard the raven's call for a while.

My thoughts turned to the white plastic bag and its contents. What was for lunch? Roast beef? Chicken? Spaghetti? Fried-egg sandwiches?

I reached the shore line and hauled the canoe, net, paddles, lines and anchor up the bank, then turned my attention to the bag.

It was gone.

I spotted it in the grass a few feet behind the chair, and the feathered behind of that master of skulduggery, the raven, was sticking out of the bag. Its head was buried in white plastic.

I charged my enemy, hurling verbal obscenities as I ran. It pulled its head out of the bag. But before I could close in to complete the kill, the raven shoved its beak back into the bag, secured a final morsel and prepared for serious flight. I could plainly see that the crook had my pastry in its beak.

In momentary blindness and confusion, symptoms of extreme anger and frustration, I ran into the chair at full tilt. I felt myself soaring into the air, once again heels over head.

As I walked up the hill, a defeated and humble man, the raven added insult to injury by gently calling with a sound that resembled a laugh – at least it sounded like a laugh to my tormented ears.

Patrick M. Polchies
Fredericton

✉ My husband and I have been feeding the birds every winter since 1976. Already this winter we have put out more than two hundred pounds of whole sunflower seeds for the grosbeaks, Blue Jays and other large birds. We are up to nearly a hundred pounds of hulled sunflower seeds for the small birds. These include gold-finches (which are no longer gold, as they now have their winter feathers of olive drab), Pine Siskins, sparrows, Purple Finches and chickadees, plus a few other assorted transients.

Our favourite is the chickadee. They are here all year round. They are the most polite bird I know – they never squabble and peck. They come to the feeders, take one sunflower seed and fly to a barberry bush near the feeder; holding the seed on the branch between their feet, they eat it completely – not wasting a morsel! Then they fly to the feeder for another seed and repeat the process. Compare that to finches and other birds, which hog the feeder and waste time and seeds fighting off other birds. Or Blue Jays, which gobble up many whole seeds and store them in their cheeks – after which they fly to the woods and hide them and come back for more. I have read that the Blue Jays often can't find them again.

Chickadees are very friendly and easy to train. They come and eat out of my hand. They especially like peanuts, which I reserve for them exclusively.

Jean Rodgers
Sable River, Nova Scotia

✉ For two years, a chickadee I call Scraggy would swoop over our lawns onto my shoulder or hands while I stood on the deck around our house. As I walked down the winding path to the Saint John River, he would call, I'd mimic him and he would come swooping down. He would follow me on my walks, sometimes to the lighthouse a quarter of a mile away.

Last year he didn't come back. I still miss him. Other chickadees will feed from my hand, but only if I am near the feeder, and they don't look right in my face and talk to me.

Berna Critchlow
Westfield, New Brunswick

✉ Unlike other birds who may or may not show up on any particular morning, chickadees are always there, even in the worst weather. They can always be relied on to appear and make a comment. If you've ever had one within your reach on a bare twig who scolded you because you were too close to the feeder, you'll know that chickadees have a sure sense of who they are and what they want and how they can get it. Chickadees are friendly individualists, companionable yet independent, never stooping to the mob panic that strikes flocks of jays or grosbeaks. With their bold, bright glance, they can take your measure in one uncomfortable instant; they are neither intimidated nor impressed by your superior size.

Common? Sure, and thank goodness they are. Let's hear it for the energy, self-reliance and unpretentiousness of the everyday, everywhere chickadee.

Cathy Simpson
Lewisporte, Newfoundland

✉ Chickadees boring? Hardly!

Please allow me to set you straight on this interesting little bird. I have some knowledge of the subject, having spent many years hand-feeding and enjoying their company. My normal day starts with a ramble in a neighbouring wood lot. The chickadees are often already waiting in a nearby tree when I step outside armed with a pocket full of peanuts in the shell. Off we go, man, dog and chickadee escort – they follow along in their unique rollercoaster flight pattern. Whenever we pause in our walk, the chick-adees gather round in anticipation of a hand-out.

If I attempt to buy them off with some seed other than peanuts, the seeds are tossed away and the birds impale me with a black beady-eyed glare. If they land on an empty palm, they drum away on my fingers or palm.

I marvel that these tiny birds can withstand the biting cold of some of our winter nights. Their secret, of course, is insulation. On a very cold morning, they appear almost twice their normal size as they arrive with feathers puffed out to resist the freezing cold.

John R. Lisle
Marmora, Ontario

✉ My husband and I operate a summer camp for children on Salt Spring Island, and we have several Muscovy Ducks.

Seven of the Muscovies were given to us by two female university students who were my husband's patients. (He is a medical doctor in addition to being a camp director.) The two girls asked him if he would take six ducks initially, as they felt they couldn't afford them. The girls were tearful at giving them up. The six ducks had arrived and settled in when we received yet another tearful call explaining the plight of Sophie and Elvis, the pair who had produced the six. Apparently Sophie had gone missing the night her children had been sent away, presumably fallen prey to a raccoon, and this left Elvis in a state of pining loneliness. Would we take Elvis also? It was cautiously explained to us that Elvis was an orphan when the girls got him, and he was brought up with a litter of puppies; ever since he'd been trying to bark. He had imprinted on people and he seemed to have a special fondness for men. With some misgivings, we agreed to accept Elvis. Elvis's character was quickly evident. He would roam around the entrance to the property, greeting all visitors with his characteristic husky, rasping throat noise, and walk with his head and neck jerking back and forth. He became affectionately referred to as our "watch duck."

Then one of our camp counsellors thought Elvis would do nicely on her boy-friend's farm back home. So Elvis was crated up – along with a female duck for a mate – and went on the train to Alberta. I've heard since that they are doing well there. I'm sure that soon Muscovies will be controlling the fly population in Alberta, too!

Carol Voorhoeve
Salt Spring Island, British Columbia

✉ On my parents' farm in the Dresden area of south-west Ontario, Muscovy Ducks were standard fare.

There were usually one or two females and one drake with his red eye patches. They were overwintered in the hen-house with the chickens. As they were let out to forage for themselves in the spring, they chased bugs and flies and butterflies, took short flights for a swim in the ditch, then the females settled down to making a nest, laying their greenish eggs and hatching out perhaps six or eight yellow downy ducklings in the cow barn.

The next event was to capture the female – usually by dropping a burlap feed bag over her head – and pinioning two kilograms of hissing, striking neck and bill, clawing webbed feet and pummelling wings. She and her ducklings were then transferred to the safety of a wooden coop – ours was always under the black walnut trees near the barn. Safe from skunks and racoons, the duck family was fed and watered. I remember removing feed and water cans from the slatted front of the coop and replacing refilled ones while trying to escape the striking bill of the protective mother. I also remember the pain of a direct hit.

After a few weeks or so of growth, the coop would be propped up during the day so the ducklings could be taught to forage for themselves. The coop was moved to fresh grass regularly and oh! the pungent area left behind! Over the course of the summer, the ducklings put out pin feathers and grew quickly. Regularly, they waddled out the lane to the ditch for a swim.

Summer baseball games often involved skidding on duck poop as the Muscovies increased their range.

A vivid memory of mine is from June of '69, coming home from a Trudeau rally in Chatham to find heavy rain had left several ducklings drenched and near death. A quick trip into the house and under a heat lamp in a box brought immediate success.

Elizabeth Dawson
North West River, Labrador

✉ When I was a child in New Brunswick, for some reason still unknown to me we kept a group of Muscovy Ducks. While some people marvel at the fly-killing ability of the ducks, I must say what we marvelled at was the ability of the ducks to make feces.

I can recall several occasions playing "500" on the lawn and going for a high fly ball and loosing one's footing in the mire on the ground.

Some experts have suggested that some civilizations employ these ducks inside the house. This just boggles the mind!

Grant Goodine
Bridgetown, Nova Scotia

✉ Beth and I suffer from a serious house-fly problem. We thought we had it licked several years ago when we had our old farmhouse insulated. It stopped the fly invasion cold – for three years. Last summer was notable for infestations of fleas and flies. We now find ourselves back in the battle hook, line and fly-swatter. We also happen to be duck fanciers, and after hearing about the fly-eating ducks we are determined to give them a try on fly patrol. (Do you think they can hover under a fly-infested skylight?)

296

We became dispirited about ducks several years ago after Andy, our Rouen drake, was killed by a neighbour's dog. Andy was following us on a walk; we didn't realize it, and the dog did him dirt. He (the duck Andy) would follow us around and play "fetch." His version was to yank on my pants leg until I picked him up and threw him in the air. Once airborne, he could fly several hundred feet. He would then race back to us on foot and worry my pants leg until I threw him again. He sort of fetched himself. He also swam with us in the pond and went for long walks through the fields with us. He was a sterling character in all regards, though he didn't eat many flies as far as we noticed.

Peter Powning
Sussex, New Brunswick

✉ Until last fall I had no knowledge of breeds of chickens. In fact, chickens as living birds held no real interest for me. And then came the science fair project. Encouraged by our oldest daughter, a student at the University of Guelph, our eleven-year-old decided to hatch chicks at home.

Approximately one hundred dollars and several months later, we had a wooden incubator in an upstairs bedroom and a pen in the basement containing Squiggles and Squeak, two Barred Plymouth Rock chickens hatched from eggs acquired through the poultry research department at Guelph. Living in a bushel basket, to keep him separate from the larger chicks, was the result of our second attempt at hatching, Jimmy.

By early March, Squiggles was an almost fully grown hen, weighing probably four or five pounds, friendly and domesticated. Squeak, on the other hand, was a slightly smaller, feisty rooster who crowed at disconcerting moments and would often startle guests because he was not limited to sunrise for his noise-making. (Some people find it a little difficult to concentrate on a bridge hand when a rooster unexpectedly starts to crow in the basement at eleven o'clock at night.)

It became quite an interesting project for all of us. We carefully balanced humidity and temperature in the incubator and turned those eggs four times every day. At the end, when they were close to hatching, it was fascinating to see that the eggs moved, and we could hear the little chicks cheeping from inside the shell. The hatching process had us all huddled around the incubator watching with bated breath while those chicks took their own time to peck their way out.

The chicks were grey-black in colour, not the traditional yellow, but they were little balls of fluff at first. As their feathers came in, they changed to the distinctive black-and-white stripes that mark Barred Plymouth Rock chickens.

Then reality set in. Chickens require care. And they are *not* clean pets. They require feeding and watering several times each day, and what goes in at one end comes out the other, on the bottom of the pen and in their food and water dishes. Cleaning the pen and bowls became a real chore. Can you picture the scene? The chicks would be captured and removed to bushel baskets (the only container of appropriate size we could come up with). Then the cleaning process would begin, accompanied by moans, groans and gags from the eleven-year-old, the ostensible owner and keeper of these chicks. When the cleaning was complete, the chicks would be returned to the pen with fresh food and water, to begin the process all over again. And chickens *smell*, particularly in the basement!

Our family did find the project fascinating and worthwhile. The cat, as you can imagine, was mesmerized by this food on the hoof (or claw), which she seemed to feel should be hers for the taking. Our golden retriever spent many hours sitting by the pen, cocking his head this way and that, while he tried to figure them out. When a dog barks beside a chicken pen, it is interesting to see how the chicks fly about flapping and screeching.

In the end, my husband found a good home for Squiggles, Squeak and Jimmy. The pen was fitted carefully into the back of our station-wagon (with great foresight, my husband had built it to fit exactly), and the chicks were transported, squawking and flapping, from our home in Oakville to a farm north of Whitby. I wasn't along but I understand that the drive across the 401 was particularly interesting, not least because of the reactions of other drivers.

Cathy Cormier
Oakville, Ontario

✉ I spent some happy summer vacations at the hobby farm of friends, at Oka, circa 1935. My late mother and our hostess made a weekly trip to "la Trappe" (the local name for the Trappist monastery and agricultural college–where the Chantecler chicken was developed, along with Oka cheese) to buy fresh vegetables, fruit, cheese, milk, poultry and Chantecler eggs. As I recall, Mother thought the eggs were particularly good so she asked the monk who was in charge if it might be possible for them to ship a few dozen each week to our home in Westmount. The shipping method chosen was, believe it or not, parcel post via the Canadian Post Office. The monks made a solid plywood box to hold several layers of papier mâché egg flats and a quantity of straw, and that is how we received our weekly supply of eggs for several years thereafter. In all the time that we got our eggs this way, only a few were ever broken or cracked. The box was put on the morning train from Oka to Montreal and a parcel post truck delivered it the same day.

M.L. de Martigny
Willowdale, Ontario

✉ We'd always wondered why the little greasy spoon down the street and around the corner was called The Chantecler. It was one of those true university haunts–open after everything else is closed, its menu priced for the student budget. It specialized in one of the worst pizzas I'll ever eat. But its most outstanding feature was outside the restaurant, on the roof. There, on top of The Chantecler, was a huge, six-foot-high, pink neon chicken.

We never knew the Chantecler was a chicken – we thought they were just trying to be fancy by giving it a French name.

The Chantecler is gone now. Like so many other lovely old spots in Halifax, it was torn down. But we will never forget the big pink chicken glowing proudly in the darkness of the early morning – its beak majestically pointing us in the direction of home.

Ron and Kelly Sherrard
Halifax

✉ Students of Chaucer will remember the Nun's Priest's Tale, which concerns Chanticler (cock or rooster) and Pertelot (or Partelot), his favourite wife. This story is believed to have derived from an old French fable popular in medieval times and perhaps much further back than that.

The name Chanticler (one of several spellings) is not difficult to explain, I think.

Chant – to chant or sing – all birds were believed to have sung in earlier times.

Cler – sometimes spelt clair, clere, or clear – signifies light, as in *au clair de la lune,* or clerestory.

Thus the name Chanticler is appropriate for a cock or rooster who sings at dawn. Of course, other birds really sing at dawn but less penetratingly than the barnyard rooster.

Betty Millway
Burnaby, British Columbia

✉ Just after the war in Europe ended, my mother and I were surviving in a displaced persons' camp in Germany. Food was even more scarce than during the war. My mother traded something, probably a ring or her watch, for an old White Leghorn hen. When the hen got broody, we traded with a local farmer twenty of her eggs for ten fertilized ones from his flock. This clutch produced two delicious roosters and eight hens. The birds grew up large and of assorted colours. Mostly darkish, red and brown and black.

The coop was very close to our barrack, and the chickens, although allowed to roam free, stayed fairly close, and in the summer when the door was left open, occasionally wandered indoors looking for special hand-outs to augment what they could scratch up for themselves. When they started laying, seven were quite happy to use the nests provided in the coop, but one, the darkest, somehow managed to lay her first egg indoors on my bunk. Thereafter she would not lay anywhere else and used to stand outside the door and complain loudly and almost panic until she was allowed in to do her thing. Having music on the radio made her even more happy.

This habit made it very easy to keep track of her efforts. This hen was very prolific and quite often produced two eggs in less than twenty-four hours. She'd lay one in the morning, making me get out of bed earlier than I would have liked, and then again in late evening. It seemed that she would do that particularly after taking a day or two off. I don't know why, and it's too late to ask, but my mother used to mark her output on our calendar.

"Blackie" ran up a total of 362 eggs in 362 days, just three days short of a year, and then decided to take a vacation. I remember our disappointment at the time that she didn't quite make an egg a day for an entire year.

We gave the flock away to other DPs when emigration to Canada became a reality. Perhaps our favourite hen did even better with her new owners, providing they allowed her access to a bed and radio.

Al Vitols
Vancouver

✉ In 1930, Hen Number Six, which belonged to a Mrs. Routledge of Sardis, British Columbia, produced 357 eggs in 365 days. I'll never forget the excitement. My father, Harold Hicks, superintendent of the Dominion Experimental Farm at Agassiz, British Columbia, checked each morning to see if the bird had done her thing!

A little background. Each year from 1920 to 1938, the farm ran a contest in which prominent poultry breeders entered a pen of ten birds, each bearing a leg band number that was used to record individual production. Good results increased the farmer's prestige when selling fertile eggs to the hatcheries.

357 eggs in 365 days sounds like a good year's work to me.

Odetta Keating
Penticton, British Columbia

✉ *The Ballad of Hen Number Six*

(To the tune of "The British Grenadiers")
Some sing of Chicken Little, some boast of Chaunticleer.
Some claim that Victorine was a pullet without peer;
But the bravest bird of bounty, you poultry heretics,
Was the fruitful, fertile, fecund, female fowl, famed Hen
    Number Six!

She laid her ovoid offerings three hundred times a year.
Conception was her cause, reproduction her career.
But now in hen nirvana, her nest no more a crib,
In her roost in the sky, her battle cry is "Long live chicken
    lib!"

Alison Mackay and David Fallis
Toronto

✉ I used Hen Number Six as a subject for the first cartoon I sold –for five dollars! –to the Vancouver *Province* in 1926 when I was 18. (I am now 18 reversed.) This Hen Number Six cartoon egged me on to hatch many more over the years.

Here's a limerick to commemorate this laying L – egg – horn.

> Hen Number Six did her stuff
> Tho' egg-laying contests are tough.
> She was able to lay
> An egg every day
> *Un oeuf* every day is enough.

E.A. Harris
Vancouver

AN EGGSELLENT EGGSAMPLE

DARK NIGHTS OF THE SOUL

In the midst of the two seasons covered by this book, one of *Morningside*'s own small band of producers was forced to stop working by unmanageable depression. Another – the redoubtable Sheri Lecker – spent many of her non-CBC hours working on hotlines with other potential victims. In my own extra-curricular life, one journalistic executive I knew more than slightly, the father of four lively young children, committed suicide; someone else I knew well wrestled all the time with un-nameable demons.

Depression – not just feeling blue, as all of us do from time to time, but something that is, as one writer says in this chapter, beyond the "continuum of sadness" – seemed all around us.

In the season of 1990-91, we did an hour on clinical depression. Here are some of the stories that came back to us.

✉ I am now thirty-six years old and as a teenager and young adult frequently but quietly tried to kill myself. I have struggled for years to be a sane, functioning human being and on the surface succeeded to some extent. All my life I felt that there was something wrong with me and only realized and accepted this past month that it was never me but what was done to me.

As a child the messages I heard were all "Don't be" messages. "Don't be so stupid." "Don't be so immature." "Don't think." "Don't feel." "Don't be so selfish." "Don't be so noisy." "Don't be so disrespectful." And so on.

By the time I was a teenager, the messages were so internalized that I believed that I should not "be" any more at all. Dying by my own hand seemed the only way to give everyone what they wanted.

A month ago I realized, accepted and believed that I was sexually abused as a child. This was the missing piece that has kept me from healing into a whole person all these years even though I had done a lot of work in therapy and on my own. I now realize how many of the "Don't be" messages were part of my family's denial of a horror they could not acknowledge let alone discuss.

As a parent I realize how black and white things are for children. My daughter, who is now fifteen years old, is the most accurate feedback I can find on how honest I'm being in my life. Adults create grey areas. They do what they want and justify it later. Children question those grey areas, frequently at the most embarrassing times. Most adults react by calling children liars or laughing about their over-active imaginations or by silencing them completely.

On the subject of teen-age suicides, I am not surprised when I hear of them, what surprises me is that there are not more.

Over and over, people wish longingly to be young again. The message to children and teens is that they are living the best years of their lives. For many young people, these best years are pain-filled nightmares. A time when they may be being emotionally, physically or sexually abused. A time when their rights are controlled by others and used against them. If these are their good years, why on earth would they want to stick around for the bad?

I keep telling my daughter when times are tough at school, "Hang in there, kid, it gets better, I promise." Any complaints I may have had as a child or teen would have been met with, "You think you've got it tough, look around, others have it a lot worse." So what was I expected to do with my "bad" feelings?

I have many people in my life who are open to questioning their own lives and don't feel the need to silence me as my family did. I do not know a woman who has not been affected in some way by incest, rape, harassment, unwanted sexual advances, physical or emotional abuse. I also know men who were sexually abused. I strongly suspect that the statistics on sexual abuse of children, particularly female, are vastly misleading. Many women effec-tively block out all memories of abuse so their response to any question would be, "No, it never happened to me."

In our society families are sacred. We need to stop treating all families as places of stability and safety.

Rose Stanton
Plantagenet, Ontario

✉ People so often think dangerous depression shows up in the "blues" – wrong, so wrong. Many of us who contemplate suicide are so fearful we *might*, the last thing we exhibit is a black mood. Ever.

When I tried it, I made sure I wouldn't be found for a whole weekend (having a fear of ending up vegetablized instead of dead); hooked the hose from exhaust pipe to inside the car (so it wouldn't leak out and be seen); went looking for the cat (remembering stories of exhaust seeping into a house from an attached garage). When I picked her up to put her outside, all by herself for a whole weekend – she reached up a small paw to my face, and that was that. I couldn't go through with it.

Anonymous

✉ "There are two kinds of people in the world . . . "

Statements that begin like that can be witty and perceptive or stupid and bigoted. But for me, the starkest and most undeniable ending to that opening is "people who *know* depression and people who don't."

To put it as simply as I can, severe depression causes such pain that the sufferer will do *anything* to get relief. "Anything" includes suicide.

Is depression the extreme end on the continuum of sadness? I say emphatically that it isn't.

There is a line, or rather an edge, that one tumbles over. And one knows it. I fell over that edge a few years ago. I was lucky. Tricyclic anti-depressants worked for me. I survived.

I survived with new understanding. The drug, a chemical, cured me. Therefore, the condition, depression, is some kind of chemical imbalance and not a punishment for failing to live up to some standard or other.

If the first drug had not worked, I would have tried others. If those did not work – and there are people for whom these drugs do not work – I would have tried ECT. If ECT did not work, I would have tried the final "anything."

Jolting a human brain with one hundred volts of electricity is an unsettling thought. But if unsettling thoughts are on a continuum, ECT is a long, long way from suicide.

Francesca Scalzo
Toronto

✉ I am one of those irrepressibly cheerful people. I am reasonably happy and am always smiling. Life is good and rich for me, and I enjoy it to the full.

Yet I am the survivor of two depressions. The first occurred while I was in grade thirteen. It almost cost me my year. I believed, foolishly, that I had learned enough to make me impervious to another episode. This was not true. Ten years later I again had the occasion to kiss the ground and mean it. The second time I was aware of what was happening to me.

The second episode is recent enough that it still pains me to think about it. I recovered, because I was grimly determined to do so. I worked very hard at it. I also owe a great debt to my friends and co-workers. They were totally puzzled by my behaviour. I will be forever in their debt for their patience and forbearance.

I cannot really describe how it feels. What does it mean when you drive to work weeping the whole way? Since I work with the public, I had to smile while they were there, but the tears were there as soon as the people were gone. In grade thirteen, I ate compulsively and in secret. I gained an enormous amount of weight, which did little for my self-esteem. This time I found that although I was desperately hungry, food was totally repulsive to me. People kept congratulating me for losing weight. Thanks, but I would rather have been fat.

I wish that I had sought help earlier when I was sick. I had to make it through both times without much help from the medical profession. The first time the GP announced that I was perfectly healthy. This time I consulted a doctor rather late in the game, but she was a great help to me. She was supportive and I felt there was someone keeping an eye on me. But going to a GP is not enough. The medical field encompasses a huge body of knowledge. A general practitioner is aware of the anti-depressants on the market, but does not deal with them on a daily basis. I would prefer to be treated by a specialist in this field.

Right now I am very happy. I have made a much-needed transfer to a new town. I have a new apartment with a beautiful mountain view. I have many friends both here and elsewhere. Life is good to me. Perhaps I am stronger for what I have endured. Perhaps I appreciate my happiness more.

Carolyn Fysh
Banff, Alberta

308

✉ One of the things I did to put myself through college was to work in the state mental hospital in my home town. We called it "The Hill" and indeed it was up on a hill, on the edge of town, and from certain points you could see down below the Susquehanna River winding its leisurely way to Chesapeake Bay and the ocean.

Some of the buildings were not unlike the older buildings at college – stone or brick, ivy-covered, with broad porches. The hospital had been conceived of as an "inebriate asylum" – I believe the first one of its kind in the United States – and must have been intended primarily as a sanatorium for high-class drunks. By the time I worked there, it had been operating as a hospital for the insane for years and years. I ended up working there as an "orderly" (O irony!). I needed a summer job, something that would pay more than waitressing at a summer resort or baby-sitting.

I took myself over to the Employment Bureau. Could I type? No. Could I drive a car? No. What was my job experience?

The woman shook her head. She had only one steady job that required no experience and that was at the mental hospital, as an orderly. Did I think my parents would let me work there? It was long hours but good pay and I would not be required to do anything that might endanger me. (That's how she put it – "anything that might endanger you.") I persuaded a friend of mine, the daughter of a doctor who did volunteer work at the state hospital a few days a month, to apply as well and, borrowing her brother's convertible, off we went.

My friend quit on the second day and I didn't really blame her. We had no idea what we were getting into (I still don't understand why her father didn't tell us), and I was so *stunned* when I entered my first ward, Ward 88, called by the rest of the hospital "The Shit Ward," that I was unable to move. There was a long corridor, with a few side rooms off it, then the nurses' station, then the general ward. The noise was dreadful, as was the smell. Thirty-eight to forty old women, all bed-ridden, muttering, screaming, cursing – some so thin all I could think of was the phrase "when we dead awaken."

This was not the only ward I worked on (I was "relief" so I was shifted around a lot) but it was my introduction to the world of the damned and I still don't know whatever possessed me (and I use that word deliberately) to stay out the summer and come back again, and again. I worked on the shock wards, both ECT, where I sometimes held down the patients' feet so they wouldn't "get in the way," and insulin, which made the women enormously fat and which I think is never used any more as it's so hard on the body. I worked in the operating theatre: I was present at lobotomies, amputations, the birth of babies. The people I worked with were tough, outspoken nurses who talked openly of abortions and sexual matters generally and who, for the most part, treated all these sad people with a compassion that amazed me. They taught me to smoke, to roll an efficient cotton swab, to get a patient into a strait-jacket or into the baths without using violence, to "think of England," as one of them used to joke, when sluicing down sheets covered in pee and shit. (I almost wrote "urine and excrement" but that's not what they said.) This was just before the big Thorazine breakthrough – now there are "chemical strait-jackets" and things like that to keep most of the wards more orderly (that word again).

I was not allowed to work on the violent ward and I was just as glad – these wards seemed violent enough for me. The door to the corridor was always locked; the elevator opened only with a key. (I wore a set of keys on a lanyard around my waist.)

You have to understand that all this had *nothing to do with me*; I was merely "paying for my education." Nothing like this could ever happen to me – I was seventeen, then eighteen, then nineteen, strong in limb and sound of mind. The other nurses and orderlies called me "the Princess."

Yet only ten years later I went through a dark night of the soul, after the death of a baby, that led me so close to madness I later wondered if that earlier time had been a kind of mithridatism (remember him? the king who took a little poison every day so that he could never be poisoned by his enemies) and kept me, in the end, from "losing my mind."

I once read a book on problems in perception that contained the phrase, "the word cat cannot scratch you." But it can – if you are in an altered state of consciousness. There are so many rituals you have to obey and so many phobias to confront. At one time certain words, either "sharp" words (knife, axe, glass, needle – especially needle) or "red" words (blood, wound, break, tear, death) would, if spoken by someone, detach themselves from the sentence and move around the walls of a room like a message at Times Square. People would become very tiny, very far away or else too big (I couldn't go to the movies at all as my mind wouldn't make the necessary optical-perceptual adjustment). I was terrified almost twenty-four hours a day.

I do think the memory of what it would be like in one of those places, plus my strong love for my family, kept me from going under. (One of the things I felt was shame – and yet I had never been allowed to grieve for my dead child! Never allowed myself nor was I allowed by others. We must always remember that to be mad also means to be angry.)

Those who perform destructive or self-destructive acts are often seeing things quite differently than those who care for them. To the mentally ill, those acts may be *necessary*. How to keep them from hurting themselves, I don't know. But the idea of using prods or water pistols or other such aggressive tools in order to control their behaviour reminds me of the tired mother who says to the crying kid, "I'll give you something to cry about."

You can't cure pain with more pain, hurt with more hurt, fear with more fear. I'd vote for compassion any day; I might even vote for a strait-jacket if an orderly could then sit next to the patient and talk quietly to him or her, but I'm not sure about this.

Audrey Thomas
Galiano, British Columbia

P.S. At which "institution" did I really get my education? I sometimes wonder.

✉ My father was invalided out of the Royal Air Force in the early 1950s because of constant abdominal pain. Doctors could find nothing wrong and he was given a unilateral lobotomy to cure him of supposedly imagined pain. (His stomach ulcers burst shortly after and he nearly died of peritonitis.)

I was seven years old when he came home from the hospital.

My mentally unstable mother decided from his changed personality that he was "insane." She goaded him constantly and his diminished reasoning ability made him an easy target.

I was put into foster care for a few months where I was treated well.

When I was returned home, nothing had changed except that my mother was campaigning to have my father put in an insane asylum, as they were then called. She lectured me on his insanity and violent nature and told me I was not to obey him, only her.

It wasn't long before I joined her in her venom towards my father and only once in all that time did he show any anger towards me.

My mother's campaign worked and my father was put in an insane asylum.

The day they took him my mother was overjoyed and was angry at me for not sharing her joy. I'll never forget the words she shouted at me – "He's gone, he's gone, aren't you glad?" Her anger didn't subside; and for what seemed an eternity, but could have been only six months, I endured one long scream of abuse from my mother. Then I was put in a group home.

Meals at the home consisted of plain bread with sugar sprinkled on it. Only the staff were allowed to use the inside toilet. The children were supposed to use a hole in the ground partially covered on three sides by rusted metal sheets. It smelled so bad that I went behind an old abandoned tram car in the yard when I could do it without being observed.

Transgressions were dealt with harshly. We would be assembled in a small hall to watch as children had to strip from the waist down, walk to a desk in the middle of the stage and lean over it to be beaten with a heavy bamboo cane. I will never forget those expressionless faces or lose the guilt I still feel at the only emotion I was capable of feeling as I watched the welts appear, to be glad it was someone else, not me.

After a while I was returned home. My mother's hostility had turned to silent loathing. She would hit me on the head with an open hand if I did not duck fast enough.

I was sent back to school, where I was ridiculed by the teachers. One teacher stood me in front of the class while he walked around me with a sneaker he called Betsy in his hand. He would say, "You are contemptuous. I hold you in utter contempt. See how my lips curl in contempt for you." A variation to this speech was, "You are a guttersnipe. You are lower than a snake's belly. You are nothing, nobody cares about you. You are the lowest form of life." By the time I was fifteen, I had been abused in similar fashion by nine different teachers.

Between the seething and unpredictable outbursts, my mother had calm periods during which she lectured me about my father's evils. She calmly explained that his operation had caused him to lose his soul, that he was now controlled by the devil. I became confused and angry but kept the anger in; any display of anger would invite retribution.

I must have started to hallucinate; I opened the door to my room and saw my father standing there. I could not see his face but I recognized his clothes, size and shape. I ran downstairs screaming. My mother explained to me that I had seen the devil in my father's clothes.

When I was ten, I swallowed all the phenobarbital that was prescribed to control my epilepsy. The last few caught in my throat and the foul taste made me throw up.

I was taken to a foster home, where I was locked in my room each night because I screamed so loudly in my sleep. My foster parents were afraid that I would sleep-walk.

I was soon home again. Mother screamed more and lectured less. Once she beat me with her fists as I tried to hide under the blankets in my bed. I would go for days at a time without speaking.

Mother had nice clothes, a fur coat, shoes. She had butter on her bread and cookies with her tea. My clothes were moth-eaten; on my bread was beef dripping or margarine.

On visits to a doctor I put on Sunday clothes and cleaned up. Mother spoke calmly and convincingly and explained that it was what my father had done to me before they took him away that made me such a problem.

She could not have been totally believable. At twelve I was put in a reception centre.

I tried to run away and was moved to another group home. Then, at thirteen, I was sent home to Mother's tender care.

Mother resumed her barrage of venom about my devil father. I looked silently at the floor. I stole books and read and read and read. I read in my room. Sometimes I played hooky from school and read all day.

When I was sixteen, I swallowed all my mother's pills. I was pumped out and put in a huge ward of about fifty men. Many were old and about five died while I was there. I watched them die alone without family or friends or any apparent attempt to prevent their deaths.

It's more than thirty years since I was locked in my room for screaming in my sleep. But I am still woken at night by the sound of my own screams. A little less since I started to recall all this poison. As the memories came back so did the pain. I couldn't stop crying. I spent two months in hospital and was given electric shock therapy. I was fired from my job. I've had six jobs in the three years since then. The memories won't stop and I have to find a place to hide so they won't see me cry at work.

There is little enough help out there for any of us. But for me and others like me for whom sex was not the instrument of abuse, there seems to be none at all. A wound is a wound and pus is pus, and for the wound to heal the pus must be cleansed. It makes no difference what filthy instrument of abuse was used to cause the wound in the first place.

Jim Wood
Halifax

✉ I am not a "latent victim!" I remember practically every incident over an eight-year period, from the age of six to fourteen – suffered enough because of it; never thought it unusual that I did. I am thirty-nine now.

I started out as a day girl at Elmwood Girls' School in Rockcliffe Park. My parents were both degreed civil servants in Ottawa (my father at the Department of National Defence; mother at the National Research Council). The sexual abuse mainly started as my mother took four years of graduate (night) school to earn her Bachelor of Library Science (as it was then). I was an "only," a good little girl in uniform; raised an obedient child.

My father was like any other in appearance. He had a temper, though. He had served in the war as a radar technician, graduated from U of T, taught in a rural school, became a civil servant. In Almonte he joined the golf club, Lions Club (edited the newsletter), and generally socialized when necessary. His hobbies included puttering in his workshop, classical music, crossword puzzles – mostly lone pursuits, really.

I think that *power* is the operative word here (for abuse in general). He had not been sexually abused as a child, but had endured not a mild dose of some proper Victorian punishment, inflicted by his father, at the whim of a step-mother. (All of *that* is another story!)

In my case, the abuse itself consisted of being required to strip naked before him while he masturbated, and then, over an hour or so period, performing oral and manual sex on him. Other usual activities included groping on the sofa in front of the television (Nathan Cohen's *Fighting Words*, *Front Page Challenge*, and so on) plus "quickies" while still suited after work and before my mother's return.

Things got worse after our move to Almonte when I was eleven, and finally, at fourteen, having had enough of his nakedness and guile, I told my mother. I sacrificed my whole little world in the process – the inevitable consequence over which I still ache.

He had tried to strangle me towards the end, and things had got so messy by then that my mother and I really only wanted to escape in safety. We lived for years in fear. My father was a charming man – who on earth would doubt *him*?

My father died last year. He was a Mensan and unofficial poet laureate for *Mensa Magazine*. Even after his death, he was published in the international version of same (poetry and cryptic puzzles, et cetera). He hadn't deserved his sorry childhood, but what help could he have got? He grew up to serve his country, to keep his pride. He, after a twenty-year estrangement, conceded that perhaps he had been the author of some of my past troubles, and he was sorry. I accepted his apology. My teens and twenties had been a write-off – suicide attempts, et cetera.

I am now the mother of a beautiful two-and-a-half-year-old girl – a role I still marvel at. I had an inherent knowledge in my twenties that I never wanted to have children (I used to faint from my periods, all psychological, I now maintain – what would birthing be like?). Anna was Caesarean – so I was spared after all! I'm also, since I married at thirty-four, a struggling musician in the Rob Roy Pipe Band of Kingston, Ontario.

Valerie Pulker Soper
Kingston, Ontario

STRINGS OF THE APRON,
STRINGS OF THE HEART

A chapter on families – their strengths, and sometimes their failings.

✉ When Remembrance Day services are held in the Memorial Hall in our town, I watch the solemn young faces as, one after the other, they march forward to the altar to lay a wreath on behalf of the Air Cadets, the Boy Scouts and the rest. To the left, in rows of seats reserved for them, are members of the Royal Canadian Legion, medals and ribbons fastened to their navy blazers. One of them, a distinguished senior, crawls into bed with me at night and shares his toast with me in the morning. He is also a crisp young flight lieutenant struggling to pilot his Dakota through the monsoons of India to drop men and supplies to the beleaguered British Army in Burma. Bearing witness is his Distinguished Flying Cross. Every medal and ribbon there is a story. And there is a need in me to have the young faces in the hall on November 11 look past the snowy heads – not to mourn, but to *know*, and to understand, on this day.

No ancient veterans, these, nor toughened warriors with noble ideals. Just kids. Your cousin, lover, brother, son. But because we speak in thousands, there are no faces. So for all the thousands of lost young faces, I want to show you just one – the one I have in my memory on the day of remembering.

His name was Jimmie. He was average height and slim. He was two years older than me. His hair was dark, his eyes were green and his grin irreverent.

He was bright, full of music, good at baseball and hockey. He could ride a horse like the wind without saddle or bridle. He had, however, one heavy cross to bear when we were small. Though he was fearless where he was concerned, when I or our two younger brothers were hurt or in trouble and wound up in tears, so did Jimmie. He considered it a horrendous weakness and hated it.

When I was six and it was time for me to start school, I was full of excitement, hopping along the three miles we had to walk, gabbling all the way. But when school began and the students settled down and silence reigned, suddenly my world became very lonely and frightening and, try though I might, the tears began.

When our kind teacher came to comfort me and asked what might help, I said I needed to go and sit with Jimmie. With his sobbing six-year-old sister beside him, of course the inevitable happened and he began to weep, too – for an eight-year-old seasoned schoolboy, the ultimate humiliation.

On the way home that afternoon, I wasn't allowed to walk with him. He made me walk a few steps behind so that he wouldn't have to look at me, because not only was I a girl, and a stupid one at that, but I was the ugliest stupid girl he had ever seen and if I ever cried at school again, he would kill me. As nearly as I can remember, I never did.

As we grew older, Jimmie, like all young boys, I guess, was sometimes a source of immense pride and sometimes the cause of collective family insanity. While he was a good student and athlete, he was not impressed with the seriousness of life in general and the family house rules in particular, so while our parents struggled with this unsinkable kid, Jimmie's brass remained bright. He felt free to hand out discipline to the rest of us, however, and did, with glee. During one of our many confrontations, I called him something off-colour, I don't remember what, and with an expression of totally artificial shock, and in spite of my fierce resistance, he scrubbed my mouth with a tooth-brush and laundry soap.

I didn't appreciate his efforts much. In fact, I don't remember appreciating him at all, particularly, at the time. He was handy to have around when I got stuck with my homework and always had a store of information on hand – mostly inaccurate, I found later – when I grew curious about things in the adult world.

When our father, like many farmers in the late thirties, had to take a job away from home, it fell to us to get the milking done and the stock fed and watered before we left for school and again in the evening. I suppose we thought it was difficult at the time, but some of our best conversations went on then, our heads butted up against the cows' warm flanks while we milked, the stable in the winter-time sweet-smelling and warm, the lantern casting long shadows on the walls.

In 1943, boys could enlist in the armed forces at age seventeen and a half. If they had not enlisted by the time they were eighteen and a half, they were conscripted. Jimmie turned eighteen that year but was able to help with the harvest before he joined the Air Force.

He took his initial training in British Columbia, then was posted to Mount Pleasant Bombing and Gunnery School in Prince Edward Island where he was trained as an air gunner. Until then, all his training had been in a classroom. His letter dated May 22, 1944, begins, "Well, folks, I have rode a airplane." He goes on to say, "Twice, in fact. We flew around for about ¾ of an hour and then all of a sudden I didn't feel so well. At about 2 o'clock we landed and the first thing I did was get the fire hose and wash the plane out. Then in about 15 minutes we were in another plane and on our way again. I was o.k. that time."

He took his commando training in Trois-Rivières in July 1944; came home on embarkation leave from Lachine, Quebec; and that fall was posted to an operational training unit in England. There they polished their gunnery skills and aircraft identification but had plenty of time to themselves. They bought bicycles and pedalled into Leighton Buzzard to the pub, a dance or show.

The British were kindness itself to the young airmen. At Christmas time, a lord and his lady opened their beautiful old home to a homesick young Canadian, provided him with a robe and slippers and, on Christmas Eve, shared a little wine, which they had hoarded, and used their weekly ration of coal to build a fire in the fireplace.

A letter dated March 28, 1945, mentions an escapade in which Jimmie and another crew member were involved. "I was a little worried about getting a severe rep.," it read. "If that had happened, my crown would have been delayed another six months. As it is, my Flight Sergeant is due March 30. And it's worth having, too, because it means another 30 cents a day."

Jimmie's Lancaster bomber crashed during a training flight on the twenty-eighth of April, 1945, one month after his twentieth birthday and one week before the war ended. He was buried May 3 in Brookwood Cemetery in Surrey.

There was a poem, most of which I've forgotten now, titled, "Letter to Saint Peter." Part of it went like this:

> Let them love, Peter, they have had no time,
> Girls, sweet as meadow wind with flowering hair.
> They should have birds songs; hills to climb.
> The taste of summer in a ripened pear.
> Let them in, Peter. They are very tired.
> Give them the couches where the angels sleep.
> Let them wake whole again to new dawns fired
> With sun. Not war. And may their peace be deep.

Margaret Hewson
Indian Head, Saskatchewan

✉ I'm twenty-four, and I've been living away from home (either in university residences or off-campus housing) for five years. I have always had a close and loving relationship with my parents, and yes, I consider myself very lucky. For me, it is the place my parents reside that I think of as home.

I did not realize how important that mental and emotional image of home was until I went on a trip this past semester. For four months, my boy-friend and I explored the mysteries of Asia (Hong Kong, Thailand, Nepal, India, Pakistan) and the Middle East and Europe (Egypt, Israel, Turkey, Italy). I saw things of incredible beauty and equally incredible desperation and poverty. For the first time in my life, I was removed from all of my support mechanisms (school, friends, sports, Western values and, most critically, my family). Although I am an outgoing, confident and intelligent individual in search of experience and excitement, there were many times when all I could think about was going home, and I had a yearning to talk with my mom and dad on the phone, just so I could hear them say "I love you" and know that everything was all right. (I hope this doesn't sound corny, but it is difficult to convey how intensely homesick I was.) I wrote them letters constantly for a period of three weeks, because it was almost like talking to them and it gave me a greater sense of emotional stability, even though I was thousands of miles away in a foreign culture.

I don't think I ever took my parents for granted when I was at university – that is not why I missed them so much. I missed them because I realized how fortunate I was to have a caring and supportive family with which to share experiences and burdens. It was suddenly very clear to me just how much effort and sacrifice and patience is required to be a good parent. For me, the words "home" and "parents" are synonymous, both conveying images of warmth, physical and emotional shelter and stability.

It's nice to tell somebody how much my parents mean to me.

Megan McKenna
Ottawa

✉ I'm twenty-five, single, female and finishing my third university degree. I left home at eighteen to start studying at Queen's, and since then I've lived in a girls' residence, a house of six girls, a mixed house of ten people, an apartment with a girl, and an apartment with a guy – just a friend. In between school years, I might return home for a month at a time, to my "permanent address." Actually, "home" is a relative term – whether I was at my parents' or in my own place, I always referred to the other place as "home." Which might make me a homeless person, right?

I really enjoy visiting at my parents'. Not because of the fridge full of food (they go on diets now that they aren't cooking for children) or the laundry (their machine is less dependable than the laundromats) but because we are *friends* now. We cook dinner for each other and pour another cup of coffee and talk about things as *adults*.

But I will also probably live with them again. That's a reality of being over-educated and under-experienced and being unable to afford the rent. At my age my mother had a marriage, a career and a child. I haven't even started my career yet. Many of my friends are in their mid- to late twenties and are still relying on their parents for a place to live, for short or long periods. It's hard on all of us. The parents lose their privacy and gain a house guest who *wants* to be independent. The child looks and acts like an adult (most of the time) so it's hard to have hosts who used to spank her for stealing cookies and can't quite relinquish that role.

This year, I'm living with my grandmother, and that's another kettle of fish altogether. There is a generation gap, but more difficult is the sharing of space and chores by two women, each of whom has taken care of herself for years, and we each feel a responsibility to look after the other. When she's asleep, I check that she's still breathing, and she feels her privacy is being invaded when she catches me. My hackles are raised when she tells me to put my slippers on or not to stay out too late. Don't even ask about dating. There *are* benefits, of course: she has a young person to fetch the groceries and put out the garbage and hang the laundry and listen to her stories; I have a room in a lovely house and a chance to hear great stories. Yes, I've heard most of them several times now, but there's always one I haven't heard.

I look forward to having a place of my own – intensely. And I am not alone. Many of us between twenty-five and thirty have finished a degree (or, increasingly, two), and returned home because we can't find jobs or we have jobs but can't afford rent or mortgage payments. This "twilight adolescence" of the economically immature is part of growing up now and deserves more attention.

Jennifer Macdonnell
Kingston, Ontario

✉ I have many memories of childhood evening meals. They were called, interchangeably, supper or dinner, but lunch was *always* lunch, even on Sunday.

I remember feeling awed and slightly intimidated by what I considered to be my father's intellectual brilliance (he was a scientist), and when he would ask me for my opinion or thoughts, I felt the onus was on me to come back with something half-way intelligent.

I think my mum tried to make Sunday suppers special, as Sundays meant something to her that they didn't mean for the rest of us. Most weekends, however, were spent canoeing, hiking or skiing, so often a Sunday meal would be a wonderful pressure-cooked stew which, when I look back, is eloquent testimony to my mother's ability to create culinary miracles within twenty minutes. Then we might sit in front of the living-room fireplace and eat that Bourguignonne with hunks of home-made bread, still in our grubbies, feeling the exquisite exhaustion of physical activity and surrounded by the fire's spreading heat.

We laughed a lot at supper. My brother, Bruce, was a great story teller, and I think we all may have tried to compete a little with his ability. Once when he came home late for supper, which was *always* at six, he gave us the lame excuse, "I was in a plane crash." Well, we gave him a hard time for that one, but he insisted we stay up late to see him on the news. And there he was, climbing out of the harbour waters onto a dock, and there was a small float plane out there somewhere upside down. My sister and I were suitably impressed.

For a year or so, we had to speak French at the dinner table. I forget now who made this rule, but for me it was a delight and a challenge, and I hope to start this soon with my own sons. It is quite likely that no one who speaks French would have understood what we were saying, but we all improved and I, at least, had great fun.

Dishes. I'm ashamed to admit that as kids we didn't help out a whole lot with dishes. I think we had a dishwasher, but my clearest memories are of Mum and Dad standing side by side at the kitchen sink, washing and drying and singing harmony, exchanging glances I didn't understand at the time, but now cherish.

Holidays like Christmas, Boxing Day and Easter brought out all the good china and silverware (or *cutrely*, as my sister Lynn called it), as well as all the ancient aunts and uncles. The crystal and teacups and fancy plates couldn't go in the dishwasher and seemed to take forever to wash and dry, and I was terrified of breaking something. (For some reason, I usually offered to wash.) On Boxing Day after supper we'd all play charades. I still remember old Uncle Ernie doing "The Naked Ape."

I know we fought and squabbled, but those aren't the predominant memories. Great food, laughter and discussion and always a dessert are what I remember, and what is still recreated when we get together now as adults, which we do far too infrequently.

Kelly Leroux
London, Ontario

✉ My name is Allan Michael MacDonald. I was born at Prince County Hospital, Summerside, Prince Edward Island, on January 11, 1979.

324

In 1981, I came to live at the home of Shirley and Ronald MacDonald. In June 1982, they became my adoptive parents. Now they are my mom and dad. When I came to live with Mom and Dad, I wore Pampers, I couldn't walk and I couldn't talk, I sucked my thumb and I cried a lot of the time because I was scared. It wasn't long before I learned how to use the bathroom. I had to or Dad wouldn't take me in the truck, and I loved going for drives in the truck. I used to stand up by Dad and fall asleep in the truck. At first I didn't like going to the barn at milking time, but I got used to it. Now I wish we had a farm. I miss it. Mom and Dad bought me all new clothes and toys because I didn't have any.

I used to go with Dad to John Deere Farm Machinery to pick up parts. One day Mom couldn't find me, she was calling and calling me. I heard her. I was on the wrong side of the road with my thumb up; I told her I was hitch-hiking to John Deere to buy a tractor. She told me I would have been there a long time. On January 9, 1982, I was baptized at St. Malachy's Church, Kinkora. My new grandparents were Ronald and Rosella MacDonald, and Harry and Agnes Simmonds.

In 1984, I started school in Kinkora. Mrs. Smith was my teacher. I cried a lot of the time and I thought that they would never take me back home again, like when I was small. I had to go to school by bus and Justin Kelly was the bus driver. It was quite a walk from the bus stop to where we lived in Rose Valley. I didn't like going to school. Mom would be waiting for me at the bus stop to drive me home. I still sucked my thumb and it used to get pretty sore. Mom and Dad had to take me everywhere with them because I would cry so much – I used to think they were never coming back home.

I have accomplished a lot since 1982. I learned how to get along with other people, and I trust my family. I learned how to skate, play ball and hockey. Dad bought me a dirt bike in 1985 and I love to drive it. He bought me a pony and his name was Mickey. I overcame my fear. I know my mom and dad love me and I never have to worry again, because they tell me every day. My whole family is so good to me. My big sister Donna is really good to me. She takes me swimming, skating, shopping and to ball games. I am an uncle to Tammy, Monica and Robin Wall.

On May 10, 1986, I made my first communion at St. Paul's Church in Summerside.

I am now eleven years old. I live in the village of Bedeque with my mom and dad. My ambitions are to become a lawyer or an accountant and get a good job, and to take care of my mom and dad because they took good care of me.

I want to buy Dad a little farm. Because he loves animals. Sometimes I go to work with Dad and help him. He pays me. I like to make my own money because I can rent Nintendo games and buy Nintendo books. If everything goes as I have it planned, I will be a great citizen and will lead a good life.

Mike MacDonald
Bedeque, Prince Edward Island

✉ Last year, we were still farming in Saskatchewan. We were struggling to keep our heads above water then. We aren't any more. The summer of 1988's drought pushed us to the point where we had to decide whether to go further into debt and risk losing everything, or to sell out while we still had something left to start over with somewhere. We were behind on loan payments and credit account payments to farm suppliers, but no one was really pressuring us too hard yet. But we felt we couldn't go on that way for another year, and we had made up our minds not to borrow any more money. We grew most of our own food including milk and meat, and we didn't buy anything except what we absolutely had to. We got used to having fun together on the farm rather than looking for entertainment or relaxation elsewhere. But it wasn't enough. There were several factors that put us into that desperate position in which we found ourselves. One was taking on too much debt for the size of our farm. Another was not recognizing soon enough that we needed off-farm income to provide our living expenses until the farm became profitable. However, the interest rates and the weather and commodity prices were out of our control. In the nine years we farmed on our own (my husband farmed with his family previously), approximately half of them were dry years. And when we started out in 1980 and 1981 we were paying up to eighteen per cent interest rates.

Despite the difficulties in those nine years, we learned a lot about what we truly valued. Our kids had an opportunity to live the life we wanted them to experience on the farm. We found out how resourceful we could be without money. If it hadn't been for the debt, we could have survived the way we were living for several more years. After several months of heart-rending consideration, we chose to book an auction sale in June 1989 and advertised our land for sale. We moved to Alberta, where my husband works at a large feed lot.

At first, the relief from financial pressure felt so wonderful, I enjoyed our new life in a rented house in a small village that was so surrounded by bush and pasture land, it felt almost like the farm still. But after a while it began to sink in the real price we had paid to get out of debt. We gave up a life-style that gave us freedom and independence in day-to-day living. We gave up being able to provide our basic needs by working with our own hands. My husband and I gave up being able to communicate with each other at any time of day when the need arose and having lunch together and listening to the farm broadcast and sharing comments as we read the farm papers. Now we have to maintain a relationship on two hours a day of being in the same location, and with five children, that time is spread around pretty thin. It was hard at first to believe that this is the way most of North America lives, and everyone seems to survive somehow. It was also hard buying *everything* at the store, even a scrap of wood to fix the screen door with. I had no idea how much it would cost to feed our family when everything had to be paid for in cash.

We had been in Alberta six months before I really understood what we had lost and would never have again, and then I really wept over it. And yet, in some ways we are happier now. We've had to become closer because we've moved away from family and friends, so when we talk, it's to each other. We've done a lot of analysing and grieving and saying "what if" to the mistakes we made. But losing what we had on the farm has focused for us what we value in life, and we realize now how much we took for granted that valuable life we had on the farm.

We hope to have that life again someday. We won't go into debt ever again, but we'll find a way to have some of what we had on the farm. Our fifth child, born last November, was a boy (after four girls), and we'd like him to grow up knowing first-hand that milk comes from a cow's udder, eggs get laid by chickens and manure is a perfume that's unbeatable.

My husband, now thirty-nine years old, had to move away from family and lifelong friends for the first time when we came to Alberta. I think we've both found out that "home" is not a geographic location, but where you are with those you love the most.

Nancy Bateman
Hughenden, Alberta

✉ I am twenty-one, the oldest of three girls. My father, Alan Kennedy, is a farmer. The truth is that farmers do not get increases the same way that other businesses do. I can't think of many people who would be willing to work at the same job year after year with hardly an inflation increase.

But even closer to my heart is the life of a farmer. To me, both my parents are incredible people. My father, like many farmers, can only be called a genius, and Mother nothing short of a saint, and an incredibly intelligent one at that. Unfortunately, *stupid* seems to be synonymous with *farmer* for many people. It was not a prejudice that I ran into until I moved away from my home community, where everyone is a farmer or at least strongly tied to the agricultural industry. But as soon as I hit the city, I was shocked to hear some of the comments. Most people see farmers as the proverbial "hayseed"–a piece of straw stuck between their teeth, plaid shirt, bib overalls, a horrible western accent and something gross stuck to the bottom of their boots. Some people even said to me, "You don't look like a farmer" and intended it to be a compliment.

But a farmer probably has more fields of expertise than the heads of corporations. My father is an expert in meteorology, accounting, bookkeeping, machinery and its repair and maintenance, negotiating with buyers and sellers, carpentry, construction, metalwork, a smattering of veterinary medicine, market analysis, all the intangibles that one must know to be able to plant and harvest a crop, and to top it all off, my father designs and builds much of his own machinery to suit his needs. Now, he is building his own glider in his "spare time." And one must remember if a farmer does not excel in all these areas, his farm will not succeed.

My mother has a degree in home economics and a teaching certificate. She has raised three kids, without the benefit of day care or nurseries, and we are the better for it, I believe. Mom has always worked by the farmer's wife's creed: You must have meals ready to serve half an hour early or four hours late and they must be filling and edible either way. My mother is a baker, chef and housekeeper for the five of us and an indefinite number of guests, as farmers often have crews of neighbours and friends in to help out in a crisis, and she must be able to look after all these people with no more notice than an hour sometimes; she must can and preserve for the winter every fall from the garden and other sources; she has to know how to operate all the farm machinery for when the big push is on to get something planted or harvested, be a secretary for all business calls my father receives, because he is never near a phone, be the absolute thriftiest of consumers, an economist, and know a fair bit of medicine to look after a family when the nearest hospital is thirty miles away. Not to mention all the volunteer work she does – church group, horticultural group, 4-H, school and the list goes on.

I am very proud of my parents and the job they do. I never

shirk my roots. I now live and work in Vancouver and am desperately homesick and waiting anxiously for the chance to go home. As my father says, the one good thing about farming is you don't have to live in the city. I never regret the way I grew up and feel sorry for those who didn't have the same opportunity. My heart bleeds for those who have lost their farms to the banks. While my father laughs heartily and does his best to discourage me every time I mention farming, it is something I still think I would like to do. I would at least want to raise any family I may have in the country. As my mother says, "Once a stubble jumper, always a stubble jumper."

Michelle Kennedy
Vancouver

✉ I heard the letter written by Michelle Kennedy.

I was deeply moved by the way she spoke of her parents and what they meant to her and to this community. I was listening in the cab of my tractor as I seeded my wheat crop. As I worked, a cloud of dust appeared across the way and moments later a tractor emerged from it. It was Michelle's dad, Alan Kennedy, preparing his cornfield for spring planting. Michelle's letter reminded me of a saying that surfaces here from time to time, "Our largest export is wheat, our second largest export is young people."

Michelle's situation is indicative of what is wrong with Prairie Canada, low grain prices, high operating costs, an uncaring federal government and drought, the latter being the only thing that might change soon. The situation has got so bad that in recent years, parents have been advising their children to get out of farming. Somehow, however, I feel that Dulcie and Alan would be pleased if Michelle became involved in agriculture in some way. As for me, I hope she does because agriculture needs young people, young people like Michelle. We in this community miss her youthful exuberance, her sparkling personality and ready wit, but most of all we miss her promise for the future, the future of our community that she and her generation represent.

Gordon Simpson
Miami, Manitoba

✉ Our daughter Carolyn (in Montreal) is, I believe, breaking new ground. She is refusing to accept an earned Master's degree from Concordia because it is too "sexist." She wants a Mistress degree! She called us recently to say that she was to be interviewed on this matter by a local Montreal radio station but we couldn't get it here.

We feel that this is probably one of the most foolish lengths to which a feminist could go. Her father explained to her the Latin background of the Bachelor and Master's degrees in which there is no sexual connotation whatsoever, but that fell on deaf ears.

What has made a dear little redhead with long pigtails come to this pass? Carolyn is the youngest, strongest and most aggressive of four children. As soon as she could jump over a high bar, she was on her way. All through UNB she played basketball and field hockey – deliriously happy with success, totally depressed in defeat. Three times she was termed "Fittest Female in Canada" during the Gillette Fitness Challenge televised in Toronto. And when she took up weight-lifting, just to keep fit, she found she could do quite a notable bench press.

After UNB, she went off to Laval to become bilingual. She continued her weight-lifting program and was encouraged by a coach there to join the Canadian women's weight-lifting team, which was preparing for a competition in Britain. Once overseas, she did a shoe-string tour of Europe, making beds in London, picking grapes in France, and so on, and it was during this sojourn that it dawned upon her that she was a lesbian!

She took this in her stride. She became a militant, placard-carrying feminist out to save the gays of the world and stamp out prejudice. And how would she do this besides preaching the gospel by word of mouth? She would become a writer – not prose but poetry. She had always been interested in creative writing, having taken a course at UNB, and she had kept voluminous journals from the time she was young. So with her new-found sexuality, the whole focus of her career changed.

She tried to enroll at the U of T as a graduate student in English, but she was told she would have to start in a Bachelor's program as her phys. ed. background at UNB (even with a number of arts courses included) was not comprehensive enough. After all, as they pointed out, the U of T had very high standards. Look what it did for such illustrious graduates as Margaret Atwood! To which Carolyn replied in frustration, "I don't think the U of T did any more for Margaret Atwood than UNB did for Anne Murray."

Carolyn did, however, take a number of English courses and was encouraged to continue writing poetry. For breaks and to earn some money, she worked for several months in Trinidad in a broccoli-growing estate, and later at McDonnell Douglas as a metal cutter in the aircraft factory.

Finally, with her UNB record, her courses at the U of T and her sheaf of poems, she was accepted by Concordia to study for a Master's in Creative Writing. There she has been fighting and writing all the way to her degree. To support herself, she has been working part-time teaching weight-lifting at the Women's Y.

For fairly orthodox aging parents, Carolyn is somewhat of an anomaly, to say the least.

Frances Gammon
Fredericton

✉ I became a mother last July at the relatively old age of thirty-one. Even though Mitchell is an easy, good-natured baby, the past nine and a half months have proved challenging as my husband and I readjust our life-style to include an infant who requires regular meals and naps and doesn't realize that weekends are for sleeping in well past six-thirty.

Being a mother has given me a whole new perspective on mothers in general and my mother in particular. The amount of love I have for my son is awesome to me. I realize now how much love was involved in things my mother did with me.

Memories of *my* childhood seem clearer these days. I can remember the sights and smells of going downtown on the bus with my mom. The sticky green vinyl bus seat with the warm oversized indentation where some adult had sat before me. The thrill of pulling the cord to let the driver know you wanted the next stop.

We'd often eat lunch in one of the department stores. Woodward's had the upside-down ice-cream cone on a plate. It came decorated as a clown with the cone as the hat. At the Hudson's Bay, the cafeteria was downstairs. We would sit at tall skinny tables, balanced on tall skinny stools eating beef barley soup.

My mom taught me how to ride a two-wheeler, how to skip rope and how to play badminton.

I remember the ritual of cleaning the silverware together. Also the treat of helping buff the freshly waxed floors with the electric buffer. You had to be careful not to let the handle point straight up or the buffer would go right out of control. Of course I had to test its power once or twice.

My mom sang when she did housework. I still remember all the words to "My Sweet Little Alice Blue Gown."

I can remember my mom walking to meet me after school. I'd discuss my day with her as we strolled home hand in hand. Later, these meetings became embarrassing to me and Mom no longer came to get me.

I remember Mom and Dad getting ready to go out for the evening—the smell of Chanel No. 5 in the air, the lipsticked kiss goodnight. I hoped they were going to a wedding. That would mean in the morning there would be two sticky, foil- and doily-wrapped pieces of cake in the fridge for my brother and me.

The telephone hung in the hall outside my bedroom door. Often I would lie in bed at night, lulled to sleep by my mother's hushed voice as she spoke on the phone.

It amazes me that these small, seemingly insignificant moments flood me with such feelings of nostalgia and remembered security. It makes me realize how important every single day is in the life of my new, beautiful son.

Six years ago on May 12, the day before Mother's Day, my mother died. As the years have passed since her death, I've felt her presence slowly slip from my life.

This Mother's Day she's with me more than ever.

Vivian Saddy Braam
North Vancouver

✉ My mother was diagnosed with lung cancer in February 1988. We packed more memories into the following year than most people have in a lifetime.

Christmas was no exception. Mom had always decorated the house to the hilt. She was not able to get about very well by December, so I became her Santa's elf. I bought the pine boughs to decorate the mantelpiece. I brought the many boxes of decorations up from the basement. We spent a whole afternoon reliving Christmases past as we unwrapped our family's history with each coloured ball, red bow and tiny Santa.

She taught me, from her vantage point on the love-seat, how to make a wreath from fresh cedar. We laughed a lot at my incompetence, and I could sense her impatience at not being able to do it herself.

I put up the tree by myself that year, the same artificial one my dad and I put up together when I was younger. Mom unwrapped the lights and tree ornaments while I carefully hung them on the tree. I wouldn't let her peek until it was finished. The look of joy and wonder on her face when she turned around lives with me still.

We discussed her Christmas list and then I did the shopping. Mom helped me wrap the gifts and took great care, as always, with the corners and the bows. Each one was a work of art. She had bought a book for each of her grandchildren and carefully wrote a short inscription in each one.

On Christmas Day, we had dinner at my brother's house. It was wonderful. Mom was well enough to make the short trip and we were together for what would be the last time.

Mom died on February 25, 1989. I think of her often, especially at this time of the year. As I made a wreath from cedar for our front door two weeks ago, Mom was there. As I made Christmas pudding by myself for the very first time, Mom was with me. When I opened the boxes marked "Xmas decorations" in my dad's familiar script, I found more than just pretty ornaments, I found my past.

Julie Wise
Paris, Ontario

✉ I am becoming more and more like my father
Especially at Christmas
I sweep through the house in a furor
Rearranging furniture
Pulling dusty boxes from closet shelves
Sorting through the remains of Christmas past
My family patiently and gingerly side-steps
Pine cones, boughs, rose hips and berries
No one mentions the grape vines soaking in the bath-tub
And they hearken to the Christmas Harridan who
    proclaims
Don't touch that! I'm making something.
Don't sit there!
You do *not* need to be in the bathroom right this minute!
Get away! Those aren't for us to eat!

So the lights are strung in the windows
And the tree goes up in the living-room

My family are cautiously co-operative
Ever mindful of infringing on yet another tradition
And they hearken to the Christmas Wheedler who cajoles
Why don't we sit and look at the tree
Let's turn off all the other lights
How about putting on some Christmas music
I think about my father

How we rearranged the furniture
And pulled down musty boxes from the garret
Sorting through generations of Christmas ghosts
How we struggled to set the tree straight in a bucket of
  rocks
While my father stood off to one side suggesting we lean it
A little more to the north

My father, never content with Nature's plan,
On his back beneath the tree
Boring holes with his brace and bit
Adding a limb here
And how about one down there
"Only God and I can make a tree"
And in our teen-age years the annual arguments over
Streamers . . . Oh Daddy, no one puts those old things up
  any more!
Garlands . . . They're old-fashioned, Dad!
Turkey . . . How can it be raw? It's been in the oven for
Twelve hours!
We would sit around the table watching our
Christmas dinner congeal on our plates
While my father asked the blessing
Describing in great and humorous detail events of the past
  year
Taking outrageous snipes at the various boy-friends

Later we would whisper and tiptoe around my father
Asleep in his chair

The tree's coloured lights reflected on the top
Of his smooth, bald head
Coming home from university on winter weekends
I would find my father
Still sitting beside a bedraggled Christmas tree

And so I think about my father
And long for one more Christmas
With all the confusion and haranguing
My family have tiptoed off into darkened corners
I sit watching the coloured lights
Reflect on the garlands strung around our Christmas tree
I think about my father
And listen to the melting ice drip from the eaves
The way it always does
In the middle of January

Betty Belmore
Halifax

✉ I told my partner I would leave him if I ever saw him in a baseball cap. Such is the depth of my aversion to the sport.

It's not the memory of my knees knocking and my heart pounding in fear while I tried to make contact between a wooden bat I could barely lift and a white ball being hurled at me while a crowd jeered and said awful things about me.

Or remembering standing all alone in the out, out, outfield, a skinny little southpaw, with borrowed right-hander's glove – terrified that someone might actually hit something out here, and then what would I do, since no one had ever taught me how to throw a ball.

There is more to the roots of my baseball phobia.

I was a baseball orphan.

My mother grew up in New York. Baseball is in her blood. She even has a picture of her uncle standing with his arm around Babe

Ruth. My parents met, married and had five children. Most of the time life was pretty great. But when baseball season started, everything changed. We knew there would be a ball game on TV when we saw Mom carrying the basket of ironing up from the laundry room. She would set the ironing board up in front of the TV, and when she licked her finger and I heard that "ttssst" as she touched it to the iron, my misery began.

"Time to play outside," she'd sing as she ushered us out into the yard. Then – *she locked the door!*

Often one or two of us would park on the front steps, our chins in our hands, elbows resting on our knees. Eventually other siblings would wander home and we'd say, "Mom's baseball is on." They, too, would claim a step, cup their chin and pray it didn't go into extra innings. Sometimes we would put our faces to the screen, watching Mom standing at the ironing board, the basket emptying and freshly ironed shirts dangling from the door frames. Half-way into the season, the screen door would be peppered with little nose dents.

I'm all grown up now, a mother of two children. When my partner puts on the ball game, I roll my eyes. When he and the kids start chanting "Mooo-key Moooo-key" – I get this incredible urge to catch up on the ironing. Thankful at least to be on the other side of the screen door!

Sharon P. O'Connor
Scarborough, Ontario

✉   my laundry room is not very big &
      it's in the basement
      it's an old Vancouver house we live in &
      the basement leaks all winter
      there are bits of insulation sticking out here & there in the
         walls
      & the furnace & hot-water tank are in there too
      there are two metal shelves with junk & three large boxes
         of

artworks, not the greatest place for art
an old wooden high chair which I was never able to part
    with
sits by the washer & holds the soap box
there's a ground-level window above the dryer & a bare
bulb overhead by an old fluorescent light we brought from
    Calgary
my bike is in there & an old wooden milk bench & beside
    the furnace
a pair of somebody's cross-country skis
it's a tight squeeze to say the least

but this room is where my son hangs his hockey
    equipment, my son
16, a strapping six footer who loves hockey & his
    equipment
he strokes his skates & cares for them with infinite love
hangs them above the washer on nails, & hangs his sweat-
    soaked
underwear there too & his stinky skate socks
between the dryer & the furnace hang his hockey pants by
    suspenders
thickly padded holding their own human shape
helped along by years of hockey sweat
a sweat-soaked blue jersey hangs beside the water tank
beside the washer on boxes of art he puts his helmet,
his jock-strap, his $100 knee pads, &
expensive smelly $200 gloves
$1200 worth of equipment stinking up my tiny laundry
    room &
to top it off
thick shoulder pads swing above the washer on a coat-
    hanger
then there's his black sweat pants on a nail &
that is exactly what they are
sweat

sometimes it's difficult to walk down the steps to the
  laundry
the stench of hockey equipment is overwhelming
i've asked other hockey parents abt this &
they say it's the same everywhere
i try to console myself imagining mothers in Sweden in
their laundry rooms
two weeks ago i told him i'd buy him a
hockey tree to hang up his equipment in his room
no, mom, he sd, i *like* the laundry room

Victoria Walker
Vancouver

✉ When my husband and I moved into an old farmhouse on the fourth line of McNab Township nearly eighteen years ago, my mother, no doubt remembering her childhood in an old rural house, gave us a spoon box. It was not an antique, but it had been made from an old design and seemed appropriate for our rustic decor. However, being part of the Rubbermaid generation, not accustomed to storing spoons in a wooden box, we eventually moved it to the top of an old pine dresser in our bedroom. There it squatted with only minor disturbances until January 3, 1991.

As a kind of New Year's purge, I was ransacking closets, sorting out unworn clothes to pass on to the Sally Ann. My husband entered the bedroom and said, "If you really want to clean out something, why don't you sort out this." He dumped the contents of the spoon box onto our bed. I was horrified when I saw the pile of junk, not to mention dust, scattered on the duvet. "Off-white" suddenly took on a new meaning. But within seconds, my curiosity seized me and I began to poke among the stuff.

The most colourful items were five Remembrance Day poppies, thirty cents in Canadian Tire money and an Alfred Sung guarantee of quality from a wallet. As I removed them, the cork from a bottle of Asti Spumante floated to the top of the pile: ah, a souvenir of a romantic evening for two? No, this one had been carried upstairs by our black Labrador one Sunday after a family brunch and had been batted around for several days by the cats before almost getting stuck in the nozzle of the vacuum cleaner. And speaking of cats, there were three photos of the ginger one, sitting between rows of corn stubble on a foggy morning.

Suddenly the organized side of my nature nudged the sentimental one, forcing me to take some action. I was tempted to put on the plastic glove from the health food store but I tucked it into my pocket for that painting job. I spread the items over a larger area and began to categorize. Office supplies: forty-five paper clips, two HB pencils, one pen, two plastic pencil sharpeners, three return address stickers, a box of 0.5 mm pencil leads and thirty-eight elastic bands. Sewing supplies: thirty-four straight pins, twenty-three safety pins, sixteen buttons, six needles and two small belt buckles. Household hardware: sixteen screws of various sizes, three S hooks, a jack for a forgotten radio, a three-inch galvanized fence nail, three nuts, six bolts and seven washers. Grooming items: three nail files, a sample of Ralph Lauren perfume, seven bobby pins, eleven cuff-links, a make-up brush and a disposable razor.

At this point I took a break. My husband and son were delegated to carry some of the items to their "proper" places. I made a pot of jasmine tea and then perused the rest. A minute package of Po Chi Pills to "regulate gastro-intestinal disorder caused by intoxication" reminded me of a hostess with a sense of humour who had served a wonderful meal in a setting of cyprus papyrus trees. Four tiny teeth brought back the sound of a child padding into the bedroom to announce that the tooth fairy had come. The clip from a tensor bandage stirred the uneasiness that I had felt as I watched my husband limp from the barn with broken toes after a calving cow had sat on his foot. Coins from Britain, Sweden, Norway and Finland filled my mind with exotic landscapes and images of foreign friends. The stud from the tonneau of a white MGB brought a flash of the swinging sixties, while a spare key to a 1964 Chevy Nova sold only five years ago made me wish to see her sitting in the driveway once again. A dog tag dated 1984 brought tears to my eyes for a departed black Labrador named Jasper.

"What are you going to do with the rest of the stuff?" asked a voice from the hall.

Without answering, I scooped up the treasures along with the useful items and gently placed them back in the box. I heard a quiet chuckle.

Diane Brearley
White Lake, Ontario

DELIGHTS OF THE GARDEN

Sometime in the season of 1989-90, according to Carole Warren, *Morningside*'s music producer until she left to take up full-time life in the country (with her garden), gardening surpassed curling as Canadians' most favoured leisure activity.

Was Carole right? I don't know. We received scarcely any letters about curling.

✉ A gardener always has a project. It is either just finished, inasmuch as anything in a garden is ever complete, or it is in progress or else in the planning stage. A gardener is never at a loss for something to talk about. Gardeners don't want the junk food of generalities but some decent protein. They want to hear what sparks other gardeners or they want information, or both.

I use the term "gardener" but should try and spell out the distinction between them and people who grow things. It is easy to tell the difference but not at all easy to say what it is. It has nothing to do with experience or how the garden is planned or laid out. A friend of mine decided to turn her back yard into a garden a few years ago. Her previous experience consisted of

buying impatiens to line the edge of her front path. She transformed the back into a magical shade garden under the pine trees.
She is a natural. I have other friends who try very hard, who take
great care and trouble but lack this indefinable something. Some
gardens look nothing very much but they are gardens. Some look
immaculately tended and yet something is missing.

Growing vegetables may be a part of gardening but there is far
more to it than that. It means total involvement in making the
area round the house a pleasant and interesting place. Some people
get it done professionally because they have no ideas or because
they are physically unable to do it themselves (or lack strong and
willing helpers). The professional garden can be identified fairly
easily: emerald lawn, foundation planting, a "feature" of some
kind, a fancy path and narrow strip alongside for the owner to
plant with favourite annuals. I think a true gardener prefers to do
it without help if possible or, if that is necessary, then to their
own design. The garden evolves according to soil, site and defined
limits. A gardener's interests may range from particular species
plants such as roses or dahlias, shade planting to xeriscaping,
wildflowers to formal bedding (and vegetables to prize begonias).
You name it and someone somewhere is interested in it.

Personally I am eclectic and willing to try most things though I
do have strong dislikes too. Perennials are my first love and I
prefer the natural (and often untidy) look. Gardening is a challenge
and very stimulating. I am always discovering something new,
something that takes to the conditions here and conversely what
doesn't work for me. In June 1988 I embarked on a roadside, bank
and ditch garden to save awkward mowing and trimming. It
turned into an immense and fascinating labour of love as, like
Topsy, it growed. The fun I had collecting common wayside plants
from waste ground and roadsides, seed collecting and watching
how things adapted was immeasurable. Now I'm sad that it is
more or less complete though one never knows what may be
affected by snow and ice and road run-off. I'm looking forward to
spring and already have some rather formless ideas about another
area that could be improved. The garden is rather a mystery, and

perhaps that is the key: endlessly exploring the mystery and being amazed at what one finds.

Gillian Boyd
Ottawa

✉ Mom was a gardener. Her vegetable garden on the farm was hedged on two sides with rows of maple, ash and elm and bordered on the third side with Saskatoon bushes and young poplars. Around a houseful of kids and threshers to feed, around eggs and cream to ready for shipping, around canning and mending and school lunches, she maintained a formal flower garden that ran the full length of two sides of our rambling old white house. It was a settled, secure old garden with cinder walks and caragana hedges, with clumps of forget-me-nots and clouds of baby's breath, a garden where humming-birds came for lunch. Trimmed round with a row of whitewashed stones, the garden held a treasury of old-fashioned perennials mixed with hand-reared annuals. Meanwhile, in the house, geraniums bloomed from each deep-sill window, and the verandah was a greenhouse year round. The Easter lilies never failed to produce the most perfect white trumpets, and her Christmas cactus bloomed twice each year, to celebrate both Christmas and Easter.

As a young adult, I moved to the city, where the smog ate the petals off my windowbox bachelor's buttons. My kids, I eventually discovered, didn't know which end of a plant produced potatoes and which end produced peas. Willing victims of a smart hardware salesman, we bought three sizes of tools – adult, pre-adolescent and play, for the baby – and we fought our way through the tangle of matted green stuff that passed for our developer's idea of a sodded lawn. Directly beneath the skin of sod, we hit bedrock, solid clay that had been bulldozed clean of top soil and nutrients.

Still, we eventually harvested a handful of peas, a meal of beans, a taste of tiny, tender potatoes and a small mountain of cherry tomatoes. Some unsavory bug got the turnips and the onions and the radishes, and the kids ate the carrots before they were big enough to see. But as I served up what were, undoubtedly, the most expensive potatoes in Canada, I reminded myself that I wasn't intending to save money. I was carrying on family tradition. The kids loved it. They despised digging and they loathed weeding, but they much admired going shopping for our spring supplies when, drunk on the promises of the new crop of seed catalogues, I could be convinced to buy at least a dozen of anything.

I learned to harvest some Beefsteak tomatoes by feeding beer to the slugs. My pup was addicted to green peppers straight from the vine and daughter Ruth's dog learned to dig and eat carrots. The Quebec robins ate all our Saskatoons, and the kids next door, where they grow nothing but grass, stripped the raspberry bushes. The strawberries never recovered from an eastern winter ice storm.

But, every February, madness would strike. I'd sit by the kitchen window, watching the sleet coat the lilacs, and I'd budget for the garden, making majestic plans for a rose bed and gravelled walks edged with feathery wands of spirea. Meanwhile, the kids left home and Jack and I took a three-week cruise on our sailboat. The idyllic sun-kissed days we had enjoyed had fried the garden. I mourned the dusty remains of my dreams and wondered if this were the end of an era.

However, down in the damp corner of our lot, clustered around a pile of rocks, the clumps of white daisy that I had rescued from a builder's lot bloomed a welcoming greeting. The ferns that I had dug from the woods near the yacht club, minutes ahead of the road-building crew, had settled in to gossip with the black-eyed Susies and the little wood violets, product of another rescue mission. The ancient stand of hollyhocks, the invincible Little Old Lady, Grandma's Icelandic fern, was, as always, encroaching on the so-called lawn, and the rhubarb was ready to pick.

For the next two years, I was content each fall to tuck a few tulip and daffodil bulbs around the clumps of fern and phlox and to sprinkle some of the wildly expensive wildflower seeds the kids had given me. But my son-in-law had gardening books out the last time we went for dinner. Convinced I was cured, I decided I'd have just a little peek.

Immediately, I could feel madness closing in. If I dug around all the Saskatoons, I could add some columbines and, although it was late, I was sure I could find a flat or two of Canterbury Bells and some candytuft, and maybe three bunches of forget-me-nots and a flat of Sweet William . . .

I chained myself to the boat for a week, at its mooring where I could watch the great blues fish off the end of the dinghy dock, down where the water lilies bloom, and I waited to be restored to sanity.

✉ I thought "Saskatoon" was the most evocative word in the English language, until I learned that the fuzzy yellow and purple and white cups that I called "crocus" are more correctly called "Pasqueflowers" in honour of Easter – which explains why I can't get warm feelings from the sophisticated true garden crocus that should appear in our lawn soon, unless the squirrels ate all the bulbs last fall. Anyway, Pasqueflowers aside, I thought "Saskatoon" was the quickest route to a binge of homesickness for the prairies.

Until, that is, I heard Don Freed sing "Hold On, Caragana." There's a lot of caragana in all of us prairie lilies, no matter where we've transplanted. There's a deep-rooted quality, and a hold-on quality that won't quit. (Ever wonder why it's so easy for rural Canadians to become free-lancers? Shucks – wondering where the next cheque's coming from is a natural feeling.)

There were caraganas on the farm where I grew up, clipped and controlled, lining the edges of the cinder walk to the front door (which no one ever used) and bordering Mom's flower beds, her solace of an evening after a day of holding on. When we moved to town, there were caraganas lining the driveway and defining the limits of our property, a mass of yellow blossoms in the spring and tiny pea pods popping in the fall.

Mom moved most of her garden into town with us but one day when I was back out at the old house, I found a rusty pair of old clippers and I ritually trimmed the caragana hedge.

Last summer, when I joined one of my Western nieces back on the old farm, I discovered that favourite shades met in the evening to walk among the lilacs and the caraganas, and they didn't mind having me join them. We told secrets in the evenings and when I said goodbye to them the night before I left, I again ritually trimmed a caragana.

Joan Eyolfson Cadham
Ste. Anne de Bellevue, Quebec

✉ I'd like to share a hint on starting seeds indoors. I use the same garden dirt they will grow in – I have less trouble with that than sterilized soil when it comes to damping off. I use old milk cartons as containers: fill three-quarters with soil, sprinkle with seeds, water well, then cover the seed with fine dry dirt – except petunias, as they require light to germinate; cover with glass or plastic wrap to keep them moist, and place in a very warm place so germination occurs as soon as possible. I place the cartons over furnace registers; a friend uses their water-bed (no daytime naps in their house!). A hot-water radiator would be perfect.

As soon as possible, I sit the seedlings outdoors where they get full sun, cooler temperatures and shelter from too much wind. Of course, they are brought in each evening as we still have frost at nights. Because we lack water, I transplant the seedlings to halves of milk cartons, two or three to a carton and let them grow that way until I transplant them in early or mid-June. Then I simply cut the bottom off the carton, set it in a hole and pile dirt up along the edges. The carton provides some protection from wind and cutworms while the plant keeps right on growing with no transplanting shock. I can pour a cup of water in each container if we've had no rain and it goes directly to the roots. I've grown tomatoes, peppers and cucumbers this way all through our drought years. Mind you, you should see the crop when we do get rain!

✉ About "orange hoary puccoon." Thirty years ago I wouldn't have known the word. It would have sounded like some ugly worm we'd find in our garden. But if you said "cowslips," my eyes would have lit up. I grew up on the Saskatchewan-Manitoba border – long-grass country – and cowslips were as essential to spring as swallows and red-winged blackbirds. They grow in the grass in the full sun but sheltered by aspen groves (sloughs). They might grow twelve inches or a bit less and are not bold flowers at all. They look a bit like an orange forget-me-not: small, orange flowerets clustered in loose heads. But what makes the hoary puccoon so special is a drop of nectar hidden in the base of each tiny flower. And if country kids can beat the bees to those flowers they can carefully pull out the florets and suck that tiny drop of heavenly sweetness. It was a rite of spring down home.

Wendy Caldwell
Ceylon, Saskatchewan

✉ Is morning glory a weed? This morning, I yanked miles of it out of my garden and woods. In fact, if I look out of my bathroom window right now, on top of a stump largely covered by ivy sits in triumph a white trumpet – *convolvulus* is what I call it – because morning glory is too fine a name for a menace such as this is.

I have been battling this creature (and blackberries) since 1949! – and the battle is still not won by either of us. With great effort – weekly – I maintain some boundaries, but I know if I were to surrender, within a few months my garden would be like the thicket in Sleeping Beauty – covered over and impenetrable.

The *cultivated* convolvulus are beautiful – pink, blue, white – easily controlled and confined to designated areas. Little resemblance to its cousin, which advances like a silent army!

Sheilah Thompson
North Vancouver

✉ When I got married, my husband and I combined our two households, which included, among other things, two coffee grinders, three pressure cookers, two woks, et cetera. Because of the over-abundance of possessions, we thought long and hard about wedding presents. We didn't need anything for the house but we certainly did for the garden. So we suggested to people that plants such as rhododendrons, azaleas, flowering trees, shrubs and so on would be well received. It was really funny going back to my apartment after the reception to find the building manager had let people drop off their presents. My apartment looked so odd crammed with burlap-wrapped trees and bushes with bows and ribbons on them.

Now, nine years later, we still marvel at how much our garden has filled out and grown. We delight in the shape and beauty of our "wedding" plants and can still pinpoint (we have had no casualties, which is quite remarkable) who gave us which plant.

Carol Tabbers
Surrey, British Columbia

✉ It is only since my husband and I bought a house two years ago that I've become interested in gardening. I now find myself staring at people's gardens and picking out the flowers that I like and trying to place them mentally in our garden. I should admit that I am by no means a hard-core gardener. I am an accidental gardener – if it lives it stays, if it dies it's out on its ear. I am one of those people who throws some peat moss and cow poop into the garden and puts in the plants. I have yet to get my soil tested for its pH (although I think I could do that myself with some litmus paper). Despite my flagrant disregard for the cult of gardening, my garden seems to be doing very well.

One of the things that I love about gardens is the sense of continuity that you get when you plant plants from other people's gardens. We have dahlias that came from my grandmother's cousin's garden, and coreopsis and baby's breath that came to Toronto in the Thirties from the Sault. (An older lady friend of our family who has been a surrogate grandmother to us brought them from her mother's garden to Toronto when she was married.) It gives one such a wonderful link with the past and a real hope for the future. I too am carrying on the tradition. Some of our dahlias are now growing in a girlfriend's garden in Washington, D.C., and cosmos seeds from our garden are being planted by friends and family.

Susan L. Maltby
Toronto

THE FIVE SWEET SONGSTRESSES OF BELLEFIELD, MANITOBA

Or, as their biographer calls them, The Shirley Group.

The Shirleys' biographer (they were all named Shirley) is Lavinia Glass, who lives in – or at least writes from – Winnipeg. She sent me the scholarly document that makes up this chapter some months after we had launched our Monday poetry club (see Chapter Two). Nancy Watson called her and made a date to talk about the Shirleys on the radio. In the course of our interview, I asked Lavinia if she had been influenced by the work of Paul Hiebert, the grand old University of Manitoba chemistry professor and theologian (and a particular hero of mine) who, in his spare time, had given the world Sarah Binks, "the sweet songstress of Saskatchewan." Yes, she said, she had.

Professor Hiebert listens to *Morningside* from heaven now. I hope he enjoyed the conversation based on this work as much as I did.

The Shirley Group, by Lavinia Glass.

The Shirley Group

✉ In the 1930s in the Manitoba town of Bellefield, a group of eleven-year-old poetesses formed an important voice in Prairie Literature.

Their founder and poetic whip was Shirley Nunnelly, the frail and albino-like daughter of the town piano tuner. She gathered together and trained up as versifiers a circle of contemporaries – Shirley Ott, Shirley McGill, Shirley Smith and Shirley Mary-Beth LeClair.

Although not dispossessed or rootless, The Shirley Group was encouraged by their leader to be aside from the intellectual mainstream of their town, to develop their own convictions on the human condition, to stand united in their belief in the importance of serviceable poetry.

A recently published centennial history of Bellefield and district makes no reference to The Shirley Group. Only the fortunate discovery of a body of their work (in a black pebbled-leather schoolbag) enables us to learn the central nature of their poetic statements and their accidental approach to form.

Group founder Shirley Nunnelly grew up in a hushed household. Her mother, Letitia, padded quietly about her daily duties and contentedly attended to her *petit point* in the evenings. Her father, Alfred, solemnly carried out his piano-tuning responsibilities, returning home to rest his ear and read his current copy of *Etude*.

Shirley Nunnelly is remembered by an elderly neighbour. "She was a wispy snip of a thing with a very, very high forehead. And was she a talker! Always piping up here and there with some weird idea (neither God nor Santa can see beyond the end of his nose). Many's the time I could have cuffed her ears."

In the following flagship poem, in uncontrolled free verse, we get a glimpse of those leading Bellefield townspeople who moved and shook in such a way as to provide Nunnelly with some of her best-loved weird ideas.

by Lavinia Glass

More Rot than Not

You see their silly faces
In every corner of town
A throng of pudding-headed creatures
Watching the free John Deere movie
Ordering Eaton Beauty dolls.

Hen-hearted tight-fisted Alex Spurgeon
Mayor of what!
Mayor of a town that will never
Vote in the waterworks
Bellefield needs a bath!

Abominable Mrs. Harvey Craddock
Going through the change
Shoving us down in our seats
At the Christmas Concert. A blessing
She never had any of her own!

Scrawny God-forsaken Rev. Mogridge
Comes to the house for tea
Five pieces of cake and to get warm
I wouldn't give you a plug nickel
For what they teach you in Sunday School!

Mouldy Mrs. Florence Hawkes
Screeched at me
"Whoever put that idea into your head, child?"
When I happened to mention her clothes smelled b.o.
She shouldn't keep her nose so otherwise occupied!

I suppose I should mention one uppity person
Who should remain nameless
What if she did come from a well-to-do family
In the Old Country?
She's still not good enough for me!

Batty Mrs. Myrtle Motts
Always hollering across the fence
"And how are you-oo this morning?
Going to be another scorcher I'm afraid."
Neighbours should be seen and not heard!

Lazy fat-bum Mr. Farquahar
Scratches himself
Where it is not courteous to do so!
Bellefield could better use a zither teacher
In order to be a well-behaved town!

And what about the big stink
Common-minded trustee Una Whatley kicked up
When Mr. Murphy taught some moral sex facts?
Of course, I'm not much for information of this kind
Or physical culture of any kind!

Thank the Lord
For true-hearted Matt Downey
Who whistles softly
And delivers fresh ice to most homes!

Beautiful Jenny Tate
Bellefield's only known slut
Always says hello to me
Very nicely, too!

Our level-headed volunteer firemen
Pull the water wagon quickly
To the scene of the belching flames
And rolling smoke!

The Oriental gentleman who runs Bellefield's café
Has never been connected with
One single white slavery incident
That I know!

Mr. Stannard our interesting butcher
Lets us watch him bludgeon
The pigs and cows and lambs at the slaughterhouse
Although this isn't a school outing!

TAKE MY WORD FOR IT!
BELLEFIELD HAS ITS ROT!
TRASH, BULLIES AND DRUNKARDS!
JUST A FEW WHO ARE NOT!

by Shirley Nunnelly

Shirley Ott was the eldest of Henry and Bertha Ott's eleven children. She is remembered by a teacher as being a dreamer of far-away places, wishing always to be from somewhere other than Bellefield, yet surprisingly, not a top geography student. In the following, we sense the young girl's desperate hope.

Homeland

Take me back to Colorado
Mid waving fields of avocado
There to smell the apricot
Sweet fruit of life o Camelot
There to stand mid bows of larch
Eating pears tho it be March
Let me wander by your berries
Pomegranates, peerless cherries
There belong I, there now I'll go
O citrus state my Colorado!

by Shirley Ott

Shirley Mary-Beth LeClair was the only child of Bellefield's only mixed marriage. Her father, Armand, arrived in the town, friendly and jobless, in the summer of '26. The first door he knocked upon, the United Church manse, was opened to him by the Reverend's daughter, Lydia Bowen-Lane, a kind and intelligent teacher who asked only what Armand took in his tea.

In the cool, shaded Bowen-Lane parlour while eating sandwiches, nine-day pickles and spice cake, Armand outlined to his hosts (the Reverend Bowen-Lane had come in from the garden) his desire for a permanent livelihood in a good place, to end his years as an unbound stray.

He acquired steady work clerking in Smith's General Store but not before living as a transient for several weeks beneath the grandstand at the Fair Grounds, calling each evening at the Bowen-Lane mealtime for sustenance and companionship.

During those weeks, Lydia and Armand took to passing the after-supper sunlight hours strolling and chatting to and from the mile corner south of town. Bellefield also chatted. For they knew, beyond question, it was not right for the daughter of the United Church minister to harbour a French stranger.

This was of no concern to the couple. Their easy friendship became genuine love; their marriage a blessed and abiding union.

Shirley Mary-Beth was born happy and strong on a blue and golden September afternoon. At age eleven, recruited into Nunnelly's poetry group, she created, willingly and playfully.

My Country

I feel so good in the morning
I feel so good at night
And in between
Everything's pea green
Everything feels quite all right I mean.
Unless a bugbear I have seen
Or catch a bout of gangarene
Unless I eat a bad sardine
Unless a blizzard is too mean
Or I rip my dress of velveteen
On the barb wire fence at Wood's ravine
Unless in quicksand I have been
Everything feels quite alright I mean.

by Shirley Mary-Beth LeClair

Shirley McGill, daughter of Sam (Bellefield's undertaker) and Grace (Supreme Grand Lady of the Order of the Mystic Realm), was a weighty child, and the Prairie winds carried the dust and pollen that gave her a constantly stuffed nose. McGill's personal concerns were mankind's physical vulnerability, germs and the inevitability of death. She expressed them in a practical manner.

Rhymes of the Red Cross Health Rules

Always stand and sit up straight
Worms and stroke we sure do hate.

Early to bed and exercise
Boils and flu we all despise.

Drink lots of milk and chew food well
To prevent a fainting spell.

Cover your mouth when you cough or sneeze
Stay away from draft and breeze.

Dirty nails can be typhoidal
Some of our troubles are adenoidal.

Never slouch or never loll
To keep your spinal column tall.

Rotten food your body fouls
Always try to move your bowels.

Have good light for both your eyes
They can go pink you realize.

Take lots of medicine from Rexall
You never know what might befall.

When you're sick and lie abed
Have two white pillows at your head.

Avoid epidemics and red, red rashes
Til earth gobbles up your dusty ashes.

by Shirley McGill

Shirley Smith seems not to have been remembered by any of the townspeople for anything, including recollection as to which of the two Smith families she was one of. The sole evidence of any association Smith had with the poetry group lies in a single scansion-free stanza that turned up on the endpaper of her school text, *The Romance of Canadian History*.

Fall

In Mr. Flanders field
There was a barley crop growing
My heart suddenly leaped up
When I saw Mr. Flanders mowing
Then threshing.

by Shirley Smith

There was exactly enough headroom beneath the east end of the CPR station platform to accommodate The Shirley Group meetings. Eight feet or so away, behind a high lilac hedge, Mrs. Daniel George, the stationmaster's wife, tended her garden and listened on occasion to the nearby poetic proceedings.

Thanks to Mrs. George's proximity and remarkable recall of one such meeting – held on a hot, dronish July afternoon – we are able to faithfully reconstruct what went on.

The poetry meeting began with Nunnelly leading the singing of "God Save the King." Then

NUNNELLY   I call the meeting to order and do the roll call. Shirley Smith?

SMITH   Here.

NUNNELLY   Shirley Ott?

OTT   Here.

NUNNELLY   Shirley McGill?

McGILL   Here.

NUNNELLY   Shirley Mary-Beth LeClair?

LeCLAIR   Here, there and everywhere.

NUNNELLY   Shush! Just say here. And of course I'm here. Now class, the last time we met I told you to bring a new poem you made up to read out loud and I told you to bring your favourite poem by a real poet to read out loud. I'll start with my own new one. It's called "Ode to the British Empire."

McGILL   My father said we shouldn't have any more to do with the British Empire.

NUNNELLY   Your father's not a poet. "Ode to the British Empire" by Shirley Nunnelly.

> The British Empire expects us all
> To do our duty daily
> Standing at attention
> While the Union Jack waves gaily!
>
> Far-flung mother country
> Though not where we reside
> Through centuries of fracases
> She's never come untied!
>
> The King watches over the Commonwealth
> Wearing his very best robe
> Brave-souled spunky-minded
> Ruling all the waves on the globe!
>
> London Bridge can fall to pieces
> The Prince of Wales marry Wally
> But never in a thousand years
> Will England not be jolly!
>
> Bellefield's few loyal subjects
> Are strong as granite rocks
> Bellefield's bigwigs the Empire hates
> Like Mrs. Florence Hawkes!

The end. Miss Ott, you go next.

SMITH   I was first after you last time.

NUNNELLY   Shush! Miss Ott?

OTT   Mine's called "Far Away." "Far Away" by Shirley Ott.

O California here I come
Shirley Temple be my chum.

Ontario let me see your quints
England let me meet your Prince.

O I am going to the coast
Where it's always warm as toast.

When a contest I have won
I am going to Wisconsin.

I will go down to the sea someday
When I drive a Chevrolet.

O Winnipeg I will not greet
Poor Queen Victoria's snowy feet.

NUNNELLY   I suppose that's fine. Miss LeClair, you're next.

LeCLAIR   Matthew Mark Luke and John
Hold the horse till I get on!

NUNNELLY   You didn't make that up!

LeCLAIR   Mary Mary quite contrary
Our milk comes from Larkin's dairy!

NUNNELLY   You only made half that one up.

LeCLAIR   Pussycat pussycat where have you been?
I went to the creek to catch a sardine
But my car ran out of gasoline!
I made up most of that one.

NUNNELLY   You can't do that! Make one verse two lines and the next one three!

LeCLAIR   Twinkle twinkle little star
  Saturday's the church bazaar
  According to the calendar
  And I like raspberry vinegar!
I made up three-quarters of that one!

NUNNELLY   It sounds so silly.

LeCLAIR   I know a girl and her name is Tilly
  Daffy down daffy down daffy down dilly
  She has eyes like a tiger lily
  And her little brother's name is Billy!
I made all that one up just now.

NUNNELLY   Miss LeClair, you do undesirable poetry. Miss McGill, you next.

McGILL   Mine's called "A Word to the Wise Is Sufficient." "A Word to the Wise Is Sufficient" by Shirley McGill.

  Never point a loaded gun
  Always make sure your pork's well done
  Never sit on cold cement
  Piles are not a good event
  Never never swallow your gum
  Or constipated you'll become
  You all know this one I suppose
  Never put a button up your nose
  This is important and good to know
  Always wash your hands after you go.

NUNNELLY   Thank you, Miss McGill. You've given us something to ponder. That's what poetry is supposed to do!

OTT   I'd rather ponder about California.

LeCLAIR   I'd rather ponder about – sardines!

SMITH   I don't like to ponder about anything!

NUNNELLY   Shush! Miss Smith, you're last. Read your poem.

SMITH   You won't like mine.

NUNNELLY   You have to read it anyway.

SMITH   I didn't know what to call it so I called it "The Bee." Is that all right?

NUNNELLY   Is it about a bee?

SMITH   I guess so. "The Bee" by Shirley Smith.

> ZZZ ZZ ZZZ
> Goes the bee
> From flower to flower
> I stand and watch them

but I couldn't think of anything to rhyme with flower.

OTT   Hour. You stand and watch them by the hour!

McGILL   Devour. You stand and watch them pollen devour!

LeCLAIR   Sour. You stand and watch them till the milk turns sour!

NUNNELLY   Shush! Order!

OTT   I've got an aunt south of the border!

NUNNELLY   Order! Shush!

SMITH   Boil an apple, it turns to mush!

NUNNELLY   You are not funny, Shirley Smith!

SMITH   Only boys can stand and pith!

NUNNELLY   Shirley Smith! You are not funny!

LeCLAIR   Nights are dark and days are sunny!

NUNNELLY   Shirley LeClair! You are too far-fetched and bothersome! Now, we're each going to read our real poems. Miss Ott, you're first.

OTT   (recites) Way down south
   Where bananas grow
   A mouse stepped on
   An elephant's toe

NUNNELLY   Good lord.

OTT   The elephant cried
   With tears in his eyes
   And said
   Why don't you pick on someone your own size?

NUNNELLY   Is that all? I suppose it's plenty. Miss McGill?

McGILL   I found this one in *The United Church Observer*.

(reads)

   If we knew the woe and heartache
   Waiting for us down the road
   If our lips could taste the wormwood
   If our backs could feel the load
   If . . .

OTT   If Shirley McGill would just forget
   About germs and sores and dying

LeCLAIR   She'd be happy as a lark
   Without even trying.

NUNNELLY   Miss LeClair? Perhaps you have a better poem?

LeCLAIR   My mother gave me this one out of her chocolate box of poems. It's called "My Kingdom" by Louisa May Alcott.

(reads)

   A little kingdom I possess
   Where thoughts and feelings dwell
   And very hard the task I find

Of governing it well.
I do not ask for any crown
But that which all may win
Nor try to conquer any world
Hey! The train is coming in!

(the train is heard from afar)

NUNNELLY That's enough of that anyway. We've got to hurry!
Miss Smith?

SMITH Mine's from the *Saturday Evening Post*.

(reads)

One for the money
Two for the show
Campbell's Tomato
Helps you grow.

NUNNELLY Good lord. I'll read mine. "Reynard the Fox" by John
Masefield.

(reads)

The fox was strong, he was full of running
He could run for an hour and then be cunning
(He was being chased by dogs and men on horses)
But the cry behind him made him chill
They were nearer now and they meant to kill!
They meant to run him until his blood
Clogged in his heart as his brush (his tail) with mud!

(the train whistle sounds)

Till his back bent up and his tongue hung flagging
And his belly and brush (his tail) were filthed wi

(rumble rumble clang clang hisssss – the train is heard overhead)

SMITH It's here!

OTT Let's go up!

MCGILL   And see who gets off!

LeCLAIR   And see who gets on!
(exit scampering – Shirley, Shirley, Shirley and Shirley)

NUNNELLY   Hmph. This meeting is now ended. Adjourned, I mean.

Author's Note

Didn't I say Mrs. Daniel George
Had recall nonpareil?
And wouldn't you say those dear poets Shirley
Showed expression most versatile?

Here's to The Group
All grannies by now.
McGill sixty-three, hale and hearty?
Wherever you are Shirley Mary-Beth LeClair
Have you managed one life-long tea party?

I wish you avocados
Miss Shirley Ott
Oranges from your very own tree
Sunny and warm in a room of your own
In that other citrus state by the sea.

O Smith. Shirley Smith
Of the barley crop growing
Where o where are you at this hour?
Under the CPR platform?
Trying to rhyme something with flower?

Shirley Nunnelly, Group Leader
I know where she is
(May nothing or no one reduce her)
Teaching in Bellefield, grades four and five
Writing poems for *The Western Producer*.

OUR OWN DIET OF WORMS

I don't know who to blame for this. Shelagh Rogers, with whom I was talking (and reading letters) about camp songs one morning when the subject of the worm song came up? Gary Dunford, the *Toronto Sun* columnist who heard us and (see below) sent us what he insisted was the proper version? Or maybe just the weird little corner of all our minds that stores away the most bizarre memories – and lyrics – from childhood.

In any case, here, I'm delighted to say, is the most disgusting chapter in all the history of the *Morningside Papers*, original, *New*, *Latest* and, now, *Fourth*.

✉ When I was a little girl and in a bad mood, or "A Charter Member of the Life Stinks Society" as my dad would say, my mother would sing "Going to the Garden to Eat Worms" to me. It rarely failed to restore me to good humour, probably as much because of the cuddle on her knee as because of the words of the song.

When my youngest sister, who arrived when I was twelve, was in ill humour, I vividly remember singing the song to her as well and the magic of the silly words, along with the necessary cuddle, always worked.

I now have four children of my own and each one in turn has received their share of cuddles along with a rendition of "Nobody likes me, everybody hates me, I'm going to the garden to eat worms." Works every time.

Cathy Cormier
Oakville, Ontario

✉ The *real* worm song . . .

Nobody loves me, everybody hates me
Guess I'll eat some worms
Long slim slimy ones, short fat juicy ones
Itsy bitsy fuzzy wuzzy worms.

First you cut the heads off, then you suck the guts out
Oh, how they wiggle and squirm
Long slim slimy ones, short fat juicy ones
Itsy bitsy fuzzy wuzzy worms.

Wiggle goes the first one, goosh goes the second one
Sure don't wanna eat worms
Long slim slimy ones, short fat juicy ones
Itsy bitsy fuzzy wuzzy worms.

Down goes the first one, down goes the second one
Sure hate the taste of worms
Long slim slimy ones, short fat juicy ones
Itsy bitsy fuzzy wuzzy worms.

Nobody hates me, everybody likes me
Never shoulda eaten those worms
Long slim slimy ones, short fat juicy ones
Itsy bitsy fuzzy wuzzy worms.

Up comes the first one, out comes the second one
Oh, how they wiggle and squirm
Long slim slimy ones, short fat juicy ones
Itsy bitsy fuzzy wuzzy worms.

Gary Dunford
Toronto

✉ I remember all the extra lines of the worm song and sing them regularly to my three children who are currently in a "bathroom" humour phase. Our last three lines are:

Hasten Jason bring a basin!
Oop slop! Bring a mop
Too late, bring a plate.

It never fails to bring down the house.

Diane Watts
Erickson, Manitoba

✉ I sang the worm song as part of a "fruit basket" at Bayside Baptist Youth Camp (outside Halifax, Nova Scotia), where I attended from 1959 to 1967. Here are the words we sang:

Nobody likes me, everybody hates me
Sitting in the garden eating worms.
Big, fat, juicy worms; long, slim, slimy worms
Itsy, bitsy, teeny, weeny worms.

In goes the first worm, in goes the second worm
In goes the third little worm.
Big, fat, juicy worms; long, slim, slimy worms
Itsy, bitsy, teeny, weeny worms.

My stomach is in a commotion.
I dare not lean over the rail.
I don't want to dirty the ocean.
Oh somebody please bring a pail.

Come up, come up
Oh come up dear supper, to me, to me
Come up, come up
Oh come up dear supper, to me.

I'm coming, I'm coming
For my head is bending low.
I hear those gentle voices calling,
Hasten Jason bring the basin
Oops, kurplop, bring the mop.

That is the *real* version of the worm song.

Peggy Bendell
Porcupine, Ontario

✉ As a child in the early 1970s, I attended a summer camp on Kootenay Lake, called Camp Koolaree. My mother and her sister went there as children thirty years earlier. To the best of all of our knowledge, the worms were always eaten in the garden – where else would you expect, really? There was no talk of Jason or the basin, but it was a church camp after all. Or perhaps we westerners are just a little bit more queasy than that. One more verse to add:

The first one was easy
The second one was breezy
The third one got stuck in my throat
(cough, cough)
Long, skinny, slimy ones
Short, fat, hairy ones
Itsy, bitsy, squishy, little worms.

The worm song was for sissies, though. We seasoned campers preferred to sing the Gopher Song:

Great green gobs of greasy, grimy gopher guts
Mutilated monkey meat
Petrified porpoise pus
All wrapped up in little piggies' hairy feet
That's what we had for lunch.

Lynn Dorward
Port McNeill, British Columbia

✉ I learned this version of the end of the worm song from my husband, who was raised in India and attended school there. This was the way it went at his school:

Quick, quick, the cat got sick.
Where? Where? under the chair,
Great Scott! what a lot,
Hasten, hasten, fetch a basin,
All in vain, all in vain
The cat just licked it up again!

Pat Beer
Sault Ste. Marie, Ontario

✉ Sure as God made little green apples with little green worms in 'em, this is the real, honest-to-goodness version that I learned at Brownies in 1960 here in Victoria. Our version carried the "hasten Jason" part a little further:

Hasten Jason, bring the basin!
Ooops kerplop, bring the mop . . .
Alas! Alack! it's all in vain –
The dogs have licked it up again,
And me without my spoon.

Monny Rutabagas
Victoria

371

✉ My four Edwardian, maiden great-aunts, genteel Edinburgh ladies, used to amuse us with the verse:

Quick! Quick!
The cat's sick.
Where? Where?
Under the chair.
Hasten Jason
Bring a basin.
Great Scott,
What a lot!

As an impressionable nine-year-old, I thought this very risqué!

Alison Cartwright
Fort Good Hope, Northwest Territories

✉ Sixty years ago, the Third Fort William Wolf Cub Pack on occasion would sit cross-legged on the basement floor of St. Paul's Cathedral, to be lead by our Akela in a rousing rendition of "The Worm Song"; the "gar-den" having been replaced by the "cub-den"; as in "sitting in the cub den," which made eminently more sense under the circumstances.

During the summer we would camp out on the banks of the Kaminisitiquoia River, winding worms made of flour and water around dirty sticks, which were then held over a smoky fire before being eaten. At least they didn't wriggle on the way down. Or on the way back up.

Deryck Thomson
Sidney, British Columbia

✉ I hope to have the final and absolutely last word on the Worm Song controversy. For, unlike your purely literary and academic debaters, I have actually eaten worms!

I ate them in Toronto several years ago, but not in a garden. I bought a pack of the creatures in an off-beat gourmet food store, the kind of place that sold chocolate-covered ants and sparrow eggs.

The worms had been toasted to a fine crisp and then chopped up into pieces about the size of large match heads. The clerk assured me they were an excellent source of protein and were indistinguishable from bacon bits. So they were.

At a dinner for friends a few days later, I dumped the package of worm bits into a bowl on the table, and my guests and I sprinkled the little devils all over our salad. We all munched away very happily and nobody knew the difference.

Of course, I didn't tell anybody. I'm sure if I had, nobody would have loved me, and everybody would have hated me!

Bill Barringer
Vancouver

It's Not Easy Being Green

Thoughts on the environment, 1989-91 – a collection of letters that arrived, without exception, on recycled paper.

A few weeks ago I started to examine what changes we have made to our life-style. Then my brain started to fizzle. After reading the list of all the things we do and realizing how unconventional we are, I became thoroughly depressed. How does one convince others that perhaps they should be doing things a bit differently? Here is my list in no particular order, things I do, as well as the changes we have made as a family. Yes, it's a full-time job saving the environment, but we all have to do what we can.

1. Recycle paper – anything with a blank side used to write letters, make lists, kids' art projects
2. Recycle envelopes – the ones that come with your VISA, hydro and phone bills; we don't use as we pay at the bank machine
3. Breast-feeding – my own children, as well as encouraging others to do so (member/librarian with La Lèche League)

4. Empty plastic squeeze bottle for juice instead of drinking boxes. I got tired of replacing the glass liners in thermoses, and while a steel thermos is too heavy for a small child to carry, it works great for an adult. Soups go in a plastic container wrapped in a towel.

5. Compost – have helped neighbours start their own as well, collect scraps from those who don't have heaps, as well as old local tradition of using capelin, seaweed and peat moss

6. Make own baby toys – give workshops to show others how

7. Friendship coupons for birthdays – a gift of a skill or time together (going skating, swimming, special supper)

8. Use clothesline instead of dryer

9. Re-use bags for department store purchases. This causes problems sometimes; the cashiers are convinced I want to put my bag inside of their bag; I've had to ask to see the manager on occasion to avoid taking home yet another plastic bag

10. Start a food co-op – allows us to buy organic food in bulk

11. Cold water to wash laundry

12. Turn off lights when leaving room

13. Put on extra sweaters when cold

14. Make our own: ice cream, yoghurt, granola, pickles, sauerkraut, baked goods, mayonnaise, soup, and so on. Avoid using processed foods

15. Use pressure cooker, microwave, wood stove for cooking

16. House designed for passive solar heating, R-2000 standards

17. Cloth diapers – for baby and now for me – yes, that's what we "environmentally concerned types" use instead of "Wings" for our monthly cycle, just like Grandma used to do

18. Interior of house and furniture all solid wood (air-dried) construction – natural renewable materials rather than plastic or synthetic wherever possible

19. Buy things that will last as long as possible even if more expensive, e.g., tools, clothes

20. More vegetarian meals

21. Wear hand-me-downs, exchange with friends

22. When tempted to eat out, we buy something special to cook for supper, or treat ourselves to exotic fruit for dessert

23. Donate to environment groups—we're doing this for Christmas with our friends instead of buying more things we don't really need

24. Buy from their catalogues

25. Walk to work, grocery store (it's too dangerous to bicycle here)

26. Hang fly paper instead of using sprays

27. Use the library – they will go across Canada to fill your request

28. Grow own vegetables in gardens, sprouts inside in winter – have plans to build a greenhouse next spring

29. Have to make three stops minimum if using car

30. Stop cutting front lawn – encourages birds and insects. Since we live in suburbia, this drives the neighbours crazy, but it's my revenge for all the chemicals they spray on their lawns

31. Plant native shrubs and trees

32. Use hand mower for back lawn

33. Pet rabbit eats kitchen scraps, donates manure

34. Learn about and practise organic gardening

35. Put TV in basement

36. Feed birds – more entertaining than TV, and they hang around in summer to eat grubs

37. Cloth bags for groceries (I haven't been able to find net bags anywhere here yet). After you have recycled the plastic ones to bits, you need to make your own re-usable bags

38. Use old onion net bags for loose veggy purchases at store, e.g., mushrooms, grapes. This really freaks out the cashiers, as they can't find a UPC sticker on it

39. Heat with wood, collect scraps to burn from building sites – solar heat isn't feasible in the fog

40. Bath water, tea-kettle water for plants

41. Don't flush toilet every time

42. Make our own cleaners with baking soda

43. Buy "friendly" shampoos, detergent, and so on. These I have to buy from the mainland when we make our yearly trek back to stock up on fresh peaches and other market goodies each summer

44. Cloth hankies from sentimental clothing that has worn out

45. Spreading "the word" via newsletters of groups we belong to

46. Support the Organic Growers Association

47. Letters to radio encouraging coverage of environmental issues

48. Try to get name off junk mail lists – not sure how yet

49. Things not needed donated to charity

50. Use rags, tea towels instead of paper towel

51. Decorate plants at Christmas instead of cutting down tree

52. Collect discarded Christmas trees to put around yard for birds and as a wind break, then burn for heat

53. Save empty tins for cutworm collars – we only have a recycling program for plastic pop bottles and aluminum pop cans here, two products we don't use. I haven't figured out what to do with my glass jars yet, there's only so much you can store in them. Perhaps I should take them back to Ottawa to put in a Blue Box?

54. Use material scraps, children's art for wrapping paper

55. Burn kitchen scraps in winter, put ashes in compost and around bushes to discourage bad bugs

56. Letters to store managers to encourage less plastic packaging, recycling bags, and so on

57. Wash plastic bags, aluminum foil to re-use

58. Use a water-saver head on shower

59. Replacing regular bulbs with energy savers where possible (someone needs to come up with a better design, as their shape precludes their use in many areas).

Cathy Smallwood
St. John's

✉ After my weekly ritual treat at a Moncton supermarket's snack bar a few days ago, I was surprised, and a little guilty, when I took notice of the amount of trash I was leaving behind me from an insignificant snack. I guess the increasing media coverage of our waste disposal problems has raised my awareness of the issue.

For what it's worth, here is an inventory of the garbage left from a snack consisting of one deliciously hot, crumbly carrot and nut muffin (freshly baked on the premises) and a cup of coffee with a smoke:

Muffin

1 cello wrap
1 paper muffin cup
1 plastic butter container
foil top from butter container
1 plastic knife
2 serviettes
(1 to act as a plate)

Coffee (large)

1 paper cup
2 plastic milk cups
2 foil tops from creamers
2 sugar envelopes
1 wooden stir stick

Smoke

1 foil throw-away ashtray
1 cigarette butt

Perhaps we should move forward by going back to a saner time when waste was considered wasteful and we actually washed used dishes and containers.

William Thomas
Kent County, New Brunswick

✉ What? Not use toilet paper? How to do without toilet paper and menstrual pads? Here are some ideas.
1. Use water instead of toilet paper. It gets you a lot cleaner! Dry off with a towel if you wish. You wash your hands afterwards anyway, right? Many countries all over the world (Turkey, India, all Moslem countries) use only water. (Toilet paper is a recent invention.)

2. Because women can't "drip dry" as easily as men after urinating and since a lot of toilet paper is used to "wipe the drips," you can use a towel specifically set aside for this purpose that you throw in the wash regularly.

3. For guests in your home, you can have strips cut from old clothes or sheets in a container next to the toilet with a note to be sure the cloths get thrown in the garbage basket and not down the toilet.

4. Use re-usable menstrual pads – a dozen should do you. I've been using these for years now. Treat them as you would cloth diapers: soak, rinse, wash and dry. I've recently sewn up a new set using my son's cloth diapers that he's no longer needing. My friend grew up in Holland with his mother re-using cloth pads.

Seems to me the main obstacle to doing these things is our cultural hang-up about our body and its fluids and excretions. It's especially difficult for women who have grown up with the attitude that menstrual blood should not be seen, mentioned, acknowledged, celebrated never mind touched by the hands of the woman whose blood it is!

It's all really not so yucky and difficult. In the words of a smart mother – "There's nothing you can get on your hands that you can't wash off." It not only can be done – it must be done.

Agnes Milejszo
Steinbach, Manitoba

✉ I have been wanting to tell other women about an alternative to sanitary napkins and tampons. For the past fourteen years I have used a natural sponge. The sponge can be cut to whatever size a woman needs. When it becomes saturated, the sponge is just rinsed under running warm water. This method would not work well in countries short on water, but in Canada it works great.

Louisa Johnson
Sackville, New Brunswick

✉ Newspapers, Loblaws and public service announcements constantly remind and chide us about the environment. Blue Boxes greet guests on stoops everywhere. Most people are happy about the new, mass environmental concern – except in some cases where it's gone too far.

What we *don't* hear about is the newest unhealthy mind-set, *enviro-neurosis*. I'm not a psychiatrist or anything, but I know that a person is called neurotic when his or her leading a normal life is impeded by problems. My overly sensitive concern for the environment is starting to cause embarrassment and discord.

I won't accept plastic bags at shops any more, but walk around Dundas with armloads of baskets. Poor clerks look at me in puzzlement as I cry, "No, not in bags, I have a basket." At my grocery store, the cashiers have been taught not to put my produce in extra bags. I made my grocer, the David Wood of Dundas, sell French string bags so I wouldn't have to use plastic. I've even brought bags back to Zehrs rather than throw them out. To my own mortification, I ask the clerk to promise they'll be re-used. I won't buy foil or Baggies. I re-use plastic bags over and over. I go through the trash sometimes to see if my man has put in recyclable things by mistake. (I usually find one or two.) When I imbibe drinks in a can or glass bottle, if the shop doesn't recycle, I put the containers *in my purse*, to my husband's dismay. And I won't buy overly packaged goods any more.

I asked the dry cleaners not to put the shirts in plastic, but they won't box them without plastic. Then I agree to a hanger, hold the plastic. Before the dry cleaning drone gave me our hangers, she tore off the protective plastic and punched it into the trash bin. My body writhed, and I haven't been back.

I refuse to fix or insure my car, because I want to live without fossil fuels as much as possible. I beg my man to boycott projects his company does with the oil company – to no avail.

I'm housebound most of the time – but will get around on my bike in a pinch. We're getting a wood stove, so I can burn cardboard. I compost all winter long, even when the racoons come for midnight snacks resulting in my dog barking all night. I only buy cosmetics at the Body Shop, since they recycle the containers. I'm a sucker for anything with an environmental claim – although I realize the biodegradable garbage bags are a swindle. I won't make copies of my business correspondence any more – unless absolutely necessary – but instead keep it on disc. Do they log trees for 3½ inch discs?

I'm even going to slow down in my profession so that I can work – for free – on an environmental film. Clearly, I've gone too far. And all this internal suffering has not helped the cause, just paralysed me in daily life. Pretty irrational, eh?

It's green guilt, like white guilt – and I feel personally responsible for our culture's decadent, energy-hungry way of life.

Hm – maybe talking about my neurosis could work out to being a good thing.

Amy Willard Cross
Dundas, Ontario

✉ I'm writing, on recycled paper, to commiserate with the woman who, I believe, termed herself an "enviro-neurotic." Perhaps we should form a self-help group.

I, too, am becoming obsessed (who am I kidding, I *am* obsessed), and it seems there is no turning back to the ignorance I once enjoyed.

Give me an "enviro-stat" – tell me something is bad for the environment and I'll stop buying, using, eating it, or at least modify my usage.

The substitutes or alternatives are a riot. I made my own dish soap, my man refers to it as "the dish soap from hell" (make some if you want to know why); walking (isn't that something the pioneers did?); a re-usable shopping bag (if you want a shopkeeper to look at you as if you have two heads tell him/her you don't want a bag); cloth diapers (need I explain?); and I have a garage full of glassware awaiting the promised Blue Box – we can just barely get the air-poisoning machine in there.

But my family is very understanding of my three garbages; it's my friends and acquaintances that I'm concerned about. How much of my obsession are they expected to endure?

I cringe and bite my tongue when my daughter's classmates all whip out juice boxes at snack time; when I see my neighbours spraying their lawns with poisons; when I see idling cars. The list goes on and on.

Last week, I had a nightmare about plastic bags—I don't remember the context, just the bags.

It has become so urgent to me – scratch the self-help group, I don't think there is a cure, except a clean environment. In the meantime, I'll continue my quest to "neuroticize" the nation.

Debbie Cousins McIntosh
Sudbury, Ontario

✉ *My friends are so useless*

Bill and Gail live in Edmonton,
they have been married for a number of years,
their oldest child, Betty, is seventeen,
and she has a brother and a sister.

Gail works at home.
Bill is a maintenance man,
he doesn't make that much money,
but enough for the family.
Two or three times he was offered a better paying job
which would have meant less time at home,
so he let it go.

They bought an old house,
and slowly renovated it themselves,
carpentry, plumbing, tiles, insulation and painting;
(well, a few friends helped them).
They bought second-hand furniture
which is functional as well as beautiful.

Too bad they didn't hire an architect, and tradespeople;
they could have fostered the economic expansion of their
    city;
and if there were more Gails and Bills,
what would happen to IKEA and Brick Warehouse?

They have time to grow vegetables in their back yard,
potatoes, lettuce, cucumbers, peas, carrots, etc.;
they produce about two-thirds of their yearly needs.
The garden demands more attention than a lawn,
but they say it is much more fun also,
and a family recreation.
But how could Safeway and Supersave prosper
if more families would become nearly self-sufficient?

They have a car which takes them wherever they want to
    go,
but it's probably the oldest car in the block.
These people really don't care
about the welfare of Ford, GM, or Toyota.
Oh yes, they own a black & white TV,
but with more of such non-TV addicts,
Sony wouldn't need new models which everyone "must"
    purchase every year.
And how could the cable TV companies become rich and
    powerful?

That's what I mean,
My friends are so useless
in our world of consumerism and commercialism.
They don't even speculate on the land and housing
    markets.

Gail has time to cook nutritious meals,
and the packaging industry
(which makes more profit than the farmers who produce
    the food)
would have to pack off if there were more people like her.

She also designs and sews some of the family clothing,
so, she doesn't help Canadian companies to reap huge
   profits
from the cheap labour provided by the Taiwan garment
   workers

Their three children don't waste money on candies or junk
   food.
With kids like them the dentists could never afford to buy
   yachts;
too bad for the yacht builders too.

Bill, Gail, and the children have a canoe and a few paddles;
for their holidays, they drive to a lake, or to the
   mountains.
Usually they camp with a few friends or by themselves,
and they really enjoy their vacations,
even if they haven't been to Hawaii yet, or to Disneyland.
They don't even seem to worry about not giving their
   money
to travel agencies, fancy hotels and foreign airlines.

Gail and Bill volunteer some of their time
in a few neighbourhood organizations.
They manage to save money
and to send it to Oxfam and Development and Peace,
for projects which promote the self-reliance of people
in what we call the Third World.

They must have their ups and downs also,
but parents and children seem to trust each other,
to communicate with great openness,
to give freedom to each other,
and to be so happy together,
which is really too bad for the psychologists and
   counsellors,
psychiatrists, remedial teachers, and welfare officers,
whose services they have never required.

Even their teen-age girl has never been in trouble with the
   police.
She has never been arrested for drunkenness,
or for possession of drugs or stolen goods,
and she hasn't smashed a car yet.
Couldn't she be like many delinquents and criminals
who bring such prosperity to professionals,
lawyers, prosecutors, police officers, jail guards
and to the builders of these beautiful jails,
court houses and police headquarters?

I'm telling you,
my friends are so useless
in our wasteful society.
They are allergic to greed,
don't lust mindlessly for money,
and don't worship the Gross National Product.
They believe that markets exist to serve people,
and not the other way around.
But how could the banks build magnificent skyscrapers
with people who don't need loans,
and who don't have to pay twenty-four per cent interest
   on their credit cards?

My friends are so useless!

René Fumoleau
Yellowknife

✉ It seems that every once in a while I must come out of hiding
again. This housewife is coming out of her broom closet to object.
   This morning I heard three ladies talking about their wonderful,
new recycling programs. They were all gushing about the wonderful things they were doing for the environment, like making a
compost heap and feeling so close to nature. Imagine, they were
sacrificing paper towels to save trees, and one lady actually has

no garbage any more. (Well, what *does* she do with all the plastic bottles, bags and wrappers so many things come in?)

Now, I don't want to knock compost heaps, for I'm very fond of mine. Every year I faithfully fill it and empty it into the garden the next year. Nor do I want to belittle trees, for I've planted a few myself and regard them as good friends. As for garbage, we all have too much of that, and one of my goals in life is to produce as little as possible.

But, really, where have these ladies *been* the last ten years? I know where I've been, right at home here, composting, recycling, re-using, doing without all those wonderful consumptive and disposable conveniences. Cloth diapers for me, and a good old wash line to dry them on. I've been busy gardening organically, canning (using those re-usable Mason jars, remember them?), freezing (using recycled milk bags, washed and dried), buying in bulk and cooking from scratch (using whole foods). Rags are recycled towels at our place, and we've even given someone else's cast-off carpet a new lease on life.

The three lady guests were quite pleased with themselves, but so seriously pointed out that these changes really meant a whole *new* life-style. Maybe we should give it a name: The New Environmental Life-style. Yes, they said, it takes time and effort to live this way.

Well, don't I know it! It takes *all* my time, and a lot of hard work. For years everyone has said that I'm crazy to stay at home and be "just a housewife." The job that I've been doing, keeping house the old-fashioned, non-polluting way, has been derided for years. I can hardly believe my ears now when the proponents of the New Environmental Life-style begin to gush. Don't they know that there is nothing *new* about what they are doing? Don't they know that old-fashioned housewives have been doing all these things all along? Why, my life-style is actually coming into style again, just like all the clothes I've been wearing all these years!

I think it only fair to warn all those eager converts to the New Environmental Life-style: if you're really serious about this "new" way of living, somebody has to take the time to run a household this way, and somebody has a lot of work to do. Who's it to be? Is it possible, do you think, that the role of "housewife" might actually be revived? Maybe we should give the old job a new name: New Environmental Life-style Engineer. Will that make it more palatable?

Do you really need *newsletters* to inform each other of your efforts (more garbage and fewer trees)? Do you really need to go to *speeches* to find out how to live this way? Just ask any old-fashioned housewife – she'll be glad to tell you, if she isn't too busy. Or is this going to be just another flash-in-the-pan movement with big organizations, government money, fancy meetings and lots of talk?

As for me, well, I'll just put on my apron and whip up a batch of bread to go with the pan of pea soup for supper tonight. The old-fashioned life-style has suited this family for many years. It's still a good way to live.

Femmie VanderBoom
Burlington, Ontario

✉ A few weeks ago, I did something that should put me in the running for the glorious title "Environmentalist of the Year" – I decided *not* to be cremated when I die.

What could this possibly have to do with being an environmentalist?

It all began with a comment made by my daughter after we'd walked past the crematorium in Parkview Cemetery. The furnace must have been stoked up, for great quantities of black smoke were pouring from the chimney.

I was quite surprised by the colour of this smoke and said something to the effect that I never thought I'd produce clouds of black when I departed this earth. (I had naively assumed that I'd depart innocuously, perhaps as pure white vapour, or even as a colourless, odourless emanation.)

My daughter responded with a typical teen-age, "Oh, Mom

. . . " and walked on, shaking her head in disbelief, or disgust, I'm not sure which.

A few days later she said to me, "You know, Mom, if you're really an environmentalist, you should be buried, not burned."

Her reasons were good. First, in our fast-growing cities of asphalt and cement, cemeteries are green, quiet spaces, treed and flowered. As the world population rushes headlong toward ten or fifteen billion, we'll need more and more such oases in our urban deserts. Good argument.

Secondly, if I (in my casket) am burned at 2000° F, it will take only two or three hours to return me to the elements whereas if nature does it, it will take several decades. Think of all that carbon dioxide being released into the atmosphere all at once; think of how I'd be contributing to the greenhouse effect! And think of the rain forest being cut to supply the wood for my mahogany or rosewood casket!

Even if I opted for a simple pine box, there's still the fact that Canada's forests are being cut at a far greater rate than they are being regenerated. I could hardly argue with this reasoning, could I?

From this point, it was a natural progression for me to enter the debate – on my daughter's side!

How could I *not* consider the energy that would be saved if I were buried instead of burned? After all, it must take a lot of electricity or gas to fire up a crematorium to 2000° F, to keep it at that temperature for several hours, then to let it cool down enough to remove the ashes before heating it up again for the next body.

And finally, I had to face the fact that I live in an area where water supply can be a problem – that alone is reason enough to choose burial. Why? The human body contains about eighty per cent moisture. Therefore, if all the bodies in the Region of Waterloo were buried, just think of the ongoing additions to our ground water!

So, after much discussion and reflection, it became quite clear to me that burial would be the better environmental solution.

I phoned my funeral director and asked him to strike out the word "cremation" and write instead "burial" in the appropriate place on my instructions.

Feeling that I'd taken the ultimate environmental stand, that I'd be leading an environmentally conscious life right to the end, I settled down to read the evening newspaper.

There, on page three, was the headline, "More in Ontario choose cremation." I couldn't believe it. Just as I'd reached this *grave* decision to be buried – for the good of the earth, the water and the air – I found I was bucking a trend.

I guess this environmentalist will have to find another way to go down (or up) "trailing clouds of glory."

Samm MacKay
Waterloo, Ontario

✉ My wife and I have been living and enjoying life without a car since 1976. This would not be so remarkable if we lived in a large metropolitan area with plenty of public transportation. (And no matter what its detractors claim, big-city public people movers are viable, reliable and convenient and would be more so if more people would use them.) We live in an isolated, rural area with no public transportation, unless you count a couple of decrepit, sometimes unreliable taxi cabs. Our only links with the outside world are a daily bus to Duluth, one hundred and seventy-five miles south of us, and a couple of commuter flights to Minneapolis, twice as far away.

Living sans car is not the impossibility that most of our friends seem to think it is. We still have legs and we have bikes. The grocery store is only about two miles away; the hardware and drug stores only about five. Riding bikes gives us a chance to retrieve for recycling all those cans that car drivers love to toss into the ditch. I suppose that our friends think we don't own a car because we can't afford one. This is true; but not in the way they mean it. I have been trying for years to convince people that the world can't afford the automobile. Of course I can't afford a car and neither can you. If I owned a car, I'd have to go to work to support it. At my age, I'm not about to do anything as ridiculous as that. Eschewing autos and rescuing beer and pop cans for the recycler are not the only things we are doing, or not doing, in our attempt to rescue the planet. We also eschew all the plastic we can. When it comes to new gadgets, we refrain from buying. We have no TV, we have no microwave oven, we have no gasoline-powered lawn mower, no rototiller, no snow-blower. Our boat has sails; our canoe has paddles. When we do buy something, it's almost always used. The machine this letter is being typed on is probably at least thirty years old. I bought it this morning at an auction. We try to avoid clothes made from synthetic fabrics. Cotton, wool and leather do just fine, thank you. The Salvation Army store has some fantastic bargains.

So that's what this funny old couple that rides bikes all over is doing about the ecological disaster. We think that, if more of you did the same, everybody would be happier.

Ray Anderson
Ranier, Minnesota

✉ I have never driven, and I agree with your guests about the risks of driving, the pollution factor, and don't forget the cost of car insurance. It's also true that driving can be solitary. But when you don't drive, that doesn't mean you can take taxis everywhere. What I find not driving has left me with is walking. In between, you take the (sociable) bus provided there will be one following the route you wish to take; you ride your bike; or maybe a friend gives you a lift; but mostly there is walking. I'm surprised at the people I know who, on their journeys behind the wheel, don't notice the details of the neighbourhoods they travel. I walk two small children to school, parks, library, store, doctor's, and so on, and not driving gives us the pleasure of finding the first chestnuts, identifying new flowers and smelling them, saying hello to passersby and stopping to watch Hydro workers atop telephone poles. Don't forget all the dogs and cats who appear each day, to whom you give your own names. There's Limping Cat, Fat Cat and Baby Cat. Sometimes a box of apples is tucked against the sidewalk marked "Free, Help Yourself." If you grumble home in a downpour, there is anticipation of a hot drink. Also, come summer, you don't have to feel too ashamed of your thighs.

The two children have other ideas. They loved the free apples, but they're determined to turn their mother into a chauffeur. Guilt is their leverage. "Mummy, if you drove, you could take us to Nan's house." "They want drivers for the field trip next week." "I wish you could pick me up at lunchtime." I remind them that neither ice in Alberta nor torrents on the West Coast have stopped us before, but the look in their eyes says, She's fanatic. I suppose I'll take up the wheel, but I'm sorry for some four-year-olds I've met who've *never* ridden the bus, and indeed for all the people driving everywhere whose pockets are empty of chestnuts and whose trouser legs don't betray the fur of strange cats.

Elizabeth Harris
Victoria

✉ Is it cheaper to have a car or go public?

I know exactly what the answer is. I had a ten-year-old Vega. A lovely yellow vehicle with one blue door and one red. It served well and in spite of the strange noises that it emitted I enjoyed driving it. I even drove it around the continent, which brought laughter to my friends and fear to my mother. But that is another long story.

Three weeks after returning, the Vega decided it had had enough of me and refused to continue another wheel turn. Since I also use my car for business, I had records telling me exactly what this luxury costs me. Instead of rushing out to replace my toy I started, every week, taking the operating costs out of one pocket and putting them into another. The other was used every time I took a bus or taxi. The other began to bulge. I had tangible proof that cars are expensive. I was elated. Look how much money I was saving.

One day I reached into that pocket, took out a wad of bills that I never had before . . . and went out and bought another car.

Lawrie Weiser
Toronto

FOREIGN AFFAIRS III: VAL IN CHINA

In contrast with virtually all the other people who write to *Morningside* from around the world, Val Boser was not only known to me and to the program before she left Canada, she worked with us. For one season, in fact, she almost ran the place – in the thankless position we call "the desk," the equivalent of the news editor of a daily paper.

Val's from Alberta. She was the host of the morning show in Calgary before moving behind the scenes, first in Edmonton and then at *Morningside*. Then, like Catherine Pigott, she got wanderlust. Through the season of 1990-91, she worked at a news agency in Beijing and, in her spare time, wrote home about her life in China.

August 31

✉ The words of an old pop song keep going through my mind. "It hurts to be in love." Gene Pitney, I think. But nowhere are those lines truer than in China. There is so much denial, separation and difficulty facing young people who fall in love here.

Li Pei is a young professional, nearly thirty and very much in love with his wife of two years. His face lights up when he talks about her, but clouds when explaining the reality of their lives together. In those two years, they have spent only a couple of months together. She is going to university in Shanghai, while he works in Beijing. Even when they get to spend time together, it's hard because he shares a dormitory room with three other men. He's waiting to see if he'll get a room of his own, waiting to see if she'll be assigned a job in Beijing when she graduates, waiting to see if somehow he can work in Shanghai. But none of these things is in his control.

Another young man, Zheng Xie, recently returned to Beijing after enjoying the privilege of studying for a Master's degree in the United States. But with that wonderful opportunity came the reality of leaving his young wife and six-month-old son for two years. There is no money for taking wives and families along, so he missed all those firsts – his little son's first steps, first words. When he returned, the child was afraid of him for some time.

For a young couple wanting to have a baby, there are a number of obstacles. First, the couple must be over twenty-five to get married and qualify for parenthood. Then, permission to get pregnant must be obtained from one's work unit. Each work unit is only allotted so many allowable pregnancies each year. One young woman I know of managed to meet all of the criteria, but now she and her husband only see their child on Sunday afternoon for a few hours. The couple lives in one small room, too cramped for one, let alone three, so the baby lives with her grandparents, a ninety-minute bus ride across town.

Yet all of this pain doesn't seem to discourage the young people or harden them to love. They remain in spite of (or perhaps because of) the problems sweetly, hopefully romantic. They walk hand in hand, arm in arm in the evening. They spend a Sunday afternoon in Yuyuantan Park or Beihai Park, sitting on a park bench, chatting or even dozing in each other's laps.

The other day, Li Pei came bursting into my office and began rooting around in a cupboard. Miraculously, he produced a paint roller and held it up like a trophy. "I have my own room," he beamed. "I'm going to paint it!" The next time his wife comes to Beijing, they will have a place of their own, ten square metres of privacy, the kind of secret hideaway lovers long for.

September 9

✉ As I sit here writing this, I can hear the gentle musical trill of bicycle bells. It's usually the first sound I hear in the morning and the last thing I hear at night. In Beijing and most of China, the bicycle is a fundamental requirement of daily life, regardless of your age, physical condition, profession or, for the most part, status in life. In my first days here, one of my colleagues, a young Chinese broadcaster, suggested we go for lunch. "How will we get there?" I asked, only to be met with a bemused look. "Bicycle, of course," he replied.

No one (except very big potatoes) has a private car. Taxis are expensive, beyond the reach of the average young broadcaster. And the city bus is a crush of humanity to be avoided if at all possible. Therefore we cycle. We cycle to work, to lunch, to shop. We cycle on Chinese bicycles with evocative brand names like Flying Pigeon, Silver Swallow, Five Rams or Phoenix. We cycle on mad, busy streets and on tree-lined cycle lanes separated from traffic by iron railings or trimmed hedges. We cycle with dinner in our carriers, children in baby seats, a new chair or TV set impossibly strapped on behind. We cycle in our finery, in business suits or high heels and white gloves.

If you simply stand on a street corner and watch, this sea of people on bicycles looks calm, ebbing and flowing in an orderly fashion. However, astride a Flying Pigeon, as one of the seven million cyclists in this city, it looks much different, more like a wild obstacle course or a musical ride gone berserk. The first and foremost obstacle is your fellow cyclist.

The first group, and by far the largest, is made up of dreamers, slowly pedalling along, lost in their private thoughts. Since they are in a dream, they don't hear the insistent ringing of bicycle bells behind them. Then there are the lovers, couples who manage to hold hands while they pedal along, lost in each other. Needless to say, these besotted folks don't hear the bicycle bells, either. Next, there are the bell ringers, cyclists who believe they can ride anywhere, anyhow as long as they keep ringing their bells, as if this tinkling provides an invisible shield. There are also the speed demons, typically young and hip, often on ten speeds, who would rather die than stop for anything. Add to this soup a whole variety of tricycles loaded down with huge cartons of vegetables, long steel pipes, kids, grandmothers or large vats of sinister sloshing substances. Throw in cyclists going the wrong way, going sideways or stopping. Now include other obstacles like pedestrians pouring off buses, smoke-belching trucks loath to use their brakes and the universally known and feared bloodthirsty taxi cabs, and what you have is an undulating, lurching, screeching, heart-stopping mixture that brings new meaning to the expression "Getting there is half the fun."

Yet, in all of this chaos, there is kindness. I saw a young man lose his cloth bag filled with groceries from the back of his bike, peaches and potatoes rolling all over the street. At least half a dozen cyclists stopped to help him, and everyone carefully avoided running over any of his goods.

When I confided my horror of the dangers of cycling to my broadcaster friend, he laughed and told me I simply didn't know the rules of the road. In fact, there is just one rule, he said. Might is right. If it's bigger than you, stop for it. If it's smaller, don't worry, it will get out of the way. If it's a draw, well, it doesn't hurt so much when you run into another bicycle.

October 16

✉ Across the street from where I live in Beijing is something a bit uncommon in China. It's a bar – not a lavish hotel bar for tourists, nor one of the hole-in-the-wall beer and noodle joints frequented by Chinese workers. This is a real alfresco bar with jaunty red umbrellas and patio lanterns. On warm evenings, artists and university students gather to sip beer or Coke and do what the young and the hip do everywhere – laugh, argue, lie, flirt, brag, all to the incongruous accompaniment of an endless string of sentimental singers from the West. Julio Iglesias. The Carpenters. Whitney Houston.

This same ageing musical mush has made Radio Beijing the choice of the city's young people for the seven hours a day it pumps out "Easy FM." In a year-old joint venture with an Australian broadcasting company, Aussie deejays named Ian and John introduce what they describe as "the best easy listening music from around the world." The programs are taped in Australia and shipped to China. Easy FM has exhumed musical has-beens like Neil Diamond, John Denver, Bread and Gordon Lightfoot and given them new life as stars in Beijing. As a joint venture hoping to attract advertising revenue, Easy FM is something of a disaster, but to the young people in my office (especially the young men for some reason), this non-stop sop is an important part of their day. Often, when one of their favourite songs comes on, they turn up the volume and sing along with great feeling. The other day, when a Dan Hill hit from a decade ago blared out of the radio, Wang Liu, a young man with big black eyes and a shy smile, started to sing. "You ask me if I love you, and I choke on my reply." I felt almost embarrassed at his intensity. Then Shu Jianfu, the office sophisticate, joined in the chorus. "Sometimes when we touch, the honesty's too much." Their impromptu duet swelled to an impressive finish. "I want to hold you till the fear in me subsides."

Pei Chu-en is a well-educated man of about twenty-eight and a big Carpenters' fan. He approached me shyly when "We've Only Just Begun" was on the radio and asked if I liked the Carpenters. I lied and told him yes. He confided that the Carpenters and John Denver are his favourite singers. He reached into his pocket and produced a tiny, dog-eared pulp booklet in Chinese that tells the life story of Richard and Karen Carpenter. Pei Chu-en asked me to explain how Karen Carpenter died. He couldn't grasp the concept of anorexia. Somehow, neither can I, any more, and I explained it badly. She thought she was too fat, I tell him. Too fat? he ponders, looking more confused than before. I ask him what other kind of music he likes. Only emotional music, he tells me gravely.

You won't hear any rap or punk or heavy metal coming from Chinese pop singers, either. Popular singers like Liu Huan and Wei Wei from the mainland and Taiwan's Qi Qin and Tan Yonglin could break your heart with the uninhibited emotion in their music.

In a recent article in the official newspaper *People's Daily*, education officials were wringing their hands in despair over young people's obsession with pop music. This is having "bad effects," the article warned, citing a lack of attention to studies and "puppy love" as the most serious consequences.

In a society that hasn't had much time or tolerance for puppy love or for that matter any emotional needs, and given the subdued mood of young Chinese since their democracy movement was so brutally crushed, I guess it shouldn't be surprising that songs expressing longing, desire and melancholy are so popular. A research scientist in his mid-twenties told me that to be Chinese means giving up so much of yourself – your privacy, your ambitions, your choices and often your dreams. His participation in last year's demonstrations cost him the opportunity to go abroad to study.

As I write this, I can hear an old Barry Manilow song wafting through the air from the little bar next door. Somehow, it doesn't seem ridiculous at all.

December 18

✉ In the late 1970s, when China adopted its policy of opening up to the outside world, there was a surge of interest in learning to speak English. Now that surge has become a fever, an obsession especially among young people. It's become very popular to wear jackets and sweat-shirts and carry bags emblazoned with English phrases, no matter that they often make little sense. On a stroll down busy Xidan Street, several young men all sport shiny bomber jackets proclaiming the "Colonies of Sparkle." A young woman declares via her sweat-shirt "He Men's World." A teen-ager in sun-glasses wears a sweater that reads "Boys and Balls." Up the street at the foreign languages bookstore, the best-selling non-fiction book in Beijing is *TV English*, a language manual to accompany an equally popular television program.

A little further up Xidan Street is a night school, a few stark unheated classrooms equipped only with desks and a blackboard. On a cold Sunday evening, a roomful of students, shop clerks and factory workers huddle in coats and gloves at the regular weekly "English Corner." It's their chance to listen to and speak English with a native speaker. Since the government shut down the infor-mal Sunday morning "English Corner" in Purple Bamboo Park after last year's pro-democracy movement was crushed, language students have few opportunities to practise their skills. The night-school students have a favourite topic–speaking English. A young brewery worker asks, "How can I learn to speak English more quickly?" Another asks, "What advice can you give Chinese students studying English?" Another hand goes up. "What are conditions like for college students in your country?" It takes only a few minutes to get to the heart of this English mania. A stylish young woman who introduces herself as Helen asks, "Can you tell me how I can go to your country to study?" The classroom is filled with murmurs, nods and poised pencils.

A Chinese education journal recently published an article lamenting what it called the current "going abroad craze." The dream of going to the United States, or Canada, or Australia, or anywhere to study is affecting the decisions of top high-school graduates. Some of the best and brightest are turning down the few previously coveted places in Chinese universities in favour of attending private colleges specializing in English. Even though the students must pay their own tuition of about sixty dollars

Canadian for each semester, when they graduate, they are free of any obligation to the state. Students educated at government expense must work at an assigned job for five years after graduation before they can get permission to study abroad. Another reason for attending private colleges is that students can pursue their goal of learning to speak English to the exclusion of just about anything else.

A young woman on the subway, anxious to practise her English for a few minutes, removes her earphones and shuts off her Walkman before speaking to me. I ask her what kind of music she is listening to. It's not music, she explains. It's an English lesson. English is my life, she tells me fervently. She says her English name is Amy and she is preparing for her TOEFL test in a few months. TOEFL, or Test of English as a Foreign Language, is just one of the many hurdles that must be jumped before a student can go abroad.

All Chinese young people know about TOEFL. They also know when and where the test takes place. They know that it costs thirty dollars in American cash. They know about scholarships and sponsors. Word of which colleges or universities are accepting Chinese students spreads like a secret password.

As the Chinese education journal correctly points out, many of these students are pursuing an impossible dream. Even if they can pass the TOEFL test, scrape together the money and get a Chinese passport, there simply aren't enough places to be had in foreign universities and colleges. Some hopeful students have been caught up in scams, paying thousands of dollars to colleges in foreign countries only to find out they aren't really legitimate.

Still, for all of the obstacles, many young people see studying abroad as their greatest hope, their greatest opportunity. It's no secret that about half of the students who go overseas to study don't return to China. The government acknowledges this and is trying to stop the brain drain by offering incentives to return. Awards, better housing, research grants, more challenging jobs are all being held out as carrots.

But there's one important element missing from the incentive package, and that is choice. For most Chinese, life is a small box with no way out of an assigned job, an assigned room, even an assigned city. The dream of going abroad, even for a little while, opens an irresistible door.

A few days ago, I was skating on a pond in Purple Bamboo Park, the site of the now forbidden English Corner. A group of students surrounded me, delighted at their good fortune in finding a native English speaker simply gliding around, there for the taking. I agreed to help them practise their English for a while, and after we'd exhausted my opinion of Beijing, my age and why I wasn't married, I asked them what they were planning to do when they graduated. They all broke into smiles and answered in unison, "Go abroad!"

January 10

✉ In China, there is no free flow of information. As a result, one must try to figure out what is going on in the Chinese government by reading between the lines, under the lines, behind the lines, anywhere but on the lines. The Chinese people are expert at this. For example, if a leader usually photographed standing shoulder to shoulder with the other big shots begins to appear in the back row or off to the side, that means he is falling out of favour. When retired leader Deng Xiaoping recently tottered out on his eighty-seven-year-old legs to vote in what passes for an election in China, he was photographed standing alone dropping his ballot in the box. This photo is meant to say (a) that Deng is alive, (b) that he is well, (c) that he still has influence, though limited, as there were no other leaders in the picture and (d) that despite China's hard line after the June 1989 suppression of student demonstrations, the country still espouses the reform and openness symbolized by Deng.

I find myself now not looking at pictures or television reports about goings-on in China, but rather I look into the corners, the background, the juxtaposition of people and objects. I've begun to analyse why, despite the country's formidable reputation for going to any lengths to crush opposition and dissent, Chinese leaders always appear kind of cosy, harmless and grandfatherly.

There are several things that contribute to this paradoxical image. First of all, armchairs. Chinese leaders are almost always photographed sitting in cushy armchairs, inevitably cloaked in a practical, if drab, chair cover. The chairs have the dishevelled look of cheap pantihose bagging at the ankle. Then there is the preponderance of doilies and antimacassars. These white crocheted bits of fluff are draped over chairs and end tables. How could anyone surrounded by lacy doilies be thinking anything other than kindly thoughts? This brings us to the next ubiquitous object – the cornflower-blue and white ceramic teacup complete with a lid to keep the contents warm. No matter who Chinese leaders are meeting and no matter the subject under discussion, there are always cups of tea nearby. A crisis, you say? Well, nothing could be so serious that we can't discuss it over a nice cup of tea.

Often in the background, you'll see a big thermos or two. Low tech and practical, the thermos is a nice common touch. The Chinese people are never very far away from their thermoses of boiling water for making tea or instant noodles. By having a thermos nearby, the leaders look like they, too, are regular folk who shuffle down the hallway a couple of times a day to the communal water boiler.

Sitting amidst this shabby but comforting environment, the leaders and officials are always smiling. Big, happy smiles. Wide, ear-to-ear grins. These guys look really happy as they dish out the day's good news. Steel production is up. The textile industry surpassed its quota. The number of schools in Tibet has doubled. Walnut production is at an all-time high.

These are powerful images, especially when seen day after day, in every newspaper and on every television newscast. One begins to understand the power of misinformation. Chinese people tell me that of course they don't believe everything in the news, but neither do they discount everything. They sift through it, trying to figure out the truth. They talk to each other, compare notes, listen to short-wave radio and grill visitors.

They are used to it. I am not. The conflicting images, the misinformation leaves me feeling unsettled, off balance. The firm foundation of facts I have always relied on crumbles here beneath my feet like a house of cards. I find myself simply not knowing what to believe, therefore believing nothing.

February 4

✉ There they were. About forty fat kids huffing and puffing and rolling their way along the Great Wall. Groups of tourists stopped contemplating the magnificence of the ancient fortification and began staring at the overweight youngsters. There were jeers and giggles as the tubby pre-teens, looking embarrassed and a bit bewildered, tried to hurry away from the crowds.

The kids were part of a group of about two hundred who were attending a ten-day camp organized by the Social Medical Institute in Beijing. Twice that many applied to take part. The response surprised even the organizers, who weren't really sure how much demand there would be for a camp that teaches children in China how to lose weight.

It's not easy being a fat kid anywhere, but in China where overeating has been the exclusive privilege of emperors and party officials, people aren't sure what to make of an obese child. One chubby lad complained that strangers sometimes pinch his arm and declare him "a good example of socialist superiority."

Today's child in China leads a life far different from that of his parents. The increasing occurrence of obesity is just one example of that. The improved standard of living over the last decade combined with the one-child policy has created a sturdy, well-fed crop of youngsters doted on by mothers, fathers and grandparents.

With a little more money in their pockets, parents spend generously on nutritious food, stylish clothing and the latest toys. When one father of a three-year-old commented on how expensive children's clothes were, I asked him why he didn't shop at a second-hand store. Given the Chinese propensity to thrift, I was sure parents would be keen to swap kids' clothing. No, he told me. This would be his only child and he didn't want to dress him in old clothes. You need only look up and down the streets of Beijing to see that many Chinese parents feel the same way. Kids bundled in bright new paintbox colours are everywhere.

These children are also different in ways not so apparent to the eye. They are part of a generation that has no brothers or sisters. They will never be aunts or uncles. They will have no nieces, no nephews, not even a sister- or brother-in-law. The one-child policy has irrevocably changed family life in China, and today's youngsters are the pioneers of this new structure.

One of the hazards of being an only child is shouldering the entire weight of your parents' unfulfilled dreams and ambitions. There is tremendous pressure on Chinese youngsters to succeed. One woman I know saved for and bought her four-year-old daughter a piano. This is all the more astonishing when you consider that a piano costs about two years' wages in China and must then be crammed into the one or two small rooms the average family calls home. The mother of the future concert pianist is mystified and hurt by the fact that her daughter isn't really interested and won't practise her lessons willingly.

A new radio program has cropped up in Beijing. Twice a week, experts in child rearing answer questions written by perplexed parents. One mother writes in to say her son won't study. All he wants to do is watch television. The experts tell her not to worry. Try to cut down his TV time, they advise, by introducing him to educational activities like stamp or rock collecting. When I heard that, I thought about something I saw in Shanghai.

I was walking down a narrow back street when I heard an oddly familiar tune. It was electronic music, but I couldn't quite place it. I followed the music through a doorway and down a hall.

There was a room with about half a dozen video games. The music was from the popular Nintendo game, Super Mario. At one machine was clearly the neighbourhood ace. He was a big fellow, about ten years old. He was wearing blue jeans, and around his neck was his Communist Party Young Pioneers scarf. He looked confident, nonchalant even, as he eased Mario through the perils of World Five, no small accomplishment, to be sure. This did not appear to be a youngster you could lure away from video gadgets with the promise of the fun to be had collecting rocks.

Where all this leads remains to be seen. One thing is certain. The lives of these youngsters are different from their parents', who grew up in the chaos of the Cultural Revolution, and chasms apart from the ageing Chinese leaders, who came of age in the mountains of Yunnan believing in revolution and class struggle.

March 21

✉ Because I am Canadian, spring is a big event in my life. Starting in early January, I am desperate for signs of spring. The fact that I am now living in China hasn't changed my instinctual Canadian longing for the relief of green grass and warm sunny days. And to my delight, northern Chinese share exactly the same sentiment.

A Beijing winter is not like an Edmonton winter. It's not nearly so long, so cold nor so snowy. Still, from November to March, it's dark, dreary and definitely chilly. Sometimes when the wind howls in from Siberia, it's extremely cold. Buildings are poorly heated, and transportation is limited to draughty buses or the ubiquitous bicycle, so even a mild winter is a trial. People bundle up in so many layers that they all look pudgy and quilted.

On a grey day late in February, when the dreaded *da feng*, or big wind, was blowing out of the north, I ventured out to the bird and fish market in search of some colour. Usually this is a place where people crowd around buying goldfish or canaries, the only practical, affordable and permitted pets in the city. Bird lovers often stroll around looking at the different breeds and comparing bird-songs. But on this cold winter day, there was a great crowd gathered at one end of the market. I pushed my way through to see what was going on. There were at least a dozen vendors selling bedding-out plants, rose-bushes and bulbs just starting to push up green stalks. People with tiny incomes and even tinier homes were buying up plants, carefully wrapping them in newspaper and happily carrying them off. Not one of them has a garden, but they put plants on the window sills of their apartments or in the doorways of their crowded courtyard homes. It was still at least a month until you could safely put a plant outdoors, but that didn't seem to dampen the enthusiasm of the crowd. The arrival of the plant pedlars was a harbinger of spring to be seized and savoured. I bought a hyacinth plant with its white flowers just beginning to bloom.

Another way Beijingers hurry the season is to deny that it is still winter and shed their long underwear and bulky coats. After one misleadingly warm day in early March, winter gear is nowhere to be seen. People would rather shiver in light coats and short skirts than admit that it's still winter. On an outing a few days ago, I wore my big down-filled coat. My Chinese friend took one look at me and announced that I looked ridiculous. It's spring, he said. I know, I replied, but it's still cold. I stood my ground and, looking ridiculous among all the light jackets and sweaters, we went to the Summer Palace, a favourite destination for Beijingers on a Sunday afternoon. There, with ice still on the edges of the lake, families were out in droves paddling little dragon-shaped boats and stuffing themselves with rice crisps, candied yaws, sausages and bean-paste doughnuts, all the while taking pictures of each other as they shivered in the early spring breeze. There was not a hint of green anywhere, not on the trees nor the ground. Then, appearing like a miracle around a corner between two old palace buildings, was a tree ablaze in tiny yellow flowers. No leaves, just bright little blossoms. People were going up to it, delicately touching and smelling the flowers as though it were some sort of religious object. Others were lining up taking photos in front of it. This was proof positive. Spring had arrived. I took off my big down coat. I *did* look ridiculous.

April 23

✉ I worry a lot about women. It seems that in most places in the Third World, they are little more than chattels and beasts of burden, abused, dominated and powerless. But I had high hopes for women in China. One of Chairman Mao Zedong's most famous quotes is, "Women hold up half the sky." As early as 1927, he was writing that the authority of the husband was getting shakier every day and that the time had come for women to lift their heads and become truly equal. For all its faults, the Chinese government has held equality of the sexes as a basic tenet for more than forty years.

In reality, though, women in China are only equal when it comes to sharing the arduous work in the factories and fields. The attitude that men are superior to women remains deeply and historically ingrained. It seems even the modern young people in Beijing, for all their pop music, miniskirts and leather jackets, still buy into the traditional Chinese ideal of a mild, modest woman who lives only to serve her husband and family. I teach English to just such a group of hip nineteen-year-olds. Recently the subject of women as political leaders came up in class. I asked them why there are so few women in the Chinese government. One young man said matter-of-factly that women don't make good leaders. Why? I asked. He grinned and looked a little embarrassed, as if he wasn't quite sure how to break this to me. Why? I pressed him. He exchanged grins with a few of the other boys, got up his courage and said, "Men are more intelligent." I asked him if he really believed that. He nodded. I asked the next boy and the next. Yes, they all agreed. The young women in the class were saying nothing. I asked them if they thought men were smarter than women. They looked blank and unsure until a girl who goes by the English name of Janet spoke up and said she thought women were just as smart as men. The other girls looked at her proudly but offered no support.

Seizing on what I thought would be a good issue for a debate, I gave them a few minutes to prepare their arguments for the proposition: be it resolved that men are smarter than women.

The boys opened. "It's obvious men are smarter than women because they run all of the countries and businesses. And men are interested in learning things or reading or doing some business while women only care about romance and looking nice."

The girls considered this. They countered with the fact that many women become skilful typists. The boys scoffed that typing is simple work and that's why women type and men run the companies.

The bravest of the girls, Janet, smelling defeat, switched tactics. Turning to science, she declared that women's brains are shaped differently from men's, as if this explained women's inability to be managers, leaders and, in this case, debaters. Everyone was a little stunned by this idea. Clearly, the debate was over. The boys looked smug in victory, and the girls looked resigned, as if the side of right had likely prevailed. I just looked depressed, and it must have showed. One of the girls offered an adage in an attempt to salvage the situation. "In China, it is said that if a woman is a success at work, she is probably a failure at home." I didn't feel better at all. In fact, I went away feeling very sad for these bright young women.

But their attitude isn't all their fault. Despite the rhetoric about equality, China is still a country where the restaurants are packed with men doing business and the trains are filled with men going places. Universities set higher entrance requirements for girls than for boys. The government is a sea of male faces whose anonymous wives are never seen in public. And in the countryside, the practice of disposing of unwanted girl babies still exists. It's no wonder that my young student thinks women's brains aren't the same shape as men's. There has to be *some* explanation for all of this.

May 14

✉ In China, there is a common greeting that goes *Chi le ma?* or literally, "Have you eaten?" Given that the reality of hunger and famine are never far from the Chinese people's memories, the question makes sense, even today. There are still parts of the country where getting enough to eat is a daily struggle. But even for those in more prosperous urban and coastal areas and for young people who haven't really known hunger, food is still a national obsession. Sunday outings with the family are one big snackfest. Festivals and holidays require days of shopping and preparation of special dishes. And of course the Chinese banquet favoured by Chinese leaders and officials is a sumptuous parade of dishes that defies even the heartiest Western appetite.

Great care is taken in the preparation of Chinese food. The ingredients are scrutinized in the market by discriminating shoppers. Often, a whole day is lovingly devoted to making a special dish. In Beijing, there is a particular passion for a picture-perfect little meat-filled dumpling called *jiaozi*. A huge bowl brimming with steaming hot *jiaozi* is not only a staple, it's a way of life, a conversation piece and an art form.

No celebration is complete without *jiaozi*. Often, the time-consuming process of making the little dumplings is a social occasion, shared by three or four people working around a table.

For me, the experience of making *jiaozi* will forever be a bittersweet one, inextricably linked with the tragedy of a certain middle-aged intellectual. This tiny woman, her body slightly misshapen from malnutrition as a child, patiently taught me the art of *jiaozi*. While we mixed, kneaded and rolled in her shabby room, her life story slowly emerged. At times, she shocked me with the ferocity of her dissidence. At other times, her cheerful smile looked pasted on, as if the upturned corners of her mouth were holding back the tears.

First she mixed a dough of flour and water, adding just a bit more flour, then more water until it was just the right consistency. Then she began to knead the dough. She told of how in the fifties, her father was labelled as a rightist, a label that has haunted her throughout her life. As a schoolgirl, she was forbidden to participate in most activities. She was harassed, hounded and denied access to university. Finally, she was accepted at a teacher's college although her dream was to be a scientist. Later, she fell in love with a People's Liberation Army soldier, but because of her family background, they were not permitted to marry until he was out of the army.

"Even at that time," she said, "even though politics had already caused me so much trouble, I still loved Mao Zedong so much. I trusted Mao and believed all of this labelling was for some greater good. Somehow, it would be good for China."

Her hair falling across her eyes, she continued kneading the dough, explaining that it must be just right, not too hard nor too soft. She gave me some mushrooms, leeks and ginger to chop, keeping a close eye on me to ensure I was cutting the pieces finely enough.

She continued her story, telling of how she finally got married and for a while was very happy with her husband and two sons. But her rightist label continued to plague her. Her husband began to beat her, blaming her background for all their misfortune. When the Cultural Revolution began in 1967, she was quickly singled out and sent to the countryside for reform through labour. She worked in the fields for five years, allowed to return to see her children only twice a year to sew clothes for them. "Even my children were encouraged to criticize me," she said softly. She began beating the mixture of pork, mushrooms, leeks, ginger and sesame oil. She tasted a sample of the mixture and frowned. "This isn't quite right. Give me some more salt and chop a little garlic."

The madness of the Cultural Revolution turned her into a dissident. She refused to repent or criticize herself. Eventually, she was sent back to the city and to her family but she was irrevocably changed. "My friends and my husband tell me I should not be so outspoken but I cannot stop. They can send me to jail, but I will not stop. I hate this government," she said fiercely. "I hate Li Peng."

Li Peng is the unpopular premier of China who ordered the army to fire on the students on June 3 and 4, 1989. This woman's fierce condemnation of the Chinese leader gave me chills. I had never heard uttered so clearly what many Chinese had hinted at.

The filling was now perfect, and she turned her attention to rolling out palm-sized pieces of dough, ensuring the centre was just a bit thicker than the edges. She instructed me in putting a spoonful of filling in each piece, then gently squeezing the dumpling shut. As she placed each perfect little *jiaozi* in a pan and added a mixture of water and vinegar, I regarded this small woman, trapped in a loveless marriage, passed over at work for any privileges or promotions because of her dissidence and bitter over her wasted life. I felt helpless; anything I could say would seem inane and facile. The *jiaozi* were ready. She lifted the dumplings onto a serving plate. "There," she said with great finality. "Now you can make *jiaozi*. Now you know what it is to be Chinese."

LOWER ECONOMICS

Our shrinking dollar, and what various listeners had to say about how to stretch it.

✉ My move to Ottawa five years ago opened my eyes to the reality of street people. Being a good middle-class white kid from oh-so-affluent London, Ontario, the move to a city-core neighbourhood where every church seemed to have some kind of shelter or soup kitchen operating out of its basement, and where it wasn't unusual to find "bag people" sleeping in the foyer of the university library because there were heat ducts there, was quite a culture shock. I lived for a while in an area of rooming-houses, with their fascinating population of poor students, welfare recipients and bikers, where it was a rare night when there wasn't at least one police call on the block. I moved, eventually, into a slightly less dangerous area, and my neighbours were the denizens of the nearby Union Mission for Men and the Salvation Army. I have watched the street people of my neighbourhood go downhill over the last few years–Bob, who used to recognize you when he came to bum a cigarette, who now can't figure out why you know his name and is bound to yell obscenities at you, or the air, or anybody else who doesn't have a butt for him; the telephone lady who screams incoherently into pay-phone receivers, who now screams incoherently almost all the time; and many more. And somehow, they all know me as a soft touch – as someone who can't say no when asked for change. And I can't – if I have money, I don't feel it's a choice.

When I try to communicate that to people I work with or the kids in my youth group at church, I get a sense of futility. They don't, and most never have, lived downtown. They've never dealt with a dead body, lying frozen in its own vomit in broad daylight, or had to step over the alcohol-redolent body of the vagrant sleeping in their stairwell (as I had to more than once in my old apartment in Vanier). Their neighbours don't change every two months, as another single mom tries to make "home" for her kids and the seemingly inevitable abusive boy-friend. One day, you have two great little boys living next door to you who always have a smile and a hello for you when you come home from work and stop to play in the snow with them. They send you thank-you notes when you drop by with baking and can always cheer you up when you're down – and then the next day they're gone, with no goodbye and no forwarding address. And another small family moves in, and the cycle of late-night yelling starts again, until they move out, two months later.

At work this year, we decided not to do a gift exchange, but to take up a collection to be given to the Salvation Army's Christmas Cheer Assistance program. We suggested that people give as much as they would have put in to the gift exchange. I was astonished at the fact that people, instead of opening their wallets more than they would to buy a small gift, closed them. It's a mentality that says, "If I'm not getting anything out of it, I'm not putting anything into it."

Lisa Kowaltschuk
Vanier, Ontario

✉ I heard a politician remark that poor people do not buy books. Some people laugh at that idea. But, in fact, poor people do not buy books. Poor people buy food and shelter and heating supplies, and at the very most sometimes can buy shoes or school supplies or other necessities. They do not buy books because they cannot afford books.

I, for example, cannot be considered poor but have limited excess funds. I buy very few books and teach my children not to buy books, except for discards from the library or second-hand books. The reason is that we can borrow books from the library. We do not have to buy books. On the other hand, we cannot borrow food, or shelter, or shoes.

Anne George
West Vancouver

✉ I am very tired. I work two jobs totalling fifty-six hours per week minimum. Sometimes I have to attend functions during evenings or weekends. I was working a minimum of sixty-four hours a week but I had to stop because my mind and my body didn't get a chance to catch up and also it put my regular job at risk. At this point in time, I work two seventeen-hour days a week, Wednesday and Friday. Thursday is my toughest day because I'm supposed to be at work by 9:00 A.M. Saturday I do get to sleep in till 11:00 A.M.

My income is just over thirty thousand dollars a year. My wife does handicrafts and makes about $4,000. We have three children – aged eighteen months, three years three months and almost nineteen years. The nineteen-year-old is putting herself (with some help from her grandparents) through university – we can't afford to help. The two little ones are at home – for two reasons: (a) quality of care; (b) after expenses, my wife might clear fifty dollars a week if she were to work at a regular job – so her knitting and sewing actually bring in more money.

We are living in and building (at the same time) our house and home in Duncan Cove, Nova Scotia. I figure I should be finished somewhere around the turn of the century. This is not a small building (twenty-seven hundred square feet) and it has a spectacular location – one hundred feet of ocean frontage. Our east and south walls are almost entirely glass. We heat using passive solar and wood, five to seven real cords per winter, which I buy in eight-foot lengths and then cut and split. I could never ever afford a location like this anywhere else in the world. This is why I live and work here.

As I said earlier, I'm tired. I work very hard and long so that we can have a certain quality of life. I don't think that I am unusual. I believe that I am lucky to have what we do have. But I can't for the life of me understand how all of the economists, politicians, business people, and so on expect someone like me to survive. Where do they think that I am going to get the money to reduce the deficit, combat inflation, pay higher interest rates, pay for a new sales tax, and so on? There is nothing left of the bullet to bite. Surely to God not all of these experts live in Toronto and southern Ontario. It seems to me that the person who continues to survive on a limited low income has a valid economic opinion to express. Because we don't have an economics degree or make over fifty thousand dollars a year does not mean we don't understand or are incapable of understanding the intricacies of higher economics. I would suggest that the higher income people don't understand or appreciate the intricacies of lower economics.

Lower economics – true financial management – is the ability to find funds to buy a 1981 Volvo (in 1988), the day-to-day budgeting that puts food on the table, fresh fruit in the children, buys the occasional beer, puts gas in the car, gets your car safety-checked once a year and finds money to pay for used clothing for your little ones – never mind luxuries like diapers, haircuts, restaurant meals, wine, magazines, a whole twenty-four of beer, a bottle (not mickey) of liquor, candy, whole milk, pistachios, life insurance, RRSPs, dental work, or how about a holiday!

It is the everyday existence with which we average and below-average Canadians have to contend. It is our everyday existence that these experts are placing in jeopardy.

I don't believe that it is my deficit. I don't believe that it is my responsibility to pay for inept management. It is not my money that should pay for bad advice and incompetence at all levels of government. I shouldn't have to pay because Ontario (or parts of) is doing too well. Why should my family suffer because some idiot in Ottawa thinks that he has to control the economy in Central Canada? I didn't create this mess, why should I have to pay to clean it up?

Let those who blew it fix it. Have the moneys come out of their salaries, not mine.

God, I'm tired! I'm tired of being ignored – I'm tired of government bureaucracy and waste, I'm tired of hearing of housing prices in Toronto, I'm tired of paying for others' mistakes as well as my own, I'm tired of working fifty-six-plus hours a week.

I guess, most of all, I'm just tired!

Jim Legge
Duncan Cove, Nova Scotia

✉ *A Taxpayer's Lament*

Mulroney and Wilson came to power
On a beautiful True Blue vote.
With words of honey, they take our money
With a diligence worthy of note.

They raise our taxes and lower our grants
With manifestations of glee,
And after that's done they'll still have their fun
Collecting the GST.

If I could convey, for a year and a day,
Them to perdition, I would!
I pay more for my liquor, my fags and my gas
Than a pensioner reasonably should.

Our property taxes go steadily up
Our income tax certainly will,
For when we get pay, it is taken away
By the turkeys who live on the hill.

They live in style, wearing crocodile smiles,
Their attitude gives me a chill
While arm in arm, with ineffable charm,
They spend and we pay the bill, the bill,
They spend, and we pay the bill.

Moira E. MacDonald
Ottawa

✉ I teach grade six. Whenever math and life intersect in my class, I seize the teachable moment. Last month, my bank afforded me just such a moment, so I'm writing you.

"Decimals *count*, folks. Have a look at this." I pulled out a GIC Renewal Notice I'd just received. It should have been for four thousand dollars, but instead it read forty thousand dollars. After figuring out my overnight net gain, the class moved beyond black-and-white arithmetic into the grey zone of ethics.

Explaining that the GIC money was locked in for a year, during which time the bank would likely discover its error, I asked my students, "What should I do?"

"Keep it, Ms. D. . . . You could buy a great car and it's their mistake." (I don't drive.)

"Play dumb. Pretend you didn't notice." (I often *don't* – I just file those papers.)

"We could have a class trip around the world!"

"No, no. Be honest and maybe they'll give you a reward!"

Students then shared stories in which *their* honesty had been rewarded for returning wallets, puppies, lost children and the like. Two students suggested honesty *irrespective* of rewards, if I wished to live with myself and sleep at night.

Together we theorized as to what might happen back at the bank. Clearly the employee who'd displaced the decimal would be dumped and some unsuspecting client would suddenly be short thirty-six thousand dollars (the Conservation of Money Principle).

One pro-honesty student illustrated the situation by lining up her marker pens on end, saying, "Ms. D., this is you; this one's the person who made the mistake; this is the guy who lost the thirty-six thousand dollars; this is his wife; and these are his two kids." She picked up the marker representing me, saying, "You've just done *this*!", and dashed all the others.

I felt like turning myself in to the Fraud Squad that afternoon. One resourceful student threatened blackmail. "What's the name of that bank again, Ms. D.?"

By and large, the grade six class recommended honesty either for fear of getting caught, hope of a reward or its intrinsic value over material advancement.

The GIC exercise proved so enlightening, I decided to try it on the grade seven and grade eight guidance classes. Predictably, the level of corporate cynicism blossomed with age. The pro-honesty faction numbered four out of twenty-seven students in grade eight:

"Thirty-six thousand dollars is a drop in the bucket for a large bank. They can afford to pay for their screw-ups out of profits. You should get the money and leave the country, or hire a cheap lawyer to help you launder the money."

Another student advised that one really needs at least three million to buy a new life in an exotic country. I marvelled at the untapped expertise of today's thirteen-year-olds.

In grade seven, I was advised to "lose" the renewal notice and phone requesting a new one. If the bank blew its *second* chance to get the decimals right, then the money was *mine*, no question. Two students demanded a consulting fee, up front, before delivering their advice. (I gave them each a penny for their thoughts.)

The most original suggestion was that I sue the bank for mental cruelty, filling me with a false sense of wealth, then alternately tempting me and racking me with guilt.

Though the grade seven class talked tough and greedy, when asked what they'd *really* do in an eyes-shut show of hands, honesty prevailed.

Our school is facing a serious financial crisis. Looking at ends justifying means, I asked what they'd think of my taking the thirty-six thousand dollars and donating it to the school (or the homeless, the ozone layer, the ANC, pick your cause). This idea received little enthusiasm. I should either be honest or *enjoy* the spoils of my dishonesty.

The bank phoned yesterday.

The decision is now out of my hands and I blew my shot at a reward. My plan had been a form of deferred honesty, waiting to see how long it took the bank to catch its own error: three weeks.

But what a wonderful three weeks! I could not have *invented* a better barometer of student values, not to mention my own.

Ann T. Davidson
Toronto

✉ I was hoping you could help me with some historical information about something that I think may be coming back into vogue very soon.

When I was younger, I can remember people making fun of those old folks who used to keep money in a sock under the mattress: you know, just in case the banks failed again. "Ho-ho-ho," these worldly people sneered. "Why don't they put the money in a nice, safe, federally insured bank? That way, the money will earn interest and grow!" This idea stuck with me for a long time, but now I find that my convictions are beginning to falter.

I opened an account a while ago at a local financial institution. I was given a choice of accounts and opted for the kind that allows you to write a couple of cheques a month at no charge. The interest on the account, which was set at three per cent, would be paid monthly. This is wonderful, I thought, and briefly recalled all those old codgers with their lumpy sums under their aging Posturepedics: the fools.

The account was meant as a secondary account, to be used for special purchases. With the freedom of writing a cheque if necessary, I thought it would be ideal for putting away the odd shekel towards some of those silly little things you really need, like maybe a Nintendo, or a custom-made umbrella: little rewards for daily toil and strife. And what the hell, if I couldn't decide, at least it would pull in some interest, right?

When I got my statement on the account the other day, I noticed two things. One, there was no interest credited, and two, there was a one dollar service charge, even though absolutely nothing had occurred in the way of withdrawals, cheques or even account inquiries. (I had heard that an American bank was now charging a dollar if you asked a teller anything about your account. Aha, I thought, there's been a mistake here. Obviously, someone had made an inquiry and charged it to me somehow.)

When I phoned to ask about all this, I was told the following:

1. When your accumulated interest for the month is less than a dollar, it isn't added on. They just pretend that there never was any. The explanation for this is that the paperwork involved makes this totally unworkable and not worth the trouble.

2. No matter what you do with this particular type of account, you get charged a dollar a month, period. The explanation for this is that the time and cost involved in sending you out a statement makes this mandatory.

This is the New Economics. No longer do financial institutions have to worry themselves over paying you insignificant amounts of interest. However, the fact that you decide to leave money with them makes you accountable for any of the resulting paperwork. I can remember the old days, when the difference between the prime rates and the interest paid on your account was supposed to do that.

A little quick figuring revealed to me that unless I kept a minimum of four hundred in the account at all times, I wouldn't even be paid enough in interest to cover the service charges. In fact, once the balance fell below the four hundred mark, I would receive absolutely no interest and have the privilege of paying the financial institution twelve dollars a year in easy monthly payments for leaving my money with them. Left untouched, the amount would be under the three-hundred-dollar mark in just ten years. And don't forget the unpaid interest, too. Why, with a little willpower, this untouched amount could produce a real net loss of close to two hundred dollars in a decade.

What I want to know is, is there a particular *kind* of sock that you should use when you put money under your mattress? Also, is there a recommended spot that one should put the aforementioned sock? I'm not all that familiar with the practice, but I do know that if I put a little under four hundred dollars there, at least I'll still have that much in ten years' time.

Bob Wakulich
Mill Bay, British Columbia

Lost (Well, Almost Lost) Arts

We started with knotting a bow-tie. On the grounds that if I couldn't see him I would ask the questions whose answers the listeners need to hear, David Scott, a lawyer who wears one every day, went into a studio in Ottawa and tried to teach me once more what my grandfather had once showed me how to do–in my grandfather's case by draping his hands over my shoulders from behind and instructing me in the mirror. Did it work? Well, I said on the air that it did–you don't think I'd lie, do you?–even though, when it's time to dress for a formal occasion, I still reach for the clip-on. What that session did do, though, was launch us on a series of instructional sessions, on everything from how to iron a shirt (a captain of the armed services set up his board in Halifax) to how to chop wood (two brothers from New Brunswick) and . . . well, read on.

✉ Like all young Brits in the 1940s, on reaching eighteen years of age I was called up and I enlisted in the army. After basic training, the army, in its desperation, thought that I might turn out to be a "WOSBie ninety-day wonder" so I was shipped off to a small town in southern Scotland for further training.

I should explain that a "WOSBie (War Office Selection Board) ninety-day wonder" was the supposed metamorphosis of a gangling eighteen-year-old into an urbane army officer with fuzz on the upper lip. The training was about as successful as the U.S. Liberty ships, which were built in ten days flat, and just as disastrous.

The cadre officer, who had either strayed inadvertently north of the border or had been posted there in an attempt to promote bilingualism, had an accent and manner of speaking about as intelligible as the young couple we see on the TV tea commercial in which they twitter back and forth and end with "pity." Among the Scottish cadets, he was known as "Pork Head."

One fateful day, I was singled out and told to describe to the other cadets how to tie a conventional knot in a tie without using my hands. Having finished my disastrous description there was a pause, then I heard Pork Head utter, "I say, I do think the army has a need for you" – another pause " – at Nuremberg, to hang the guilty." An obvious reference to the war crimes trials taking place in that city.

Nowadays, I don't wear a tie as the moustache has, like a virus, spread around my face and just about covers where a knot would be.

If ever the occasion arises that I must wear a tie, I'll opt for a clip-on any day.

Don MacKenzie
Nepean, Ontario

✉ A few weeks ago, my teen-age son Bryan headed off to the city to take his friend Robin to her school formal. As he had errands to do on the way, he left here in teen-age attire – jeans, sneakers, and so on, and planned to change at her house.

About three hours later, I received a phone call from Robin – who sounded a touch frantic. "Bryan can't tie his bow-tie, and I can't either, and Mom is trying to find a neighbour who can help and we don't know what to do!" Gasp!

Eureka! said I. If Peter Gzowski can tie one over the radio with help from a lawyer in Ottawa, then I should be able to give telephone instructions! She got her arms around his neck, and on we went, step by step. On the third try, her mom arrived – having had no success going up and down the street for help, only to cry out in excitement, "That looks great" as she walked in the kitchen and saw them getting help by phone! The party was a smash, and Bryan's tie looked great.

I'm now going to darn a hole in my husband's favourite sweater.

Lynn Pady
Aurora, Ontario

✉ My mom taught me the art of ironing on Sundays as we talked about everything and she ironed – bless her, it helped me avoid many a detention at school. But even then I was not a neophyte; I had watched my grandmother iron my grand-dad's shirts when I was just a kid, forty years ago.

In those days, in Belgium, it took two irons to press a shirt. Mind you, my grandmother had a gas stove to heat those up. As well, the starch was applied *en masse* as the shirts were rinsed. After air drying, one was faced with a wrinkled board. The goal was to have a perfectly smooth garment but both cuffs and the collar had to have a slight shine. The shine was obtained by pressing the outside, or visible part, of the cuffs and collar. To prevent scorching and patina, ironing of the front and back panels was done from the inside. The sleeves were covered with another piece of fabric, then pressed.

The finer points of the art and the proper sequencing of the rite I picked up from my mom. Although her iron was electric, it did not have steam, automatic shut-off or any type of blinking lights.

With her, the first step in the ritual involved softening the clothes. This was done with a bowl of water and a limp hand. The clothes to be ironed were sorted, sprinkled with water and rolled up in bundles to get slightly damp – steam to be. Here are the steps in the proper order. Bear in mind that you must talk about music, politics, food, travel or love at the same time:

1. The collar

Place the shirt, opening down, on the narrow end of the table and start with the inside of the collar. Fold over and pat down with the iron. Insert the collar stays (which you had removed before doing the wash).

2. The cuffs

Place the shirt along the table, cuffs at the narrow end, openings facing up. Iron the inside of the cuffs and, using the tip of the iron, press the pointed tab ends. Button the cuffs.

3. The buttonhole placket

Drape the shirt over the side of the board closest to you, collar facing the wide end. Stretch the shirt so that the buttonhole placket is flat and taut. Place the tip of the iron at the bottom end of the placket and, holding the shirt by the collar, run the iron to the top of the placket.

4. The button placket

Drape the shirt over the side of the board farthest from you, collar facing the wide end. Stretch the shirt so that the buttoned placket is flat and taut. Place the tip of the iron at the bottom outside end of the placket and, holding the shirt by the collar, run the iron to the top of the placket on the outside of the buttons. Still holding the shirt by the collar, press in between each button from the inside out. Then, to finish, place the tip of the iron at the bottom inside end of the placket and, holding the shirt by the collar, run the iron to the top of the placket inside the buttons.

5. The yoke and sleeves

Place the shirt across the narrow end of the board, collar on your side. Stretch the sleeve towards the wide end, holding the cuff and the collar. Smooth the yoke and sleeve with your hand (the crease should be in the middle of the yoke). Press, starting from the yoke and running to and over the cuff. Turn the shirt over and press the sleeve again. Repeat for the other sleeve. Note that you will have to reverse the shirt's position on the board.

6. The side panels

Drape the shirt over the pointed end of the board, collar at the end. Stretch the shirt so that the buttonhole panel is flat and taut. If there is a pocket, iron it first. Then, place the tip of the iron at the bottom end of the panel right against the placket and run the iron to the top of the panel. Repeat for the other panel. Note that you will have to reverse the shirt's position on the board.

7. The back

If your shirt has a gather in the middle of the yoke in the back, you must iron from the outside. If your shirt has no gather, you can iron from the inside. Drape the shirt over the pointed end of the board, collar at the end. Stretch the shirt so that the back panel's buttonhole placket side is flat and taut. Starting at the bottom, iron to the top of the panel (or to the bottom of the sleeve). Rotate the shirt and repeat. When you reach the back gather, shape it by hand and press it. Then keep on doing the back panel.

The shirt must hang in a well-aerated location until entirely cold and dry. Then it can be stored or worn. Wearing a just-pressed shirt is like eating pasta out of a tin can; it'll work but it's from another galaxy.

Olivier Schittecatte
Gabriola, British Columbia

✉ My mom taught me that you ironed the collar first. It was the most important part of the shirt and if you goofed on it there was no need to finish ironing the rest.

Ruth Hutchinson
Ottawa

✉ Ironing an army shirt took me back forty-eight years to Kitchener. I was a parade square sergeant, paid two dollars a day (oh yes, we all know what an RSM is). In the last ten days of the month most of us were broke. At least I was. No TV or other entertainment, this was no fun. What did I do for money to go for a steak dinner on Queen Street in Kitchener? Right after breakfast Saturday morning, I stood in the centre of the hut and yelled, "Anyone need their shirts washed and pressed by 5:00 P.M.?" I washed all morning and pressed all afternoon. I know how to press a shirt and starched collars, too.

It doesn't take long to learn to iron a shirt with a little encouragement from a six-foot, one-inch, two-hundred-pound RSM.

Josie Hjorleifson
Duncan, British Columbia

✉ My grandmother taught me to iron before I was ten. And judging from the superior looks talking about it elicits, I may be the only thirty-something woman left doing it.

Time stops, worries crumble and stress evaporates on Sunday evenings when my overflowing laundry basket comes out. Small piles of folded clothes dot the bed in the ironing room. Soon the preliminaries are over and the iron is hot. I grip the cool handle of the Braun iron in my hand.

We move slowly over the collar, yoke, sleeves, cuffs, back and sides of the shirts. One by one, the shirts cover the hangers that are suspended from the door-frame, and form a curtain redolent of an indescribably clean and warm odour.

Louise Béland
Fredericton

✉ My mother made us learn to darn properly. We had to do it right. Not like one of my grandmothers, a mother of eight, who much preferred to play the piano than darn socks. She sewed around the hole then pulled the stitches tight together in a gather. This closed up the hole and, although a bit lumpy, served the purpose.

My grandmother's sin of sloppy darning was often used as an example of what I should not be doing. The fact that my grandmother was a delightful, talented woman was not a justified excuse. So now, I never darn socks. I hate to admit it but I stuff the holey socks into the bottom of the bathroom garbage can with a guilty pang every time, then heave a sigh of relief when they are out of sight. My family, however, is constantly bewildered by missing socks.

Lynne Smith
Newmarket, Ontario

✉ I was recently reminded of all the great things my mom does for me. You see, on any given day, my job requires me to clean stalls (hot work), train dressage horses (warm work) and teach lessons (absolutely freezing cold work!). I find that wearing layers of wool sweaters keeps me warm and dry no matter in what order my tasks must be completed. I enjoy wearing these sweaters and am often buying a new one "for the barn." However, by the time I get it home I realize that it looks much better with "these pants" than with "those grubby old riding breeches." Thus, I find myself wearing the same barn sweaters for years on end. Thankfully, my mother knows how to darn. I have a number of well-loved sweaters worn thin at the elbows and cuffs that have been repaired by my mom. Each time I screech that "I can't throw it out, it's my favourite one!" Mom comes through. Mom comes through a lot. No matter how thoroughly we argue, she makes sure I always have home-made bread in my freezer, helps my husband and me renovate our house *and* darns sweaters for me!

Janet Fortin
Listowel, Ontario

✉ When I was a young person I tried, at my mother's knee, to learn the intricate finger work related to knitting. I failed. My mother, despite her patience, could not understand my ineptitude at a craft that she so enthusiastically enjoyed and to this day, at seventy-one, still creates unique knitted gifts for my children and others in our family. She is one who will walk into stores and examine knitted apparel, turning the pieces inside out and upside down, all the while her brain is measuring and taking notes so she can duplicate the same item at home (without a pattern) adding her personal touch.

My husband, who has been collecting "fur" from our Old English sheep-dog and had it spun into beautiful wool, wanted to create a unique gift for a close friend who was moving to the Northwest Territories. When I informed my husband there was no way I could help him knit something, my mom came to the rescue and sat with my husband and the two of them painstakingly knit a beautiful scarf to be worn around our friend's neck to keep the ultra-cold away. It proved to be a "family" effort – grandma, hubby and dog!

Barbara Snelgrove
Meaford, Ontario

✉ I heard a mention the other day of darning, and the light bulb and needle and wool.

I was reminded not of a light bulb, but of a solid wooden "mushroom," a device designed to be slotted into the end of an artificial arm. It was one of two devices – the other was a simple rod with a rubber-cushioned knob on the end, designed to hit typewriter keys. They were attachments I was given (along with a "hook" just like the fellow in *Peter Pan*) to use in my arm when I was eight years old. These two gadgets surely told me all I needed to know about my place in the world.

I was born with no left hand. I predated Thalidomide, my mother took no drugs, it was just one of life's mysteries, a clump

429

of cells whose switch didn't flick at the right time. On a doctor's advice and at the request of my teachers – God forbid I went unarmed to school, it might upset the other children – I started limb-fittings at an early age and at age eight attended Roehampton hospital, London, as a resident to learn the mysteries of this new arm with the gadgets.

The arm was a prehistoric monster – hot, heavy and useless and worn with strap contraptions that crossed over the shoulders at the back and under the right armpit. It was dumped in the cupboard whenever possible so that I could better spend time tree-climbing. At Roehampton I met the mushroom and its mates. More importantly, I met men from both world wars, many still struggling to rehabilitate, to learn the use of prosthetics, to recover from shock long after the war was over. I had it easy.

I also had friends like young Albert, who would walk us three young girls, all of us between eight and twelve, into Putney, where we would sit on a bench outside the pub and sip shandy while he downed his pint and told us how it was "over there." He had lost a leg. There was the Danish pilot who had lost his leg at the knee and his arm at the shoulder. He was in constant pain but endlessly kind to us rambunctious kids.

I was not there for long and in some childlike way recognized the mushroom for what it was – an albatross. By age eleven, I shed any pretence of wearing an arm and since then have only wandered once into the world of prosthetics. At twenty-two, I tried again. Again the arm ended up in the garbage, a useless encumbrance.

There have been hazards along the way to wholeness. As a potential school-leaver, on applying for a job in a bank I was told psychiatric assessment would be necessary in case I suffered mental as well as physical incompleteness. A library job in my teens disappeared when I argued about being "kept out of sight of the public." Luckily these incidents were isolated and served only to harden my resolve.

I have raised two children – large and heavy both – and suffered the frustrations of opening doors and hanging onto kids while my arms were full of groceries, carrying infant seats, wrestling squirming babies into clothes before the birth of Velcro, putting all the dishes down to turn on taps . . . I am glad it's over.

I knit, sew, swim, cross-country ski, play squash, tennis, badminton, learned to cycle at forty, varnish my own five nails and have driven for twenty-seven years all manner of vehicles in all kinds of conditions. I loathe tying shoelaces and shovelling snow.

I can also type much faster than many a two-handed two-finger pecker—and I can darn a mean sock without benefit of mushroom. But frankly I don't bother in spite of the obvious economy. It is my remaining rebellion to the original gift, which at the age of eight could so easily have sealed my womanly fate.

Angela Mackay
Ottawa

✉ I don't know how or when my son picked up the rudiments of knitting, but when he was in university he decided to create some marvellous pieces of wearing apparel with very bright yarn. His pieces were always made with the wearer in mind. There were jester caps with three or four pointed peaks and bells, a sputnik-like cap for me, a foot-tall mountain with climbers, mittens with two wrist parts and only one mitt for engaged friends and many, many other one-of-a-kind creations.

Always having been a practical and very handy person, he approached knitting in the same way he'd approach the building of a shed or a piece of furniture. If you want to go this way, you add stitches, and if you want to go in, you decrease, and so on. But every once in a while he'd meet a problem he couldn't solve. His solution was to board a bus in Oak Bay, Victoria, and search out an older woman who looked as though she'd know how to knit. He had some very pleasant encounters and the women were always pleased to share their knitting knowledge.

Helen Gerow
Hornby Island, British Columbia

✉ I learned to waltz back in 1918-19 when we lived in Midhurst, Sussex.

I attended a Church of England school that the vicar visited two or three times a year. The vicar of my time was quite odd – eccentric, I suppose – he always wore "velveteens" rather than an ordinary suit. His velveteens were dark green, as I recall. Velveteens were the garb of game wardens on private estates. Maybe the Rev. Tatchell saw himself as a warden for God.

Anyway, he arranged dancing classes for twelve-, thirteen- and fourteen-year-old girls. I don't remember if it was strictly for girls or whether no boys decided to attend. We learned folk dances and the waltz.

However, the waltz we learned was 1-2-3-4-5-6, 1-2-3-4-5-6. The first three steps were similar to the usual three, but on 4 you put your left foot forward, on 5 you placed your right toes to the heel of your left foot and on 6 made a little pirouette on your toes, ending with your right heel against your left instep. Try it – remember to always begin with your right foot.

As I live alone, I've been practising by myself and can't quite figure out just how a partner would fit in!

Sybil Willard
Dryden, Ontario

✉ For the record, the waltz is alive and thriving in the Rideau heartland of Eastern Ontario courtesy of the Rideau Lakes Ballroom Dancing Club. The club sponsors a monthly dance where we trip the light fantastic to our hearts' content. Many of us take weekly dance lessons where we practise an increasing array of steps and twirls in a seemingly endless string of classic and Latin dances.

There are a few things you should know about ballroom dancing that they do not teach in grade eight dancing lessons. (Remember them, the boys hiding in the cloakroom, the girls trying to be nonchalant?) Dancing is the last refuge of the male chauvinist. All major decisions on the dance floor are taken by the male; the female simply follows his lead. It gives the male a tremendous sense of power and awesome responsibility from the time the couple gets to the dance floor (what the heck dance is this anyway?) to the ultimate in identifying the numerous possible moves and making the appropriate lead in such a way that his partner is clearly impressed with his abilities. The flip side of this responsibility is the perfect opportunity to make an idiot of yourself.

You can have your lambadas! Give me a tango or a merengue with Cuban motion. These dances done properly are enough to raise hormone levels in both sexes to dangerous levels.

The most important thing one should remember about dancing is that it is indeed a body contact sport.

Doug Green
Athens, Ontario

✉ *Tree Planter's Waltz*

Buy me some shoes with steel in the toes
a silver gardenia, a jonquil, a rose
I'll wear a dress of gossamer lace,
rings in my ears, stars on my face

Though you step on my toes,
I'll still dance like Kain,
a sunbeam, a willow,
a clear drop of rain

Don't eat garlic soup
or too much red wine
and I then will be yours
and will you be mine

Mavis Jones
Vancouver

✉ I grew up in Bruce County, Ontario, and came in contact with square dancing at an early age. My father played the fiddle and was often asked to play for dances at the school, community centre or some neighbour's house. I played the piano and occasionally went along to chord.

I remember asking a caller about the term "allemen left" years ago. His explanation was that it grouped together the words "all the men left."

At one house party, there was a set of square dancers in the living-room and a second set in the dining-room. A room off to the side was emptied and a third set was dancing in there. It was particularly difficult for this last set to hear the caller amid the din of people chattering, feet shuffling, fiddle, guitar and piano music. Occasionally this set would get behind, and someone would come to the doorway to catch the caller's instruction. I remember some wag running to the doorway, taking a quick look, then yelling back, "Elephants left."

Bill Zettler
Portage la Prairie, Manitoba

✉ For the better part of ten years, Max (and I, too, when he was away or too busy) doggedly trudged to the barn morning and evening through wind, rain, snow, ice and lots of good weather to milk a succession of Jersey pets—Eunice, Millie and her daughter Floss, The Herd, Calfé au Lait, DeCalf, Stella and Daphne. All the while, we enjoyed the gifts of these creatures, including their gentle natures and the rich milk that provided us with more than enough yoghurt, butter and cheese, much to our contentment and the delight of our guests.

Then one day last summer, Daphne defied the electric fence for the umpteenth time and invaded Max's garden just when the lettuce, Swiss chard, beans, peas, beets, broccoli and corn were about to be harvested for table and freezer—*not* for belly of cow. That was when the first serious grumblings about some other fate for cows began to be heard. The loudest finally came on a bitterly cold February morning following one of our more significant Maritime snowfalls. Three hours after leaving the cosy house, a frostbitten Max burst into the kitchen to announce: "That's it! I've finally had it! Two hours to shovel snow out of the barnyard [that's so the animals can exercise without walking over the fence] and twenty minutes to shovel frozen manure . . . All for two lousy bottles of milk. That's it!"

It took less time for the grapevine to start buzzing than it does for some people to discover the work involved in milking cows. Several days later, Daphne and her four-month-old granddaughter had found appreciative homes elsewhere. Our relief was immediate, and so was the length of a good night's sleep. Now, though, as our hands and arms weaken from lack of milking exercise, we keep looking out to our little barnyard expecting to see our doe-eyed Jerseys peacefully chewing their cuds while soaking up the warmth of the winter sun and realize it's more than our palates that miss our gentle friends.

Willi Evans Wolfe
Lower Jemseg, New Brunswick

✉ I'll be thirty-six years old next month, and ten years ago, if anyone had told me I'd be milking a cow, I would have thought they were right out of it!

About four years ago, my husband and I became foster parents for a teen-aged boy, a boy of five and a girl of three years.

My husband thought that it would be more healthy and a good learning experience for the kids if we had a cow.

Enter Daisy. She was a gentle Jersey that we bought from a dairy farmer in the area. She was due to be sold as her milk production was too low for a commercial farmer. The deal was that I would not have to have anything to do with her, except to bottle the milk. To make a long, boring story short, I ended up being responsible for her well-being, as well as milking her twice a day.

The first few times, it took me forty minutes or more to completely milk her. But, as the saying goes, practice makes perfect, and I soon cut my time in half, for which I'm sure Daisy was grateful. As a matter of fact, I was soon enjoying myself!

During the winter, I always wore mittens while doing the other chores first (i.e., feeding and watering the chickens and Daisy), so that when it came time to milk, my hands weren't like a couple of blocks of ice.

As I sat there, with my head pressing into her warm flank, her tail often swished into my face, or she would reach around and lick at me. (Once warm weather came and I didn't need a jacket, it felt like she was using the roughest sandpaper ever made on my poor arms and back!)

Surprisingly, the best thing to get her to settle down was to sing. Then, she would just turn her head and stare with those beautiful brown eyes of hers. However, I'm not sure if my voice was soothing, or if she just couldn't believe the noises I was making.

I put up a big fuss at the thoughts of the work involved with having her here, but that's one experience that I'm grateful for.

Debbie Sayles
Apsley, Ontario

✉ Early in our marriage, my wife prepared what she thought would be a special treat for me. I am a soup freak, and she was on the look-out for new and different soup recipes. This time she thought she had a winner, and I must confess that the mouth-watering aroma that greeted me when I opened the door had me drooling in a matter of seconds. Then she told me what it was – oxtail soup. I had to tell her I would not taste it nor would I ever taste it. When she asked why, I asked her if she had ever seen the tail on a live ox. She said she had never seen a live ox and wouldn't lose any sleep if she never saw one, and what did that have to do with my peculiar position. I told her of a traumatic experience I had on the farm when I was a child.

I had nagged Uncle Charley for almost a month to let me milk a cow. I told him I had watched him and Aunt Hannah at evening and morning milking and was sure I knew how it was done. He finally agreed to let me milk old Bonnie, who had been giving milk since before I was born.

I lost no time getting into action. I positioned the pail and the stool, sat down, grasped two of the four milk-giving appendages and squeezed. Nothing happened. I switched to the other two, but still no milk. I tried all possible combinations until my fingers were aching, but Bonnie held fast to her milk.

Convinced she was deliberately holding out on me, I spoke to her with the kind of language I'd heard adults use when they were very angry. I didn't know what some of the words meant, but I suspect that Bonnie did. With an attitude like hers, she must have heard them many times before that day. Under the pretext of swatting flies on her flank, which up to that point she had ignored, she lashed out with her tail.

My head and face took the full force of the blow. The blow did not hurt, but it caused severe mental anguish. That Bonnie had been careless in her toilet that day was revealed in the foul smear she deposited on my face and in my hair.

In my haste to prove I could milk a cow, I had forgotten to wash her udder, dugs and her offensive tail. What was offensive to Bonnie, however, and what probably triggered her action, was the fact that I had tried to milk her from the wrong side. As a reminder of my stupidity, she gave me a lasting legacy – an intense feeling of revulsion at the mention of oxtail soup or any reference to any kind of bovine tail.

Royal Shepherd
Scarborough, Ontario

✉ On rural Vancouver Island we have much wood, and hydro that tends to flutter out at the first sign of a storm. Wood fires are part of our survival, along with the candles and coal-oil lamps.

My wood warms me three times. The first time is when my cord is delivered in the fall and left for me to stack in the wood-shed out of the weather. There is satisfaction in making a neat stack, and I stand back, sweat pouring down my brow, to admire my handiwork. I think it looks like a patchwork quilt and it pleases me. But an acquaintance on Salt Spring goes one better. He creates a happy face in the middle of his wood stack that grins at him all summer and then slowly loses its personality come winter as the wood disappears into his airtight stove.

The second time my wood warms me is when I split it into fireplace-sized pieces and kindling and restack it close to the house. I can work up quite a lather doing that, and it's a good way to relieve tension.

And the final time my wood warms me is when it burns merrily, spitting and crackling in the hearth, while I sit with my feet up, reading a good book and sipping a cuppa. Not bad for a lost art, eh?

Patricia Landry
Shawnigan Lake, British Columbia

✉ I was in first grade and had my first homework assignment: a spelling lesson. I had studied hard and, wanting to show off, I presented my open speller to my father with the request that he hear my lesson. Dad put his newspaper aside and accepted the book. "Yes, dear," he said, and waited. I pointed to the words I had learned – the first six words of a set of twelve – and explained that he was to ask me a word and I would spell it. Dad replied that if I really knew my lesson, I would be able to recite it, and he provided the formula he had had to use a generation earlier: state the word, spell the word, use the word correctly in a sentence, state the word again and move on. It was too late to back out, so I took the book, studied some more and returned to recite. More than fifty years later, I can still picture those six words as they appeared on that page.

soft	lake
boat	park
silver	watch

I have no recollection of the second set of six words, and no subsequent lesson was ever as well learned, for I avoided the risk of recitation by never again asking Dad to check my homework. My loss.

June Manson
Ottawa

✉ I remember a poem I was often asked to recite at my mother's tea-parties. Over the years I have forgotten the title but I think that's not too bad a record as my next birthday will be my eightieth. Dressed in my perfectly ironed, best white dress, white shoes and white knee socks with horrible garters – elastic bands – I went into the drawing-room. My mother announced to her friends I would say a little piece. At first I was very nervous but over the years I learned to enjoy my small performances. My mother's favourite, which invariably made her cry, was the following:

Here is the nursery where they slept, three little beds in a
  row
Over the floor I softly crept, so the children would not know.
But red and scratched the nursery bath still in the corner
  stands
And the little tin dish with the scrap of soap
That washed their baby hands.
Over the floor the soapsuds flew. It was a splendid play
But the soap we have found is hard and brown; the children
  have gone away.

(At this point tears would come into my mother's eyes.)

No babies wash in the bathtub now
They have gone with their smiles and their tears,
One and all they have trodden the road
That leads to the height of years
And out of our ken, as women and men,
Into the grown-up lands,
And all we hold is the scrap of soap that washed their baby
    hands.

By this time the tears were running down my mother's face and her friends were sniffing and blowing their noses and mumbling "Such a lovely little piece" and my mother always added, "So simple." Applause followed. I made a quick curtsy and dashed from the room.

Doris Skerl-Mackedie
Vancouver

✉ This month I received, with the utmost pleasure I might add, my first pension cheque.

I thought that, for a senior citizen, I wasn't doing too badly. Granted, this past year when I attended the ex-overseas evacuees' reunions and discovered that I could remember more than fifty years back with the utmost clarity, I got a bit of a shock. Still, there's a bit of spring left in my step and when I get done up and dusted, I don't look too bad provided the light isn't too strong.

But lost arts? Tying a bow-tie? Well, yes, it is a bit tricky, but I've done many a one in the past and assumed that people were still tying them. Granted, I was brought up in the U.K. but I was always told that no gentleman *ever* wore a made-up bow.

Then there were the "lost arts" of darning, reciting, waltzing and ironing a shirt. Am I so antiquated and out of touch that I can do all these things? My mum taught me to darn, and when first I was married, before nylon socks came in, I used to sit down with a big pile every week. Reciting (again, granted that I was raised in England)–bet I could give you a good run for your money on "And still of a winter's night they say, when the wind is in the trees, And the moon is a ghostly galleon tossed upon cloudy seas." I well remember on (what we used to call) Armistice Day, being the one chosen to recite Rupert Brooke's "The Soldier" in front of the whole school, that would be grade five, and when I was in grade seven we had what were called our Anthology Books. Any time we had learned by heart a poem (any poem) of our own choosing from our poetry reader, we could recite it out loud in front of the class for our English mistress, get some points for our school house and then copy it into our Anthology Book. It was no chore. It was fun. I could waltz the Merry Widow off her feet any day, we all could, and we never had ballroom dancing lessons, and as for ironing a shirt. Well, I still do my nice ones sometimes, though granted it isn't as great a chore as when they had to be dampened down and done with an ordinary iron before the steam ones came along.

I'm a bit miffed at being made to feel that I came out of the Ark because all these "lost" arts were part of my growing up.

Maggie Morris Smolensky
Toronto

FURTHER ADVENTURES IN THE NAME GAME

Remember a girl called Bruce, and other misadventures of names from *The Latest Morningside Papers*? The sagas continue.

✉ The other day I was reminded of an early-morning conversation I had with my then four-year-old son Oliver.

Lying in bed with him nestled at my side, I was tuned into the morning show, on which they were discussing the various pleasures encountered by art gallery goers.

The commentator made some remark about how nice it was to be sitting in a room surrounded by works by the likes of Michelangelo. She went on to name a few other masters of note. But I didn't hear her finish. At the sound of the name Michelangelo, Oliver's apparently sleeping head suddenly popped up and he stammered, "Michelangelo, Michelangelo," as if he expected to see a life-size Ninja Turtle stride into the room.

"Calm down, Oliver," I said. "They aren't talking about *that* Michelangelo."

"Which Michelangelo are they talking about then?" he asked accusingly.

"The one who painted the ceiling of the Sistine Chapel in Rome," I replied.

Oliver thought about that for a second, then said, in all seriousness, "Why would a turtle want to paint the Sistine Chapel?"

Allison Brewer
Fredericton

✉ Because of our last name, which some people apparently find a bit peculiar, my seven-year-old son and I have both developed a special interest in the Teenage Mutant Ninja Turtles phenomenon. The link our last name provides between the TMNTs and us has led my son to form a very special affinity with these green titans, and he has become his school's guru on mutant turtle matters.

What strikes me is that, unlike his father and paternal aunts and uncles, my son has not had to put up with schoolyard taunting about his name; to the contrary, his name has made him a bit of a cult hero in these Turtle-crazed days. My siblings and I were not held in such high regard. We endured the jokes about being slow, about being green, about the Mr. Turtle kids' wading pool, about Turtle Wax, about Howie the Turtle and about turtle soup.

I had some occasional relief, however; when attractive Canadian singer Gail Dahms cooed her innuendo-laden line, "Oooh, I love Turtles" in the chocolate commercials of the mid-seventies, I could imagine she was singing to me. As well, I was able to have my sadistically bent little league coach dismissed partly because, his left brain unable to accept the fact that my name was "Turtle," he was convinced I was lying to him and he benched me.

Having a strange name toughened us a bit and taught us a repertoire of witty responses to those people who felt compelled to make jokes that they somehow thought we hadn't heard a million times already. We emerged, and remain, proud of our family name.

My son's pride has been acquired a bit more easily, though I know his toughest days are still ahead of him. But the link between Chris Turtle and Raphael, Michelangelo, Donatello and Leonardo is almost cosmic, and we know that unlike those mutant teen-age terrapins, we will remain turtles far beyond our teen-age years.

Gordon Turtle
Edmonton

✉ I have run across people who share my name, Bill MacLean, but not always with amusing consequences.

The first instance occurred just after my wife and I had moved to Toronto and had applied to our local bank for a car loan. We were turned down because, in doing a credit check, the bank found that Bill MacLean had previously defaulted on a number of car loans. It took a while to convince them that I was not that Bill MacLean.

A few years later, I made an appointment with a writer-in-residence at our local library to have a couple of my short stories critiqued. This writer seemed hesitant to keep our appointment. As I found out when we eventually met, she had once lived with a Bill MacLean who had not been, shall we say, a model mate. She was worried that I was he, trying to trick her into renewing their acquaintance.

The oddest coincidence took place when I called a brokerage firm to sell some stocks my wife held. Once I was routed through the system, the man who answered the phone said, "Sales, Bill MacLean." Maybe it was the way he said it, or maybe it was the shock at hearing my own name come back at me, but for an instant I wasn't sure if he had the same name as myself, or by some psychic power knew it was me on the line without my having identified myself. After a few confused and confusing questions from each of us, we sorted the mess out. Later, when my wife went down to fill out the papers, she said it was the strangest experience to be introduced to someone with her husband's name, and yet who looked nothing like him.

Which brings me to my final name conundrum. I have recently entered the world of broadcasting only to discover that I share my last name with a host of other broadcasters: Stuart McLean, Ron MacLean, Elizabeth MacLean, Bob MacLean and Wayne MacLean. It appears that for many of us MacLeans, being enamoured with the sound of our own voices is a family trait.

Bill MacLean
Toronto

✉ Unless a sizeable inheritance hangs in the balance, becoming a Junior or a III isn't worth the muddle that goes with sharing a parent's first name.

I didn't know that when we baptized our first daughter with my name. The hospital threatened to hold her hostage until we filled in all the birth certificate blanks.

We didn't make her my namesake to worm her into a rich grandparent's will, had that been possible. We both liked the name: all the letters stay above the line; it looks good as a signature. And I've especially been fond of it since it's a diminutive of my father's name, Claude.

Until I was twenty, Claudette Colbert was the only namesake I knew of, unlike all the Kims or Marys. Every classroom had several of those. Then a neighbour six-year-old showed up answering to my name. She even adopted the nickname my baby brother had given me, Detta. I felt robbed, as if she'd stolen my private property, yet I was helpless to complain.

Though I liked my moniker enough to divvy it with my offspring, she was ten months old before I could conquer my self-consciousness and call her anything but Sweetheart. Even today, twenty-three years later, while I'm comfortable referring to her as Claudette, I still prefer to speak to her as Sweetheart, a quirk that causes heads to swivel if I try to capture her attention in a public place like an airport waiting-room.

Had I known what my daughter and I were in for, she'd be Vera, or Melissa, or Ingrid.

Insurances (both life and medical); hospital and doctor's records; letters to the editor – all are prone to confusion.

Optometrists sort her contact lenses from my bifocals. The family doctor separates her fractured ankle from my arthritic wrist.

Co-owners of names carry extra responsibilities, too. Suppose one of us passes a bad cheque, deals drugs or submits a rotten article to a publication (fortunately, we have no worries along these lines).

Phone calls were a special mix-up. We determined her calls from mine by asking, "Did you want to speak to Big Claudette or Little Claudette?" When both our weights zoomed, we revised the question to "Old Claudette or Young Claudette?" Later when Grecian Formula no longer did the trick for me, we compromised with "Claudette, the mom, or Claudette, the daughter?"

Then she graduated from journalism school and moved to Castlegar. We thought distance would solve our dilemma. Not so.

Within weeks of her byline appearing on the front page of the *Castlegar News*, a former Terrace resident – now living in the Kootenays – phoned her expecting to renew acquaintance with me. The caller's cheery greeting was met with my daughter's puzzled silence.

We also adopted our daughter's suggestion that Father sign any cheques we sent to her. Otherwise, when she took the cheque to the bank, tellers huddled with the Fraud Squad.

"Having the same first name opens some doors, but doesn't hit any balls for you," golfer Jack Nicklaus, son of the Golden Bear, said.

How true.

Claudette Sandecki
Terrace, British Columbia

446

✉ I once had an encounter with two people sharing more than just a name. It happened in a busy emergency room in Saskatoon where I was the doctor on duty. The patients' charts were lined up in order of appearance on the desk and I would start at one end and work my way through the row. One of the first charts I picked up one morning described a patient, let's call her Jane Williams, date of birth September 8, 1964, who had suffered a knife injury to her left wrist. Jane told me she had accidentally cut her wrist with a utility knife while opening a cardboard box at work that morning. I stitched the cut and sent her on her way. About an hour later, I again encountered Jane Williams's chart, again listing a laceration to the left wrist. I wondered what had prompted her return and noted in passing that the admitting clerk had gotten the date of birth wrong – it now read September 8, 1959. However, when I went in to see Ms. Williams, it was not the woman I had sutured earlier. She confirmed her name, she confirmed the date of birth and told me that, yes indeed, she had cut her left wrist with a utility knife while opening a cardboard carton at work that morning. I don't know if the two women ever met each other, but it wouldn't surprise me if they did. I somehow think the coincidence would not be complete otherwise.

Steve Rollheiser
Chase, British Columbia

✉ There are few situations that are quite as confusing as the first time you realize that someone else answers to your name. I had been married for just over a year and was working with the speech therapist for the schools in town. We saw each other only off and on during the week and used the office bulletin-board to keep in touch. She would post work to be done and letters that needed to be filed from parents, teachers and "reference professionals" (doctors, occupational therapists, audiologists and so on, whom we would meet with to help confirm diagnoses, and help with programs among other things). There, one morning, was a letter signed with my single name. Although the confusion was only slightly longer than momentary, it was intense. The signature was my name . . . but not . . . and in handwriting that was done by a pen not held in my hand. The person to whom this letter referred was a child I knew about, yet it was saying things I had no knowledge of. Did I type this letter for my boss? Why would I sign it? Just a minute, I hadn't been signing that name since I'd been married. I took a closer look, settled into the office chair and smiled at the thought of another Linda Barr, a reference profes-sional. A few weeks later my boss and I met with her to complete the business referred to in the introductory letter. She was about the same age as me – within five years I'd guess – and did all her business settled in a wheelchair.

I knew her for less than half a day. I smiled with her over the coincidence of names, said maybe five sentences to her and admired her for her position and ability to achieve it from a wheelchair.

She was one of those people we all run into in our professional and business lives and forget about after all the "i's" are dotted. Yet a few years later when I read that Linda Barr who worked at the Calgary Children's Hospital had died, I knew and remem-bered her and felt a little pain that could only have come from sharing the same name.

Linda Barr Hajash
Brooks, Alberta

✉ I get riled up every time I think about what happened to me, a shy, unassuming little girl starting grade one in 1956. There are not many things that occurred during my childhood that I can recall as vividly as this.

The first thing that happens when starting school is to be identified by your teacher and classmates. As you can see, my name is Diane. I was not the only little girl in that class with that name. That seemed to be a problem that couldn't be allowed to continue. The teacher, in her wisdom, asked each of us what our middle names were. The other Diane had as a middle name Mary.

Guess what? There already was a girl named Mary in this grade one class. That meant it fell on me to be called by my middle name.

I think my middle name is rather unusual and I don't really mind it in its entirety. It is Gwendith – I don't know where my mom dreamt that up from. Anyway, Gwendith seemed a much too complicated name, so Teacher shortened it to Gwen, which I hate with a passion, and so I was called until a far more understanding third grade teacher asked me if I would rather be called Diane.

Unfortunately, growing up in small town Alberta, you never entirely get away from your past. Gwen kept raising its ugly head at the worst possible moments.

My schoolmates quickly got used to me being called Diane and forgot all about my alias. Not so the public health nurse. She was around to haunt me all through junior high school and into high school.

If I thought I was shy going into grade one, by the time I was in grades seven, eight and nine I positively wilted at the thought of being singled out in public.

Every year the public health nurse provided us with our eye check-ups, booster shots and whatever else was required for our physical well-being. Each year she would appear at the door of the classroom and call out the name of the student she wanted to see next. It never failed she would arrive at the door and in a very clear voice ask Gwen Scheibner to please come with her.

You can rest assured that every boy and girl in the class would be craning their necks to get a look at who this Gwen was. I would then, red-faced and trying to fade into oblivion, slink out into the hall cursing the day my grade one teacher needed a solution to a problem of what to do with two Dianes in the class.

Diane King
alias Gwen Scheibner
Calgary

✉ I was born Maureen Sullivan. My dad had been talking to someone in Ireland just before I was born and discovered Maureen was the Irish form of Mary – my mom's name. The name was fine by me until the first day of school when a fifth of my grade one class turned their heads when my Irish name was called out. It was a natural, I guess, for an Irish Catholic convent.

I quickly adopted part of my dad's nickname for me, "Maureen, Dean the Bean" – I kept the Dean part. No more loss of identity. From then on only my mother, the government and the bank called me Maureen Sullivan. It helped me to tell if it was a friend or the tax department.

My new name worked. People remembered me, often remarking how unusual my name was. I left Maureen only to officialdom. I almost forgot it. Years passed as Deannie. I married, had children and took up photography as Deannie.

Photographing flowers had led to a botany class given by Erindale College, part of U of T. I had become enthralled, much to my horror, with flowers. Even the dried pressed lifeless varieties were gardens of wonder under the microscope. I worried I'd be planting gardens next and weeding hedges in 30° weather – this I had done growing up as unpaid gardening assistant to my mother the horticulturist.

Much to my surprise, I did very well. The prof encouraged me to sit in on his university class, unofficially of course. He then said it would be all right to write the exam, no credits, just to see how I would do. When I received the second highest mark, he encouraged me to legitimize my status and sign up.

For this I was told I needed a transcript of my marks. After high school I had gone to an art school that was a part of Concordia University. I didn't think this would count in the world of academia. Yes, it did, the registrar encouraged me. With little time before the deadline for the next semester, I called Montreal for my transcript. I almost forgot it would be filed under Maureen.

I was excited when it arrived. I checked the marks. Maureen Sullivan had graduated from a two-year course in Commercial Art. I raced downtown where the registrar shook her head. I would have to take a year of university prep classes, and a transcript had to be sent directly to her.

I decided I would take the prep classes, and I sent for another transcript with a special note to have the marks sent directly to U of T.

Months passed. Then a large white envelope arrived, and I opened it. "Transcript for Maureen Sullivan." The marks were wonderful—not an art school Maureen Sullivan but a summa cum laude Maureen Sullivan of literature and history . . . she would ensure entrance to any university. The only snag, this literate accomplished younger woman hadn't paid her graduating fee. Fifteen dollars was the only thing standing between me and legitimate university botany. This and her middle name, which was not the same as mine.

I struggled for days, weeks. I wouldn't have to spend a year studying things I didn't want to. I could get right at it . . . I could study plants in the rain forests. All I'd have to do is pay up and ensure that this time these glorious marks made it straight to the registrar.

In the end it came down to values. I valued my honesty. However, I never did carry on. My life abruptly changed, as my marriage of twelve years split apart, my ex-husband vowing not to give me my settlement if I were to fritter it away on botany.

I realize now how little time we have to achieve the things we want. I have yet to see a rain forest, and at the rate things are going, I probably won't. Sometimes I wonder what would have happened if I had let that younger clever Maureen Sullivan open the door.

Deannie (Maureen) Sullivan Fraser
Dartmouth, Nova Scotia

✉ How fitting that after a week's break for the Christmas holidays I should return to find a parcel on my desk addressed to Mr. Ken Dunn. "Why?" you may ask. Because, alas, my name is Kim Dunn. And I am a mister.

This is not a new experience for me. Perhaps it is because I am a mister that leads people to change my first name.

"Kim," they seem to reason, "is a woman's name. I must have misheard. His name must be Ken, Tim, Cam, Jim, et cetera."

The mail addressed to me from people with whom I have not spoken or whom I have not met is usually accurate as far as my name goes. They get "Kim" right. However, it is my sex that is changed. I become Ms., Miss, Mrs. Kim Dunn. At age sixteen, I received my Social Insurance card addressed to Miss Kim Alexander Dunn.

Of all the alternatives to my name that I have read on envelopes, my favourite is one that came to my place of business from my company's bank. Each February, the bank sends all employees an invitation to take advantage of its RRSP. Everyone got one except me. It wasn't until later that the office manager decided that what appeared to be a misaddressed envelope was indeed meant for me.

In bold blue type, perfectly centred, was my bank's version of "Kim Dunn":

King Duran

So if someday you pick up a novel that begins, "King Duran, Foster in hand, looked out over his 500,000 acre sheep station . . . " you'll know whence it comes.

Kim Dunn
Montreal

✉ I heard a comment that shocked me with its suggestion that Sherlock Holmes might have been a woman.

You see, Sherlock Holmes was my father.

Of course Dad was no Great Detective but he was born in 1894, just seven years after the publication of A Study in Scarlet, and his father (William Harry Holmes), either because he was a very early Holmesian or because of the weird sense of humour he certainly had, could not resist the coincidence of the surname and christened his son "Harry Sherlock."

Dad always went by the name Sherlock until, in his sixties, he remarried and his new wife re-named him Sherry.

Being the daughter of Sherlock Holmes was not always easy: even before I'd heard of Conan Doyle or Dr. Watson, I ran into trouble with my grade two teacher. One day she went round the class asking for the first names of students' fathers. When Eleanor Holmes innocently and truthfully replied, "Sherlock," the balloon went up. Unfortunately I can't remember what she said, only the fury of her reaction and my own feeling that once again I had offended an adult without understanding why.

However, some years later I was fully able to appreciate the satisfaction of the reporter or editor of a small-town newspaper with the headline of his career. Dad had been convicted of a very minor traffic offence and next day the front-page inch-high headlines read, "Sherlock Holmes Not Right This Time."

Eleanor Wise (née Holmes)
Bloomfield, Ontario

✉ I gave up a perfectly nice, simple name like Carlson, to marry a guy with an M-name. Not only is it an M-name, it is a Mac-name, spelled Mac small kay, and pronounced Mac Eye!

I once accused my husband of having a very common name. "I have *not*," he answered, getting a wee bit shirty. "And not only that," I argued, performing the *coup de grâce* with very little *de grâce*, "it's impossible to file, impossible to pronounce, and it's at the *middle* of the alphabet!"

When you have spent your childhood at the *front* of the alphabet, going *first*, it is really hard to be patient.

It is a myth that Catholics have the largest families. Have you ever seen the pages of Mcs and Macs in the phone book? Those Scottish Presbyterians have been busy doing more than sniffin' heather and kirkin' the tartan.

The Ms take forever, especially at convention registration booths. The M-lineup stretches all the way to the elevator, and we are still shuffling forward long after the C-names have gone for their first Fuzzy Navel.

Expecting the correct pronunciation is like debarking at Ellis Island and is proof of my long-held suspicion that not all Canadians get the same education.

Now, in bonny Scotland, you'd never have to explain. Of course, the original spelling was something like "McAoidh," which is what happens when you are isolated in the highlands with only sheep and a bottle of twelve-year-old malt for company.

We have had years of really interesting mail, and I take my bonnet off to the postal service, who do a wonderful job of finding us under the name McKi, MKI, Maki, McKie, McKye and (my all-time favourite) McHigh.

There is only one thing more foolish than marrying a man with an M-name, and that is naming your son the *same name*! I admit it, I'm not as smart as I look. I paid the grandparents off. I gave my son the same name. Now we have another generation of M-names, and, of course, my son gets my husband's mail, my husband gets my son's mail, they both get an uncle's mail, and they share the mail with another Vancouver barrister and solicitor.

We recently received an invitation to a wedding where the groom was taking the bride's surname. I thought that that was a highly original and perfectly reasonable idea.

Bob has this special look. I call it his "Dr. No" look. That's what he gave me when I said, "Bob Carlson. Now that's a distinguished name!"

Gail Mackay
North Vancouver

✉ I heard someone say that naming would be much simplified if people would only marry others of the same surname.

My parents did just that back in 1946 when George Cairns married Frances Cairns and settled in Charlottetown. That seemed simple and neat enough in itself, but read on for the implications.

First there was the naming of grandparents. As youngsters, we couldn't use the term Grandpa Cairns without confusion because there were two of him. The problem was relatively easily surmounted by calling them Grandpa Stanchel and Grandpa Freetown, after the districts in which their farms were located.

The matter of uncles was more challenging. Each of my parents has a brother named Robert Cairns, both of whom had moved to Ontario. One became known as Uncle Robert Ancaster after the place in which he lived. However, the other, who lived in Toronto, was referred to as Uncle Robert B.C., based on his initials. Then of course there were the great-uncles to be distinguished because, as you might have guessed, both my mother and my father had uncles named Robert Cairns. Mercifully, one generally went by his middle name while the other was identified by tacking his city on after the Uncle Robert.

Before you heave a sigh of relief, let me hasten to add that the multiplicity of Robert Cairnses didn't end there, for there were also two first cousins of that name in my parents' generation.

As some of the more elderly Robert Cairnses have been dying off, the confusion has been gradually diminishing. However, in recent years Uncle Robert B.C. has moved back to P.E.I., and Uncle Robert Ancaster has moved to B.C.

Now what was that about simplifying things through samesurname marriages?

Winifred (Cairns) Wake
London, Ontario

AND, IN CLOSING, A LOVING AND LINGERING LOOK AT THE LAND

This is one of a series of panels that, in the spirit I alluded to in the introduction to these *Papers*, we presented at various times and from various places in the season of 1990-91 – produced, once again, by Nancy Watson. In Newfoundland, with the artist Christopher Pratt, among others, we talked about the rugged and compelling power of the island and the surrounding sea. In Quebec, with the novelist Roch Carrier (again among others) we looked at the hold of that province's – that nation's, in some of our panelists' views – varied landscapes on its artists and its people. At other times and with other people, we felt the pull of the North I talked about in the introduction, and the majesty of the mountains.

This is the Prairie – along with the North, perhaps the most distinctively Canadian landscape of all. The panelists are the poet Lorna Crozier, who was in Saskatoon, the landscape artist Robert McInnis, in Edmonton, the sculptor Joe Fafard, in Regina, and the singer-songwriter Connie Kaldor, who was in Montreal when we recorded this conversation. I began, in fact, by asking her what she missed about the west.

Connie Kaldor

I miss the light, the quality of light. The grey is different out here. I miss the clarity of light. It's unusual, and it's no place else in the world other than home.

Peter Gzowski

Joe Fafard, give me a snapshot of your favourite place.

Joe Fafard

My favourite place is the place where I was born, in Saint Marth, Saskatchewan, which is rather like parkland, or was before they cut down a lot of the trees. It's a little bit rolly but has a lot of bush and a lot of fields. Saint Marth is on the way to Winnipeg from Regina. When you cross the Manitoba border on the Trans Canada, you go thirty miles north, and there's Saint Marth, a little hamlet of French Canadians holding out.

Peter Gzowski

Lorna, take me to a place on the Prairies.

Lorna Crozier

Probably my favourite place is home, too, about thirty miles north of Swift Current where the Saskatchewan River cuts through the landscape. It's surrounded by beautiful old, bare hills that in the fall look like the backs of an animal's hide. A kind of golden, short hair. The Swift Current Creek, which is very sluggish when it goes through town, by the time it gets to the river it's rolling. Where it meets the Saskatchewan River has to be one of my favourite spots. There are gorgeous prickly pear cactuses; I always see antelope and deer. I found a buffalo stone there, the stone where the buffaloes rub their backs. The edges of the stone are smooth as glass and there's an indentation around the stone where hundreds of creatures walked. I get a very strong sense of the past and of what the Prairies used to be like as well as what they are like now.

Peter Gzowski

Robert McInnis, you're a Prairie-ite by adoption?

Robert McInnis

Yes, I grew up in Saint John, New Brunswick. I left there at age twenty to travel all across Canada for my painting career, and I was in the Air Force as a photographer, as well. That sent me around for the first five years, and since then I've been on my own.

I'm really at a loss to pick a favourite place on the Prairie because I love it all. A hundred kilometres in from the Ontario border heading towards Winnipeg, suddenly the land opens up, and the sky, and it's perfectly flat for miles. I can see everywhere. The minute I reach that area I breathe a sigh of relief and say, "I'm home." I'm still two thousand miles away from Edmonton at that point but I feel like I'm home. I claim the whole southern Prairie for my inspiration, all the way from Winnipeg right across to the Number 2 Highway in Alberta. That's quite a space to claim, but for those native Prairie people, they can have their little corners, I'll take the whole thing, thanks.

Peter Gzowski

The first time I ever experienced that landscape was on a train. We're talking 1956, I guess, and we had just pulled out of Winnipeg. There was a guy, it was his first time in Canada, and unlike me he hadn't seen this landscape in his head and in books all his life, and he had been looking out the window steadily for about three hours. I said, What do you make of it? He turned to me and said, It's the biggest expanse of {blank} all I've ever seen in my life. Which is what a lot of people think, that it's all just a big nothing, all flat. But Prairie people know that's not true. Right, Connie?

Connie Kaldor

You bet. We were sitting around looking at wedding photos last night – a real Prairie thing, looking at wedding photos from Willowbunch, Saskatchewan – and there's one shot where one of my nephews is sitting on a promontory, where you can see for miles – probably all the way to Moose Jaw, about a hundred miles. It's absolutely breath-taking. That's the point where the Métis used to look for the buffalo herds to come in. It was like a painting. It was in the fall, with all those browns, those subtle little changes of colour that are exquisite. My friend was looking at it and she started to cry. She said, nobody else would think this is beautiful. The little changes are like an emotion. And it's quiet. It's this large, large sky. Don Freed used to call it "Prairie under glass." The colours change subtly and beautifully, and that "expanse of nothing" is filled with all these little tiny changes that I watch.

Joe Fafard

When we talk about the Prairies, we talk about experiencing it only in terms of space. The Prairies is something that has to be experienced in time, day to day and season to season. Because the landscape changes all the time. That's the nice thing about the Prairies. You don't have just one Prairie – you have a whole year's history. From fall to winter to summer you have many different countries right here in the Prairies.

Lorna Crozier

I heard it described in another way once – that the Prairies were like a huge yawn by God. But only God would be bored with it. The rest of us aren't. I find the crops here absolutely beautiful. I'm not a farmer, and I don't depend on them for my income, so I can look at them in a more artistic or aesthetic sense. When I drive out of Saskatoon about thirty miles, I hit an area that grows a lot of canola, which has a bright yellow blossom. When I see that huge field beside a field of flax, which has a mauve-blue blossom – it's probably one of the most extravagant things I've ever seen.

I'm going to read a poem about a field of wheat, which I think is equally beautiful but more subtle. When I stand near a field of wheat, I get a sense that there's more there than just a field of wheat. There's a presence. It has a feeling to it that is hard to describe. But that's what poets try to do, is describe the indescribable.

The poem is called "Field of Wheat."

The wheat is flattened
in a small circle
where a deer lay down
in the night to sleep
or an angel danced.

If I had a choice,
I'd choose the deer,
that perilous reality,
indigenous, its big eyes
full of wonder
when it looks at you
as if you come from somewhere else.
And you do, a place far beyond
its knowing.

A deer then.
Though the wheat rustles like wings
as if it's calling something down.

Strange, a field of growing wheat
seems the most silent thing
though it is seldom so.

Even when the wind is still,
there is this sound,
this small breath
drawn in
          and held.

Peter Gzowski
Among other things, this morning will be remembered in my life
as the day Lorna Crozier solved the mystery of the circles on the
Prairie landscape. A deer lying down to sleep, or angels. I like
angels. I want to move to winter for a moment.

Lorna Crozier
We're moving there quick enough as it is.

Robert McInnis

We only have three seasons out here. We have a green season, we have a white season and we have a brown or yellow season.

Peter Gzowski

Robert, you paint outside in the white season.

Robert McInnis

That's right. That's my favourite season to be outside.

Peter Gzowski

But it gets cold, Bob. It gets very cold.

Robert McInnis

I've learned how to dress for the weather out here.

Lorna Crozier

Do you paint with mitts on?

Robert McInnis

I do at the start. A lot of the work can be done with my gloves on just for the roughing in. But for the finer work at the end, I will work with my gloves off. I keep my white paint in my pocket because it seems to seize up quicker than other colours. I take it out of my pocket at the last minute when I need it, squeeze it out and finish up the whites at the end, which is most of the colour anyway.

It is an incredible experience to be standing out on the Prairie. In some of these isolated areas I paint, I can be standing out there in the middle of what appears to be nothing, trying to pick up a few little brush strokes here and there of fields and very little sky. Most of the time, it all blends together. People in the east cannot experience this. It's hard to imagine. The closest I can come to it is the fog I grew up in, in Saint John, New Brunswick. That's probably why I like it out here. I have the effects of fog, the simplicity, and at the same time I have sunshine.

Peter Gzowski

What other colours do you have in your palette when you're out on a day that looks all white to the non-artist?

Robert McInnis

I have all the colours on my palette, and they all somehow enter into the white painting. It's a full palette—two reds, two yellows, two blues and the white.

When I paint other seasons, I'm more into yellows and ochres. So I tend to put one squeeze of ochre paint. That's the only change I'd make for a different season.

Peter Gzowski

When I suggest it gets bitterly cold, no one yet has said dry cold. I'm grateful for this.

Joe Fafard

It's hell but it is a dry hell.

Peter Gzowski

There is some myth among westerners that when it's fifty below and it's dry your lungs don't freeze.

Robert McInnis

I find our winters are more bearable than any place I've lived in Canada, and I've lived in just about every region of Canada for a length of time, except the north. We do not have really cold weather. The sun here is hot, even in winter the sun is blazing hot on your south side, and then on your north side you're freezing cold. But you can walk around outside in the winter and get a sun tan. The sun is blazing hot and the snow is so powdery you can sweep it, you don't have to shovel. We have an awful lot of good things going for us in this cold, cold climate.

Lorna Crozier

Everybody here has a parka. I think that's how we get through it.

Peter Gzowski

In Newfoundland, artists talked about the jaggedness, the hard edge to the landscape, how it gave them a sense of living on the edge, how it affected their work and the spirit with which they worked. Joe, do you have thoughts about that?

Joe Fafard

I think we live here because we like it here. We're not feeling like we're living on the edge. I feel like I'm living on the top. Whenever I go anywhere, like if I go to the mountains in British Columbia, suddenly the landscape's coming up higher than I am. But when I'm on the Prairies, I'm on the top, I'm on the highest point all around me; I'm on the horizon; I'm in the middle.

Peter Gzowski

Do you feel closed in when you're on the mountains or in a city?

Joe Fafard

I experience it when I leave the mountains. After I've been in British Columbia for a couple of weeks and I come back to the Prairies, there is a tremendous sense of exhilaration as I approach the landscape and see it open up.

Robert McInnis

You can't believe the incredible feeling of peace you suddenly get when you see that sky and vast land. You don't have that feeling when you're closed in by all the trees and hills. And the person who made the statement that he didn't like the mountains because they spoiled the view, I find that to be absolutely true.

Connie Kaldor

In other parts of the country, people are concerned with the land and the shape of trees and things that are on the land. On the Prairie, the land is a little less significant on a certain level. It's the sky that is so huge, and it changes all the time. I think that affects how people think about things. Nothing is static. We see the sky changing; we see the things coming at us, in a way. Maybe it makes us more conservative. We get nervous if we can't see what's going to happen next.

I don't know if it's only Prairie people who feel it, but I know when I get off the plane in Regina, my shoulders relax. I feel too big in lots of places. I feel like I'm too big for cities. When I get off the plane and I see that expanse, it feels like there's room.

There's room to breathe. There is an enormous sense of having nothing over your head.

Robert McInnis

Your eyes have a place to travel, as well, that's the nice part of it. When I lived in downtown Toronto, my eyes had no place to go. I'd run up against a tree or red brick building immediately. Here my eyes have places to travel. It's restful for the eyes to look at this kind of scenery.

Lorna Crozier

I was reading a poem not too long ago by Jan Zwicki, who I believe grew up in Alberta, and she had the lovely line, "When I was a child the sky was a song." Maybe that's what we're doing here – we're finding words for this space, this release, this openness, this spirituality. A British philosopher said he suddenly understood the necessity to write poetry when he arrived on the Canadian Prairies. He tried to describe the peculiar feeling that all that space gives a person. Maybe those of us who grew up here can understand that in a particular way.

Connie Kaldor

So much has not been said about the Prairies. Oh, well, it's that large blank spot before you get to Banff. A sense that there's nothing to say about it. But I heard all the stories, all the things people talk about, all the things I know. What we thought was history, my father thought was current events – that kind of thing.

Lorna Crozier

Our parents are full of stories, particularly about the dirty thirties and the Depression. Those stories started to get told, and people thought most of them were lies. We grew up thinking they were the truth, whether they were or not.

Joe Fafard

I read Canadian history all the time, and I find that in travelling across the Prairies I'm following what I read in history. There are people living who are part of history. I would challenge any Canadian to read *The National Dream* by Pierre Berton, or *The Last Spike*, or *The Company of Canadians* by Peter Newman, and then travel across the country and say that the Prairie is bland and boring. This country, the roads, the cities have all been formed by the river routes, the Hudson's Bay people, then by the railway people after that.

Lorna Crozier

I also think it's a real gift to live in a piece of a country that has not had so many years of history over the native history, too. We still have a presence and a sense of that in our country.

Robert McInnis

I drove through the area where Treaty 7 was signed at Gleichin, Alberta. I'm driving right through this little valley and I'm aware of what took place on either side of the road a hundred years ago, where thousands and thousands of Indians all camped from various places, and the Mounties were there, were wearing their white helmets.

We have this history right in front of us, and we can look at it.

Joe Fafard

This Prairie, I was born here, but it is certainly the nicest part in Canada. I've been to all the provinces. But the Prairies, especially Saskatchewan, certainly is my choice.

Peter Gzowski

Connie, will you ever feel at home in Montreal?

Connie Kaldor

I don't know. I don't know if I've ever felt at home anywhere other than on the Prairies. I think of the Newfoundland expression, "where you belong to." No matter where I live that's where I belong to, that's where my soul is at peace.

INDEX OF AUTHORS